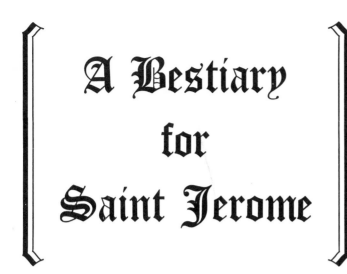

A Bestiary for Saint Jerome

Animal Symbolism in

European Religious Art

HERBERT FRIEDMANN

Smithsonian Institution Press

Washington, D.C., 1980

Frontispiece: Cosimo Tura, *Saint Jerome in Penitence*,
ca. 1477–1481. London: The National Gallery. Copyright NL.
Photo by John Webb.

Library of Congress Cataloguing in Publication Data
Friedmann, Herbert, 1900–
A bestiary for Saint Jerome.
Bibliography: p.
Includes index.
1. Hieronymus, Saint—Art.   2. Painting, European.
3. Animals in art.   4. Animal lore.   I. Title.
ND1432.E85F74   1980   704.94′6   79–607804
ISBN 87474-446-6

IN MEMORY OF GUY EMERSON,
WHOSE COMBINED INTERESTS IN ART
AND IN NATURAL HISTORY MADE HIM
THE IDEAL READER I HAD IN MIND
WHILE WRITING THIS BOOK.

Contents

Preface

Anyone who has frequented the great art museums in this country or abroad will have noted numerous intriguing and striking representations of Saint Jerome, many of which include a lion and often one or more other kinds of animals. For years I have wondered why these creatures were present; what meanings, if any, they were intended to convey, and what degree of knowledge of them the artists may have had, particularly in past centuries when the opportunities for such knowledge, personal or second-hand, were far fewer than they are today.

It was not until interest had developed into serious study that I realized that the story of Saint Jerome was one of the few themes within the conventional limits of church art that lent itself readily to extensive use of natural history material. Prolonged and intensive study of this surprisingly large corpus of both natural history and of art has resulted in the present work. The book may, therefore, be of some interest to naturalists and historians of the natural sciences, as well as to iconologists and art historians. With the former group of readers in mind, I have thought it necessary to deal with the nature and the special logic of symbolism and allegory, since without these attributes the whole artistic effort would have been meaningless and probably would never have developed.

After many years of gathering materials, and especially of looking, with the mind as well as the eye, at works of art showing Jerome and his animal entourage, I began to explore the thinking behind the icons involved. Each attendant animal had to be carefully identified; unfortunate earlier published misidentifications had to be discarded; and the use in art of each of the species had to be charted by artist, by country, and by period. The fact that these creatures had to be understood and properly interpreted made it necessary to ascertain, in each case, what meanings were intended. These meanings were not necessarily in the conscious minds of the artists as they created each image, but stemmed from the culture of the time and place. Then these thoughts had to be aligned with Saint Jerome and with the legends that had grown up around his known biography.

In a very large part of the total mass of art devoted to his story, the saint was shown chiefly in two quite dissimilar, but equally significant roles: in penitence and self-chastisement in the solitude of the wilderness on the one hand, and, on the other, in peaceful absorption in meditation and scholarship, either in the open or in his study. It is chiefly in these two settings that Jerome is accompanied by his animal associates. This is particularly true of the animals other than the lion, which, as his emblem, often accompanies Jerome in other types of pictures as well. Furthermore, all of these creatures, large or small, prominent or inconspicuous, frequently or infrequently included by the artists, are carriers of meanings, seemingly concealed, but waiting to be grasped by the viewer.

The book has been kept largely free of other considerations that could justifiably enter into a discussion of the iconography, in order to demonstrate most clearly the meaningful way in which the many kinds of animals have been used in connection with Jerome. It starts with a general introduction presenting a brief account of Saint Jerome, of his place in the world of Christianity, of how he came to be a central figure around whom an enormous corpus of art developed. There is also a discussion of the nature of the symbolism that came to surround his story. Then follow two chapters, one on the theme "St. Jerome in his Study" and one on "St. Jerome in the Wilderness," the two chief settings in which the saint is accompanied, in art, by animal associates. Inasmuch as both of these compositions became the occasion for visually expressing much more than their titles indicate, they are discussed with their historical and philosophical background and with their due interpretation.

In order to elucidate more explicitly, and in greater depth, the complexity of the ideas and concepts involved in the use of animals in the Jerome theme, six chapters are then devoted to detailed treatment of renditions by six diverse, but great and original artists, three chosen from north of the Alps—Albrecht Dürer, Lucas Cranach the Elder, and Hieronymus Bosch—and three from Italy—Antonello da Messina, Francesco di Giorgio, and Cosimo Tura. These were selected because they made extensive use of animals in their renditions of the Jerome story. I hope that these detailed accounts will demonstrate that careful study of the different kinds of animals and of their symbolic significance may serve to increase our ability to "read" these works of art with more precision than has been possible hitherto.

Then follows the Bestiary, an account, species by species, of the many kinds of creatures that have been found in the great mass of paintings, prints, drawings, and carvings of the story of the saint. This includes not only a listing of the artists by whom each was used, and how frequently, but also a discussion of the symbolic significance of each, its antecedent use as expressed in folklore and mythology, and its degree of applicability to the Jerome theme. The depiction of the legend of Saint Jerome removing the thorn from the foot of a lion is dealt with in detail in the account of that animal in this Bestiary. Inasmuch as the lion was more often present than not, merely as Jerome's attribute, and because of the rather involved legend about it, this beast receives more detailed study than do most of the other animals. Similarly, because of the iconographic problem it raises and the complex nature of the data required for its solution, many pages also have to be devoted to the lioness.

It is because of the large number of kinds of animals that occur in art in depictions of the Jerome story that I have ventured to title this book *A Bestiary for Saint Jerome*. Strictly speaking, it is not a bestiary for him but one for the people who may look at or study the great corpus of art devoted to the saint.

The bulk of the descriptive material in the Bestiary, reporting and identifying many kinds of animals, is new to art literature. Also, many of the interpretations of the symbolic meanings of these creatures, and of the works in which they occur, are new at this point, although carefully based on old thoughts and concepts contemporary with the works in which they occur. I have tried to indicate the degree of certainty (probability might be considered a safer term) of the validity of some symbolic interpretations, particularly in cases, happily few, where the iconologist finds himself working with incomplete and fragmentary data.

In each such instance I have been at some pains to state explicitly the attendant uncertainty and to point out the degree of tentativeness of my conclusion. In each of these cases I have come back again and again to contemplation of the work, usually in photographic reproduction, and have strenuously tried to avoid an easy acceptance of any pat explanation. To increase the chances for objectivity I have made a point of allowing long intervals, up to several months, between such returns, and it was only when inclination was transmuted into conviction that I dared to make a decision. I realize that this does not constitute proof, and that is why each such decision is presented with a statement of its tentativeness. Fortunately, these instances are very few in number, actually only three: the meaning of the lioness; part of the reading of Albrecht Dürer's great engraving of 1514, *Saint Jerome in His Study*; and the interpretation of the owl and of the wall creeper in Cosimo Tura's *Saint Jerome in Penitence*, in the National Gallery, London.

As indicated earlier, it is anticipated that this book will be of interest primarily to art historians and iconologists, and only secondarily to biologists. Relatively few of the latter, at least in the United States, have as yet developed the type of historical interest in the background of their subject that might tempt them to roam in the fields of allegory and symbolism and that might enable them to feel comfortable with the regulated iconography of religious thought and dogma, often so different from the logic and the approach of the natural sciences. For the benefit of those biologists who will look at the book, I have felt it proper to include statements, here and there, concerning thoughts and facts already familiar to the art historian. I hope that these inclusions will be pardoned by those to whom they may otherwise seem needless.

The present study makes no attempt to discuss, or even to list, *all* of the paintings, engravings, etchings, woodcuts, drawings, or sculptures that portray Saint Jerome. Although I have studied great numbers of altarpieces and other works that include Jerome as one saint among others in attendance upon a central "Madonna and Child" or "Crucifixion" or other episode from the life of Christ, or that show him enthroned as a cardinal, as a doctor of the Church, or that depict his last communion or his death, I have not thought it necessary to mention them here unless they included some animals or other points of special interest. Even in renditions of those parts of the Jerome cycle that are usually faunally embellished I have tried to be selective rather than merely statistical.

The general survey of Saint Jerome in art, particularly in Italian painting, brought out in 1924 by Adolfo Venturi, and the history of the "Saint Jerome in His Study" theme published in 1925-26 by Anna Strümpell, have made it superfluous for me to go over again in detail what they have covered. I have made much use of their descriptive works and acknowledge my indebtedness to them. However, neither studied the faunal and symbolic contents of the individual works of art. It need hardly be added that many more representations of Jerome are known today than Venturi or Strümpell were able to list half a century ago.[1]

1. There were two earlier studies of the Jerome theme in art, neither of which is mentioned by either Venturi or Strümpell: a two-volume work by Angelo Ficarro (1916, 1920), dealing with Jerome's place in the history of culture and including some references to art; and Father Ansgar Pöllmann's 1920 survey of the saint in early Christian art. More recently, two other works have appeared: a book by Rudolf Eiswirth, *Hieronymus' Stellung zur Literatur und Kunst* (1955), too brief in its presentation to have supplied discrete data for the present study; and Renate Jungblut's *Hieronymus Darstellung und Verehrung eines Kirchenvaters* (1967). This work includes references to 588 representations of Saint Jerome, the great majority of which are also included in the present survey. The chief differences between her list of paintings, graphics, and sculptures and my own is that her selection was not faunally oriented as is the case here to a large degree.

Acknowledgments

Early in the course of this study it became obvious that there were many paintings of Saint Jerome that either had, or seemed likely to have, significant details not readily studied, or too small to be more than barely visible, in the published reproductions, or that contained creatures whose accurate identification necessitated knowing their coloration, not revealed in black-and-white photographs or in imperfect colored prints. Accordingly, a list was prepared of what I termed "problem pictures," paintings of which it was essential to study the originals. These were widely distributed in galleries and churches of many countries. Two generous travel and study grants from the Samuel H. Kress Foundation made it possible for me to examine them at first hand. Together with memories and notes from many earlier visits to the major art museums of Europe and the United States, this enabled me to feel secure in my identifications of the innumerable creatures that are to be found in the many hundreds of paintings, graphics, and sculptures of the Jerome story. Without these grants, many of the most significant discoveries of the Hieronymite faunal iconography could not have been made. Some paintings that I thought I knew intimately from reproductions turned out to contain surprising additions in the way of tiny or shadow-concealed creatures. I need hardly add that first-hand study of the originals at close quarters and in good light cannot be overrated. Furthermore, the accumulation of photographs with which to illustrate this report would have been much curtailed, had the grants not included a budget for such items. I am glad to express my deep gratitude to the Kress Foundation, to its executive vice president, Mary M. Davis, and to its panel of experts, who allocated the grants, for their support. I cannot help but venture to add that the potential readers of this publication are similarly indebted to them for the much more complete coverage of its theme they may derive from it. Furthermore, the actual publishing of this book was made possible by a very generous grant from the Kress Foundation.

Of necessity, the bulk of the research on the art works themselves, on the artists who created them, and on the nature of the demands made on the artists by the changing aspects of the cultural milieu of the various periods and places in which they worked, had to be carried on in libraries with extensive holdings in these and related fields. It is a pleasure to express my appreciation and thanks for their invariable helpfulness and cooperation to the following of these repositories of knowledge: the Library of Congress and the library of the National Gallery of Art, Washington, including the Richter Photographic Archives; the Frick Art Reference Library, New York; the university research library and the special art library of the University of California at Los Angeles, including its set of the Princeton Index of Early Christian Art and of the I Tatti photographic files; the library of the Los Angeles County Museum of Art; the Henry E. Huntington Library, San Marino, California; and the Bodleian Library, Oxford. The Joseph Regenstein Library of the University of Chicago kindly made for me a photograph of a reproduction of a lost painting by Paul Lautensack from a rare book in its collection, and J. G. Pollard of the Fitzwilliam Museum sent me a photograph of a small relief by Filarete in his collection.

At the University of California at Los Angeles I have enjoyed the opportunity of discussing special items, as they arose, with a number of friends on the faculty, who have given me help in their special areas. Among these, the following are particularly to be mentioned with gratitude for their interest: Karl M. Birkmeyer, art history; Claus-Peter Clasen, history of the Reformation period in Germany; Wayland D. Hand, European folklore and comparative mythology; and Philip Levine, classics, especially Latin inscriptions.

At the National Gallery of Art, I have enjoyed the benefit of informal discussions of special problems concerning some of the paintings of Saint Jerome and their makers with Fern R. Shapley and the late John Shapley, and am indebted for specific information about items in the gallery's photographic (Richter) archives to Anna Voris. The curators of the various art museums in Europe and the United States, with whom I have had correspondence, have been uniformly cooperative and helpful. Burton Fredericksen, of the J. Paul Getty Museum, Malibu, California, examined at my request photographs of a few Italian paintings of uncertain authorship and made suggestions as to their attributions. He also very kindly gave me advance copy of the proof sheets of the Jerome material in the subject index of the *Census of Pre-Nineteenth Century Italian Paintings in North American Public Collections* by himself and Federico Zeri, which enabled me to see if I had overlooked any pertinent material in American museums.

The late Dr. Wolfgang Stechow called to my attention a publication by Renate Jungblut that furnished me with some much desired information, which was extended in correspondence with Dr. Jungblut (now Dr. Miehe). Dorothy Yamamoto, of Somerville College, Oxford, sent me information about the fourteenth-century English poet, John Gower, and his comments on the harpies. Edwin Hall, Wayne State University, kindly sent me his unpublished interpretation of the lion in van Eyck's Detroit "Saint Jerome" as a sign of the zodiacal Leo, with permission to include it in the present discussion of that realistic plus symbolic creature.

Philip Hofer, Librarian of the Norwich Library, supplied information on Bishop Joseph Hall, the seventeenth-century Norwich divine; Jaroslav Pelikan, of Yale University, answered some questions dealing with the writings of Martin Luther; and Dr. William A. Emboden identified the plants in Cosimo Tura's *Saint Jerome in Penitence.*

A particular debt of gratitude is due to Dr. Karla Langedijk of Duke University, and an even greater one to Dr. William S. Heckscher, formerly of the same institution, both of whom were so kind as to read the entire manuscript of an earlier version of this book, and who made innumerable helpful suggestions, from which the work has benefited greatly. Any errors of fact or of judgment that it may still contain are the responsibility of the author, but the unusual extent and meticulous detail of the criticisms of these two scholars have certainly eliminated many dubious suggestions.

Thanks are hereby expressed to the Harvard University Press for permission to quote from such books as Erwin Panofsky's *Early Netherlandish Painting* and F. A. Wright's *Select Letters of St. Jerome* (in the Loeb Classical Library series); to Stanford University Press for a quotation from E. W. Martin's *The Birds of the Latin Poets*; to Longmans Green, through David McKay Company, for material from *The Golden Legend of Jacobus de Voragine*, translated by Granger Ryan and Helmut Ripperger; to the Princeton University Press for a quotation from George Boas's *The Hieroglyphics of Horapollo* and one from Jean Seznec's *The Survival of the Pagan Gods*; to the *Gazette des Beaux-Arts* for a quotation from an article by the present author first published in that journal in 1949; to the Istituto Editoriale Electa, Milan, for permission to reproduce plate xxvi from Mario Salmi's *Cosmè Tura*; and to E.H. Gombrich for the use of a brief quotation from his 1948 paper on "The Visual Image in Neo-Platonic Thought."

To the staff of the Smithsonian Institution Press, under the direction of Edward F. Rivinus, I express my thanks for their understanding and patience, and for their expertise in handling the many and varied details involved in turning a manuscript into a book. A special note of gratitude is due to three members of the staff, Hope Pantell, Judith Wilder, and Elizabeth Sur, who devoted a great deal of time and effort in this connection. From the day of its arrival at the Smithsonian, the manuscript has had an interested and sympathetic response from Mr. Rivinus, who has continued to expedite its progress.

Mrs. Reese Hale Taylor very kindly volunteered to type the manuscript of this book for me. Aside from an unusual and most generous expression of friendship, which I deeply appreciate, this act of hers had the added benefit of making her a stimulating and interesting person with whom to discuss various aspects of the interpretations suggested in the text. The degree to which the subject matter and meanings of Jerome's animal associates came to interest Mrs. Taylor as she typed the manuscript has encouraged me to think that other readers may also find this book worth reading.

During crowded days and hours in the great collections of Europe and America, as I tried to see as many "Jeromes" as possible—and yet take the time to write down full notes on each, and even tangential thoughts they suggested—the planning and maintaining of an effective travel schedule and work pattern were greatly expedited by the competent and devoted collaboration of my wife, Karen J. Friedmann. She became an expert "Jerome spotter" in her trips through endless rooms of many galleries, and her superior sense of direction saved me from losing myself in the innumerable and not always clearly marked streets leading to some of the churches and smaller museums in many towns in Italy and in Europe north of the Alps.

Note: To help the reader identify and locate works of art mentioned in the text, the Appendix gives a listing—alphabetically by artist or period —of more than a thousand Hieronymite pictures and sculptures. When the present location is unknown, there is a reference in most cases to a published illustration or to an available archival photograph.

Unless otherwise noted, English translations of quoted material are the author's own.

The Legend of Saint Jerome in Art

Saint Jerome and His Animal Associates

Saint Jerome (Eusebius Sophronius Hieronymus), one of the four Fathers of the Latin Church, was born about A.D. 341 in Strido, a town on the border of Dalmatia. He was the foremost Christian scholar of his time, a remarkable linguist, and a man of great industry and devotion. His translation of the Scriptures from Greek and Hebrew into Latin, the Vulgate, is still used by the Roman Catholic Church, in revised form, as its authorized version of the Bible. This achievement, Jerome's greatest contribution to the growth and dissemination of Christianity, made the Gospels available to the world of the Latin West; until then, the Holy Writ had been accessible only to the small number of churchmen who were able to read it in earlier versions and languages.[1]

In his youth Jerome had devoted himself wholeheartedly to the study of classical Roman literature. After a serious illness in 373, he went through a spiritual crisis and renounced pagan scholarship in favor of the Holy Scriptures. He retired to the deserts of Chalcis in Syria, and spent some four years as a hermit, undergoing stringent mortifications while pursuing rigorous scriptural studies. This is the period that provided later artists with the important "Saint Jerome in the Wilderness" theme, of which more later.

Following these years of solitude, Jerome was ordained a presbyter at Antioch. The remainder of his life was devoted to further studies, teaching, and writing. He was a very active participant in the theological controversies of his day; his many correspondents included Saint Augustine. Jerome's final years were spent in a monastery in Bethlehem, where he died in 420.

Saint Jerome was noted more for his scholarship than his sanctity, and his life offered little drama of the kind that distinguished the lives of certain other saintly figures. Few miracles were attributed to him, aside from the legend of his extracting a thorn from the paw of a lion. This episode, as it happens, was apocryphal, having been transposed to Jerome, inadvertently but early, from the legend of the less prominent Saint Gerasimus. According to Alberto Vaccari,[2] the old story of the lion of Gerasimus was repeated by word of mouth among the monks long before it was officially translated from the original Greek, and the names of Gerasimus and Geronimus (Jerome) were so similar that the monks confused the two.

1. It is true that there were, before Jerome's work, some parts of the Scriptures available in Latin, but these were not in agreement among themselves. They have been studied and reviewed by Dora Panofsky ("The Textual Basis of the Utrecht Psalter Illustrations," p. 50), who concluded that before Saint Jerome "there was no standard Latin version of the Psalter. There existed only a number of slightly divergent translations, based on the Septuagent, which are loosely referred to as *the Itala* or, more appropriately, the unrevised Old Latin versions. . . ."

2. "Le antiche vite di San Girolamo," *Miscellanea Geronimiana*, pp. 1–18.

The legend of Saint Gerasimus was included in the *Pratum spirituale*, a collection of biographies of the Holy Fathers and ascetics, brought together by Joannes Moschos (died 619) in collaboration with his friend, Sophronius, Patriarch of Jerusalem. As it came to be applied to Saint Jerome, the story is found in the *Legenda aurea* (*Golden Legend*), compiled in the late thirteenth century by Jacobus de Voragine, a prominent member of the Dominican order and archbishop of Genoa. This work, a collection of the legends and lives of the more important saints, became one of the most popular and widely copied religious books of the late Middle Ages, and served to make Jerome's experience well known to a wide circle of readers, and to a much wider circle of listeners, who learned of it from those readers. The extent to which material of this kind was familiar to the largely illiterate public of Europe apparently was much greater in past centuries than it is today with a far more literate public. Such stories were part of the everyday conversation and knowledge of people living very drab existences. To them the lives of the saints were very real and interesting topics.

An English translation of de Voragine's story of Saint Jerome is given here in full, since it helps to explain the Saint's close association in art with a lion (see footnote 3 for the Latin version, followed by the Latin and English versions of the Saint Gerasimus story, for comparison):

One day, as evening was drawing on, and Jerome sat with the brethren to hear the sacred lessons, suddenly a lion came limping into the monastery. At the sight of him all the other monks fled, but Jerome went forward to meet him as a host his guest. The lion then showed him his wounded foot, whereupon he called the brothers and ordered them to wash the lion's feet and to dress his wound with care. When they did this, they found that the lion's pads were wounded by thorns. By their care, however, the foot was healed, and the lion, losing all his wildness, lived among them as a tame beast. Jerome judged from this that God had sent the lion not merely to have his foot healed, but to serve the monks; wherefore, after consulting the brethren, he put the lion in charge of the ass which carried wood from the grove to the monastery. Thereafter the beast cared for the ass as a shepherd for his sheep, constantly accompanying it to pasture, guarding it on all sides as it fed in the fields, and bringing it home at the same hour daily, when its work was done and it had fed. But once when the ass was in pasture and the lion was overcome with drowsiness, certain merchants who were passing that way with their camels saw the ass alone, and straightway stole it. But roused from sleep, and not finding his companion, the lion ran roaring this way and that, and finally returned sadly to the doors of the monastery, not daring to enter, as he used to do, for shame at having lost the ass. When the brothers saw that he came back later than was his wont, and without the ass, they thought that he had been forced by hunger to eat the ass, wherefore they refused to give him his customary portion of food, and said to him: "Go and eat what is left of the little ass, and so have thy fill!" Yet they were reluctant to believe that the lion had done this wrong, and went into the pasture looking for traces of the ass; but finding none, they reported the matter to Jerome. At his behest they gave the ass's work to the lion, and loaded upon his back the wood which they cut; and this the beast bore patiently. And one day when he had finished his work, he went out to the pasture, running about and looking for his comrade; and all at once he saw the traders afar off, marching along with their loaded camels, and the ass walking in the lead; for it was common in that region, when camels were going on a long march, to have an ass lead them by

3. The story as it came to be transposed to Saint Jerome is here transcribed from the standard Latin edition of the *Legenda aurea*, edited by Th. Graesse, pp. 655–57:

"Quadam vero die advesperascente cum Hieronymus cum fratribus ad sacram lectionem audiendum sederet, subito leo quidam claudicans monasterium ingressus est. Quo viso cum caeteri fratres fugerent, Hieronymus ei quasi hospiti abviavit. Leo igitur dum pedem sibi laesum ostenderet, vocatis fratribus pedes sibi praecepit ablui et diligenter ejus plagam inquiri. Quod cum fuisset, invenerunt leonis plantam a sentibus vulneratum; adhibita igitur diligenti cura leo convaluit et omni feritate deposita inter eos quasi domesticum animal habitavit. Tunc Hieronymus videns, quod non tam pro sanitate sui pedis, quam pro eorum ultilitate dominus leonem misisset, de fratrum consilio eidem hoc injunxit officium, ut asinum, quem habebant, qui ligna de nemore deferebat, ipse leo ad pascua duceret et ductum ibidem custodiret. Quod factum est. Nam injuncta leoni asini cura more pastoris industrii eundo ad pastum socius incessanter itineris rure pascendo undecunque defensor tutissimus erat, verumtamen ut se cibaret et asinus solitum perficeret opus, consuetis semper horis cum eo domum redibat. Quadam igitur vice pascente asino et leone graviter soporato meratores cum camelis inde transeuntes asinum solum viderunt et eum quantocius rapuerunt. Expergefactus itaque leo cum socium non inveniret, rugiendo huc illucque ibat, quem tandem non inveniens ad portas monasterii tristis adiit et intus, ut solitus erat, prae verecundia ingredi non praesumsit. Et videntes fratres, quod tardius solito more et sine asino venisset, putaverunt, quod fame compulsus asinum comedisset, nolentesque ei annonam attribuere consuetam dicebant; vade et reliquam partem aselli, quae tibi remansit, mande et tuam ingluviem reple. Haesitantes tamen, utrum hoc malum perpetrasset, exierunt ad pascua, si forte aliquod indicium invenirent, et nihil invenientes hoc Hieronymo retulerunt. Tunc monitis ejus officium asini leoni injungunt et ligna caedentes leoni imponunt. Quod cum leo patienter ferret, quadam die expleto opere agrum exiit, hac illaque discurrit scire desiderans, quid de suo fuisset socio factum, et ecce vidit a longe negotiatores cum onustis camelis praecedente asino venientes. Mos enim illi regioni est, ut, quando cum camelis longius gradiuntur, cameli, ut directius vadant, praecedentem et collo funiculum gestantem asinum subsequantur. Recognito igitur leo sino cum ingenti rugitu super eos irruit et omnes homines in fugam convertit. Et leo terribiliter rugiens percutiebat cand fortiter terram perterritosque camelos, sicut errant onusti, ante se ad cellam ire coegit. Quod cum fratres vidissent et Hieronymo nuntiassent, ille ait: hospitibus nostris, fratres carissimi, pedes abluite, escas praebeti et super hoc voluntatem domini expectate. Tunc leo per monasterium coepit, ut solebat, laetus discurrere, singulorum fratrum vestigiis se prosternens et quasi de perpetrata, quam non fecerat, culpa cauda alludens veniam postulabat."

The story of Saint Gerasimus, as told in the *Pratum spirituale*, is as follows (from Migne, *Patrologia Latina*, vol. 74, cols. 172–74).

"Vita abbatis Gerasimi.

"Uno fere milliario distat a Jordane monasterium advenientibus nobis narraverunt qui illic morebantur senes de abbate Gerasimo, quod die quadam ambulans super Jordanis ripam, obvium habuit leonem valde rugientem, suspenso pede, cui infixus erat ex calamo aculeus, adeo ut ex hoc pes ipse intumuisset, et sanie plenus effectus esset. Cum igitur vidisset leo senem, ostendebat illi vuleratum ex infixo aculeo pedem, flens quodammodo et obsecrans ut illi curam adhiberet. Cum ergo vidisset eum senex tali necessitate constrictum sedens apprehendit ejus pedem aperiensque vulnus eduxit aculeum infixum, cum magna put-

redinis copia diligenterque depurgato vulnere, et panno alligato, dimisiteum. Leo autem cumse curatum vidisset, noluit senem deserere sed utcharus discipulus, quocunque pergeret, magistrum, sequebatur, ita ut admiraretur senex tantam ferae gratitudinem. Igitur ex tunc senex nutriebat eum, mittens ante illum panem et infusa legumina.

"Habebat autem ipsum monasterium asinum unum, ad ferendam aquam pro necessitate fratrum de Jordane. Consuetudinem autem fecerat senex, ut curum pascendi asini leo haberet. Itaque abiens cum illo juxta Jordanis ripas, pascentem observabat. Quadam autem die dum pasceretur asinus, leo se ab illo longiuscule avertit; cum ecce camelarius ex Arabia veniens, inventum asinum accepit et secum duxit. Leo vero, amisso asino, rediit in monasterium tristis valde, et dejecta facie ac cervice, ad abbatum suum. Abbas igitur Gerasimus putavit quod asinum comedisset leo, et ait illi: Ubi est asinus? Ille vero quasi homo stabat tacens, et deorsum aspiciens. Dicit ei senex: Comedisti eum; benedictus Dominus. Quidquid faciebat asinus, amodo facies tu. Ex tunc igitur leo, jubente sene, portabat canthelium capientem amphoras quatuor, ferebatque aquam in monasterium.

"Die vero quadam venit miles quidam ad senem benedictionis gratia. Qui cum videret leonem bajulantem aquam, didicissetque causam, misertus estejus, proferensque tria numismata dedit senibus, ut emerent asinum ad ipsius aquae ministerium, et liberarent ea necessitate leonem. Brevi autem transacto tempore, postquam liberatus a labore fuerat, camelarius triticum, ut venundaret illud in sancta civitate, habens et asinum secum. Et cum transisset Jordanem accidit ut occurreret leoni; quo viso, dimisit camelos et fugit. Leo autem, cognito asino, cucurrit ad eum, et ore, ut solebat, ejus capistrum mordens traxit eum cum tribus camelis, et gaudens simul et rugiens, quod perditum asellum reperisset, venit ad senem. Senex vero, qui prius putabat quod asinum leo comedisset, tunc vero didicit quia insidias passus fuisset leo. Imposuit autem nomen leoni Jordanem. Egit itaque leo in monasterio cum fratribus plus quam quinque annos, nunquam recedens a sene. . . . Hoc autem totum factum est, non quia animam rationalem habuisse leo putandus sit, sed quod Deus voluerit glorificantes se glorificare, non solum in vita hac, sed etiam post mortem, et mon-

strare nobis qualem primo homini habuerint subjectionem bestiae, priusquam inobediens esset mandato, et antequam excideret e paradiso deliciarum."

In English, this reads as follows:

"The Life of Abbot Gerasimus

"About one mile from the Jordan there is a monastery, which is called the monastery of Abbot Gerasimus. When we came to this monastery, the old men who lived there told us about Abbot Gerasimus: one day, while walking on the bank of the Jordan, he found himself opposite a loudly roaring lion, who held up his paw, into which a splinter from a reed had been driven so violently that, as a result, the foot had swelled and become infected. Therefore, when the lion saw the old man, he showed him the paw wounded by the embedded splinter, weeping, as it were, and begging that the man treat him. So the old man, when he saw the creature in such need, sat down, took his paw, opened the wound, extracted the embedded splinter along with a great deal of pus, cleaned the wound carefully, wrapped a cloth around it, and sent the animal on his way. The lion, however, when he saw himself cured, did not want to leave the old man, but, like a dear disciple, followed his teacher wherever he went, so that the old man marveled at such great gratitude of a wild beast. So the old man from then on fed him by throwing before him bread with vegetables sprinkled on.

"The monastery, then, had a donkey, whose purpose was to convey water from the Jordan for the use of the brethren. Now, the old man had established the custom for the lion to watch over the donkey while he grazed. So the lion went off with him to the banks of the Jordan and watched him as he fed. But one day, while the donkey was grazing, he went away from him a little too far, when, behold, a camel driver from Arabia came along, seized the donkey that he had come upon, and carried him off. But the lion, having lost the donkey, returned to the monastery very sad and went, with face and neck lowered, to his abbot. The abbot Gerasimus therefore thought that the lion had devoured the donkey and asked him, "Where is the donkey?" But the lion, like a man, stood in silence looking down. Then the old man said to him, "You have devoured him, bless my soul (lit.: the Lord is blessed). What the donkey did, you will do from now on." Therefore, from that time on the lion, at the command of the old man, carried a container holding four amphoras (= about 7 gallons each) and brought the water into the monastery.

"One day, however, a soldier came to the old man for his blessing. When he saw the lion carrying water and learned the cause, he felt pity for him and, producing three pieces of money, gave them to the old men so that they would buy a donkey for the hauling of the water and free the lion from this drudgery. But a short time after the lion had been freed from the labor, the camel driver who had carried off the donkey came again with wheat to sell in the holy city and brought the donkey with him. When he had crossed the Jordan, it happened that he met the lion. As soon as he had seen him, he let go of his camels and fled. The lion, however, having recognized the donkey, ran towards him and bit off with his mouth, as was his wont, the donkey's halter. Then he dragged him along together with the three camels and, both roaring and rejoicing at the same time, because he had found the lost donkey, came to the old man. The old man, however, who earlier thought that the lion had eaten the donkey, then in fact learned that the lion had been victimized (lit.: had been ambushed). He then gave the lion the name Jordan. So the lion spent more than five years in the monastery with the brethren, never leaving the old man. . . . All this, then, happened not because the lion must be thought of as having a rational soul, but because God wanted to glorify those who glorify him, not only in this life, but also after death and because he wanted to show us how much the beasts had been subjected to the first man, before he had been disobedient to his command and before he was banished from the paradise of delights."

4. *The Golden Legend of "Jacobus de Voragine,"* trans. Granger Ryan and Helmut Ripperger, pp. 589–90.

5. *Hieronymianus.* In the account of Saint Jerome by Father Joannes Stiltinck, in the Bollandist Fathers' *Acta sanctorum, Septembris,* viii, pp. 657–63, Andrea's book is referred to as "Joannes Andreas Hieronymianum suum edidit posterioribus vitae suae annis, sive inter 1342–1348, quo obiit." Although quoting (p. 660) Andrea's express desire that Jerome be shown with his tame lion, "cum . . . leone mansueto," the Bollandists, apparently aware of the uncertainty of the pertinence of the legend, deny the lion to Jerome: "leonem omnino repudiamos, quia leo ille modo prorsus improbabile est conflictus."

Grete Ring ("St. Jerome Extracting the Thorn from the Lion's Foot," p. 190) writes that the "last version" of Andrea's manuscript was "about 1342." and adds that "we may . . . safely contend that without Joannes Andreas, the actual representation of St. Jerome would not have been introduced into the domain of visual art."

6. Ring, pp. 188–94.

7. Justus Bier, "Riemenschneider's St. Jerome and Other Works in Alabaster," pp. 226–34.

8. Joseph Klapper, *Aus der Frühzeit des Humanismus, Dichtungen zu Ehren des Heiligen Hieronymus.*

a rope tied about his neck. When the lion recognized the ass, he uttered a tremendous roar, rushed upon the caravan, and put the men to flight. Then, still roaring frightfully, he beat his tail upon the earth, and forced the terrified camels, laden as they were, to go before him to the monastery. When the brethren saw this and related it to Jerome, he said: "Beloved brothers, wash the feet of our guests and give them to eat, and further await the will of the Lord!" Then the lion ran happily about the monastery, as he had used to do, lying down in the path of each of the brethren, and wagging his tail, as if begging pardon for the wrong he had not done.[4]

The impetus that inaugurated the popularity of Saint Jerome in art was provided by an account of the saint's life and work written by Giovanni Andrea,[5] professor of canon law at the University of Bologna in the first half of the fourteenth century. As Grete Ring noted, this learned man's activities centered on the revival and intensification of the Jerome cult, and this indeed became the chief objective of his career.[6] Jerome became his chosen hero, and he recognized in him the obvious figure to use as the patron of humanism on the one hand, while on the other he also stressed the story of the saint calmly attending to the afflicted lion, as this tale of the savage nature of the ferocious beast tamed by Jerome's kindness and fearlessness seemed more likely to appeal to the masses of the faithful than would the relatively unapproachable image of the great church scholar at his literary labors.[7]

Andrea commissioned pictures of his favorite saint for a number of churches, and even accompanied them with original verses, several of which made reference to the legend of Jerome's extraction of the thorn from the lion's foot.[8] It was largely because of Andrea's efforts that Jerome became one of the most frequently represented saints in European art from the fourteenth through the sixteenth centuries. In earlier times when Jerome figured in art, he was often portrayed without his lion and without any pictorial reference to his penitence in the wilderness. We may illustrate this by two examples from the Carolingian renaissance in the ninth century. In the Vivian Bible, or First Bible of Charles the Bald, of about 846 (now in the Bibliothèque Nationale, Paris), Jerome is shown in three scenes: leaving Rome for Jerusalem, dictating his transla-

tion of the Bible, and distributing copies of his translation. In the San
Callisto Bible of twenty years later (now in San Paolo fuori le Mura,
Rome) the same three scenes occur.[9]

From the early decades of the fourteenth century onward, the art
devoted to the story of Jerome blossomed rapidly, both in the number of
paintings, graphics, and sculptures, and in the variety of scenes and settings in which the saint was portrayed. The great popularity of the
"Jerome in Penitence" theme provided the occasion for the inclusion of
animals with the saint. This, in turn, may be attributed in part to the fact
that Jerome happened to have written a letter which, some nine centuries
after his death, had the wholly unexpected and unintended effect of
stimulating artists to study and to portray many kinds of animals. In this
letter to Eustochium, daughter of his friend Paula, Jerome wrote that
during his lonely penitential sojourn in the Chalcidean wilderness,
scorpions and wild beasts were his daily companions.[10]

As religious art gradually freed itself in the fourteenth century from
some of the conventions within which it long had been contained, artists
began to instill an ever greater degree of verisimilitude in their pictures. To them the statement that Jerome had had daily association with
scorpions and wild beasts seems to have been an incentive to include in
their paintings such of these animals as were deemed symbolically proper
and pertinent by their clerical advisers and their clients. The degree to
which this was reflected in art may be sensed from the fact that in the
thousand or more representations of Jerome discussed in my present
account, there are no fewer than twenty-two identifiable kinds of mammals, not counting "realistic" domestic ones (ass, camel, sheep) needed
by the story. These are the badger, bear, beaver, cat, cheetah, deer (four
kinds), dog, fox, genet, ichneumon, jackal, leopard, lion (the lioness is
treated separately from the lion in the Bestiary, for iconographic reasons), monkey, mouse, otter, rabbit, squirrel, and wolf. Also to be found
are thirty-three kinds of birds: chaffinch, cock, crane, dove, duck, eagle,
goldfinch, guineafowl, hawfinch, heron (three kinds), hoopoe, jay, kingfisher, magpie, owl (three kinds), parrot, partridge (two kinds), peacock, pheasant, porphyrio, raven, robin, stork, swallow, swan, titmouse,
wall creeper, and woodpecker; four kinds of reptiles and amphibians:
frog, lizard, snake, and tortoise; and six kinds of invertebrates: ant, butterfly, fly, "insect" (probably scarab), scorpion, and snail. To this total
fauna of sixty-five species should be added three mythical creatures: the
dragon, harpy, and unicorn, and, to be complete, a number of unidentifiable, poorly rendered small birds.

It seems that no single subject in Christian art, with the possible exception of the "Creation of Animals" or "Noah's Ark," has been more
copiously embellished with animal forms. It is not certain that even those
two themes have a greater total fauna, although some paintings of them
contain a much greater variety of animals than does any single picture of
the Jerome cycle. Furthermore, in depictions of the "Creation of Animals" and "Noah's Ark," there was little need for choosing creatures of
particular symbolical or allegorical meaning, as was the case to a large
degree in selecting the animals to be used in the Jerome story.

To some extent Saint Jerome himself may have suggested specific animals, although how well known his letter *Ad Heliodorum epitaphium*

9. J. Porcher, in J. Hubert, J. Porcher,
and W. F. Volbach, *The Carolingian
Renaissance*, pp. 137, 141.

10. The original text of the pertinent part
of Jerome's very long letter to Eustochium (Epistle xxii) runs as follows: "De
cibis vero et potu taceo, cum etiam lan-
guentes aqua frigida utantur et coctum
aliquid accepisse luxuriae sit. Ille igitur
ego, qui ob gehennae metum tali me car-
cere ipse damnaveram, scorpionum tantum socius et ferarum." (F. A. Wright,
Select Letters of St. Jerome, p. 66). This
was shortened in de Voragine's *Legenda
aurea* (Graesse ed., p. 655) as follows:
"De cibis et potu taceo, cum etiam lan-
guentes aqua frigida utantur, et coctum
aliquid accepisse luxuria sit, et dum scorpionum tantum essem socius et ferarum."
The statement was translated by Ryan
and Ripperger in their version of the
Golden Legend (pt. 2, pp. 588–89): "Of
food and drink I say naught, since even
sick men drink cold water, and to them
also it is somewhat of a luxury to eat
cooked food. Yet, while I lived thus,
the companion of scorpions and wild
beasts...."

nepotiani was to the artists generally or to their advisers is not certain. In this letter he wrote: "For just as we marvel at the Creator when we behold not only heaven and earth, sun and ocean, elephants, camels, horses, oxen, panthers, bears and lions, but also tiny creatures—ants, gnats, flies, worms and the like—their forms are better known to us than their names."[11] In still other writings, explored for their natural history references by Father Leopold Fonck,[12] Jerome discussed ants, bats, chameleons, cranes, dragons, eagles, herons, hoopoes, locusts, and owls, as well as a few plants. Hugh Pope has similarly extracted notes on birds found in Jerome's writings.[13]

While the theme of "Jerome in the Wilderness" gave an impetus to artists to look at the world of nature, the matter of direct observation of animal life was not new; it was its expanded use in pictorial art that was new. During the later centuries of the Middle Ages, men showed much, even intense, interest in nature. Evidence of this interest and knowledge may be seen on every page of Lottlisa Behling's great study of the naturalistic accuracy of the plants in medieval paintings; in the similarly correct drawings of animals in the *Fiori di Virtu* described and reproduced by Otto Lehmann-Brockhaus; in Lilian M. C. Randall's study of images in the margins of Gothic manuscripts; in Otto Pächt's article on early Italian nature studies; and in Ernst Robert Curtius's lucid and stimulating study of the literature of the Latin Middle Ages, in which he reviews and explains much of the enormous mass of naturalistic description in medieval writings.[14] Aside from these publications, which are merely important samples of a much larger number, one may mention the great mass of animals and plants carefully carved by largely unknown hands in the decorations of the great Gothic cathedrals, where their function is decorative and not intended to be symbolic. These reveal patient observation by their carvers in their accuracy of form and lifelike movement.

Although the representations of animals and plants became more varied and numerous in the Renaissance, their use in art was still limited by the prevailing attitude that their chief importance was in their allegorical significance rather than their external form or coloration. Yet artists had to know the outer appearance in order to depict the creatures in readily recognizable form in their paintings or carvings. Artists thus became, in effect, the first naturalists in the period of intellectual transition from medieval to modern Europe. As a matter of historical fact, the European tradition of employing the visual arts to embellish and to make more explicitly intelligible the stories, morals, and personages they were used to illustrate was of the very greatest importance in the development of zoology and botany. It is, indeed, impossible to imagine the early, descriptive phases of biology arising without such an antecedent, pictorialized interest in animals and plants.

A case in point that illustrates this role of the artist as naturalist, an instance of unusual zoological accuracy in a religious painting, produced at a time when devotional art was still expressed within traditional modes of representation, is an early Riminese picture that I studied many years ago. This painting, *Madonna and Child with Angels*, then attributed to Giovanni Baronzio, now to the Master of the Life of Saint John the Baptist (Washington: National Gallery of Art), has been dated about

11. Epistle lx: "Ad conparationem quidem superiorum modica sunt, quae dicturi sumus, sed et in parvis idem animus ostenditur. Ut enim creatorum non in caelo tantum miramur et terra, sole et oceano, elefantis, camelis, equis, bubus, pardis, ursis, leonibus, sed et in minutis quoque animalibus, formica, culice, musces, vermiculis et istius modi genere, quorum magis corpora scimus quam nomina, eandemque in cunctis veneramur sollertiam, . . ." (Wright, *Select Letters*, p. 288).

12. "Hieronymi scientia naturalis exemplis illustratus," pp. 481–99.

13. "St. Jerome: Bird-Watcher and Naturalist," pp. 237–52.

14. Behling, *Die Pflanze in der mittelalterliche Tafelmalerei*, a detailed and meticulous account of the naturalistic accuracy of form and movement in the rendition of plants of many kinds in medieval paintings; Lehmann-Brockhaus, in "Tierdarstellungen der Fiori di Virtu," pp. 1–32, describes and illustrates a treatise of about 1400, in which the virtues and the vices are represented by animals; Randall, *Images in the Margins of Gothic Manuscripts*, a comprehensive study of these images, including animals; Pächt, "Early Italian Nature Studies and the Early Calendar Landscape"; Curtius, *European Literature and the Latin Middle Ages*. Also, Klingender's *Animals in Art and Thought to the End of the Middle Ages* is useful here.

1340.[15] It includes a rarely used animal, the grasshopper or locust, held in the Christ Child's hand. This creature is rendered with such fidelity to nature as to contrast forcibly with the stiff, lifeless, wooden representations of the ox, the ass, and the horse in paintings by the same or related artists done at the same time and in the same town. It is obvious, as I pointed out in an earlier publication, that the painter, "like the vast majority of his fellow artists, followed iconographic tradition when he could. Paintings containing horses and the beasts of the Nativity abounded in Italy, and he had no need to look beyond them for his models and ideas. The grasshopper, on the contrary, was practically non-existent in art available to a Riminese trecento painter, and he was therefore obliged to go to the real creature for his model. This accounts for the accuracy he achieved in his rendition of the locust as contrasted with the lack of it in his horse, his ox, and his ass. From this there follows a thought not kept in mind nearly often enough in looking at or studying early 'primitives.' It was not lack of artistic talent, or ability to draw what they saw, that seemed to limit their achievements, but rather the crushing weight of formalized tradition from which they were either unable or unwilling to extricate themselves. . . . But when they looked with eyes momentarily freed from the influence of their Medieval heritage they were able to see clearly and to render accurately within the limits of available media and techniques. . . ."[16] An even earlier instance of "drawing from nature" is the sketch of an elephant by Matthew Paris, done in 1255.[17]

Millard Meiss pointed out in another connection that the theme of "Saint Jerome in the Wilderness" exemplified, more than any other single subject, the emergence and growth, within the scope of church art, of the late medieval and early Renaissance interest in the unspoiled world of nature.[18] He stated that in such works of art the animals were partly representatives of the fauna that might be found with anchorites in their wilderness retreats and partly were indicative of the general current love of the natural world.

Meiss cautioned, however, that it was not always possible to say whether animals were also included because of their connection with events in the stories of the saints or because they were symbolic carriers of religious concepts. It seems that especially in the earlier decades of their use in illustrations of the Jerome cycle, they were largely of legendary pertinence or of identifiable symbolic meaning, and, as such, served to enhance the story-telling or moralizing function of the art in which they were included. The public for whom these works were created was largely illiterate, and carefully *read* pictures as we now read texts. Details that we, in our hurried glance, are apt to pass over unnoticed, were carefully deciphered by these viewers, and to them the meaningful creatures represented offered anecdotal or legendary information as well as pleasure in their contemplation. Religious art presented subject matter they had already heard about in sermons, but spread it all out before them so that they could examine it at leisure and return for further looking if they wished.

What to the modern viewer seems evidence of fantasy was to them expressive of deeper thoughts and meanings. The medieval mode of thinking was worded largely in symbols. As Henry Osborn Taylor put

15. Fern R. Shapley, *Paintings from the Samuel H. Kress Collection: Italian Schools, XV–XVI Century*, p. 68.

16. Herbert Friedmann, "The Iconography of a Madonna and Child by Giovanni Baronzio in the Kress Collection," pp. 345–52.

17. William S. Heckscher "Bernini's Elephant and Obelisk," pp. 164–65.

18. Millard Meiss, *Painting in Florence and Siena after the Black Death*, pp. 19–20.

it, the mentality of those times exalted the principle of symbolic expression into what amounted to an ultimate description and explanation of the whole visible universe.[19] An early Byzantine scholar, Dionysius Areopagiticus, used the phrase *Spiritualia sub metaphoris realium*, "Spiritual things under the metaphor of real things." This mode of thought was applied to the art that grew up around the legends and the history of Saint Jerome. The many kinds of animals in pictures of the saint are realities, and at the same time are carriers of spiritual messages, and may be enjoyed and studied in both ways.

In later paintings and sculptures, created when church art became freer, there were included some creatures that to us, in our present understanding of those times, seem only dubiously symbolic or pertinent. These are here looked upon as bits of discursive naturalism, as evidence of the growing interest in nature as such. They do not intrude upon, or interfere with, the serious content of the works they adorn. It is possible that some of these may yet be found to have had special meanings as more of the old documents in the archives of the churches and of the religious orders are studied and published.

19. *The Medieval Mind*, p. 86.

To naturalists who consult this book, a word of caution is necessary with regard to the symbolic meanings of animals. It must be admitted at the outset that it is almost always impossible to demonstrate beyond all doubt that the specific meaning of a given object (animals in the present study) arrived at by the iconographer today actually was in the mind of the artist at the time when he created the work of art in which that very object was included. The most we can hope to do is to show what meanings were current for each of such objects in the places where, and in the periods when, they were used by the artists, and to point out how closely or loosely they seem to fit the content of the work of art. While we think of each painting or carving as the work of an individual artist, the fact remains that each was also a product of its age and place. In this latter sense, iconographic interpretation does have a real validity. The agreement of the symbolism decoded may not be with the conscious thought of the artist but with his cultural milieu. A specific item involved may have been something he copied without special reason or thought from a work by an admired predecessor or friendly colleague, but still it was something that belonged in the intellectual climate of the place and period. Further, it should be said that when item after item can be shown to have a significance pertinent to the works in which we find them, this great frequency of agreement cannot be dismissed as mere coincidence.

As one example of the recognized validity of recent studies explaining the presence of otherwise meaningless items in old paintings, items whose very presence was baffling heretofore (baffling, that is, to the iconologist who was the only person who registered any awareness of them), we may take the little wooden mousetrap that occurs, unobtrusively to our eyes, in a relatively few paintings, such as Lorenzo Lotto's *Nativity* in the National Gallery of Art in Washington. It was not until 1945 that the symbolic meaning of this object was rediscovered in a revealing statement in Saint Augustine's Sermon cclxiii: "The devil exulted when Christ died, but by this very death of Christ the devil is vanquished, as if he had swallowed the bait in the mouse-trap. The cross of the Lord was the devil's mouse-trap."[20] Since then, it has been tacitly assumed that in every religious painting containing this humble object it is there as a symbol of Christ's sacrifice, although in no one case has anyone brought forth evidence that the artist necessarily knew Saint Augustine's statement. It is accepted because it "makes sense"; it helps to explain what would otherwise seem inane and meaningless in a context where everything was supposed with good reason to be relevant.

Many years ago Bernard Berenson, who, as an art historian, was more interested in the aesthetic qualities and the authorship of the paintings he studied than their "content," was led to react to iconographic interpretations by saying "it is difficult if not impossible to avoid finding a meaning even where none was intended and to cherish this meaning more perhaps than the object it sprang from. . . . We may call this . . . the 'over-meaning,' for it is probably over and beyond what the artist himself had in mind, and considerably beyond what he could hope to convey with precision."[21] Berenson's statement holds true only if we think in terms of the individual artist, but not if we consider his work as an expression of his immediate cultural ambience. In relatively few instances is it possible to establish, or even to suggest, a definite connection between the meaning and the individual creative artist.

I anticipate that some readers, particularly biologists unfamiliar with the modes of thought underlying medieval and Renaissance art, may wonder how and why the use of symbols came to be so widespread and important. Symbols were employed in all cultures, ancient and recent, but never more so than in the periods and areas that concern us here. Christianity, organized in the Church, provided the great motivating and unifying force in the development of medieval civilization out of the chaos of the Dark Ages, and Christian doctrine was presented to, and apprehended by, the medieval world of western Europe in the work of the four Latin Fathers of the Church: Ambrose, Augustine, Gregory, and Jerome. Three of these theologians grew up in the fourth century and all had studied, as part of their education, literature, grammar, and rhetoric stemming from the Greek philosophers of pre-Christian centuries. Greek philosophy, as exemplified in the wide-ranging interests of Aristotle, had grown from direct observation of the physical world, but, largely because of Socrates, Greek thought also encompassed consideration of the distinction between fact and truth. It was argued that truth was the human understanding of fact, and this caused direct observation of physical reality to be replaced gradually by an ever-increasing interest in the *meaning* of the known, observed facts.

As a result, the perception of discrete entities, such as kinds of animals and plants, came to be looked upon as dealing with merely the external actualities of inner, mental understandings, or ideas. While the physical existence of the observed facts was admitted, it was considered that their true reality lay in their agreement with the highest truths of human logic and thought. Even the mode of perception of such facts had to be defined in these terms. Every factual item came to have a primary intellectual or spiritual significance. It was accepted that the valid interpreta-

20. This was "rediscovered" by Professor Meyer Schapiro in his study of the iconography of the Merode altarpiece. He explained that the little wooden mousetrap, like other lowly objects of the ordinary household, had to be of some interest before its theological significance could justify its inclusion in a picture of religious subject matter. "But even as a piece of still life, the mousetrap is more than just an object in a home; it takes its place beside the towel and the basin of water as an instrument of cleanliness or wholeness, and may therefore be regarded as an overt symbol of the Virgin's purity in the same sense as the others and, like them, independent of a theological text."

The exact Latin of Saint Augustine's sermon (from Migne, *Patrologia Latina*, vol. 38, col. 1210) is: "Exsultant diabolus quando mortuus est Christus, et ipsa morte Christi est diabolus victus, tanquam in muscipula escam accepit. Gaudebat ad mortem, quasi praepositus mortis. Ad quod gaudebat, inde illi tensum est. Muscipula diaboli crux Domini; esca qua caperetur, mors Domini."

21. *The Study and Criticism of Italian Art*, vol. 3, p. 10.

tion of each one could be arrived at only by placing it in relationship with accepted moral and spiritual truth.

So important was this heritage of the ancient Greek writers to the outlook and the reasoning of the Latin Fathers that Henry Osborn Taylor, in his great work, *The Medieval Mind*, went so far as to title one of his opening chapters "Greek Philosophy as the Antecedent of the Patristic Apprehension of Fact."

Once this intellectual attitude was established, the need to objectify mental concepts or experiences, especially on the part of a church faced with the obligation to convey its teachings to the masses of largely uneducated people, resulted in a rich profusion of readily recognized "symbols." It is with some of these, which came to be used as illustrations of the Jerome story, that we are here concerned.

Saint Jerome in His Study

The number of kinds of animals that occur in representations of Jerome in his cubicle is barely a quarter of the total found in pictures of him in the wilderness. None of the most explicitly dangerous or "evil" of the wilderness species, such as snakes, dragons, scorpions, frogs, tortoises, cheetahs, and leopards, have been found in pictures of the saint's chamber. Nor has a lizard been noted there. (Although it is not an evil creature symbolically, it looks evil to many observers because of its reptilian appearance.) No owls have been found in Jerome's study, although in one of their meanings, as emblems of Wisdom, they would seem to be suitable there. However, because owls were considered basically creatures of ill repute, they were not admitted into the scene of the scholar-saint's bookish toil. The frequency with which the lion occurs is due to the fact that it had become a tamed and docile companion of Jerome, as well as his identifying attribute. Only two animals have been noted in paintings of the saint in his study that have not been found in pictures of him in the wilderness, and these two appear but a single time each—a cat in Antonello da Messina's London painting (fig. 119) and a mouse in Colantonio's painting in Naples (fig. 1).

Thus, from the standpoint of his faunal companions in art, Jerome in his study provides much less to engage our attention than he does as a penitent in the wilderness. On the other hand, such creatures as were introduced into pictures of his study chamber were apt to consist of a more significant, if smaller, assemblage. Indeed, we find that a number of very important artists, including Antonello da Messina in Italy and Albrecht Dürer and Lucas Cranach in southern Germany, did portray a considerable number of kinds of animals in such pictures of Jerome. A number of other, lesser, but still notable and delightful artists included one or more kinds of creatures along with Jerome's lion, and more than half of all representations of the theme include at least the lion. Out of more than a hundred versions of the theme examined in the present study, less than a third contain no animals of any kind, but of these at least two-thirds are merely half-length figures of the saint in front of a background suggesting his study room and do not extend down to include the floor, where the lion or other animals would most likely be placed. Of the compositions that do include such space and that do have one or more animals in each, all contain the lion, with or without other creatures, except two: Catena's Frankfurt picture, in which Jerome has a

Figure 1. Colantonio, *Saint Jerome in His Study*. Naples: Museo Nazionale.

guineafowl but no lion, and Joos van Cleve's Cambridge (Mass.) painting in which there hangs a cage containing a goldfinch. It is doubtful if this odd choice has any special meaning. Catena, so far as may be judged from the bulk of his work, was not particularly interested in symbolism as such, and van Cleve absorbed from other sources many of his motifs and compositions. I consider Carpaccio's well-known painting in San Giorgio degli Schiavoni, Venice, to represent Saint Augustine, not Jerome, as often stated; thus, the absence of the lion in it is quite understandable. Its sole animal is Augustine's alert little white dog.

Eight of the pictures of Jerome in his study contain from one to as many as seven kinds of animals in each, along with the saint's lion. Thus, a somnolent lion and sleeping dog occur in Dürer's great engraving of 1514 (fig. 83); a lion and a white dove in Michael Pacher's Augsburg panel; a lion and an insect in a painting by Joerg Pencz; a lion and a

Figure 2. Vincenzo Catena, *Saint Jerome in His Study*. London: The National Gallery.

partridge in a painting by Catena (fig. 2), in London; a lion, cat, peacock, and partridge in Antonello da Messina's London picture (fig. 119); a lion and a mouse in Colantonio's Naples painting (fig. 1); a lion, dog, a family of pheasants, and two partridges in one by Cranach, in Darmstadt (fig. 103); and an astonishing assemblage of a lion, a beaver, a roebuck, a parrot, a rabbit, a squirrel, two partridges, and two pheasants with a brood of eight chicks in another work by the same master, in Sarasota (fig. 104). To this total of fourteen species in nine pictures may be added the guinea-fowl in Catena's Frankfurt picture and the goldfinch in van Cleve's Cambridge painting.

Each of these creatures is treated individually in the Bestiary. Furthermore, a number of them occur in the works of three artists, Dürer, Cranach, and Antonello da Messina, whose pictures are discussed in detail and interpreted in separate chapters of this book.

The pictorial concept of "Jerome in His Study" spans many decades of art from 1352 (Tomaso da Modena) to the 1530s, in the many Flemish pictures stemming from Dürer's Lisbon painting of 1521.

In this connection, Anna Strümpell's comprehensive survey of "Jerome in His Study"[1] is an indispensable reference compilation, as is also Adolfo Venturi's slightly earlier book.[2] Neither offers much discussion of the animals, however, and little of some of the other objects that help to invest the whole Jerome cycle with much symbolic content. Otto Pächt's study[3] also makes no attempt, in its brief presentation, to interpret or to decode the meaning of the saint's faunal associates. As a matter of fact, no one seems to have been much concerned about them. How little they have been studied may be sensed from the fact that a conscientious pioneer compiler like Strümpell concluded that the composition of the saint in his study seemed chiefly to afford artists the opportunity to present the great church scholar as an ordinary townsman with all the accoutrements and paraphernalia familiar to the urban laity. Strümpell thought that this theme was of importance largely because it permitted the characterization and suggestion of the godly and the supernatural in the commonplace of everyday, earthly existence. This had the effect of deflecting attention from the ideas implied by the creatures shown with Jerome in his room. Strümpell also concluded that only a single period in the history of European art provided the proper intellectual climate for the inception and development of this combination of sacred, humanistic, and mundane ideas—the span of years between the waning of the Middle Ages and the beginning of the Renaissance. What she did not mention was that this happened to be also a period of renewed and expanded interest in the natural history of man's earthly home, and, consequently, of increasing use in art of various kinds of creatures, with their overtones of symbolic content derived from earlier legend, myth, and folklore.

While originally the thought behind the figure of Jerome at work on his translation of the Bible was merely a recognition of his scholarship in the service of theology, it rapidly came to imply still more: a coincidence, in one person, of classical, humanistic lore, and ecclesiastical knowledge.[4] The combination of the ecclesiastic and the humanist was readily accepted and easily appreciated because it expressed a timely intellectual concept. It is almost ironic, in a historical sense, that this should have happened to Saint Jerome, who was deeply disturbed by his conflicting love of the pagan, Latin authors, on the one hand, and his devotion to Holy Writ, on the other, a conflict that so preoccupied him as to cause him acute distress.

Inasmuch as the inner, psychological problems of Jerome do have relevance to the development of the particular theme in art showing him as a great scholar—eventually as the unofficial patron saint of the Renaissance humanists—it is necessary to give some attention to them. The intensity of the emotional conflict Jerome's duality of interests engendered was, however, passed over, or little noted, during the Renaissance, but it became a topic that appealed to the artists of the baroque. They and their audiences seemed to enjoy the exaggerations of self-accusation, of pathos, and of upsurging feeling involved in Jerome's famous dream, describing the sudden and startling arousal of the penitent anchorite by a trumpet

1. "Hieronymus im Gehäuse," pp. 173-252.

2. L'arte e San Girolamo.

3. "Zur Enstehung des 'Hieronymus im Gehäuse.'"

4. Renata Jungblut gives an excellent account of the interplay of humanism and the Church in Hieronymus Darstellung und Verehrung eines Kirchenvaters, pp. 107-36.

Figure 3. Simon Vouet, *Saint Jerome and the Angel*. Washington: National Gallery of Art; Samuel H. Kress Collection.

Figure 4. Domenichino, *Saint Jerome and the Angel*. London: The National Gallery.

blast from the angel announcing the Last Judgment and summoning him for trial. Thus A. Pigler listed some twenty-five baroque paintings of this theme, twelve by Italian artists, including Guercino, Gentileschi, Salvator Rosa, Magnasco, Langetti, Gandolfi, and Nasini; seven by Spaniards (six by Ribera alone); three Flemish (Rubens, van Dyck, and Janssens); two German (Troger and Matthäus Günther); and one by a French artist (François-André Vincent).[5] A good example, not listed by Pigler, is Simon Vouet's fine, emotionally intense painting in the National Gallery of Art, Washington (fig. 3). By the very nature of its distraught psychological content this particular theme did not lend itself readily to the inclusion of Jerome's faunal companions other than his identifying lion. Even this beast is absent in many such paintings, present in others. Thus, to mention but a few renditions of this subject, no lion occurs in the Vouet or in the paintings by Piero Francesco Mola in the Vatican, by Luca Giordano in Madrid, by Guercino in Leningrad, or by Procaccini in Milan. A lion is present in a painting by Langetti, in the Cleveland Museum of Art, in each of several by Domenichino, such as those in London (fig. 4) and Madrid, and in one by an unidentified Bolognese painter in the Corsini Gallery, Rome.

Saint Jerome tended to overdramatize in his own writings, but allowing for that, we may attend to the story of his dream as reported by Fray José de Siguenza:

5. A. Pigler, *Barockthemen: Eine Auswahl von Verzeichnissen zur Ikonographie des 17. und 18. Jahrhunderts*, vol. 1, p. 430.

To such an extreme depth of weakness was I reduced that my bones could scarcely hold together. And meanwhile that the necessary preparations were being carried out for my approaching burial, and at the very moment when the vital heat of the soul had withdrawn from all the parts of my body which had already grown cold, and could only be felt in a slight degree in the heart, I was suddenly ravished in spirit and taken before the tribunal of the Judge, where the brightness was such and the resplendency which emanated from all those who were present was so brilliant, that casting myself down to the ground, I never once dared to raise my eyes. I was questioned as to my condition and state. I freely replied that I was a Christian. "You lie," replied He Who presided at that audience. "You are not a Christian but a Ciceronian, for where your treasure is there is your heart." I was dumbfounded at the moment, and between the lashes (for I was being lashed by order of the Judge) I was more fiercely tormented by the fire of my conscience, and in my heart I considered that versicle, "Lord, who shall confess to Thee in hell, or praise Thee?" I began to call out and to say imploringly, my eyes streaming with tears: "Lord, take pity on me, have mercy on me!"[6]

This description has been followed quite closely by Juan Gomez, a late sixteenth-century Spanish artist, in a painting hanging in San Lorenzo el Real de el Escorial. It shows two angels beating the recumbent saint, while Christ and a number of angels look down from heaven. Jerome's lion is squatting, unaffected by the scene, in the lower-right corner of the picture. I have found surprisingly few Italian or French, and no Flemish or other paintings that include the lashing of the saint or the apparition of the Judge in the sky above him. There is an unusual series of twelve scenes of Jerome's life, probably by Jean de Limbourg, in *Les Belles Heures de Jean, Duc de Berry* (figs. 5–9), that contains one picture of the saint being scourged by angels before Christ, the Judge, shown as a dream above a recumbent, sleeping figure of Jerome. Furthermore, the series contains another scene showing Jerome listening to a lecture on pagan philosophy, a clear reference to the saint's love of the ancient, pre-Christian authors, the very reason for his punishment by scourging in his dreams.[7] In neither of these pictures is Jerome accompanied by his lion or by any other animal.

There is also a miniature illustration of the dream of Jerome, by an unknown French artist around 1480, in *Les Heures de Louis de Laval* (fig. 10). In this depiction, a few of the attendant angels hold small bundles of reeds, presumably instruments of flagellation; Christ is on the same level as the saint, not in the sky above him. The only Italian pictures I have found showing the actual scourging of Jerome are a predella panel by Francesco di Antonio, in Paris, and a painting by a follower of Fra Angelico (attributed by Berenson to Domenico di Michelino), in Chartres. A predella panel by Matteo di Giovanni, in the Art Institute of Chicago, has been identified as representing this theme, but it seems to me a dubious interpretation: it does not show the lashing; it *does* have a judge, seated on a throne at the left, but with no indication of anything supernatural about him; and the bound figure at the column is certainly no emaciated, imploring penitent. In the Gomez painting there is no trumpeting angel; that part of the episode is already past. Aside from this one, I have found no other Spanish work containing flagellators or Judge.

The story of Jerome's dream or vision is, however, only a side issue in our present study. Jerome did condemn the study of classical, pre-

6. Translated by Mariana Monteiro in *The Life of Saint Jerome*, pp. 183–84. Fray José's text is based on Jerome's own account in his letter to Eustochium (Epistle xxii), but does not follow it in all details. Jerome's text is as follows:

"Interim parabantur exsequiae et vitalis animae calor toto frigente iam corpore in solo tam tepente pectusculo palpitabat, cum subito raptus in spiritu ad tribunal iudicis pertrabor, ubi tantum luminis et tantum erat ex circumstantium claritate fulgoris, ut proiectus in terram sursum aspicere non auderem. Interrogatus condicionem Christianum me esse respondi: et ille, qui residebat, 'Mentiris,' ait, 'Ciceronianus es, non Christianus; ubi thesaurus tuus, ibi et cor tuum.' Ilico obmutui et inter verberanum caedi me iusserat-conscientiae magis igne torquebar illum mecum versiculum reputans: 'In inferno autem quis confitebitur tibi?' Clamare tamen coepi et heiulans dicere: 'Miserere mei, domine, miserere mei'" (from F. A. Wright, *Select Letters of St. Jerome*, pp. 126–28).

7. Millard Meiss and Elizabeth H. Beatson, *The Belles Heures of Jean, Duke of Berry*, pp. 134–40.

Figure 5. Jean de Limbourg (probably), *Saint Jerome Attends a Course in Pagan Philosophy*. *Les Belles Heures de Jean, Duc de Berry*. New York: Metropolitan Museum of Art; The Cloisters Collection, Purchase 1954.

Figure 6. Jean de Limbourg (probably), *Dream of Saint Jerome*. *Les Belles Heures de Jean, Duc de Berry*. New York: Metropolitan Museum of Art; The Cloisters Collection, Purchase 1954.

Figure 7. Jean de Limbourg (probably), *Saint Jerome Translating the Bible*. *Les Belles Heures de Jean, Duc de Berry*. New York: Metropolitan Museum of Art; The Cloisters Collection, Purchase 1954.

Figure 8. Jean de Limbourg (probably), *Saint Jerome Pulls the Thorn from the Lion's Foot*. *Les Belles Heures de Jean, Duc de Berry*. New York: Metropolitan Museum of Art; The Cloisters Collection, Purchase 1954.

Figure 9. Jean de Limbourg (probably), *The Lion Brings the Caravan to the Monastery*. *Les Belles Heures de Jean, Duc de Berry*. New York: Metropolitan Museum of Art; The Cloisters Collection, Purchase 1954.

8. David Knowles, *The Evolution of Medieval Thought*, p. 67.

9. *Animals, Men, and Myths.*

10. *Hieronymus im Gehäuse*, p. 182, fn. The earliest picture of Saint Jerome is the seventh-century Boethius diptych in the Biblioteca Civica, Brescia, illustrated in M. Salmi, *Mostra storica nazionale della miniatura*, pl. 10.

11. Joseph Klapper, "Schriften Johanns von Neumarkt," pp. 17, 499. Something of Neumarkt's uncritical enthusiasm for Saint Jerome may be sensed from the following excerpts (freely translated):

"This, our father Jerome, is the true Israhel to whom God has opened his heart. . . . He is also the great teacher on whom God has bestowed Christianity. . . ." (p. 17.)

"Jerome is the wholesome water of the deep well spring from whose gentle flow all ailing humanity may slake its thirst. Jerome is a growing tree whose crown reaches the heavens and under whose green limbs all the birds of the sky and the beasts of the field may find sweet nourishment. By the birds of the sky I mean all knowing, or adroit people; by the beasts of the field I mean such people of limited reason who will learn the sweet fruits of his magisterial lessons." (p. 499.)

Klapper's transcript of von Neumarkt's two statements, from which the above summary has been extracted, follows:

Christian literature, but he did not lose any of his fluency in the language of the ancient Roman writers. Many years after his dream Jerome continued to write pure, even idiomatic, Latin, and he could not restrain himself from embellishing his sentences with frequent quotations from his former idol, Cicero.[8] His linguistic expertness made the Vulgate the unassailed Latin version of the Bible for centuries to come. When Jerome first came to be portrayed as a scholar in his cubicle, it was as an ecclesiastical savant, as the great translator of the Bible. It was only later that the concept of him as a great humanist was added to that of the student of Scripture.

In studying the art that grew up around the composite image that came to be implied in renditions of Saint Jerome, and particularly the symbolic use, in that art, of animals, we must remember that while the original, late medieval humanist movement continued to pursue a relatively self-contained course, oblivious, to a considerable degree, of growing knowledge of the external world, including its natural history, the advent of Renaissance thought did not tend to make that movement notably more objective or rationalistic. The intellectual leaders of the Renaissance were not mystics, aimlessly probing around in supernatural unrealities, but they accepted as real, indeed they gave a new reality to, the mythological monsters and fabulous beasts of antiquity, to a far greater degree than these imaginary creatures had ever achieved "rational" acceptance in the Middle Ages. In the works of such respected and historically important naturalists as Konrad von Megenberg, Konrad Gesner, and Ulysses Aldrovandus, all these animals became part of contemporary zoology, where they were given as serious consideration and were thought as real in every way as the creatures that had actually been seen by human eyes. Renaissance scholars, with a few outstanding exceptions, were what Morus Richard Lewinsohn has called surrealists, people who added to reality more than they could experience through their sense organs.[9] They took the traditions and legends of antiquity, and even the products of their own imagination, as valid material to project into their concept of reality, and in this way they believed they were extending the scope and the range of their vision without necessarily forsaking the factual plane of what they really knew.

Although the great stimulus for artists to portray Jerome as a scholar in his study stemmed from the writings of the Bolognese academician Giovanni Andrea in the second quarter of the fourteenth century, the theme had already begun to attract attention before then. The earliest extant large painting of the saint in his cubicle seems to be one of 1352 in the church of San Niccolo in Treviso, by Tomaso da Modena (fig. 11). A pre-Carolingian miniature "portrait" of Jerome of as early as the first quarter of the eighth century is mentioned by Anna Strümpell.[10]

North of the Alps the Jerome cult was furthered by Johann von Neumarkt, Chancellor of Emperor Charles IV, who returned to Prague in 1368 from an Italian journey, bringing back with him an enthusiasm for the saint and a great desire to see him properly honored.[11] The early (about 1400) manuscript illumination of Jerome in his study, with his lion on the floor nearby, by the Bohemian Master of the Gerona Martyrology, in the Korczek Bible, Vienna, may be a result of von Neumarkt's influence.[12]

Around the last decade of that century, or the first years of the next one, an anonymous Franco-Flemish artist, the so-called Boucicaut Master, created a small, but often reproduced picture (fig. 12). In this work, as well as in the one by Tomaso da Modena, the lion is included. In the first years of the next century (about 1405), a little illumination showing Saint Jerome in his study was made by a member of the studio of Herman Scheere, in London, for a Book of Hours, the *Millar Hours* (fig. 13). In this early English version, the saint has no lion with him.

By the middle of the fifteenth century, French and German artists had begun to work on this theme, as Italian painters had then been doing for

"Dieser unter uater Jeronimus ist der warhaftig israhel, der noch dem herczen des almehtigen gots erwelt ist. Er ist auch der selb, der an geuerd alles das geredt und furbraht hat, das im empfolen ist von got, gegen kunigen, fursten und gegen aller werld. Er ist auch der lerer, den got seiner cristenheitgegeben hat, auf di red das er verderben, vernichten, ausrewten und vertreiben schull allen dorn, alle unfletickeit und warhaftige weisheit pawen, pflanczen und stercken schulle. Er hat lip gehabt seine bruder. Er ist der selbe, der so vil bucher von ebreischer und krichischer czungen in lateynische czunge braht hat mit groszen erbeiten. Er ist, der di heilig ordenung der ampt, di man in den heiligen kirchen heldt, des ersten funden hat. Er hat auch alle irrickeit der heiligen schrift verunfticleich geslicht. In des liht hab wir gewandert und mit dem brot seiner heilsamen ler sei wir also gespeist und gesterckt, das wir gen mugen uncz auf den heiligen berg unsers herren. Der selb unser liber vater sant Jeronimus ist auch ein seliger flusz des lebendigen waszers das gleicher weis als ein cristall lawter ist und in Kreften gots mitten durch di heiligen kirchen flewsset, auf des beiden seiten lebendigs holcz wechset, das wirdige frucht in seinen czeiten bringet, des bleter czu geistleichem gesunde seint allem Kristenleichem volk." (pp. 17–19.)

"Jeronimus ist des heilsamen waszers guellendiger brunne, uon des milden flusz alle gebrechsam leut iren durst uerleschen. Jeronimus ist ein werder baum, des hohe des himels tron beruret. Under seinem grünen laub nemen des himels fogel und alle tyr der erden ubersisze speis. Mit des himels fogel meine ich die behenden, weisen leut. Mit den tiren des feldes meine ich die sulchen, die swacher vernunft sint, wann allermenicleich getrostet wirt suszer frucht seiner meisterleichen ler. Diser Jeronimus, mein geselle, ist mir gleich und mit mir ein einsidel gewesen auf der erden und hat sein fleish mir gleich in hunger und in durst alleweg betwungen. Er ist mir gleich reiner, keuscher und schemiger gewest in allen tugenden. Mit mir hat er enpfangen den warhaftigen, lichten geist gotleicher prophecien. Mit mir ist er gewesen ein lerer der warheit czu trost der cristenleichen Kirchen." (pp. 499–500.)

12. This picture is illustrated in Mojmir S. Frinta, "The Master of the Gerona Martyrology and Bohemian Illustration."

Figure 11. Tomaso da Modena, *Saint Jerome in His Study*, 1352. Treviso: S. Niccola.

some decades. Examples of early fifteenth-century French versions are a painting by an unidentified hand, about 1440, now in the Boymans-van Beuningen Museum, Rotterdam, and the frontispiece of the famed Bible Moralisée, in the Bibliothèque Nationale, Paris (fig. 14). An early German instance is the painting attributed to Stefan Lochner, said to have been done about 1440 (fig. 15).

The fact that in the following century, Dürer, one of the supreme artists of the northern Renaissance, produced a very great and immedi-

Figure 12. Boucicaut Master, *Saint Jerome in His Study*, ca. 1400. Paris: Musée Jacquemart-André.

Figure 13. Herman Scheere Studio, *Saint Jerome in His Study*, ca. 1405. *Millar Hours*, English. San Marino, Calif.: Henry E. Huntington Library, HM 19913, f.122.

ately successful and much admired version of the theme, the famous engraving of 1514, *Saint Jerome in His Study* (fig. 83), did much to accelerate the popularity of this icon in Germany and the Low Countries. Dürer's engraving, and his painting, done seven years later, of a half-length figure of Jerome (now in Lisbon), are reflected in literally dozens of pictures by lesser artists, turned out to satisfy a growing demand. Because of its great aesthetic quality, because of its importance as a "source" document, and because of its revealing content, Dürer's 1514

Figure 14. *Saint Jerome in His Study*, French, early fifteenth century. *Bible Moralisée*. Paris: Bibliothèque Nationale.

engraving merits detailed analysis and appraisal and is dealt with in a separate chapter of this book.

In Italy there was no one rendering of the theme of "Saint Jerome in His Study" that had quite the same seminal influence as Dürer's engraving did north of the Alps, unless it was Jan van Eyck's two pictures (originally in Naples, one is now in Detroit [fig. 16], the other lost), but the pictorial composition began much earlier. It may be said to have started with the concept of the half-length picture, which arose practically simultaneously in Padua and in Siena. In the former city it is associated with Giotto, whose frescoes in the Arena Chapel (1305–1306) include such pictures of the evangelists, church fathers, and prophets. In Siena in 1315 Simone Martini painted four writing evangelists in roundels in the painted "frame" of his *Maestà* in the Palazzo Publico. It had been

Figure 15. Stefan Lochner attribution, *Saint Jerome in His Study*, ca. 1440. Raleigh: North Carolina Museum of Art.

suggested that Martini may have gotten the idea for these compositions from the tax-rate books of the city done in the preceding century, which were decorated with half-length figures of the tax collectors sitting behind tables on which were depicted money bags and coins.[13]

It was shortly after this period, when half-length pictures were giving artists the idea for compositions of Saint Jerome behind his desk or work table, that Tomaso da Modena painted his full-length portrait of Jerome, as noted above (fig. 11). Another painting, by Altichiero, not of a church figure but of Petrarch, similarly shown full-length in his study (Padua: Liviano), is more or less contemporaneous, although probably a little later than Tomaso's Jerome. It parallels the latter in that it includes a little dog curled up on the floor at lower right; the Jerome painting has a similarly small lion in its lower-left corner. A slightly later and much

13. A. Lisini, *Le tavolette dipinti di biccherna e di gabella del R. Archivio di Stato in Siena.*

Figure 16. Jan van Eyck, *Saint Jerome in His Study*. The Detroit Institute of Arts; Purchase, City Appropriation.

Figure 17. Cecco di Pietro, *Saint Jerome in His Study*, ca. 1370. Raleigh: North Carolina Museum of Art; Samuel H. Kress Collection.

Figure 18. Jacopo della Quercia, *Saint Jerome in His Study*, 1422. Lucca: S. Frediano.

14. Fern R. Shapley, *Paintings from the Samuel H. Kress Collection: Italian Schools XIII–XV Century*, p. 73; Luigi Coletti (*Catalogo delle cose d'arte e di antichita d'Italia*, pp. 440-44) noted that Tomaso da Modena's Saint Jerome and Altichiero's Petrarch were examples of a number of portrayals of learned men in their study chambers.

15. Fabio Bisogni, "Contributo per un problema Ferrarese," fig. 45.

smaller picture is a full-length *Saint Jerome in His Study* by Cecco di Pietro of Pisa (fig. 17), dating from about 1370.[14]

Another trecento Pisan picture (fig. 52), by an unknown artist, is unusual in that its surface is divided medially into equal, lateral halves, the left half of which shows Jerome in penitence, the right half in his study. In both parts he is accompanied by his lion.

In some of the early pictures of Jerome in his study the artists included the motif of the saint extracting the thorn from the lion's foot. A striking example of this is Colantonio's painting in Naples (fig. 1). Other examples are a painting in the same gallery by an unknown fifteenth-century Neapolitan artist; a picture by an Upper Rhine master of about 1480, in the Städelsches Kunstinstitut, Frankfurt; a woodcut by a Cologne master of about 1470; the famous relief sculpture by Jacopo della Quercia, in San Frediano, Lucca, dated 1422 (fig. 18); manuscript illuminations, already mentioned, by the Boucicaut Master (fig. 12); and the Limbourgesque grisaille frontispiece to the *Bible Moralisée* (fig. 14). In these last two examples, Jerome is not exactly extracting the thorn, but is about to do so, as the lion holds up its injured foot. A painting by an unknown mid-fifteenth-century Ferrarese artist is unusual in its setting.[15] Jerome is seated on the porch of the monastery at the edge of the water; at his right are three monks, one of them showing some apprehension of the lion from whose foot Jerome is extracting the thorn. The use of the open porch is a substitute for Jerome's study.

A curious variant is a Spanish picture by an early fifteenth-century artist, Nicolás Francés, in which the lion is holding up its foot to one of Jerome's attendant monks to have the thorn extracted, while the saint has returned to his literary labors.[16] A German picture, by Rueland Frueauf the Younger,[17] shows Jerome seated with the lion's head and front paws on his lap, and the saint gently patting the beast's head. Strümpell singled this out as showing the transition in the treatment of the lion from its original state as a wild animal to its future one as a domestic household pet.

In later versions of Saint Jerome at work in his monastic cubicle, the lion is usually present, merely as his identifying attribute. Out of more than sixty renditions of "Saint Jerome in His Study" that include the lion, the thorn-extraction incident is depicted in only eight instances, all mentioned above, and all of them done prior to the end of the fifteenth century.

What may be looked upon as early steps in the process of combining the "outdoor" and "indoor" settings of the Jerome-lion theme are two very similar, late-fourteenth-century Veneto-Byzantine paintings, one in the National Gallery, London, and one in the David and Alfred Smart Gallery, University of Chicago (fig. 19). In both of these Jerome is indeed out in the wilderness, but is seated on an elaborate, thronelike chair with a lectern to hold his book. It is, in effect, as if he had taken the furnishings of his study chamber with him into the rocky waste, behind which looms his church. A comparable but much later painting is Giovanni Santi's *Saint Jerome Enthroned in the Wilderness* (fig. 20). The setting of the small painting by Cecco di Pietro is outside the monastery building, but hardly in the wilderness (fig. 17).

In other versions of the subject the artists combined more than one episode of the saint's story. Thus, in a painting by the Master of Saint Gudule, a follower of Hugo van der Goes, we see Jerome in his chamber, but through the open door of the room we can discern in the "wilderness" background the saint in penitence, accompanied by his lion and with a snake nearby.

In some of the many Flemish half-length pictures of Jerome in his study, stemming from Dürer's Lisbon painting of 1521, the artists represented the saint as if he were in the wilderness, largely nude to the waist and with a stone clenched in his right hand. Examples are the Joos van Cleve workshop pictures at Princeton and West Palm Beach, Florida.[18]

While renditions of "Saint Jerome in His Study" were almost always pictorial entities in themselves, the idea of showing him in his scholarly activities occasionally was carried over into altarpieces where Jerome was merely one of several lateral attendant figures. What may be looked upon as an early and unusual recognition of the scholar in the attendant church father may be seen in an altarpiece painted in 1469 by Benedetto Bonfigli, *Pietà with Saint Jerome and Saint Leonard*, in the church of San Pietro in Perugia (fig. 21). In this remarkable altarpiece we find Jerome seated at his desk with his books and with even a semblance of his study around him, his lion nearby, filling the left side of the painting. In view of the fact that Bonfigli was far from the most original of painters, this unusual presentation would seem to reflect the growing popularity of the combined "humanist-ecclesiastic" image of Jerome.

16. Chandler Rathfon Post, *A History of Spanish Painting*, vol. 8, p. 682, fig. 319. Actually, this rendition is closer to the original legend than are those showing Jerome extracting the thorn. The saint, in the original version of the *Legenda aurea*, bade one of his monks to attend to the lion's foot.

17. Ernst Heidrich, *Die Altdeutsche Malerei*, pl. 7, p. 262.

18. John Hand, *Joos van Cleve and the Saint Jerome in the Norton Gallery and School of Art*, col. 6, states that the idea of placing the penitent Jerome in a study setting originated with van Cleve.

Figure 19. *Saint Jerome and the Lion*, Veneto-Byzantine, late fourteenth century. Chicago: David and Alfred Smart Gallery, The University of Chicago; Samuel H. Kress Collection.

Figure 20. Giovanni Santi, *Saint Jerome Enthroned in the Wilderness*. Vatican: Pinacoteca.

Figure 21. Benedetto Bonfigli, *Pietà with Saint Jerome and Saint Leonard*, 1469. Perugia: S. Pietro.

Saint Jerome in the Wilderness

The great popularity of the "Saint Jerome in the Wilderness" theme in religious art resulted from the value people generally placed on the implications behind the purely factual story of Saint Jerome's long, penitential sojourn in the Chalcidean wilderness. It is difficult for us today to appreciate fully just what the concept of the religious recluse or "holy hermit" meant to the common people of the early Renaissance. These anchorites, sometimes called the "desert fathers," were looked upon as men whose gruelling experiences had given them some concept of an existence where matters of the spirit take precedence over material desires, an existence patterned on that of the future world, a world that transcended in significance the mundane one of the ordinary man. Because of this, anchorites were regarded with particular esteem on their return from the wilderness.

It should be understood, in regard to the "wilderness" setting in various paintings, that wilderness meant not only a remote and wild region, but, in some instances, any area outside the protective walls of the cloister or a town. It is, therefore, neither illogical nor indicative of conceptual inadequacy on the part of the artists concerned when we find the saint's monastery, or even a view of a city, in the near background of a picture of "Saint Jerome in the Wilderness."

Renditions in art of "Jerome in the Wilderness" are roughly of three main types: the saint kneeling in prayer before a crucifix, beating his chest with a stone; the saint sitting in the landscape reading the scriptures; the saint simply sitting in the desolate solitude (sometimes not so desolate), quietly meditating. Many of these compositions include the episode of Jerome removing a thorn from the lion's foot; Jerome listening to the trumpet of the angel announcing the Last Judgment; and, more rarely, Jerome being harassed by disputatious heretics or by demons (as in a painting by the Spanish artist Francisco de Herrera the Elder in Rouen); or being tempted by visions of alluring nymphs (as in Francesco Zurbaran's painting in Guadalupe).

In the great majority of these renditions, Jerome's lion is included. The animal has been found in more than three-fifths of such representations, but the significant frequency of its occurrence is actually greater. This is so because more than half of the pictures in which no lion is present show only half- or two-thirds-length figures of the saint and do not extend down far enough to include the ground, upon which the lion would have had to be placed. It could, therefore, be estimated that the lion is present in more than 80 percent of all renditions of the theme that provide room for it.

The sojourn in the wilderness, during which, as described in his famous letter to Eustochium, Jerome had daily encounters with "scorpions and wild beasts," was a subject that provided an outlet for artists to express, within a religious context, the growing curiosity about the natural world. This subject, together with the somewhat comparable "Saint John the Baptist in the Wilderness" theme and, to a lesser extent, "The Stigmatization of Saint Francis," brought together in art for the first time the world of nature, with its various animals and plants, and that of man, as exemplified by the type of the "holy hermit." In the great mass of naturalistically accurate faunal and floral carvings that adorn the medieval Gothic cathedrals, the animals and plants, delightful as they are, are more or less by and of themselves; in depictions of the "Creation of Animals" and of "Noah's Ark" they are again independent entities, mere random examples of the world of nature. On the other hand, in the "saint in the wilderness" theme, a man, deliberately forsaking the civilized world to do penance and seek salvation in desert solitude, became, as it were, part of nature, and a new and more intimate connection arose between him and the creatures who were his fellow dwellers in the arid wastes. This was apt to be stressed chiefly in the art of the early Renaissance, when an effort was made, either by the artists, or in an advisory but authoritative capacity by the clerics, to select symbolically meaningful animals and to exclude others deemed less relevant or suitable, in depictions of the theme. This selectivity did not apply to all such minor creatures as insects or snails, many of which were "sufficiently on the fringe of the medieval cosmos to be free from symbolical ties and therefore, more accessible to unhampered curiosity."[1]

On the whole, the dangerous or predatory beasts that were used by early artists, such as Jacopo Bellini, to emphasize the perils of the wild surroundings of the penitent Jerome, were replaced in later versions by more harmless creatures. Dragons and cheetahs (or leopards) tended to be replaced by deer and rabbits. Exceptions to this trend, however, were scorpions and snakes, both of which continued to be included in such compositions. However, as is often the case with generalizations, the trend was upset or obscured by some artists who either ignored, or were not aware of, the original limiting considerations, and filled their pictures with needless (symbolically) numbers and kinds of animals. This was particularly true of many Venetian and other northern Italian painters, such as the three Bellinis (figs. 22–29), Bastiani (fig. 30), Carpaccio (figs. 31, 32), Cima (figs. 33, 34), Crivelli (fig. 35), Mansueti (fig. 36), Montagna (fig. 37), and Tura (frontispiece). The trend also appeared in other schools: in the works of Botticini (figs. 38, 39) and Sellaio (fig. 40) in Florence; of Francesco di Giorgio (fig. 120) and Sano di Pietro (fig. 41) in conservative Siena; in a painting attributed to Civerchio of Brescia (fig. 42); in a bronze plaque attributed to Filarete (fig. 81), and, north of the Alps, in the art of Lucas Cranach (see p. 115 ff.).

1. Otto Pächt, "Early Italian Nature Studies and the Early Calendar Landscape," pp. 21–22.

Figure 23. Detail of hawk from figure 22, Giovanni Bellini's *Saint Jerome Reading in the Wilderness*. Washington: National Gallery of Art; Samuel H. Kress Collection.

Figure 24. Detail of rabbits from figure 22, Giovanni Bellini's *Saint Jerome Reading in the Wilderness*. Washington: National Gallery of Art; Samuel H. Kress Collection.

Figure 25. Detail of squirrel from figure 22, Giovanni Bellini's *Saint Jerome Reading in the Wilderness*. Washington: National Gallery of Art; Samuel H. Kress Collection.

Figure 22. Giovanni Bellini, *Saint Jerome Reading in the Wilderness*. Washington: National Gallery of Art; Samuel H. Kress Collection.

Figure 26. Gentile Bellini, *Saint Jerome in Penitence*. Toledo, Ohio: Toledo Museum of Art; gift of Edward Drummond Libbey, 1940.

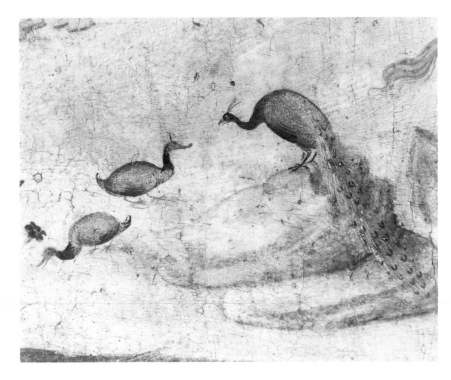

Figure 27. Detail of ducks and peacock from figure 26, Gentile Bellini's *Saint Jerome in the Wilderness*. Toledo, Ohio: Toledo Museum of Art; gift of Edward Drummond Libbey, 1940.

Figure 28. Detail of deer and badgers from figure 26, Gentile Bellini's *Saint Jerome in the Wilderness*. Toledo, Ohio: Toledo Museum of Art; gift of Edward Drummond Libbey, 1940.

Figure 29. Jacopo Bellini, *Saint Jerome in the Wilderness*, ca. 1430–1449. Verona: Museo di Castelvecchio.

Figure 30. Lazzaro Bastiani, *Saint Jerome in the Wilderness*. Milan: Pinacoteca di Brera.

Figure 31. Vittore Carpaccio, *Saint Jerome Leading the Lion Back to the Monastery*. Venice: S. Giorgio degli Schiavoni.

Figure 32. Vittore Carpaccio, *Meditation on the Passion of Christ*. (Saint Jerome is at left; Job at right.) New York: Metropolitan Museum of Art; Kennedy Fund, 1911.

Figure 33. Cima da Conegliano, *Saint Jerome in the Wilderness*. Washington: National Gallery of Art; Samuel H. Kress Collection.

Figure 34. Cima da Conegliano, *Saint Jerome in the Wilderness*. London: The National Gallery.

Figure 35. Carlo Crivelli, *Saint Jerome in Penitence*. London: The National Gallery.

Figure 36. Giovanni Mansueti, *Saint Jerome in Penitence*. Bergamo: Accademia Carrara.

Figure 37. Bartolomeo Montagna, *Saint Jerome in Meditation*. Bergamo: Accademia Carrara.

Figure 38. Francesco Botticini, *Saint Jerome in the Wilderness*. London: The National Gallery.

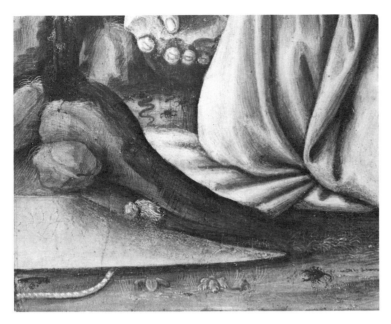

Figure 39. Detail of scorpions and snakes from figure 38, Francesco Botticini's *Saint Jerome in the Wilderness*. London: The National Gallery.

Figure 40. Jacopo del Sellaio, *Saint Jerome and Saint Francis*. El Paso, Texas: El Paso Museum of Art; Samuel H. Kress Collection.

Figure 41. Sano di Pietro, *Saint Jerome in the Wilderness*. Paris: Musée du Louvre.

Figure 42. Vincenzo Civerchio attribution, *Saint Jerome in the Wilderness*. Present whereabouts unknown; in E. L. Tross Collection, Los Angeles, prior to 1932.

Whether the motivating interest was in natural history or in expressing penance and asceticism vicariously through the person of the religious hermit, the fact remains that the theme of "Jerome in the Wilderness" became more popular in Venice than in other Italian art centers; it seemed to satisfy a larger demand on the part of the proud, rich, and luxury-loving Venetians. Millard Meiss wrote that the theme became a Venetian one *par excellence*.[2] However, I know of no single Venetian painter who turned out as many versions of the subject as did the Florentine artist Jacopo del Sellaio, to whom are attributed at least seventeen pictures wholly or partly devoted to the penitent Jerome. The number of Florentine paintings and graphics of this theme found in the course of this study is as great as the total produced in Venice.

In pre-fifteenth-century art, as covered by the Princeton Index of Early Christian Art, there are numerous pictures of Saint Jerome seated, writing at his desk, or standing, fully clad in cardinal's robes, with or without his accompanying lion, but none showing the saint in the wilderness. According to Meiss, the image of Jerome as a penitent eremite appeared first in Florentine art in the early years of the fifteen century, and was there primarily inspired by the Order of the Hermits of Saint Jerome, a group that received official papal approval in 1406.[3] If this group was the responsible factor, it apparently took some time for it to exert its influence, because the earliest Florentine renditions of this aspect of the Jerome theme that I have found date from not earlier than the third decade of that century. They are a painting hanging in the Lindenau Museum, Altenburg, attributed by Robert Oertel and Luciano Berti to Masaccio with studio assistance, possibly by Andrea di Giusto, to whom Berenson ascribed it *in toto*; and another in the Museum of Fine Arts of Montreal (fig. 43), listed by Berenson as by "Domenico di Michelino (?)," but attributed to Andrea di Giusto by its present owner.[4] After about 1435 the subject became popular, as is attested by large numbers of renditions by at least thirty-two Florentine masters, including Bartolomeo di Giovanni (fig. 44), Biagio di Antonio da Firenze, Bicci di Lorenzo, Botticelli, Francesco Botticini (figs. 38, 39), Desiderio da Settignano (figs. 45, 46), Domenico di Michelino, Fra Diamante and Filippo Lippi (fig. 47), Leonardo da Vinci (fig. 48), Filippino Lippi, Zanobi Macchiavelli, Mariotto di Nardo, Mino da Fiesole (fig. 49), Antonio Pollaiuolo, Andrea della Robbia (fig. 50), Antonio Rossellino attribution (fig. 51), and Jacopo del Sellaio (fig. 40). In both Florentine and northern Italian art the subject of "Jerome in the Wilderness" appeared early in graphic works—especially in engravings—along with its use in paintings and in relief sculptures in the middle decades of the fifteenth century.

The two earliest of the Florentine paintings mentioned here show remarkable disparity in their faunal inclusions. The one attributed to Masaccio and his studio includes several unidentifiable insectlike creatures (called noxious insects, "Ungeziefer," by Oertel), and below them and Jerome a large scorpion, but there is no sign of Jerome's lion; the one by Andrea di Giusto shows not only the lion but also a scorpion, a lizard, a snake, and a jay and two other birds. The "Masaccio" rendition is unique in that it is the lower part of a single panel, divided horizontally in the middle, the upper part depicting the "Agony in the Garden." In

2. *Giovanni Bellini's St. Francis in the Frick Collection*, pp. 19–20, and *The Great Age of Fresco: Discoveries, Recoveries and Survivals*, p. 153.

3. In a later study ("Scholarship and Penitence in the Early Renaissance: The Image of St. Jerome," p. 135), Meiss wrote that actually three congregations under the patronage of Jerome were founded in the late fourteenth century. One was established in 1377 at Cessano, near Urbino, by Pietro Gambacorta of Pisa; the second, founded in Spain prior to 1374, spread early to Italy, where its members were known as the "monaci eremiti di San Gerolamo di Lombardia"; the third, begun in Fiesole, by the Florentine Guidi of Montegranelli family, around 1360, was given official confirmation by Pope Innocent VII in 1406.

4. Oertel, *Frühe Italienische Malerei in Altenburg*, pls. 55, 57, pp. 140–41; Berti, *Masaccio*, pp. 93, 164; Berenson, *Italian Pictures of the Renaissance: Florentine School*, pp. 5, 60.

Figure 43. Andrea di Giusto, *Saint Jerome in Penitence*. Montreal Museum of Fine Arts; Horseley and Annie Townsend Bequest.

Figure 44. Bartolomeo di Giovanni, *Saint Jerome in Penitence*. Florence: Galleria dell' Accademia.

Figure 45. Desiderio da Settignano, *Saint Jerome in Penitence*, ca. 1455–1460. Washington: National Gallery of Art; Widener Collection.

Figure 46. Detail of lioness from figure 45, Desiderio da Settignano's *Saint Jerome in Penitence*. Washington: National Gallery of Art; Widener Collection.

Figure 47. Fra Diamante and Filippo Lippi, *Saint Jerome and the Lion*. London: The National Gallery.

Figure 48. Leonardo da Vinci, *Saint Jerome in Penitence*, ca. 1481. Vatican: Pinacoteca.

Figure 50. Andrea della Robbia, *Saint Jerome in Penitence*. Assisi: S. Maria degli Angeli.

Figure 49. Mino da Fiesole, *Legend of Saint Jerome*. Rome: Museo di Palazzo Venezia.

Figure 51. Antonio Rossellino attribution, *Saint Jerome in Penitence*. Present whereabouts unknown; in Bardini Collection, New York, prior to 1940.

each segment an angel descends to the orant figure. The heavenly messenger offers a golden chalice to the praying Christ, a palm frond to Jerome. In no other picture of the latter have I found this offering; it may have been an attempt to bring together the two wholly disparate parts of the panel.

Florentine artists seldom attempted to include as many kinds of wild creatures as did numerous artists of other schools, particularly the Veronese and the Venetians, but there were some Florentines who did; the names of Botticini (figs. 38, 39) and Sellaio (fig. 40) come to mind as examples. If we accept the attribution to Antonio Rossellino of a relief sculpture of *Jerome in the Wilderness* (fig. 51), his name would have to be added.

The very earliest Italian pictures of "Jerome in Penitence" were produced, however, not in Florence, where the influence of the Hieronymite Order might have been expected to show its effect first, but in Pisa. Two such Pisan paintings may be mentioned. One, said to date from the late thirteenth or the early fourteenth century, by an unknown artist, is in Cracow, Poland; the other (fig. 52), similarly anonymous, said to be of the early fourteenth century, is in the Galleria San Matteo, Pisa.[5] In the latter painting, the saint is shown beating his breast with a stone. This self-punishment occurs again in the early quattrocento pictures attributed to Masaccio and to Andrea di Giusto. All of these are earlier than might be inferred from Frederick Hartt's statement that the type of the kneeling Jerome beating himself with a stone arose around the middle of the fifteenth century in Florence and became rare after the early part of the following century.[6]

The history of the "Jerome in the Wilderness" theme in other Italian (and non-Italian) schools of art may be sensed from the large number of paintings, graphics, sculptures, and other works mentioned in this study. The earliest paintings associated with Venice are the two late fourteenth-century Veneto-Byzantine pictures, mentioned earlier, of Jerome in a rocky landscape, accompanied by his lion, but not clad as a hermit and not in a penitential attitude (London and Chicago). Otherwise, the earliest Venetian versions are to be found in the work of Jacopo Bellini, in a number of unfinished sketches in his notebooks, preserved in London and in Paris (figs. 53–55); in at least one painting (fig. 29); and possibly in another, at one time in the Viezzoli Collection, Genoa. All date from the third or fourth decades of the fifteenth century.

Jacopo Bellini's sons, Gentile and Giovanni, quickly incorporated the theme in their own work, and made it more widely known. From then on "Saint Jerome in Penitence" became one of the most frequent subjects in Venetian art. In the hands of innumerable Venetian painters, dozens of such pictures were produced from the middle of the fifteenth century onward, even as late as the eighteenth century in the work of Giovanni Battista Tiepolo. Just to mention a few of the other important Venetian masters who have left us versions of this theme we may note: Antonello da Messina, Basaiti, Bonifazio, Buonconsiglio, Campagnola (fig. 56), Cariani (fig. 57), Carpaccio, Catena, Cima (figs. 33, 34), Crespi, Carlo Crivelli (fig. 35), Diana, Fogolino, Girolamo da Treviso, Mansueti (fig. 36), Marconi, Montagna (fig. 37), Oliverio, Paris Bordone (fig. 58), Rondi-

5. The dates and attributions are those in the catalogues of the two museums; neither picture is mentioned in Berenson's lists.

6. *Michelangelo Drawings*, p. 335.

Figure 52. *Saint Jerome in His Study and Saint Jerome in Penitence*. Pisan, early fourteenth century.
Pisa: Museo Nazionale di San Matteo.

Figure 53. Jacopo Bellini, *Saint Jerome in the Wilderness*, ca. 1430–1449. Paris: Musée du Louvre.

Figure 54. Jacopo Bellini, *Saint Jerome in the Wilderness*, ca. 1430–1449. Paris: Musée du Louvre.

Figure 55. Jacopo Bellini, *Saint Jerome in the Wilderness*, ca. 1430–1449. London: British Museum.

nelli, Tintoretto (both Domenico and Jacopo), Titian (fig. 59), Veronese (fig. 60), and Alvise Vivarini (fig. 61).

Either because of Venetian examples and impetus or because of the influence of Bologna and Padua, the theme became exceedingly popular in most of the northern Italian lesser art centers, such as Bergamo, Brescia, Cremona, Ferrara, Genoa, Milan, Parma, Pavia, and Verona. Among the earlier (fifteenth-century) northern Italian artists who applied themselves to this subject may be mentioned Bergognone, Bono da Ferrara (fig. 62), Butinone, Civerchio (fig. 42), Foppa, Francia, Pisanello follower (fig. 63), Roberti, Tura (frontispiece), and Zoppo (fig. 64).

Just as the theme spread over northern Italy from Venice, so too the artists of Umbria responded to the influence emanating from Florence and from Pisa. Among Umbrian designers of penitent Jeromes may be listed Antonio da Viterbo, Bartolommeo da Forlì, Bonfigli, Mezzastris,

56

57

58

Figure 56. Domenico Campagnola, *Saint Jerome in the Wilderness*. Los Angeles County Museum of Art.

Figure 57. Giovanni Cariani, *Saint Jerome in Penitence*. Bergamo: Accademia Carrara.

Figure 58. Paris Bordone, *Saint Jerome in a Landscape*. Philadelphia: John G. Johnson Collection.

Figure 59. Titian, *Saint Jerome in Penitence*. Milan: Pinacoteca di Brera.

Figure 60. Paolo Veronese, *Saint Jerome in the Wilderness*. Washington: National Gallery of Art; Samuel H. Kress Collection.

Figure 61. Alvise Vivarini, *Saint Jerome in the Wilderness*. Washington: National Gallery of Art; Samuel H. Kress Collection.

Figure 62. Bono da Ferrara, *Saint Jerome in the Wilderness*. London: The National Gallery.

Figure 63. Pisanello follower, *Saint Jerome in the Wilderness*. Present whereabouts unknown.

Palmezzano, Perugino (figs. 65, 66), Pinturicchio, Raphael, Signorelli, Lo Spagna, and Tiberio d'Assisi.

In Siena the theme first appears in the first half of the quattrocento, in works by Sassetta and by Sano di Pietro (fig. 41). It was quickly taken up by other Sienese artists, such as Beccafumi, Benvenuto di Giovanni, Francesco di Giorgio, Fungai, Girolamo di Benvenuto, the Master of the Osservanza Triptych, and Sodoma. For some reason, as yet unclear, the subject had considerably less popularity in Siena than elsewhere, but it still was a definite part of the iconography of religious art in that city.

After its establishment in Italian art, the theme spread to the Low Countries by the last third of the fifteenth century (as witnessed by paintings by Hieronymus Bosch, Gerard David, and the Master of the Saint Ursula Legend). It had already had a somewhat earlier start there in the art of Rogier van der Weyden (fig. 67). In his work, however, we do not encounter Jerome as a penitent hermit, but as a fully clad cardinal in a rocky, arid landscape; not in prayer or meditation, but engaged in removing the thorn from the lion's foot (Brussels and Detroit). Bosch not only painted the saint as penitent, but penitent to a degree far more extreme in psychological stress than any other artist ever attempted (Ghent). Bosch's two versions of the subject (Ghent and Venice) are

Figure 64. Marco Zoppo, *Saint Jerome in Penitence*. Baltimore: Walters Art Gallery.

Figure 65. Pietro Perugino, *Saint Jerome in Penitence*. Washington: National Gallery of Art; Samuel H. Kress Collection.

Figure 66. Pietro Perugino, *Saint Jerome in Penitence*. Panel of triptych, *The Crucifixion with the Virgin, Saint John, Saint Jerome, and Saint Mary*. Washington: National Gallery of Art; A. W. Mellon Collection.

Figure 67. Rogier van der Weyden, *Saint Jerome and the Lion*. Brussels: Musées Royaux des Beaux-Arts.

Figure 68. Aelbert Bouts, *Saint Jerome in Penitence*. Brussels: Musées Royaux des Beaux-Arts.

dealt with in detail elsewhere (p. 137 ff.). The subject became very popular in the Low Countries, where it was treated, often repetitiously, by many artists such as Aelbert Bouts (figs. 68, 69), Jan de Cock (fig. 70), Jan Gossaert (fig. 71), Jan van Hemessen, Herri met de Bles, Adrian Isenbrandt (fig. 72), Lucas van Leyden (fig. 73), Patinir, Rembrandt (figs. 74, 75), Rubens, and van Dyck.

Figure 69. Aelbert Bouts, *Saint Jerome in Penitence*. Los Angeles: The Norton Simon Foundation.

Figure 70. Jan de Cock, *Saint Jerome in Penitence*. Cologne: Wallraf-Richartz Museum.

Figure 71. Jan Gossaert, Saint Jerome in Penitence. Washington: National Gallery of Art; Samuel H. Kress Collection.

Figure 72. Adrian Isenbrandt, *Saint Jerome in Penitence*. Leningrad: Hermitage Museum.

Figure 73. Lucas van Leyden, *Saint Jerome in Penitence*. Berlin-Dahlem: Staatliche Museen.

Figure 74. Rembrandt van Ryn, *Saint Jerome in Penitence*. Washington: National Gallery of Art; Rosenwald Collection.

Figure 75. Rembrandt van Ryn, *Saint Jerome Reading in a Landscape.* Washington: National Gallery of Art; Rosenwald Collection.

The earliest rendition in German painting of the penitent Jerome seems to be a picture attributed to Albrecht Dürer, dated about 1498, in the collection of Lt. Col. Sir Edmund Bacon, Raveningham Hall.[7] There is, however, an earlier German work, not a painting but an engraving, said to date from the second half of the fifteenth century, by the Master B. R., a member of the Lower Rhine circle of Martin Schongauer.[8] This shows Jerome, accompanied by his lion (inconspicuous), kneeling before a crucifix. A somewhat later engraving, of the late fifteenth or early sixteenth century, is one by the so-called Master P. W. of Cologne. Mention may be made here of a painting in the Alte Pinakothek, Munich, by an anonymous German (Lower Rhine) artist of about 1430–1440, showing Jerome in a landscape with his lion, although the saint is not in a penitent attitude.

Later, in the hands of painter-engravers such as Albrecht Altdorfer (figs. 76, 77), Lucas Cranach the Elder, and Dürer, the subject of Jerome

7. David Carritt, "Dürer's St. Jerome in the Wilderness," pp. 363–67. Dürer made an engraving of "Jerome in Penitence" in 1497.

8. A. H. Mayor, *Late Gothic Engravings of Germany and the Netherlands*, no. 434.

Figure 76. Albrecht Altdorfer, *Saint Jerome in Penitence*. Cologne: Wallraf-Richartz Museum.

Figure 77. Albrecht Altdorfer, *Saint Jerome and His Lion in a Cave*. Washington: National Gallery of Art; Rosenwald Collection.

in a wilderness setting became an occasion for portraying animals. All three of these artists were much interested in wild creatures, and Cranach, in particular, tended to crowd his pictures with them, almost as much so as the Bellini-Mansueti group did in Venice. Cranach did this even in paintings of Jerome in his study, as exemplified by two of his pictures, one now in the museum of Darmstadt (fig. 103) and one in Sarasota (fig. 104). (Cranach's work is treated in detail elsewhere in this study (p. 115 ff.). This interest in animals was not characteristic of all Teutonic artists. Examples of the opposite tendency are Hans Leonhard Schäufelein's painting in Nuremberg and Adam Elsheimer's Bergamo picture (fig. 78).

In France at the close of the fifteenth century, an unidentified Burgundian artist portrayed a penitent Jerome as an illumination in a manuscript of about 1490, now in the Henry E. Huntington Library, San Marino, California (HM 1148, f. 27). This is the earliest French version of the subject that I have found. From the standpoint of this present study it is unrevealing, as it is a two-thirds-length figure of the saint before a crucifix, with a stone clenched in his right hand. Because the lower part is not included, it is not even certain whether Jerome is kneeling or standing, and, of course, there is no room in which the artist could have placed the lion had he wanted to portray it. Approximately a

Figure 78. Adam Elsheimer, *Saint Jerome in a Landscape*. Bergamo: Accademia Carrara.

decade later (about 1500), another Burgundian artist did a similarly par-tial figure of "Jerome in Penitence," also without a lion (Beaune: Hos-pital St. Esprit). By and large, French artists apparently did not busy themselves to any extent with this theme. In the Henry E. Huntington Library there is a sixteenth-century French manuscript (HM 1124, f. 180) containing an illumination of the saint kneeling in a landscape, holding an open book in his right hand and a tall, slender cross in his left, while his lion rests on the ground in front of him. More than a century later two very dissimilar French artists returned to the theme: Nicolas Poussin (Madrid) and Georges de La Tour (Grenoble), but no other French versions of the subject have come to my notice. French artists of the early Renaissance were more interested in depicting Jerome in his study than in the wilderness, but even in his study he was never a favorite subject with them.

Aside from one fourteenth-century picture by Paolo da San Leocadio in Barcelona;[9] one of very uncertain date by the Ecija Master; one by the Urgel Master, a Spaniard painting under Flemish influence; and Bartolome Bermejo's *Pietà* in the Barcelona Cathedral, Spanish artists appear to have produced few pictures of "Jerome in the Wilderness" prior to the sixteenth century. In that century, however, many such paintings were created in Spain. Among the artists were Antonio de Comontes, El Greco (fig. 79), Juan Fernandez de Navarrete, Juan Gomez, Morales, and Vasquez. The seventeenth century witnessed the production of still other renditions of Cerezo, Montañes, Murillo, Antonio di Pereda, Ribera, Saavedra, and Salzillo, while the work of Goya extended Spanish participation in this aspect of Hieronymite art into the early nineteenth century. Some of these later pictures portray the saint's lion and others do not, but none of them include other faunal associates. Furthermore, a good many of the late (seventeenth-century) pictures of the penitent Jerome are "half-lengths" and, as such, do not include the ground of the setting, thereby excluding the possible inclusion of animals.

Of the approximately 570 versions of the "Saint Jerome in the Wilderness" theme examined, more than 400 were created in Italy, about eighty in the Low Countries, twenty or more in Germany, and a similar number in Spain, while French artists were responsible for only six. It is possible that these figures may be slightly weighted in favor of Italy, because of the more complete and more readily accessible lists available for Italian paintings than for those of some of the other countries. On the other hand, it seems almost certain that the Reformation, with its violent repercussions, resulted in wholesale destruction of earlier church art in northern Europe—but of this loss there is no listing. How many northern "Jeromes" may have perished without a trace or a record we have no way of knowing.

While the lion occurs in the majority of pictures of "Jerome in the Wilderness," none of the saint's other animal associates do so with anything like that degree of frequency. The relative occurrence of the other creatures in some 570 renditions of this theme may be summarized as follows: deer (of four kinds, varying in number in different works) in forty-three cases; snakes (from one to as many as ten in one picture) in thirty-seven; lizards in twenty-five; scorpions (from one to three per picture) in twenty-seven; unidentifiable "small birds" in seventeen; hawks (including eagles and falcons) in fourteen; owls (of three kinds) in twelve; rabbits in eleven; partridges (of two kinds) in ten; parrots (including two identifiable kinds) in nine; frogs, bears, and squirrels, in eight each; ducks and goldfinches in seven; dragons, guineafowl, jays, and pheasants, in six each; herons (of two kinds), hoopoes, peacocks, snails, and tortoises in five each; cheetahs, dogs, and titmice (of two kinds) in four each; beavers, cranes, flies, monkeys, storks, and swallows in three each; genets, magpies, otters (including ichneumons), swans, and woodpeckers (two kinds) in two each; ant, badger, cat, chaffinch, cock, dove, fox, harpy, hawfinch, "insect," jackal, kingfisher, leopard, mouse, porphyrio or purple gallinule (?), crab, raven, robin, unicorn, wallcreeper,

9. A. de Bosque, *Artisti Italiani in Spagna dal XIVe siecolo ai re cattolici,* p. 184.

Figure 79. El Greco, *Saint Jerome in Penitence*, ca. 1610–1614. Washington: National Gallery of Art; gift of Chester Dale.

and wolf in one each. In this listing no mention is made of domestic animals as the cow, sheep, ass, and camel.

Each of the above creatures is discussed in detail in the Bestiary section of this book, where, in most cases, it will be found that the particular creature has a symbolic meaning that "suits" it as part of the icon of the penitent saint. The ape, snake, scorpion, tortoise, frog, dragon, and partridge all have essentially evil connotations, and either refer to vices and errors that Jerome was seeking to escape or to shed by his penitence, or illustrate the danger of the wilderness. Other creatures, such as the deer, lizard, goldfinch, hoopoe, otter (or ichneumon), swallow, and beaver, are allusions to virtues. A very few are not individually meaningful, so far as is known; these may be considered as evidence of interest in natural history on the part of the artists or of their patrons.

The great extent to which the "Jerome in the Wilderness" theme was used as the occasion for expressing some of this natural history interest may be sensed from the following brief annotations on a selected few of the more faunally embellished renditions of the subject.

Hieronymus Bosch included in his famous panel, now in Ghent (fig. 108), not only the lion but a pair of ducks with four ducklings, a sleeping fox, a cock, three lizards, an owl, a tit, two woodpeckers, a chaffinch, and a heron! This painting includes all these creatures, many of them too small or too obscure to be seen a foot away from the picture, but does not include such symbols of evil as the scorpion (specifically mentioned as one of his daily companions in the desert by Jerome) or the snake.

In the central panel of his triptych of Jerome with other saints, in London (fig. 38), Botticini included the saint's usual lion as well as a scorpion, a scarab, a snake, an unidentifiable grayish dovelike bird, and a distant, dim, and tiny heron, most of them too small to be seen without a special search. In a painting in the Toledo (Ohio) Museum of Art, catalogued as by Gentile Bellini but attributed to Lazzaro Bastiani by Berenson,[10] we find Jerome associated with a lion, two rabbits, two squirrels, two ducks, two guineafowl, two pheasants, a scorpion, a lizard, a frog, a peacock, a deer, and two not wholly distinct quadrupeds that may possibly be badgers! (fig. 28).

Jacopo Bellini's Verona picture (fig. 29) includes the lion, two dragons, a wolf, a possible genet (not distinct enough in its drawing to be certain), a dark, long-tailed bird with a rounded but heavy beak (possibly intended as a parrot), and an eagle. In two drawings by the same artist we find equal or even greater numbers of animals. In one, in the Louvre (fig. 53), there are a lion, a lioness, two dragons, two rabbits, two roedeer, a monkey (plus another possible one, too indistinct for positive identification), a tortoise, and two eagles; in another, in the British Museum (fig. 55), a lion, a lioness, three deer, two dragons, and a rabbit! In two of Giovanni Bellini's versions of the Jerome theme we find a lion, a lizard, a squirrel, a hawk, and two rabbits in the one in Washington (fig. 22); a lion, a lizard, a squirrel, a hawk, and a deer in the one in Florence.

A painting remarkable more for its iconographic interest than its aesthetic qualities, attributed to Civerchio, a Brescian, stresses more than any other single work the unpleasant and dangerous aspect of Jerome's penitential environment. The kneeling, self-lapidating anchorite is surrounded by no fewer than ten snakes, three dragons, two scorpions, three cheetahs, a hawk, and, in the far distance, a number of unidentifiable, heavy-bodied, short-limbed mammals apparently drinking from a stream, while the saint's lion looks up at him with an almost pitying expression, quite different from the human skull that grins at him from the foot of the cross (fig. 42). Three paintings by Sano di Pietro, one in Paris, one in New York, and one in Siena (figs. 41, 80), also primarily stress the evil nature of Jerome's desert companions; each has several snakes and scorpions and a "bug," while the work in Paris also has two deer and a

10. *Italian Pictures of the Renaissance: Venetian School*, p. 26.

Figure 80. Sano di Pietro, *Saint Jerome in Penitence*. Siena: Pinacoteca Nazionale.

fly. A bronze relief attributed to Filarete (fig. 81) similarly includes dangerous animals—lions, bear, wolf, snake, and scorpion.

Lucas Cranach crowded his paintings of Saint Jerome with animals. In one of his pictures (Innsbruck, fig. 94), the penitent Jerome is surrounded by a lion, a tortoise, a scorpion, a beaver, a white stork, two squirrels, six deer, a parrot, and three large birds, two of which are harpies and have human faces; in another (Berlin, fig. 102), there are a lion, a rabbit, a beaver, a pheasant, and a stag!

In a little predella panel in London, Carlo Crivelli included with the orant figure of the penitent Jerome a lion, a snake, two rabbits, an eagle,

Figure 81. Filarete (Antonio di Pietro Averlino) attribution, *Saint Jerome in Penitence*. Cambridge: Fitzwilliam Museum; on indefinite loan from the J. G. Pollard Collection.

11. *Nature in Italian Art*, p. 4.

12. Mention may be made of one very interesting, but iconographically uncertain, instance of faunal richness—a painting by the fifteenth-century Spanish artist Bartolome Bermejo, called to my attention by Eric Young. This picture, in the Cathedral of Barcelona, shows a typical Pietà group in the center with Saint Jerome at left and the kneeling figure of Archbishop Luis Despla at right. C. R. Post (*A History of Spanish Painting*, vol. 5, pp. 144–45) considered that this work, dated 1490, and other pictures of Bermejo's Barcelona period, "reveal an advance towards the mature style of the Cinquecento . . . in the Pieta he has almost passed, with Leonardo, into the fuller reproduction of nature, with fewer

a deer, a dragon, a dog, a crane, and a small flock of ants (fig. 35). Francesco di Giorgio did in bronze relief sculpture what other artists did in paint; his version (fig. 120), discussed in detail elsewhere (p. 164 ff.), includes a lion, an owl, a tortoise, a snake, a lizard, two purple gallinules, two storks and a scorpion.

Giovanni Mansueti of Venice was exceedingly prone to fill his pictures with animals. Thus, in his *Saint Jerome in Penitence* in Bergamo (fig. 36), he included the following incredible assemblage: lion, dog, bear, otter, squirrel, ape, two rabbits, two cheetahs, a deer, an eagle, an owl, a dark, long-tailed parrot (?)—like one we have already noted in Jacopo Bellini's Verona picture—and an unidentifiable small mammal. It was this needlessly crowded picture that caused Emma Salter to write that scenery in paintings is "actually spoilt by an over-insistence on details such as results in the menagerie let loose in Mansueti's St. Jerome in the Bergamo Gallery."[11] In another version of the same subject (formerly in the Arthur Hughes Collection, London), Mansueti included a lion, partridge, guineafowl, rabbit, tortoise, a hawk with a sizable but unidentifiable bird it had killed, and an unidentifiable small bird. In still another (Bristol), he painted a lion, guineafowl, partridge, and rabbit. These are relatively meaningless assemblages of animals, some creatures with good, others with evil, and still others with little or apparently no pertinent symbolic content.[12]

primitive eliminations, that denotes the dawn of modern art." The picture includes an astonishing wealth of animal life besides Jerome's lion: two lizards, two snakes, two snails, three butterflies, six ladybird beetles, one bird (unidentifiable in a small, poor, black-and-white reproduction), and a line of distant flying birds silhouetted against the sky at the top of the panel. It also includes a number of flowering plants in the lower foreground.

Faunal inclusions are certainly not usual in pictures of the Pietà, but it is not at all certain that most of these creatures can be "explained" as being symbolically connected with the figure of Saint Jerome either, as he is quite removed from them all. In this particular painting Jerome, beardless, but with a few days' growth of whiskers, and wearing spectacles, is not wholly a penitent figure. While he is kneeling, he is not about to beat his breast with a stone, is not praying or even looking at Mary and Her dead Son, but is reading a book, a curious combination of penitence (kneeling) and of scholarly preoccupation that would seem to preclude a simple, direct, symbolic connection with any of the creatures in the picture. Aside from his lion, only three of the other kinds of animals—lizards, snakes, and snails—are otherwise known to occur in the Hieronymite context in art, the first two with considerable frequency, the third relatively seldom. On the other hand, lizards, snakes, and butterflies are all symbolically oriented references to the Resurrection, the theme in the story of Christ to which the Pietà is a natural precursor. Furthermore, the ladybird beetles are also symbolically connected with Mary, not with Jerome. The "lady" in the name ladybird is definitely a reference to "Our Lady," the Virgin Mary (mariquita or little Mary, in Bermejo's Spanish).

That the butterflies and the ladybird beetles may have had some wider usage, albeit a minor one, in religious symbolism is suggested by their presence on the ornamental border of a page (f.147b) of the Ormesby Psalter, a fourteenth-century manuscript (Bodleian Library, Oxford, Douce MS. 366).

Figure 82. Ivan Mestrovic, *Saint Jerome the Priest*. Washington: House of the Croatian Franciscan Fathers. David Blume, photographer, Washington, D. C.

To bring this survey up to the middle of the present century it seems fitting to include mention of a modern (1954), and utterly different, version of "Saint Jerome in the Wilderness," even though it has no animal associates, not even the usual lion. This is the bronze figure of the saint by the Yugoslavian sculptor Ivan Mestrovic (fig. 82). Jerome, nude save for a loincloth, is seated in a squatting position, his knees extended laterally, his head bent down over the Bible he is reading with complete absorption, his head supported by his right hand, the arm braced at the elbow against his leg. The saint's face, wholly in shadow and largely obliterated from random viewing because of the steep inclination of the head, is strongly and expressively carried out in its rough modeling. The granite pedestal beneath the statue bears the words "St. Jerome the Priest, A.D. 341–420. Greatest Doctor of the Church." This impressive statue stands directly in front of the residence of the Croatian Franciscan Fathers in Washington, D.C. Despite the word "priest" in the title, the figure really conveys the idea of Jerome the recluse. He is not shown as a priest in proper regalia for his ministry, but as a "desert father," a hermit removed from the society of his fellow men. This representation, stressing a lack of worldly goods, would have appealed to, and may have been requested by, its present owners, a group of Franciscans, dedicated to personal poverty. The absence of the saint's lion may reflect a Bollandist influence, but this is uncertain.

Finally, the theme of "Jerome in Penitence" has been rendered in at least one tapestry, an early sixteenth-century Brussels weaving, presently in the tapestry museum at La Granja de San Ildefonso, Spain.

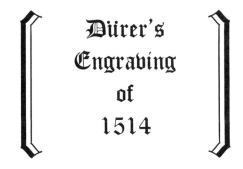

Dürer's Engraving of 1514

Albrecht Dürer's great composition of 1514 (fig. 83) is, in the opinion of many, the supreme rendition of the "Saint Jerome in His Study" theme, and is of compelling interest, not only as a masterpiece of art but also as a response to the emotional climate of its period by an intellectually outstanding artist. In its atmosphere of quiet, of complete detachment from outside events, Dürer's engraving may be said to have been anticipated by the little Detroit panel by Jan van Eyck (fig. 16), by Antonello da Messina's London painting (fig. 119), and even by Domenico Ghirlandajo's fresco in Florence (fig. 84), but it has a more penetrating, all-enveloping feeling of the tranquillity and serenity of scholarship imperturbably devoted to a high and noble purpose. By comparison, the paintings by van Eyck and Antonello, beautiful as they are, are almost genrelike records of a man in a place; they do not evoke the same intensity of response from the viewer that Dürer's engraving inevitably produces. So readily do we succumb to the pervasiveness of its spiritual calm that we accept, almost unthinkingly, the fact that the lion and the dog at the bottom of the picture are peacefully slumbering. Even they, dumb brutes without intellectual understanding, seem to be captured by the quietude and peace that surrounds them. It is not until we realize that this is one of the very few versions of "Saint Jerome in His Study" that include a dog, and the only one in which we have found only these two animals, dog and lion, to occur close together, that iconographic interest is aroused and causes us to ask why they are there and why they are in the particular attitudes that Dürer has given them. To this question we shall return, as it provides a remarkable insight into the ulterior meaning of the whole composition, but first we may note some other features of this magnificent design, not found in other renditions of the same theme.

In his study of the religious renaissance of the leading German humanists, Lewis W. Spitz[1] ventured to suggest that, in designing the setting for his Jerome, Dürer may have reproduced the actual study room of the artist's closest friend, Willibald Pirckheimer, the leader of the group of Nuremberg humanists, or else the library of the sanctuary in Erfurt, which another leading humanist, Konrad Mutian, had named his *beata tranquillitas*.[2]

Erwin Panofsky, in his biography of the artist, considered the three great engravings Dürer produced in 1513 and 1514, *Knight, Death, and the Devil, Saint Jerome in His Study*, and *Melancolia* (fig. 85), as parts of a single connected theme, each representing a different aspect of the Christian ethos.[3] The Knight of the first sheet is the courageous, militant

1. *The Religious Renaissance of the German Humanists*, p. 1.

2. Konrad Mutian (1471–1526), also known as Mutianus Rufus because of his red hair, gathered about himself at Erfurt a number of writers and thinkers, including, among others, Eoban Hess, Justus Jonas, and Crotus Rubeanus. This group was, along with Pirckheimer's Nuremberg circle, very influential in humanistic thought in Germany. Mutian had known Erasmus since their school days together at Deventer, and in the early years of Martin Luther's career both men sided with the leader of the Reformation, but both departed from this association later. Mutian, in particular, was against breaking off from the Church of Rome, but only wanted to reform it from within.

3. *Albrecht Dürer*, p. 151.

Figure 83. Albrecht Dürer, *Saint Jerome in His Study*, 1514. Washington: National Gallery of Art; Rosenwald Collection.

Christian venturing out into the dark and dangerous world, fraught with Death and with Satan; Jerome is the contemplative Christian scholar and writer, seeking in his studies the answers to his problems; Melancolia is a curious combination of the introspective Christian moralizer, weighing and discarding such human temptations as worldly power and wealth, on the one hand, and, on the other, standing for the totality of worldly

Figure 84. Domenico Ghirlandajo, *Saint Jerome in His Study*, 1480. Florence: Ognissanti.

Figure 85. Albrecht Dürer, *Melancolia*. Washington: National Gallery of Art; Rosenwald Collection.

knowledge, which is not always easy to relate to inner morality. As a result, the sad figure of Melancolia is a brooding, inactive individual. The fact that she is shown rejecting power and wealth is in close agreement with Martin Luther's tirades against the Church for its activities in these two areas of human (not divine) endeavor. According to Panofsky's convincing analysis, *Melancolia* is, in a sense, a spiritual self-portrait of the artist.

Dürer appears to have considered these three engravings to be closely interrelated in their symbolic meaning and content, because, when asked for one of them, he took pains to see that all were distributed as a set and not as self-sufficient single sheets. He seemed to be particularly concerned that the Jerome sheet and *Melancolia* be kept together, as both Jerome and Melancolia are personifications of erudition, coupled with intellectual discrimination.

Further evidence of the extent to which Dürer invested his picture of Jerome in his study with the concept of the saint's perceptive learning has recently been brought out by Peter W. Parshall, who studied a prominent, but strangely neglected, item in this magnificent engraving.[4] In the upper-right corner is a very large, pear-shaped gourd suspended from the ceiling rafter that frames the top of the picture. Long before Parshall's study, Wilhelm Waetzoldt[5] explained the gourd unconvincingly as a symbol of the saint who has renounced the world, in accordance with an old belief that it was a "mellow, ideal fruit," the struggles of its period of bloom being past and forgotten.

The gourd still has its leaves and stem and curled tendril, indicating that it was freshly cut from the garden and newly installed in the saint's cubicle. As we shall see, the gourd as used by Dürer is a veiled reference to a famous philological dispute in which Jerome was actively and acrimoniously concerned for at least a decade, and it is intended as a reminder of the saint's careful weighing of available evidence concerning an item of biblical translation.

A passage from the Book of Jonah (4:6) tells how Jonah, after having gone to Nineveh at God's command and warned the people of that sinful city of their impending destruction, waited in vain for the prophecy to be realized. In his discomfiture as a discredited prophet, he complained that the sun was beating down on him. In response, God caused a gourd to grow over Jonah, to give him shade. But the next day the gourd died and a fierce hot wind blew down on Jonah, who then complained to the Lord about the destruction of the gourd. To this, God's answer was that if Jonah, a mere man, could feel so sorry for the gourd, should not the Almighty have pity on so great a city as Nineveh. The story is a moral lesson to man not to stress immediate punishment at the expense of long-range wisdom and forbearance.

Jerome, in his Latin translation of the Bible, chose to translate the Hebrew term for the plant in the Jonah story, *kikayon*, as *hedera*, a kind of ivy. He knew that *kikayon* was the castor bean, but he knew no Latin name for that plant and thought that *hedera* was more similar to the castor bean than was the previously suggested *cucurbita*, or gourd. As Parshall pointed out, the ancient debate, long since settled in favor of the gourd interpretation, was something that not only indicated Jerome's

4. "Albrecht Dürer's 'St. Jerome in His Study': A Philological Reference," pp. 303–5.

5. *Dürer and His Times*, p. 72, based on R. Wustmann, "Von einigen Tieren und Pflanzen bei Dürer," pp. 109–16.

abilities as a textual critic, but also revealed his familiarity with the natural history of plants, and his desire to establish as definitely as possible the physical plausibility of the biblical stories he was translating. Jerome's decision to translate *kikayon* as ivy (*hedera*) led to a prolonged and not always amicable correspondence with Saint Augustine, who disagreed with him.[6] By the theologians and humanists of the fifteenth and sixteenth centuries, who were inclined to regard Jerome as particularly praiseworthy for his critical scholarship, this controversy was looked upon as a prime revelation of his acumen and knowledge. The fact that the gourd, and not the ivy, had come to be accepted—in Dürer's time, as it is today—did not militate against Jerome for his support of the ivy translation. It was the controversy, not its eventual solution, that was important, and it was easier to refer to it visually in terms of its then long-established solution than to rekindle a settled debate by using a sprig of ivy. The same pear-shaped gourd that Dürer used, identified by S. Killermann as *Concurbita lagenaria* Linnaeus,[7] is repeated in a similar position, hanging from the ceiling rafter, in Crispin van de Passe's composition of what could readily be called "Saint Jerome in His Study," were it not titled *Saint Marcus* (fig. 86).[8] It seems that Crispin took over the gourd from Dürer's engraving without realizing what it stood for in that work.

As is usual in pictures of Jerome's study chamber, symbols of transience, such as the hourglass, the candle, and the skull, occur in Dürer's engraving. It so happens that the gourd also was used as a symbol of transience, based on the fact that in the Jonah story it was said that it came up in a night and perished in a night at the Lord's command.[9] The gourd figured particularly in sixteenth-century emblems denoting "Vain Pride" and "Fleeting Pleasure," as in Alciati's emblem entitled *In momentaneam foelicitatem* (fig. 87).

6. Y. M. Duval, "Saint Augustin et le commentaire sur Jonas de Saint Jérôme," pp. 9–40.

7. "A. Dürer's Pflanzen und Tierzeichnungen," pp. 38–39.

8. In F. W. H. Hollstein, *Dutch and Flemish Etchings, Engravings, Woodcuts, 1400–1750*, vol. 15 p. 157, n. 2.

9. Patrick Reuterswärd, *Sinn und Nebensinn bei Dürer*, pp. 424–29.

Figure 86. Crispin van de Passe, *Saint Marcus*. Boston: Museum of Fine Arts; Harvey D. Parker Collection.

Figure 87. *In momentaneam foelicitatem*. From *Emblemata*, A. Henkel and A. Schöne, col. 331 (after Alciati's emblem cxxiv).

The erudition with which Jerome was credited was the primary reason why he was looked up to as the great exemplar of humanistic studies at the time Dürer made this engraving. Inasmuch as there was at that time much tension and disagreement in the intellectual atmosphere surrounding the relationship between humanism and theology, and inasmuch as the poignantly meaningful animal symbolism in Dürer's great engraving is a reflection of this tension, it is necessary to digress for a moment and to outline the emotional and intellectual ambience of the artist as well as of his work.

Dürer was an admirer of Luther, and was deeply sympathetic to his views. At the same time, he was a member of the Nuremberg group of humanists, with whose philosophical speculations and leanings he was familiar. Luther was violently opposed to their views, and to the use of symbols in religious thought and art. Thus Dürer was the recipient of much conflicting thought and opinion. Besides, he continued to work for Cardinal Albrecht of Brandenburg, Archbishop of Magdeburg, and was thereby aware of both sides of the growing schism in the Church. In one of his famous "table talks," Luther admitted that Jerome had accomplished the greatest feat of translation and interpretation in his rendering of the Bible into Latin, but at the same time he criticized him severely for his interest in classical, pre-Christian, writers, and said in so many words that humanism was over and done with.[10] Johan Huizinga has reminded us that Luther wrote of the dangers of the use of symbols in an invective aimed directly at some of the leaders of scholastic theology— Bonaventura, Durand, Gerson, and Denis the Carthusian—wherein he stated that these allegorical studies were the work of men who had little else to do, and added: "Do you think I should find it difficult to play at allegory-making about any created thing whatsoever? Who is so feeble-witted that he could not try his hand at it?"[11]

To a highly intelligent, intellectual artist like Dürer, with an artist's facility for thinking visually, it must have been disturbing that such tirades against symbolism and humanism should be fomented by Luther, who was not only his image of the proper and courageous Christian, but the man whom he came to regard as the one great leader who could bring about the reform of the Church. Dürer's sympathies with Luther continued to grow deeper,[12] but at the same time he did not divest himself of the intellectual values of the humanists. He greatly admired the writings of Erasmus, the most influential humanist in Europe at that time. It is interesting to find that in his little essay on Dürer, the philosopher Giorgio di Santillana found the artist's great engraving of Jerome in his study "Erasmian . . . in its glorification of peaceful learning . . . another medieval theme transfigured."[13]

While the mental and spiritual attitude of Dürer's thought was increasingly on the side of the Reformation, he never felt the need to sever his adherence to the Roman Church. He lived in a period of intense psychological and religious unrest, and it is to his credit that he was able to cling to his beliefs and to invest his art with what he gathered from both sides of the great disputation. I am aware of the uncertainty and the danger of interpretation without the support of incontestable documentation, but it does not seem farfetched to see some such reconciliation of conflict in Dürer's engraving. It includes a sleeping dog, unafraid of the lion whose

10. Anna Strümpell cites this with commentary in "Hieronymus im Gehäuse," p. 178.

11. *The Waning of the Middle Ages,* p. 213.

12. The impassioned language of Dürer's lament when he heard the (false) rumor of Luther's death, in 1521, seven years after the great Jerome engraving, and the urgency of his appeal to Erasmus to bestir himself against the papacy, leave no doubt as to the depth and sincerity of the artist's feelings.

13. *The Age of Adventure: The Renaissance Philosophers,* p. 129.

powerful paw is so close to its hind legs, while the lion is peaceful, almost somnolent, yet alert, as its eyes are not quite closed. The dog was an old symbol of Fidelity, which meaning is still associated with it even today in the continued use of the abbreviated name Fido commonly given to dogs; the lion, among other meanings, signified Courage or Valor. In many sepulchral effigies of the Middle Ages, it is common to find a dog at the feet of the wife and a similarly posed small lion close to the feet of the recumbent figure of the husband. That Dürer was well aware of this is borne out by his sketch for a tomb of a knight and his lady, now in Christ Church, Oxford, where the man stands on a lion and the wife on a dog.[14]

We know from the wording of his impassioned appeal to Erasmus, in 1521, that even then, seven years after he made his great engraving, Dürer still felt a strong loyalty to the Church, and also that his opinion of Luther included a high regard for his courage and valor. In all objectivity, is it not possible, even probable, that the profound serenity that pervades this engraving, showing the great scholar working quietly and placidly at his task for the Church, and the animal symbols of Fidelity and Courage, equally placid alongside each other, is an expression of basic hope that the current strife and friction in religious opinion would be peacefully resolved to the benefit of all? Only in such a condition of peace, and of mutual amity, could Fidelity and Valor afford to relax with safety. This wonderful engraving is a prime illustration of "emotion recollected in tranquillity."

The figure of Jerome in this engraving is the same as in Dürer's 1511 woodcut (fig. 88), but turned to the left; it has the same face also in his 1512 *Saint Jerome by a Pollard Willow* (fig. 89). In these two somewhat earlier works, the absence of the dog (Fidelity) and of the gourd (Jerome's philological acumen) and of such a symbol of transience as the skull (the hourglass is present, however) suggests that these were consciously added in the 1514 version, and hence that they were meaningful to the artist as items that would enhance the composition and give it greater significance as a symbolic statement. This is particularly true of the sleeping dog, even though it is, in a purely art-historical sense, a descendant of the little poodle or Pomeranian often depicted in renditions of scholars' study chambers, where, originally, it was a nonallegorical companion in the "iconography of portraits of scholars, who were at the same time the liberal arts personified."[15] Like other artists, Dürer made use of such available pictorial elements approved by earlier custom in similar situations, and invested them with iconographic significance.

As mentioned earlier, Dürer's great engraving is the only rendition of the "Saint Jerome in His Study" theme in which we have found only the dog and the lion to occur close together; not only together but almost in direct physical contact with each other. Dürer was too much of a thinking artist not to have meant something important by this iconographic innovation. Dürer was not a revolutionary; he wanted to see wrongs in the Church corrected, he wanted to see truth and virtue victorious; but he also hoped it might be possible to save what was good from both sides of the great argument that filled the air of his time, not merely to overthrow the one and to replace it with the other. This was in keeping with the fact that Lutheranism started as a reform and not as a revolt. It was not until some years later that Dürer was convinced that there was little

14. The whole history of the lion and dog symbolism has been reported in detail by Vital Huhn in "Löwe und Hund als Symbole des Rechts."

15. This was pointed out by Raymond Klibansky, Erwin Panofsky, and Fritz Saxl in *Saturn and Melancholy: Studies in the History of Natural Philosophy, Religion, and Art*, p. 315.

or no reason for hoping for this reconciliation, and then he became and remained a fervent supporter of Luther. The fact that Dürer continued to go to confession and to work for Cardinal Albrecht of Brandenburg is no proof to the contrary.

The sleeping dog occurs in the *Melancolia* engraving as well as in the *Saint Jerome*; it is a unifying common feature of both. Fidelity, especially blind (sleeping) fidelity, is obviously important in the multiple layers of meaning in the *Melancolia* design. Furthermore, the very fact that the somber, brooding figure dominating the engraving is, herself, rendered inactive by the conflict of ideas she is attempting to understand, to realign, and to coordinate, puts her in no position to need, or to make use of, active support (fidelity). Her situation is one provoking thought, rather than deed, a situation in which inactive fidelity is sufficient.

It seems highly probable that Dürer's *Saint Jerome in His Study* does express the artist's deep-seated desire for the reconciliation and eventual harmony, in an Erasmian sense, that study of, and reliance on, the Scriptures might bring into being. This was, in itself, a remarkable intellectual achievement when we consider the extreme unrest and the acute mental and psychological distress that the populace of southern Germany was experiencing at the time. It should be remembered that throughout the late Middle Ages the city of Nuremberg had supported the emperors in their struggles with the popes. In Nuremberg there had long been a much freer spirit, less blind servility to the prestige and mundane influence of the papacy than elsewhere. It was this greater freedom of the mind that was largely responsible for the fact that the Reformation took hold there more rapidly than in any other German town. As early as 1498 Dürer produced a famous series of woodcuts of "The Apocalypse," which clearly reflect the religious and intellectual unrest that so deeply discomfitted his townsmen. One of this series, *The Whore of Babylon*, a figure that traditionally stood for "Imperial Rome," has been interpreted as here signifying "Papal Rome."[16] It is to be remembered, however, that even this degree of disapproval of the state of the papacy would not, in itself, spell revolt. Michelangelo and other Italian artists were well aware and highly critical of much that went on in and around the Vatican in the sixteenth century, but they did not revolt.

Welcome light is thrown on the meanings inherent in Dürer's engraving by the fact that about seventy years later, when Luther had long been dead and the break between the Lutheran Church and the papacy had become firmly established, another southern German artist, Wolfgang Stuber, produced an engraving closely based on the earlier one by Dürer (fig. 90). Stuber's picture is a reverse image of the Dürer of 1514, but with two very important differences: Saint Jerome is given the face of Martin Luther and while the symbol of courage, the lion, is retained as in the original, the sleeping dog, symbol of blind fidelity, is left out. Stuber's engraving was actually titled, not *Saint Jerome in His Study* but *Martin Luther in His Study*. It is obvious, however, that the reformer was a replacement, a new "version" of Jerome, a new figure of a great church scholar, and that it was from the latter that theological wisdom was henceforth to be expected. Possibly through ignorance of its reference to Jerome's personal erudition, Stuber retained in his design the pendent gourd of Dürer's earlier engraving. The gourd did not matter to

16. Ivan Fenyö, *Albrecht Dürer*, p. 25.

Figure 88. Albrecht Dürer, *Saint Jerome in His Study*, 1511. Washington: National Gallery of Art; Rosenwald Collection.

Figure 89. Albrecht Dürer, *Saint Jerome by a Pollard Willow*, 1512. Washington: National Gallery of Art; Rosenwald Collection.

PESTIS ✱ ERAM ✱ ΓΙFVS
MORIENS ✱ TVA ✱ MORS ✱ ERO ✱ PAPA

Figure 90. Wolfgang Stuber. *Martin Luther in His Study*, ca. 1584. Vienna: Graphische Sammlung Albertina.

17. Roland H. Bainton, *Studies on the Reformation*, pp. 67–74.

Stuber, but the sleeping dog apparently did. To Luther the dog was, at best, a creature of simple, unsophisticated faithfulness.[17]

When Stuber engraved his picture, about 1584, there was no reason to include any vestige of the symbolic reference to blind fidelity to the old church, and, indeed, the old church was presented with a new face. A Protestant artist like Stuber, aware of the dog's implication of fidelity, would have left it out, as Luther certainly did not express blind loyalty but had fomented a reformation. The church that Luther had founded was still new enough, and was faced with external difficulties enough, to need continuing courage in its support (as evidenced by the lion), but for blind loyalty there was no desire. There had been too much of the latter in what had preceded it, and blind loyalty was precisely the opposite of what Luther expressed in his revolt from the Church of Rome.

This is further emphasized by the Latin inscription Stuber added at the bottom of the engraving, *"Pestis eram vivus, moriens tua mors ero, Papa,"* ("Alive I was your bane. Dead, I shall be your death, oh Pope.").

Before leaving Stuber's engraving, it may be noted that the replacement in it of Saint Jerome by Martin Luther does not alter the original concept of the composition as a representation of ecclesiastical scholarship. Both Jerome and Luther were very prolific writers; both translated the Bible, the former into Latin and the latter into German; both men were noted as great scholars as well as preachers; both were the epitome of literary churchmen; and both were unyielding zealots in their work. In his funeral oration, the scholar and religious reformer Melanchthon referred to Luther as a God-inspired leader worthy to stand beside Isaiah, John the Baptist, Paul, and Augustine. He did not specifically mention Jerome, but it was no great step for Stuber to add the latter, at least in his mind, and to superimpose the features of Luther on the figure of the saint in his engraving.

About 1521, while on a visit to Antwerp, Dürer painted a half-length *Saint Jerome in Meditation*, a picture now in Lisbon. This is, in effect, another "Saint Jerome in His Study," although it shows less of a setting behind the saint. Jerome is seated at his work table, only that part of him above the table showing in the painting. His right hand is supporting his head, while his left rests on a human skull, to which one of his fingers is pointing, as if to direct the viewer's attention to it. The skull, of course, is a symbol of the transience, and hence the vanity of human life. Other symbolic objects on the table are an ink pot, an open book, and a crucifix. There is no room in the picture for the lion or any other creature. In his study of this painting Erwin Panofsky was led to remark that it reflected the spirit of Luther, while the great engraving of seven years earlier conformed to the ideal of Erasmus. It appears that what Panofsky had in mind was that a Lutheran version of Jerome would be an unadorned presentation of the saint, while an Erasmian one would include the symbols and overtones of Humanism. This distinction, which seems valid and penetrating, would, it seems, further support the thought of reconciliation, as opposed to revolt, as characteristic of the earlier, 1514, picture. Erasmus was certainly no revolutionary; he was an eloquent intellectual critic and philosophical dissenter, and later, when he made his final stand, it was against Luther, whose excesses he found objectionable.[18]

In his elaboration on Panofsky's observation, Lewis W. Spitz[19] pointed out that while Dürer had for many years been deeply disturbed by the accusations made by the anti-papists in Nuremberg, with whom he tended to sympathize, in 1519 he was suddenly helped out of his deep personal doubts and worries and acute spiritual distress by the teachings of Martin Luther. Spitz corroborates this by quoting the artist's words, "At last I have found certainty!" and his expressed desire to make a portrait of the reformer, "as a lasting memory of the Christian man who has helped me out of great anxieties." This statement, five years after the engraving of 1514, shows that, when composing that wonderful design, Dürer was by no means ready to break with his past religious adherence and pattern, and still hoped for calm and understanding to effect a peaceful reconciliation. After 1519 Dürer's art increasingly reflected his strong loyalty to Luther's teachings. This is clearly shown in the difference

18. The nature of the controversy between Erasmus and Luther has been discussed by Grisar Hartmann (*Luther*, vol. 2, p. 121) and by John M. Headley (*Luther's View of Church History*, pp. 171–73). We find Luther quoted as saying, "I prefer Augustine to Jerome in the same proportion as Erasmus prefers Jerome to Augustine." Later, in one of his "table talks," of 1533, Luther gave full expression to his feelings when he wrote, "I hate Erasmus from the bottom of my heart."

19. *The Religious Renaissance of the German Humanists*, p. 263.

Figure 91. Albrecht Dürer, *Saint Jerome in His Study*, ca. 1521. Berlin-Dahlem: Staatliche Museen-Kupferstichkabinett.

between the Jeromes of 1514 and of 1521. In the former, Jerome, the patron saint of the Christian humanists and of the Brethren of the Common Life, the favorite saint of Erasmus, is surrounded by all the symbols of learning. In the later painting he is shown with much simpler surroundings, the most prominent feature of the background being a crucifix, although, as mentioned earlier, he does have a few books, an ink pot, and a death's head on his table.

Finally, it may be noted that at about the same time that he painted the Lisbon picture, Dürer made a further rendition of the same theme, a pen drawing now in Berlin (fig. 91). This is very different from both its contemporaneous painting and its predecessor of 1514. Jerome, only slightly clad and very emaciated, sits at a crude, bare table in very sparse and austere surroundings. On the table there is a human skull, but no lion or other beast is present. This unusual composition combines the penitent with the scholar, showing the saint dressed as a hermit, although sitting in his study. In this, it anticipates the pictures by Joos van Cleve in which Jerome is shown as a penitent hermit in the midst of his civilized surroundings.

Cranach's Versions of the Jerome Theme

The fact that Lucas Cranach the Elder painted at least eight versions of Saint Jerome suggests that the subject appealed to him as well as to the people who commissioned his work. He also did an engraving of the penitent Jerome, dating from 1509. The paintings, with one exception (1502), are later—1515 to 1527. Three of these and the engraving are simple in their iconography and may be dealt with briefly. The painting in Vienna (fig. 92), divided by a vertical in the middle, possibly once a diptych, depicts in the segment at left a full, standing figure of Jerome, clad as a cardinal, in the act of removing the thorn from the lion's foot. (This is the only time Cranach depicted the thorn extraction incident.) In the section of the painting at right is a standing figure of Saint Leopold. The other iconographically uncomplicated paintings are one in the Berlin-Dahlem gallery, dated 1515-1520, and one of about the same date, once belonging to Julius Böhler, Ltd., with the lion leaning against the kneeling saint's left thigh.

The remaining five paintings are rich in their faunal inclusions and require more detailed discussion. To start with the earliest (1502) and, from the point of view of its fauna, the simplest, we may take the *Saint Jerome in Penitence* in Vienna (fig. 93). This, one of Cranach's most beautiful works, was hailed by Otto Benesch as the first painting in which the main figure, the emotional "action" of the piece, and all the items in the elaborate and detailed setting were conceived and rendered as completely integrated and mutually related, a "microcosm" mirroring the "macrocosm."[1] Here we find the saint's lion resting in the lower foreground in front of the kneeling Jerome, who is about to beat his chest with the stone held in his right hand. In connection with this, Cranach has Jerome raising, with his left hand, his long, unkempt beard, as if to keep it from lessening the effect of the imminent lapidation—a curious detail of uncertain, if any, special meaning. In the luxuriant foliage of the tree above and to the left of Jerome we find a green and red parrot and a dark brownish-streaked owl with a dead, small yellow-breasted bird in its talons. The parrot and the owl, again with a yellow-bodied bird in its claws, also occur in the pair of portraits that Cranach had just painted of Dr. Johannes Cuspinian, an eminent historiographer of the University of Vienna, and his wife, Anna.[2] These were wedding

1. In *The Art of the Renaissance in Northern Europe*, p. 50, Benesch was referring to the use of the term "microcosm" as employed by philosophers to suggest that man, the "microcosm," was a mirror, on a small scale, of everything in the universe, the "macrocosm." This presupposed the latter to be integrated in all its parts to the degree that it could almost be likened to an organism. It appears that Benesch was impressed with Cranach's ability to portray the detailed landscape as a vast, connected unity in structure and in atmosphere, an achievement of importance in the development of landscape painting. It is true that in this picture the foreground and the background are tied together remarkably well for a work done in the first decades of the sixteenth century. Benesch traced the concept of the microcosm as the macrocosm on a small scale from the philosophical writings of W. Windelband, "Makrokosmos und Mikrokosmos", in *Lehrbuch der Geschichte der Philosophie*, p. 29.

2. Both in the Reinhart Collection, Winterthur.

Figure 92. Lucas Cranach the Elder, *Saint Jerome and Saint Leopold*. Vienna: Kunsthistorisches Museum.

3. Ludwig Baldass ("Cranach's büssender Hieronymus von 1502," p. 77) and Heinz Lüdecke (Lucas Cranch d. Ä. im Spiegel seiner Zeit, p. 28) both wrote that the owl in the portrait of Johannes Cuspinian is to be looked upon as an astrological and, at the same time, a personal symbol, and that the parrot in Anna's portrait is similarly symbolic in a sidereal as well as in a personal way. The owl with a dead small bird in its talons is mentioned as a sign of mortality (death-bringing owl) by Heinrich Schwarz and Volker Plagemann ("Eule," col. 287), who note its presence in Cranach's Cuspinian portrait, but make no mention of it in the picture of Jerome.

4. Benesch, *The Art of the Renaissance in Northern Europe*, p. 64; Jakob Rosenberg, "Lucas Cranach the Elder: A Critical Appreciation," pp. 33–36.

portraits, and the birds, the owl, with a small bird in its talons in the picture of Johannes, and the parrot in that of Anna, are looked upon as the couple's astrological emblems, as hints of their characters.[3] In the portraits the owl is an emblem of the planet Saturn and of the melancholy temperament; the parrot, of the Sun and of the sanguine temperament. The fact that just these birds occur again in the picture of the penitent Jerome has been looked upon as suggesting that the painting may have been a wedding gift from the artist to his friends the Cuspinians, or may have been commissioned by them.[4]

It seems justifiable to extend this sidereal rather than churchly interpretation to these birds in the Jerome picture as well, although it is probable that their religio-ethical connotations, more usual in church pictures, may also be involved. The owl, malevolent in its appearance and demeanor, could easily include some of its usual evil significance in the setting of Jerome's penitence. The owl does not occur in any other of Cranach's versions of the Jerome theme. Inasmuch as owls occur but seldom in pictures of Jerome, the presence here of such a bird might enhance the thought that this painting is connected with the Cuspinian

Figure 93. Lucas Cranach the Elder, *Saint Jerome in Penitence*, 1502. Vienna: Kunsthistorisches Museum.

5. Cranach did paint a picture of Cardinal Albrecht kneeling before a crucifix in a landscape (Munich: Alte Pinakothek), but it seems uncertain whether the cardinal is a "substitute" Jerome in this case. He is not given any of the saint's usual attributes or faunal associates, although his pose is similar to that usually used for the penitent Jerome. Also, the crucifix in pictures of Jerome is usually small, a portable representation of its subject, but in this painting it is not only large, actually as large as the cardinal, but seems to be the real Crucifixion, not merely a crucifix. In spite of this the cardinal's face exhibits no particular feeling of piety or yearning; it is merely a portrait of a prominent churchman in a pose made familiar by earlier pictures of Jerome.

6. This is, of course, the European robin, *Erithacus rubecula*, not the very different and much larger American "robin," *Turdus migratorius*.

7. In one of his letters (Epistle xccv, *Ad rusticum monachum*), Saint Jerome wrote, "grues unam sequuntur ordine litterato" ("cranes fly behind one of their number in the shape of the letter V"). From F. A. Wright, *Select Letters of St. Jerome*, p. 422.

8. In Joseph Klapper, "Schriften Johanns von Neumarkt," p. 7; and Renate Jungblut, *Hieronymus Darstellung und Verehrung eines Kirchenvaters*, p. 172.

9. This squatting on the haunches is the same pose as given the squirrel in a number of Italian versions of the Jerome theme: paintings by Giovanni Bellini (Washington), Filippino Lippi (London), and Mansueti (Bergamo), and in one relief sculpture attributed to Rossellino, and in another painting by Cranach of Jerome in his study (Sarasota). In the painting by Gentile Bellini (Toledo, Ohio), the squirrels are scampering on the ground. If, as I suggest, the squirrel gnawing on a nut is a "seeker after divinity," it may be that this squatting pose is the nearest a squirrel can assume to the orant one of the penitent Jerome.

10. Jacob Grimm (*Teutonic Mythology*, pp. 796–97) noted that the tree, used as a reference to the tree of the Cross, gave rise to numerous concepts and speculations, such as that the top of the tree, like that of the Cross, points to heaven, its widespreading branches, like the arms of the Cross, to the ends of the world, and the base of both to "this earthly plain. A

portrait. On the other hand, the parrot does occur in two other pictures of Jerome by Cranach, pictures in which no reference to the Cuspinians may be sensed. This suggests that the parrot may have, in the Vienna painting as well as in the other, some of its usual connotation of the Immaculate Conception, a theme related, in Jerome's thought pattern, to his recurring interest in the perpetual virginity of Mary (see p. 281).

To complete the list of the faunal contents of this picture, it may be mentioned that a small, unidentifiable bird is perched on a bare twig in the background near the right edge of the painting, horizontally on the level of the knees of the figure of the crucified Christ, obscure and small enough to suggest that it is probably a decorative detail of no particular meaning.

Cranach's five other paintings of Jerome have been dated 1525 (Innsbruck and Darmstadt), 1526 (Sarasota), and 1527 (Zollikon and Berlin); in other words, all were created within a period of two years. Four of these portray Cardinal Albrecht of Brandenburg as Saint Jerome; the other (Innsbruck) does not, and it is the only one of the four to depict the saint in penitence.[5] In these two important elements the Innsbruck work agrees with the Vienna painting just discussed, and it may be taken up first (fig. 94). It has a similarly luxuriant landscape setting, but contains a much more varied fauna. It does not have the owl or the same kind of parrot found in the Vienna version (the parrot in the Innsbruck painting is a West African red-tailed gray parrot), but does include the lion; two squirrels; a jay (fig. 95), almost hidden in the arborescent foliage near the upper-left corner of the picture some distance above the squirrel on the tree trunk; a robin (fig. 96) above and not far from Jerome's head, on a bare twig in front of the rocks;[6] a beaver at the bottom of the picture near the left corner; a dark, blackish tortoise just below Jerome's knees toward the lion; a black scorpion behind the tortoise; a white stork and a herd of half a dozen red deer in the mid-right background; a pheasant close to Jerome's left foot, below the stork and above the lion; three large, stocky birds near the beaver at lower left, two of them with human heads, one a bearded male, the other with a female face and well-developed breasts (the third bird has a heavy hooked bill and stout toes and would seem to be intended as an eagle); a flock of nine flying cranes (fig. 97) forming a flatly rounded dark arch in the dusky sky at the top of the picture;[7] a hoopoe (?), a crested bird with a fairly long bill, here given cheek wattles (unnatural for a hoopoe!), perched on a branch in the upper right background, silhouetted against the light sky (fig. 98); and a red-tailed, gray parrot at the very top of the picture.

Iconographically, the lion calls for no comment other than to mention that it is one of Cranach's poorest renditions of the beast; it has the appearance of having long, drooping ears, quite untrue to nature; possibly these are meant to be parts of the animal's mane. This is one of the relatively few instances in which Jerome's lion is shown drinking from a stream. This may possibly suggest an influence of Johann von Neumarkt's eulogy of Saint Jerome, wherein he called him the wholesome water of the wellspring from whose mild and gentle flow all creatures may quench their thirst.[8] However, the fact that the lion is shown drinking in a few pictures by Italian artists, who would hardly have known of von Neumarkt's writings, makes this suggestion, uncertain as it is, of only limited applicability—i.e., to German pictures.

At the same time, Cranach's Innsbruck painting does seem to illustrate some of von Neumarkt's lavish praise of Jerome, whom he likened to a great tree, whose crown reaches to heaven, and in the shelter of whose branches the beasts of the field and the birds of the sky may find protection and nourishment. Von Neumarkt explained that by the birds of the sky he meant the knowing people, and that by the beasts of the field he implied the people of more limited mentality who still could profit from the teachings of the saint.

One squirrel, climbing up the trunk of the tree to the left (fig. 99), on a level with the cross beam of the crucifix, is in an active pose, unlike the other one squatting on its haunches, gnawing on an acorn, on a horizontal branch higher up in the picture, some distance above the crucifix.[9] The position Cranach has given the first squirrel is such as to recall the old Teutonic myth according to which the squirrel runs up and down a tree, sowing discord between the snake at the bottom and the eagle or falcon in the topmost branches (neither shown in the present picture). In this myth, the tree is taken to be a reference to the Cross, which is very close to it in the painting.[10] The second squirrel, on a branch above the crucifix, is in a squatting pose much like that of the squirrel in Cranach's Sarasota painting of Jerome in his study. In both pictures the squirrel is gnawing on a nut or acorn, and in its attempt to reach the kernel, the animal would seem almost to represent the "seeker after divinity." We may recall that Adam of Saint Victor said of the nut that it is an image of Christ, the hard shell is the Cross on which He was sacrificed, the green sheath is His flesh, His humanity, while the kernel within, from which nourishment may be derived, is His hidden divinity.[11]

Near the lower-left corner of the picture is a beaver (fig. 100). This animal has been found in only three pictures of Saint Jerome, all by Cranach. As explained in the Bestiary section, the beaver was a symbol of spiritual peace attained by total and deliberate elimination of carnal desire, based on the ancient legend that the sex glands of the beaver had great medicinal properties, for which it was hunted, and that when hard pressed by its pursuers the beaver would castrate itself and leave to the hunters what they wanted, and then go off in peace. The fact that Cranach alone of all artists made use of the beaver seems due to his knowledge of the presumed value of the medicine "castoreum" made from the glands of the beaver, knowledge that he would have had in his experience as an apothecary in his native city.

In the mid-background, to the right of Jerome's left foot and directly above the lion, is a stork (fig. 101). This bird is naturalistically very accurate and may be positively identified as the black-winged white stork of Europe, *Ciconia alba*. It was a symbol of "filial devotion" because of a legend to the effect that when it grew old and could no longer take care of itself, its grown young would watch over it and feed it until it died. Curiously, this legend is also applied to a very different, much smaller bird, the hoopoe, which is also present in this painting, although unrealistically altered, as noted above. The stork was very rarely included in representations of the Jerome story; the only other instances known to me are a painting attributed to the Lombard artist Pier Francesco Sacchi,

noble tree in a garden grows, and high the skill its making shews; its roots the floor of hell are grasping, its summit to the throne extends where bounteous God requiteth friends, its branches broad the wide world clasping. . . ." This also recalls von Neumarkt's comparison of Jerome to a great tree. Furthermore, many symbolic connotations came to be involved in the concept of "the tree," including the tree of knowledge of the Garden of Eden, the tree of the cross (either the tree that served as the cross or whose wood was used to make it), and the dead tree or tree stump, with or without a living branch. The dead tree represented not only death, in a physical sense, but also life through death, in a spiritual sense—the eternal life for which physical death is a necessary prelude. We may recall that in many pictures Jerome's crucifix is hung on, or attached to, a dead tree, emphasizing this concept. A prominent example is Gossaert's Washington painting (fig. 71); another, in the medium of sculpture, is Francesco di Giorgio's bronze relief, also in Washington (fig. 120). The application of the composite mass of thoughts, centering on "the tree," to the Jerome theme has been discussed by Susan Donahue Kuretsky ("Rembrandt's Tree Stump: An Iconographic Attribute of St. Jerome"), who concluded that the dead tree stump was an iconographic attribute of Saint Jerome chiefly, but by no means exclusively, in northern European art (Altdorfer, Dürer, Goltzius, Gossaert, Rembrandt, van Leyden, van Staveren, and others). Among Italian artists who used this motif may be listed Bastiani, Filippo da Verona, Francesco di Giorgio, Ridolfo Ghirlandajo, and Zoppo.

Furthermore, Kuretsky points out that the theological argument connecting the concepts of "tree" and "cross," and showing both as instruments involved in the process of redemption, dates from the early centuries of Christianity, and was even expressed by Jerome himself, in one of his letters to his friend Pope Damasus. His statement in translation is as follows: ". . . we have been reconciled to God, having as propitiator the Lord Jesus, who forgave us our sins and expunged what was the handwriting of death against us, nailing it to the cross; and He made principalities and powers a show, triumphing over them on the tree. . . ." The complex iconography of the tree is dealt with in detail by O. Schmitt, "Baum," pp. 63–73.

11. *Sequentiae*, in Migne, *Patrologia Latina*, vol. 196, col. 1433.

Figure 94. Lucas Cranach the Elder, *Saint Jerome in Penitence*, 1525. Innsbruck: Tiroler Landesmuseum Ferdinandeum.

Figure 95. Detail of jay (left) and parrot (right) from figure 94, Lucas Cranach the Elder's *Saint Jerome in Penitence*. Innsbruck: Tiroler Landesmuseum Ferdinandeum.

Figure 96. Detail of robin from figure 94, Lucas Cranach the Elder's *Saint Jerome in Penitence*. Innsbruck: Tiroler Landesmuseum Ferdinandeum.

Figure 97. Detail of cranes from figure 94, Lucas Cranach the Elder's *Saint Jerome in Penitence*. Innsbruck: Tiroler Landesmuseum Ferdinandeum.

95

96

97

98

99

101

Figure 98. Detail of hoopoe(?) from figure 94, Lucas Cranach the Elder's *Saint Jerome in Penitence*. Innsbruck: Tiroler Landesmuseum Ferdinandeum.

Figure 99. Detail of squirrel from figure 94, Lucas Cranach the Elder's *Saint Jerome in Penitence*. Innsbruck: Tiroler Landesmuseum Ferdinandeum.

Figure 100. Detail of beaver, hawk, and harpies from figure 94, Lucas Cranach the Elder's *Saint Jerome in Penitence*. Innsbruck: Tiroler Landesmuseum Ferdinandeum.

Figure 101. Detail of pheasant, stork, and deer from figure 94, Lucas Cranach the Elder's *Saint Jerome in Penitence*. Innsbruck: Tiroler Landesmuseum Ferdinandeum.

100

showing Jerome together with Anthony Abbot and a third, unidentified saint, and in a bronze relief by Francesco di Giorgio (fig. 120). In the latter example, a monochromatic dark bronze sculpture, it is not possible to say whether the stork is or is not the white stork, as there is another species, the black stork, also found in Europe. Symbolically the two are probably interchangeable, so the question is of only minor importance. The white stork is the one that nested on housetops and was beloved by the people; it is the stork that usually comes to mind in folklore. In the Sacchi painting the stork is definitely of the same species as in Cranach's Innsbruck picture, but it is in the more distant background and is neither more nor less "associated" with Jerome than with Anthony Abbot or the third saint. The symbolism of the stork is not particularly pertinent to the Jerome theme.

Immediately below Jerome's left knee, and near the lion, is a dark, blackish tortoise with light yellow spots on the underside of its head and neck. Tortoises were very rarely depicted in the Jerome context. I have found only four other instances of their inclusion: in the bronze relief by Francesco di Giorgio just mentioned; in a painting by Mansueti (formerly Arthur Hughes Coll.); in an anonymous Italian engraving of the last quarter of the fifteenth century (Hind, no. 86); and in a drawing by Jacopo Bellini, in the Louvre (fig. 53). The tortoise is rare, not only in the Jerome context but in the whole of European religious art, the only other instances known to me of its use in church paintings being one by Botticini and one by an imitator of Andrea Mantegna.[12] A search through the comprehensive Princeton Index of early Christian Art, from earliest times through the fourteenth century, revealed no entries for the tortoise as a figure in religious art other than in a fourth-century mosaic in the Cathedral of Aquilea, where the tortoise is shown in combat with a cock. This design is an early Christian symbol of moral combat, the forces of darkness (the tortoise) against those of light represented by the cock in its capacity as the herald of dawn.[13]

In spite of its rarity in religious inconography, the tortoise had a number of meanings attached to it, discussed in full in the Bestiary. The meanings pertinent to "Jerome in Penitence" are as follows: the tortoise was a symbol of chastity, a "stay-at-home" (it cannot leave its shell), as contrasted with a wanton wandering about; it was also a symbol of reticence, being a silent animal. At the same time it was a symbol of evil, and in Jerome's own words a heretical beast living by its own volition in filth and scum.[14] In its positive, favorable symbolism the tortoise fits in with Jerome's continual plea for continence and chastity of women; in its negative, evil connotation it is a sign of the sinful and perilous world from which the penitent saint was seeking to escape. The fact that Cranach chose to make his tortoise very dark suggests that its evil nature may have been the aspect he wished to stress. Close behind the tortoise is a poorly rendered, equally blackish scorpion, another "evil" creature frequently included in pictures of the penitent Jerome. It may be recalled that Jerome explicitly mentioned scorpions, as well as "wild beasts," as his daily companions in the wilderness.

Immediately above the lion, its head very close to Jerome's left foot, is a male pheasant, somewhat difficult to make out in the verdure that surrounds it (at least in a black and white photograph). The pheasant is

12. Botticini, *Madonna and Child Enthroned with Saints Benedict, Francis, Sylvester, and Anthony Abbot*, in the Metropolitan Museum of Art, New York, and Mantegna imitator, *The Holy Women at the Sepulcher*, in the National Gallery, London; both are analyzed and discussed by Herbert Friedmann, "Footnotes to the Painted Page: The Iconography of an Altarpiece by Botticini," pp. 10–11.

13. Rudolf Egger, "Ein altchristliches Kampfsymbol," pp. 791–95.

14. Jerome wrote of the tortoise: "haereticorum gravissima peccata significat, qui suis, en coeno et volutebro luti erroribus immorant" (Andres Holguin, *La tortuga, simbolo del filosofo*, p. 24). The exact source and precise wording of Jerome's statement are, unfortunately, uncertain. Holguin took his version from J. Corominas, *Diccionario critico etimologico de la lengua castellana*," vol. 4, p. 513, where the Latin is slightly different (the last word is given as *immolant*) and the whole statement is ascribed to Jerome "en una de sus obras" ("in one of his works"). I have not been able to locate it in the great assemblage of Jerome's writings in Migne's *Patrologia Latina*.

Figure 102. Lucas Cranach the Elder, *Cardinal Albrecht as Saint Jerome*, 1527. Berlin-Dahlem: Staatliche Museen.

rarely found in the iconography of Jerome. Cranach included it in four of his pictures: one in Berlin (fig. 102), one in Darmstadt (fig. 103), and one in Sarasota (fig. 104), as well as in the present Innsbruck one. Only three other artists have been found to include it, once each: Pisanello follower (fig. 63); Gentile Bellini (fig. 26); and Carpaccio (fig. 31). The pheasant, as explained in the Bestiary, became a symbol of redemption

after the flood, and, by transference from its relative, the peacock, it was connected with the concept of immortality. As a symbol of redemption it is pertinent to Saint Jerome, the penitent seeker after exactly that state of bliss.

The dark, V-shaped flock of flying birds in the dusky sky are suggestive in their form and in their flight formation of cranes (fig. 97). They are

Figure 103. Lucas Cranach the Elder, *Saint Jerome in His Study*, 1525. Darmstadt: Landesmuseum.

Figure 104. Lucas Cranach the Elder, *Saint Jerome in His Study*, 1526. Sarasota, Fla.: John and Mable Ringling Museum of Art.

Figure 105. Detail of partridges, lion, and pheasants from figure 104, Lucas Cranach the Elder's *Saint Jerome in His Study*. Sarasota, Fla.: John and Mable Ringling Museum of Art.

flying toward the picture plane, toward the scene of Jerome's penitence. A flight of cranes, or even a single flying one, is explained in Horapollo's *Hieroglyphica*[15] as an old Egyptian symbol standing for a "man who seeks higher things." While Horapollo's interpretations and explanations of Egyptian hieroglyphics are now suspect, his book was eagerly accepted as a reliable font of information, first in mid-fifteenth-century Florence, then in Venice, and shortly thereafter in Germany, where Dürer made a notable series of drawings to illustrate the copy owned by his friend Pirckheimer. Both the text of Pirckheimer's copy and the drawings by Dürer were commissioned by the Emperor Maximilian, which attests to the high esteem this work commanded at the time. It would

15. George Boas (*The Hieroglyphics of Horapollo*, p. 107) translated Horapollo as follows: "When they [the Egyptian priests] desire to indicate a man who knows the higher things, they draw a crane in flight. For the crane flies extremely high [if the cranes were any higher, they would be out of the picture] that it may see the clouds in order not to be storm-tossed, and to remain in the calm." Dr. Gert Amman of the Tiroler Museum, where Cranach's painting hangs, has written me that these birds are assumed to be cranes.

seem not unlikely that Cranach knew of the book and its accepted, if unsupported, explanations; it was the very sort of "tool" that practicing artists would be apt to talk about, because it gave them new hints as to how to portray many esoteric themes and also gave them the appearance of being alert to such new information.

The small herd of red deer in the right background of the painting (fig. 101) cannot be interpreted other than as examples of the denizens of wild places, the kind of area in which the penitent saint had absented himself from his fellow men.

In the dense foliage in the upper-left corner of the painting are two birds, a jay (closer to the corner) and a parrot. The latter is definitely the West African red-tailed gray parrot, the best "talker" of all the parrots and highly esteemed in Cranach's time for this ability. As discussed more fully in the account of Cranach's Sarasota painting later in this chapter, the parrot was a visual reference to the Immaculate Conception, and thus, by inference, to the perpetual virginity of Mary.

The jay was primarily a creature that "sheds light on the road," mentioned by Isidore of Seville and others, as explained in the account of this bird in the Bestiary. In this sense it is understandable in a picture of Jerome. The jay also shared with the parrot an ability to imitate the sounds of human speech, but to a lesser degree.

This leaves to be considered the three largish, stocky birds near the bottom of the picture. The one to the left has a sharply hooked beak and stout, strong feet, and can only be interpreted as a large hawk or an eagle. The other two are much greener, less brownish in color, but are similar to it in the general configuration of their bodies and legs, but are utterly different in their heads, one having the bearded face of a man, the other the face and breasts of a woman. No comparable creatures have been found in any other rendition of the Jerome theme, regardless of artist, period, or country.[16] The one with a woman's face is bending down toward her reflection in the water. The male's reflection is also shown in the water, but he seems less interested in it. They are sirens, or harpies, the human-faced birds of classical Greek art and legend, here surprisingly reappearing in the sixteenth century.

These two harpies are here to be looked upon as symbols of penitence and remorse. Renate Jungblut[17] has shown that the presence of these creatures in Cranach's painting is proof that he was familiar with Konrad von Megenberg's *Das Buch der Natur*, the earliest German book on natural history, first printed in 1475.[18] In this book it is stated that harpies have truly human faces, but no human virtues; they kill the first people they meet. Later, when the thirsty harpy comes to a pond and bends down to drink, it sees reflected a face that is not merely its own but somehow includes that of the person it has slain. Thereupon the harpy is stricken with remorse, and weeps and repents for the rest of its life.

A point that calls for comment is that one of Cranach's harpies has the face of a man. In classical art harpies were always given faces of women; in fact, that was part of their original role as sirens, luring their victims to destruction, as in Homer's Odyssey. However, there is reason to think that the original concept of these creatures had changed considerably over the centuries. To take as evidence from a completely unrelated

16. A grotesque bird with a hooded human face occurs in the decorative border of a manuscript illumination showing Jerome at his desk with his lion, in an early twelfth-century (1148) Bible in the British Museum (Add. 14788-90 Bible, I, f. 1 ᵛ.), but this is not a harpy and is not really part of the picture.

17. *Hieronymus Darstellung und Verehrung eines Kirchenvaters*, p. 172.

18. *Das Buch der Natur*, 1962 ed., p. 212 (1499 ed., unpaged, examined in the Huntington Library; because unpaged, however, specific reference is made to the 1962 revision by Franz Pfeiffer).

source, John Gower, the fourteenth-century English poet, wrote in his "Confessio Amantis" that the harpy is a cruel bird of prey with a man's face. He tells much the same story as Megenberg, whom he actually antedates by nearly a century. His version of the tale differs chiefly in its greater intensification of the remorse felt by the harpy, causing it to die the same day, but the important point for our consideration is that Gower's description informs us that harpies were thought of as having men's faces as well as women's.[19] Still, the majority of renditions, even as late as Ulysses Aldrovandus's work (1642),[20] show harpies with female heads.

To come back to Cranach's "source," Konrad von Megenberg consistently used the masculine "he" when writing about the harpy, possibly because the German word for bird, "Vogel," is masculine. It is possible that this influenced Cranach's conception of the creature. What is more puzzling is the third bird, seemingly related to the harpies and with a fierce look upon its "normal," avian, nonhuman head. No plausible explanation has yet been found for its appearance. It does seem, however, that this third, "normal," eaglelike bird may yet be discovered to have a meaning, as has everything else in the painting. It is clear enough that the two human-headed harpies are here intended as symbols of penitence; indeed, penitence for crimes originally far greater than Saint Jerome had cause to consider his own relatively minor errors. It is a commentary on the peculiar logic of symbolism, and on the moralizing changes brought about by Christian use of pagan icons, that the harpies, originally standing for calculated temptation and seduction, as in Homer, have been altered into signs of remorse and repentance. In this latter meaning they are not out of place in a picture of the repentant Jerome.

We come now to four paintings in which Cranach portrayed Cardinal Albrecht of Brandenburg as Saint Jerome, not in penitence, but as a church scholar engaged in his literary labors, presumably on the Vulgate. Two of these, now in Berlin (fig. 102) and Zollikon, show him in a landscape setting, while the other two, in Darmstadt (fig. 103) and in Sarasota (fig. 104), show him in his study. As numerous scholars have pointed out, it was quite acceptable and natural for an artist of the sixteenth century to portray a humanist cardinal, a correspondent of Erasmus and a patron of Ulrich von Hutten, as Saint Jerome. While there seem to be no extant documents pertaining to the actual commission of any of these pictures, it would seem that the cardinal was responsible for them, or at least gave them his approval. It would seem further that he must have approved the choice of the various animals Cranach painted in these four pictures.[21] It is safe to say that Cranach was too practical, too worldly wise, to have included anything that might conceivably have met with the cardinal's displeasure. We may recall, in this connection, that Cranach was at one time burgomaster of Wittenberg, was attached to the court of the electoral house of Saxony, and was a business man, an apothecary, in his hometown, as well as an artist and head of an active art studio.

In all four of these paintings we find the lion and also the pheasant, already noted in the Innsbruck picture. In each of the pictures of Jerome in his study there are two pheasants with their brood of chicks—seven chicks in the Darmstadt painting, eight in the Sarasota one (fig. 104). In

19. "Confessio Amanti," ed. G. C. Macaulay, bk. 3, 11.2599–2616:
"Among the bokes whiche I finde
Solyns spekth of a wonder kinde,
And seith of fowhles there is on,
Which hath a face of blod and bon
Lich to a man in resemblance.
And if it falle him so per chance,
As he which is a fowhl of preie,
That he a man finde in his weie,
He wol him slen, if that he mai:
But afterward the same dai,
Whan he hath eten al his felle,
And that schal be beside a welle,
In which whan he wol drinke take,
Of his visage and seth the make
That he hath slain, anon he thenketh
Of his misdede, and it forthenketh
So gretly, that for pure sorwe
He liveth noght til on the morwe."

Among earlier writers considered as "source" are these: Pierre de Beauvais, thirteenth-century French prose bestiary in *Mélanges d'archéologie, d'histoire et de litterature*, ed. C. Cahier and A. Martin, vol. 2, no. 16, p. 157 ("De La Arpie, sa nature"); Odo of Cheriton, *Les Fabulistes Latins: Odonis fabulis addita, collectio secunda*, XXI, ed. L. Hervieux, vol. 4, p. 401 ("De quadam bestia que vocatur harpia"); Vincent of Beauvais, *Speculum naturale*, cols. 1211–1212, bk. 16, chapter 94 ("de Harpya").

20. *Ornithologiae hoc est, de avibus historiae*, bk. 12, p. 337.

21. Anna Strümpell ("Hieronymus im Gehäuse," p. 229) considered the Darmstadt painting probably executed in compliance with a wish of Cardinal Albrecht as a free adaptation of Dürer's great engraving of 1514.

the Berlin work there is only a single male pheasant, as in the Innsbruck version. The use of a pair of pheasants with seven or eight young is unusual in the iconography of Saint Jerome, and is clearly meaningful. Fortunately, it is possible to suggest the meaning, which seems obviously connected with the old Germanic legend (originally a classic one) concerning the origin of the Pleiades.[22] So widely was this known in Germany and adjacent countries that a picture of a hen and seven chicks became the most popular graphic representation of the constellation. The legend tells us that one day Christ was passing a little baker's shop, from the open door of which emanated the enticing aroma of freshly baked bread, which caused him to send one of His disciples to ask for a loaf. The baker refused the request, but his wife and six young daughters were nearby and heard the request, whereupon, unknown to the baker, they secretly gave the bread to the disciple. For this act of charity they were set in the sky as the seven stars of the Pleiades.

Because of their astronomical identity in the visible pattern of the night sky, these seven characters of the Teutonic legend became connected with those of the ancient Greek myth of the seven daughters of Atlas and Pleione, who were changed into stars because of their grief on the death of their father. This constellation became important in the lives of the common people of Europe as a celestial sign to the farmers, who watched for and timed their planting and reaping by the spring rising and the autumnal setting of this group of stars.

Through their beneficent guidance to agriculture, the Pleiades thus became a source of security, a heavenly guide helping to assure food for the people, just as the original baker's wife and daughters had given food to Christ and His disciples. It involved no great feat of inventiveness for the pheasant—already a symbol of redemption—and its young to be substituted for the hen and chicks as a pictorial device. Actually, this transposition extended even to the peahen in some sixteenth- and seventeenth-century emblems. In one such, a peahen and her chicks illustrate the motto *Certa securitas* ("assured security") (fig. 106).

In all depictions of "Saint Jerome in His Study," such as Cranach's Darmstadt and Sarasota paintings, the content implies that Jerome is working on his translation of the Bible into Latin, to make newly available the guidance of the Scriptures to people who could not read the original Greek or Hebrew texts. It is in this sense, as a parallel type of "divine guidance," that the pheasants and their brood, avian symbols of the Pleiades, are to be understood in the two paintings. This would explain why the lion is watching them so intently in both cases!

Although expressing a different basic thought, it may be that this sign of divine guidance bears some relation to another old use of the "hen and chickens" device as a symbol of God's providence. This has been connected with a story to the effect that one day Christ, mourning over the guilty city of Jerusalem, declared that if its inhabitants had acted properly they would have been shielded by divine providence, "even as the hen gathers her young beneath her wings and guards them" from all harm.[23] In neither of Cranach's paintings are the chicks sheltered by the parent birds, however.

One cannot help but ask why the brood of young pheasants was not included in Cranach's Berlin painting of Cardinal Albrecht as Saint

Figure 106. *Certa securitas.* Emblem from Jacobus à Bruck, 1518, in A. Henkel and A. Schöne, *Emblemata,* col. 810.

22. Grimm, p. 729.

23. F. Edmund Hulme, *The History, Principles, and Practice of Symbolism in Christian Art*, p. 193.

Jerome, in which only a single adult pheasant was included. The answer would seem to be that Jerome's work on the Vulgate was done in his study. While it is true that in this Berlin picture Jerome is writing, the fact is that such compositions usually refer to other aspects of the saint's literary efforts, and, by the very nature of their landscape setting they approach the more frequent works of the penitent Jerome writing, while still in his solitary wilderness retreat. In such a situation the dominant theme is his seeking redemption, a concept adequately symbolized by an adult pheasant. Even this use of the avian symbol of redemption was rare, as there was little need for such double statements. Carpaccio used the pheasant one time, in his painting of Jerome bringing the lion to the monastery, causing precipitate fleeing by some of the monks. Inasmuch as this picture shows no literary effort on the part of the saint, the pheasant is merely a decorative addition, not a symbol of anything.

To return to the Berlin *Cardinal Albrecht as Saint Jerome*, we may note a beaver just above and behind the lion and the pheasant. The meaning of this creature has already been discussed in connection with the Innsbruck *Saint Jerome in Penitence*, and we find a beaver again in the Sarasota *Saint Jerome in His Study*. The herd of red deer (*Cervus elaphus*) in the Innsbruck picture occurs again, in the left background, of the Berlin work, but in the latter there is also, in the right foreground, a very prominent figure of a roebuck (*Capreolus capreolus*) with its head close to Jerome's improvised table. This deer, smaller in life although larger in the picture because of perspective, has smaller, less multi-branched antlers than the red deer. It is remarkable among European deer in being monogamous, whereas the more common red deer is highly polygamous, the stags often battling over their harems. It seems likely that Cranach, with his interest in natural history and hunting, would have known of this difference in habits of the two species, and it may be that he gave the roebuck its place of close proximity to Jerome, the ardent advocate of continence, because of its much more regulated, less extravagant, breeding habits. This, however, is only a surmise, but it would give a clue as to why the artist placed it as he did. That the roebuck was connected with Saint Jerome in Cranach's iconographic program is shown again by its inclusion in the lower-left corner of the Sarasota picture of the saint in his study (fig. 107). In this painting there is a curious chandelier over Jerome's desk, composed of antlers, not of the roebuck but of the red deer. In southern Germany chandeliers were often made of stags' horns, collected as hunting trophies.[24] The chandelier here would seem to be an allusion to the cardinal's and the artist's interest in the chase.

To the left of, and below Jerome's table is a rabbit, an old symbol of the sanguine temperament, of meekness and timidity, of sensuality and of fecundity. The rabbit occurs again in Cranach's Sarasota picture of Jerome in his study, as well as in others by various artists named in the Bestiary account of this creature. To complete this survey of the Berlin picture, I may merely note that in the upper-right background the lion is driving a caravan of camels and asses to the monastery, a part of the legend of Jerome's lion frequently included.

Cranach's two pictures of "Saint Jerome in His Study" both contain two partridges, the so-called gray partridge, *Perdix cinerea*. The various

Figure 107. Detail of beaver, roebuck, and rabbit from figure 104, Lucas Cranach the Elder's *Saint Jerome in His Study*. Sarasota, Fla.: John and Mable Ringling Museum of Art.

24. Charles L. Kuhn, *German and Netherlandish Sculpture 1280–1800*, pp. 86–87.

meanings attached to this bird are fully discussed in the Bestiary. Here it may be noted that Jerome himself considered it to be a satanic creature, even the devil himself, because of an ancient belief that in its overwhelming desire to breed, the partridge stole eggs from the nests of other birds and then hatched them. In this it was a despoiler of homes, an evildoer, but like so many symbolic creatures it had, at the same time, favorable implications. For one thing, by Cranach's time the egg-stealing story had been given a supplemental ending to the effect that, on hatching from the stolen eggs, the chicks always returned to their rightful parents. This caused Leonardo da Vinci to consider the partridge a symbol, not of evil but of "the eventual triumph of truth." It would be good to think that in the quiet and peace of Jerome's study, the partridges had this favorable message, but we know that Cranach used the pair of partridges in a drawing of *Adam and Eve*[25] as an expression of "increase and voluptuousness." Also, in a woodcut of 1529 of *Martin Luther as Saint Matthew*, Cranach inserted two partridges on the floor near the middle of the lower part of the work. Luther was no advocate of continence; in his letters and his "table talks" we find him even boasting of his sexual experiences. The whole range of contradictory meanings associated with the partridge makes it risky to select which ones are uppermost in the two Jerome pictures.

This question arises again, and even more pertinently to our present concern, in a recent addition to Cranach's known oeuvre, *Cardinal Albrecht as Saint Jerome Reading in a Landscape*, a picture in a private collection in Zollikon, Switzerland.[26] In this painting there are two partridges with five, or possibly six chicks, in the lower-right foreground. This is the only time such a group has been found in a rendition of Jerome. It immediately brings to mind the similar groups of pheasants and their young in the Darmstadt and Sarasota pictures. However, it is doubtful that a similar meaning is involved here, and this is borne out by the fact that the saint's lion is paying no attention to the partridges, as it would if they had been, like the pheasants, a sign of divine guidance. In this picture the chicks are still with their "satanic" foster parents, and, according to the legend, should shortly be returning to their legitimate ones. One cannot help but wonder about this painting: its inconography appears to be a conflation of items from several of the artist's other works—Jerome, the lion, and the stag from other pictures of Cardinal Albrecht as the saint; the partridges and their young from pictures of the "Nymph of the Spring." The Zollikon painting shares one curious detail with the Berlin one (fig. 102)—a large stone on the saint's table, against which his book is leaning. The stone can hardly be one the saint would use to beat his chest; it looks too large and heavy for him to lift!

Cranach is the only artist I have found to use the gray partridge in the Jerome context. Other artists, all Italian, who included partridges— Antonello da Messina, Basaiti, Catena, Cima, and Mansueti—used the red-legged, or chukar, partridge (*Alectoris*; two species). However, in their symbolic content the several kinds of partridge seem to have been interchangeable. In Cranach's case, the gray partridge was the species, native to southern Germany, with which, as a hunter, he was well acquainted.

Cranach's two versions of Jerome in his study contain still a few more creatures, but none that are common to both. There is a small dog in the

25. See Michael J. Liebmann, "On the Iconography of the 'Nymph of the Fountain' by Lucas Cranach the Elder," pp. 434–37.

26. Dieter Koepplin and Tilman Falk, *Lukas Cranach Gemälde Zeichnungen Druckgraphic*.

Darmstadt painting, a squirrel and a parrot in the Sarasota one. The small dog was a traditional companion in the iconography of scholars or humanists at their literary labors;[27] similar use of the small dog occurs in pictures of Jerome by Crivelli and others.

The squirrel we have already discussed in Cranach's Innsbruck painting of "Jerome in Penitence"; it has the same significance here as the similarly posed one in that picture. The parrot has also been considered in Cranach's two versions of the penitent Jerome. It is worth mentioning that in the Sarasota and Innsbruck paintings, the parrot is definitely identifiable as the West African red-tailed gray parrot, *Psittacus erithcus*, which it certainly is not in the others. Inasmuch as the gray parrot's fluency with words caused it to become a symbol of the Immaculate Conception, it would seem fitting for the saint to have not merely a parrot, but the best "talker" of all the parrots.

Looking back on what we have found in Cranach's pictures, we must credit him with unusual originality in his choice of faunal associates for Jerome, and with remarkable perspicacity in gathering unusual, yet meaningful, creatures for his purpose. This is quite the opposite from Eberhard Ruhmer's conclusion about the Sarasota painting; his praise for Cranach's gifts as a naturalist and for his careful depiction of so many kinds of animals comes to naught when he dismisses most of them as "irrelevant to the central theme."[28] I have found reason to think differently, even though I have no documentary proof that the artist had in mind all I have been able to discover about the many creatures involved. If anything, Cranach's pictures of Jerome are often so crowded with items, each one potentially meaningful, that one might wish he had been content with fewer of them in some instances. Cranach's pictures may be thought to suffer from visual prolixity, but not from meaningless clutter. That adverse criticism might easily be applied to an artist like Mansueti, but it is out of place with Cranach. In the long list of artists who worked on the Jerome theme, Cranach was the only one to use the beaver; the family group of pheasants with their chicks; the bizarre, sirenlike harpies, or human-headed birds; the West African gray parrot; the gray partridge; and the robin. He was one of the very few to include the stork and the tortoise, and to differentiate so clearly between the roebuck and the red deer. In his paintings of Jerome in penitence he saw no need to stress the dangers of the wilderness, and he did not include the usual snakes and scorpions, to say nothing of dragons, with which so many other artists chose to harass the saint. Cranach had more personal interest in, and knowledge of, natural history than most artists, but in his Jerome series he used that knowledge with control and with much discretion.

Even though it does not involve any animal, one further inclusion in Cranach's Sarasota picture may be noted. On the drape-covered table in the left middleground of the painting are two pieces of fruit immediately below and to the left of Jerome's cardinal's hat and two clusters of grapes near the squirrel. One of the two larger fruits seems to be an apple; the other is a pear. In the somewhat similar painting in Darmstadt there is a large dish of fruit—apples, grapes, and cherries (?). The grapes in both pictures are obvious references to the wine of the Eucharist; they are symbols of the Christian religion. The little squirrel is eating something, probably a grape (there are no nuts visible in the painting). Whether it is

27. Raymond Klibansky, Erwin Panofsky, and Fritz Saxl, *Saturn and Melancholy*, p. 315.

28. *Cranach*, p. 84. Renate Jungblut (*Hieronymus Darstellung*, p. 91) to some extent anticipated my conclusions about the Darmstadt and Sarasota pictures, when she wrote (free translation) "almost all the animals (present) are also signs of chastity and of steadfast faith." She did not attempt to explain a number of them explicitly, but did note that the parrot was "Mary's bird" because it could say "Ave," and she also approximated the sense conveyed by the beaver legend in moralistic terms.

gnawing a nut or eating a grape, it is symbolically a "seeker after divinity," as explained earlier in this chapter.

The apple and pear are a little more involved in their meaning. Apples occur in a few other pictures of Jerome in his study, notably the small one by Jan van Eyck in Detroit and the large fresco by Domenico Ghirlandajo in the church of Ognissanti in Florence. The symbolic meaning of the apple in religious art is usually a disguised reference to the idea of "original sin." There was a belief, accepted by the Church, that the fall of man was the fateful event that first brought death into the physical world.[29] Disease that might cause death was looked upon as a result of original sin, and this reasoning eventually brought about the equivalence of disease and sin. The argument proceeded further to state that the only true and valid medication for man against sin was that offered by Christ, Who, through His incarnation in the Virgin and through His sacrifice on the cross, had brought redemption to mankind. This salvation, easily equated dialectically with "healing," came to be implied in the Virgin in Whose body the incarnation began. She became, in effect, a vessel of the true medicine, and, through the power of Her intercession, She came to be looked upon as a remedy. Thus, in one of the medieval Latin hymns devoted to the adoration of Mary we find one verse urging all to rejoice in Her, the universal healer, the rose without thorns

Gaude mundi medicina
gaude rosa sine spina. . . . [30]

In both van Eyck's and Ghirlandajo's paintings of Jerome in his study, there are jars or carafes of medicines to counteract the evil implied by the apple, and these objects are all placed close together, visually confirming their mutual relationship. Cranach gives us no such close juxtaposition of apple and antidote, but in the far background of the picture there is an elaborate, ornate ewer on the upper shelf near Jerome's right shoulder. How much Cranach may have known of the reasons for the inclusion of these objects in the paintings of his great predecessors is not known, but he clearly did not attempt to connect them as van Eyck and Ghirlandajo had done. It is quite probable that he may never have seen their earlier paintings, or even copies of them.

However, the presence of a pear on the table is most suggestive, since this fruit seems to be used in art chiefly in connection with the incarnate Christ. The pear would then be a reference to Mary as well, as the bearer of that Incarnation, and hence as a container of healing power. As Yjro Hirn has pointed out, fruits and flowers have figured in legends as causing virgins to be transformed into mothers.[31] Similarly, in one medieval flagellant song, the angel of the Annunciation offers the Virgin Mary a sweet-smelling fruit.[32] Related to this fecundive, maternal aspect of fruit is the fact that in Germanic folklore the pear is frequently used to denote the female form, as contrasted with the apple, used as a masculine symbol.[33] The use of the pear in connection with the incarnate Christ is illustrated in three paintings in the National Gallery of Art, Washington. In two by Carlo Crivelli, *Madonna and Child* and *Madonna and Child Enthroned with Donors*, there are pears and apples hanging as decorative-symbolic objects. In *Madonna and Child in an Enclosed Garden* by the

29. Ingvar Bergström, "Medicina, Fons et Scrinium," pp. 5, 6.

30. Franz Joseph Mone, *Lateinische Hymnen des Mittelalters*, vol. 2, pp. 196, 198.

31. *The Sacred Shrine: A Study of the Poetry and Art of the Catholic Church*, p. 300.

32. Paul Runge, *Die Lieder und Melodien der Geiszler des Jahres 1349 nach den Aufzeichnung Hugo's von Reutlingen*, p. 85. Runge's account of the lavish paeans (Laude) of the flagellants of 1349, here translated from his German text, describes and connects the angelic offer of fruit in the Annunciation with the theme of the Incarnation. In one of these laudatory anthems, the angel Gabriel gives into Mary's hand a palm branch with a sweetly fragrant fruit ("con un fructo molto aulente"), while he advises her not to ponder over it, but to accept the God-given gift. Of Mary's pregnancy and of the birth, the paeans are quite plainly expressive: for example, "God sent His holy Son, who, In Mary, came to assume human flesh (encarnato) and was carried in Her womb for nine months." In 1349, a period of devastating plague, the divinely sent fruit would have been of the greatest symbolic import, as an antidote to the black death then raging in epidemic proportions.

33. For the statement that the pear often represents the female, the apple the male, in Germanic folklore, I may cite the wording given in Hans Bächtold-Stäubli's *Handwörterbuch des deutschen Aberglaubens*, vol. 1, col. 1340: "Überhaupt gilt häufig der Birne (im Gegensatz zum Apfel der des männliche Geschlecht symbolisiert) als weiblich" ("Generally the pear (in contrast with the apple, which

studio of the Master of Flemalle, Saint Barbara offers a pear to the Christ Child. To mention still another instance, there is a garland of pears and apples hanging above a half-length *Madonna and Child* by a follower of Andrea Mantegna, in the Kress Collection, Philbrook Art Center, Tulsa.

As further evidence of the symbolic pertinence of the pear to the Virgin Mary, it may be noted that near Sielenbach, Bavaria, there is (or was) a retreat, or place of pilgrimage, called *Mariabirnbaum*, or Mary Pear Tree, concerning which Friedrich Panzer cites a wording, "Unsere liebe Frau unterm B(irnbaum) verehrt" ("our dear Lady honored beneath a pear tree"),[34] which, it is suggested, may possibly be a relic of an old fertility legend. Also in Germany, the pear tree was sometimes called "Dreykönigsbaum" (Three Kings' Tree) in reference to the theme of the "Adoration of the Kings" in religious art. In Greek and Roman mythology the pear was used as an attribute of Aphrodite or Venus, who was, at times, likened to Mary in later, postclassical centuries.[35] In a general way, not necessarily connected with any of the Holy Personages, fruits, regardless of kind, were also used to symbolize peace and joy, the "fruits of the spirit."

The fact that in Cranach's picture the pear and the apple are near each other would serve to connect the antidote closely with the source of sin and disease. This might relieve the ewer, at the far rear wall of the room, from the symbolic role it plays in the two earlier paintings mentioned, but, at the same time, the distant ewer may still have its old meaning.

The apple and the medicinal container (jar, carafe, or ewer) are more often included in pictures of the Annunciation than of Saint Jerome. In renditions of the former theme the inclusion of the curative containers reflects the idea advanced by Saint Bernard that in the act of the Annunciation the antidote was provided against disease and death, both of which, in turn, had resulted from original sin. In one of his sermons (*Sermo II. in festo Pentecostes*), Saint Bernard said, "missus est interim Gabriel angelus a Dio, ut verbum patris per aurem virginis in ventrem et mentem ipsius eructaret, ut eadem via intraret antidotum, qua venenum intraverat" ("the angel Gabriel was sent by God to eject the Father's word through the Virgin's ear into her womb [ventrem] and mind, that thus the antidote might enter by the same way as the poison"). The "poison" here refers to the word of temptation that the serpent of Eden hissed into the ear of Eve. Bernard was not the first to draw a comparison between the serpent and the angel Gabriel, both of whom conveyed their messages into the ear, in one case of Eve, in the other, of Mary. This had been done earlier by Saints Zeno and Ephraim in their discussions of aural impregnation.[36] This is one of the many instances in which characters of the Old Testament were looked upon as prefiguring others in the New.

It follows, from the above, that the ewer, or the jar, or the carafe are interchangeable symbols of Mary the Healer, and it seems that Cranach used the pear in this sense as well. So far as I know this is the only time the pear has been used in this way in any picture of Saint Jerome. But the question still remains why this matter of sin and redemption, understandable in renditions of the Annunciation, should appear in paintings of Jerome. It so happens that the saint had a deep and lasting personal attachment to the cult of the Virgin, to the whole, complex material of Mari-

symbolizes the masculine sex) stands for the female"). In another place (col. 1339), we are informed that the pear is sometimes a symbol of fertility.

In her unfortunately undocumented but descriptive book, *The Floral Symbolism of the Great Masters*, p. 252, Elizabeth Haig refers to a picture in the Corsini Gallery, Florence, attributed to Hugo van der Goes, in which the Madonna holds a pear, and the little Christ Child an apple. She assumes that the artist has distinguished between the apple, symbol of damnation, and the "sweeter, mellower fruit, which may be the symbol of Redemption," and supports this contention by the pose of the Child, Whose action she interprets as attempting to exchange the fruits, one for the other. She adds that a similar thought may have been expressed by "the French ivory-cutters of the fourteenth century [no names or specific works cited], who, not infrequently, put an apple in the Christ Child's hands and a pear in His Mother's." (The painting attributed to van der Goes is not listed by Max Friedländer.) Possibly the most prominent use of the pear in connection with Saint Jerome is to be found in Moretto's *Madonna and Child with Saint Jerome and Saint Bartholomew* (Vatican). In it the Christ Child holds a pear as if offering it to Saint Jerome, while on the floor in front of the base of the Madonna's throne are two groups of pears.

34. *Beitrag zur deutschen Mythologie*, vol. I, pp. 2, 14.

35. Alfred E. P. R. Dowling. *The Flora of the Sacred Nativity*, p. 183.

36. Johann H. Dierbach, *Flora Mythologica oder Pflanzenkunde in Bezug auf Mythologie und Symbolik*, pp. 100-101.

ology. Very early in his career he became a most ardent and effective advocate of the concept of "the perpetual virginity of Mary," as exemplified by his forceful and successful tract *Adversus Helvidium*. The fact that Jerome had this involvement with the cult of the Virgin, who became a universal healer, explains why the concept of original sin, and its consequences, on the one hand, and the medicinal-theological antidote, on the other, came to be included in occasional pictures of Jerome in his study. These occasional inclusions seem comparable to the similarly occasional addition of the lioness to the lion in renditions of Jerome in penitence in the wilderness (see p. 253 ff.). In his study of van Eyck's Detroit picture, Ingvar Bergström suggested that the inclusion of the apple and the antidote may have been caused by the artist's thought that Jerome, as a linguist and as the translator of the Bible into Latin, may have been especially concerned with the *verbum*.[37]

37. "Medicina, Fons et Scrinium," p. 14.

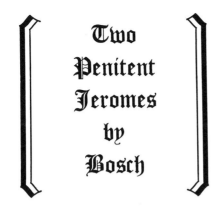

Two Penitent Jeromes by Bosch

As might be expected of their creator, the two versions of the "Saint Jerome in Penitence" theme by Hieronymus Bosch, one in Ghent (fig. 108) and one in Venice (fig. 109), are among the most remarkable, most intensely felt, and yet, iconographically, most baffling versions of the subject. This enigmatic quality permeates almost all of Bosch's work.[1] While this is also true of the two "Jeromes," my discussion here is limited chiefly to a study of the various creatures they contain in the hope that this may contribute to our understanding of the content of these paintings. In the Ghent picture, and in some others, such as the famous *Garden of Earthly Delights*, Bosch showed that he knew very well a considerable number of kinds of birds and other creatures, and painted them with a naturalist's accuracy. This gives us reason to think that he intended to portray exactly the species he did in each case, and this, in turn, makes it necessary to identify them properly before attempting to interpret them. As shall be seen, this has not always been done in the past. In the matter of faunal identifications, the Ghent picture is more amenable and important than the one in Venice; at least all the creatures in the former work are more realistic, hence more certainly identifiable than some of those, especially the partly mythical, fantastic ones, in the latter. Since the Ghent picture has been considered to be the earlier of the two versions,[2] it will be studied first.

Before discussing each of the creatures that are presented or, quite literally, hidden, in this work, it may be pointed out that an unusually tense mood pervades the painting. The composition is roughly divided by a diagonal; the lower, darker part suggestive of evil and of trouble; the upper, lighter part hinting at bucolic peace. The very pose the artist has given to the penitent Jerome is certainly the most emotionally extreme one ever given him by any artist. No longer content to have the saint kneeling in prayer before a crucifix, Bosch has depicted him prostrate on a slightly sloping rise of ground, holding the nearly horizontal crucifix between his orant arms so closely that the figure of the crucified Christ is largely in direct contact with them. Charles de Tolnay concluded in his monograph on Bosch that in this picture Jerome's ardor is so great that he experiences a mystic union with God, and that the little figure of Christ on the cross in his arms is similarly merging into a living fusion with the saint.[3] This may have been suggested by the fact that the eyes of the Christ figure are wide open, not closed as in many crucifixes.[4]

1. Erwin Panofsky (*Early Netherlandish Painting*, pp. 357–58) summed up the persisting enigmatic quality of Bosch's art as follows: "In spite of all the ingenious, erudite . . . research devoted to the task of 'decoding Jerome Bosch' . . . the real secret of his magnificent nightmares and daydreams has still to be disclosed. We have bored a few holes through the door of the locked room; but somehow we do not seem to have discovered the key." Charles de Tolnay (*Hieronymus Bosch*) has made some penetrating observations, and C. A. Wertheim Aymes (*Hieronymus Bosch*) has inclined to Rosicrucian symbolism in his interpretation of the pictures he discussed. Unfortunately, he did not include either of the two Saint Jeromes in his study, but his comments on animals, where pertinent to these paintings, are mentioned in the text, as are also Wilhelm Fränger's suggestions in *The Millennium of Hieronymus Bosch*.

2. Tolnay, p. 366.

3. Ibid., p. 36.

4. While it is true that in many, possibly in most, renditions of the crucifix the eyes of the Christ figure are closed, Bosch's open-eyed version is by no means unique. To take a single instance of comparable geographic and temporal origin, the triptych attributed to Patinir, in the Metropolitan Museum of Art, shows the eyes open in the crucifix before the penitent Jerome.

Figure 108. Hieronymus Bosch, *Saint Jerome in Penitence*. Ghent: Musée des Beaux-Arts. Copyright A.C.L.

Figure 109. Hieronymus Bosch, *Saint Jerome in Penitence*. Venice: Doge's Palace.

This depiction of Jerome shows the most abject, all-absorbing penitence imaginable, far more completely self-mortifying than even such emotionally intense renditions as those by Leonardo da Vinci (fig. 48) or by Cosimo Tura (frontispiece). So complete is this self-mortification that there is no need for the self-lapidation portrayed in the vast majority of such Jerome pictures. The sheer spirituality of this Jerome, as contrasted with the physical corporeality is heightened by the fact that his body seems to be floating over, rather than resting on, the conveniently sloping ground. This is suggested by the lack of weight on the front of the saint's ragged tunic and by the distance below his chest to the foot of the crucifix. The intensity of this rendition has caused it to be considered as involving penitence for longstanding evils, and as suggesting exorcism, a radical purging of these evils.[5]

Bosch has included in this painting many creatures that are too small or too obscured in shadows to be visible, except on very close inspection. It is not possible to say why the artist went to all the trouble of putting them there. It was clearly not done for a general audience, such as a throng of churchgoers. Even at very close range (not more than fifteen inches!) and in the relatively good light of the Ghent gallery, most of these can easily go unnoticed. At a respectful distance in the dimmer illumination of a church they would be impossible to see. In this pseudo-secretive inclusion of faunal elements, Bosch is not unique, however. Similar examples occur in works by such widely different artists as Botticini (fig. 38) and Francesco di Giorgio (fig. 120).

The fauna of Bosch's Ghent painting is as follows: a lion, two lizards, an owl, a tit, a pair of ducks with four ducklings, a fox, a cock, a chaffinch, a heron, three woodpeckers, and two indistinct and unidentifiable birds—a total of twenty creatures, most of them invisible to the casual viewer! One wonders which, or how many, of these creatures, especially the small ones hidden in the shadows, were in Max Friedländer's mind when he wrote that in this picture "even the fauna and flora seem insidious so that a devilish spook appears to be lurking everywhere."[6] He must have been thinking of at least the more conspicuous creatures: the lion, here reduced to a small, thin, curved beast, quite unlike the real animal (and, as Patrick Reuterswärd noted, hardly a protector for the saintly hermit, and far removed from him, near the left side of the painting);[7] the two blackish lizards in the area above the lion (fig. 110); and the owl perched on a dead branch above and to the right of the recumbent Jerome's hips (fig. 111). The lion was not a "devilish" creature, but was the saint's devoted friend. The lizard was a seeker after salvation, like the penitent saint himself. The two lizards here are depicted quite blackish in color, much darker than the olive greenish real creature on which was based the pertinent legend of the sun-seeking lizard. This change in color was probably made to suggest the urgency of the need for salvation after a life of sin (darkness). The legend of the sun-seeking lizard tells us that when the animal grows old and its eyesight becomes impaired, it seeks out a place in the rocks or on a wall facing to the east. Then, in the morning, it stretches its head toward the rising sun, whose bright rays give new strength to its sight. The moral involved in this tale has. been expressed as follows. "In like manner, O man, those who hast on the old garment, and the eyes of whose heart are obscured,

5. Carl Linfert, *Hieronymus Bosch: The Paintings*, p. 18.

6. *Early Netherlandish Painting from Van Eyck to Brueghel*, p. 62.

7. *Hieronymus Bosch*, p. 272.

Figure 111. Detail of owl and titmouse from figure 108, Hieronymus Bosch's *Saint Jerome in Penitence*. Ghent: Musée des Beaux-Arts. Copyright A.C.L.

Figure 110. Detail of lizards and lion from figure 108, Hieronymus Bosch's *Saint Jerome in Penitence*. Ghent: Musée des Beaux-Arts. Copyright A.C.L.

seek the wall of help, and watch there until the sun of righteousness, which the prophet calls the dayspring, rises with healing power, and removes thy spiritual blindness."[8]

The owl is the only one of all these creatures that has a primarily evil connotation, standing for heresy, willful blindness, death, and so forth. It may be recalled that Saint Jerome himself defined the owl as a symbol of "false deity."[9] There is no doubt that Bosch knew his birds remarkably well, but how much he knew of ancient Greek mythology is less certain. However, the curious fact is that the kind of owl he chose to depict in this painting is the little owl, *Athene noctua*, which was the bird of Minerva and a symbol of wisdom in the ancient Hellenic world, whereas the owls that were the primary symbols of evil connotations were the scops owl, *Otus scops*, and the larger, paler barn owl, *Tyto alba*. Iconographically, it might seem that Bosch would have done better had he used the scops owl rather than the one he did, but, as we shall see, he may have had other reasons. In his famous drawing, *Owls in a Hollow Tree*, the implications of which are essentially evil, Bosch may seem to have been inaccurate inconographically again, as there he drew little owls, not scops owls.[10] On the other hand, in *Garden of Earthly Delights* he painted an eared, scops owl in the group called "Satan's Nets."[11]

It is probable that in Bosch's time, and, indeed, for a considerable time before and after him, owls of all kinds were indiscriminately looked upon as creatures of the darkness, as birds of decidedly ill repute. Even the ancient Athenian owl of wisdom was really a bird of pre-Christian, pagan wisdom, not too unlike Saint Jerome's designation of "false deity."

8. Edward Payson Evans, *Animal Symbolism in Ecclesiastical Architecture*, p. 94.

9. Heinrich Schwarz and Volker Plagemann ("Eule," col. 273) give extensive references to Jerome's comments on owls, such as his Commentaries in Joel 3, in Migne, *Patrologia Latina*, vol. 25, p. 980; Epistle 40.2.2; 22.22.8.

10. This drawing has been studied in detail by Jakob Rosenberg, "On the Meaning of a Bosch Drawing," and by Dirk Bax, *Ontcijferung van Jeroen Bosch*.

11. The identification of the group as "Satan's Nets" is that of Jacques Combe (*Iheronimus Bosch*, p. 91).

It may be, therefore, that Bosch's choice of this particular kind of owl was knowledgeable and deliberate. Of this we cannot be certain, but the range and complexity of Bosch's symbolism clearly suggests a good deal of antecedent cultural knowledge on his part.

In the Ghent "Saint Jerome" the owl is posed frontally, staring at the viewer from its perch on the dead branch. This recalls the description in the thirteenth-century moralized poem "The Owl and the Nightingale," in which we find:

There stood an old stump beside
Where the owl sung her hours. . . .
It was the owl's dwelling place.

It may be noted that in this famous poem the owl is more a proponent of the serious, thoughtful attitude toward life than merely a symbol of the "creatures of darkness" and of the evil of their ways. Whether Bosch, like Cosimo Tura, attempted to retain good as well as evil connotations in his owl I cannot say.[12]

To come now to the less conspicuous creatures in the Ghent picture, we may begin at the bottom of the panel. In the lower-left corner there is a fox curled up asleep (fig. 112), while near it, to the right, also at the lower edge of the picture, is a cock. This is a visual reference to Fraud or Deceit. The legend tells us that the fox pretends to be asleep and lets the unwary cock come close; then it suddenly seizes and kills the foolish bird for its dinner. An illustration of this tale occurs in an eleventh-century manuscript,[13] and a similar story, using the wolf rather than the fox, is to be found in a twelfth-century Latin bestiary.[14] The same legend, with the fox, not the wolf, is also to be found in the various versions of the old *Physiologus*, the forerunner and basic source of all the medieval bestiaries.

Bosch made one drawing of the "Fox and Cock" motif, now in the Boymans-van Beuningen Museum, Rotterdam (Koenig's Collection). This sketch shows the fox, not asleep but crouching in a hole in the earth, waiting to spring on the cock that is approaching over the crest of the ground a little above and to the left. Jacques Combe interpreted the cock as a visual reference to the Savior, the ever-watchful shepherd who warns the faithful against the wiles and ruses of the devil (the fox).[15] This could also apply to the Ghent painting, in which Combe apparently did not detect the presence of these creatures. In this rendition the cock is shown in a more dangerous position than in the drawing.

A little to the right of, and above the cock, and a short distance below Jerome's body is a little pond, on which is floating at left a torn, bright reddish, thin-walled object, identified by Combe as "a strange cucurbit [or gourd], an emblem of alchemic heresy,"[16] while further to the right, in the center of the light area of the pond, rests a swimming duck, possibly, but not certainly, intended to be a male widgeon, *Anas penelope*, or a teal, *Anas crecca*, to which it also bears a general resemblance. Both of these are common European pond ducks. In the dusky area at the lower-right end of the pond are a barely discernible female duck and four small ducklings (fig. 113). As indicated, their identification to species is uncertain, since the birds, even the male in better light, are sketchily rendered. However, this is not too important, as the legend behind

12. Bax (Ontcijferung van Jeroen Bosch, p. 215) suggested that the owl in this painting might be connected symbolically with the story of the prodigal son, but he did not document or elaborate the suggestion. Inasmuch as the prodigal son ends as a penitent character, in this respect not wholly unlike Jerome in this painting, such an involvement would suggest some retention of favorable meaning in the owl. If Bax was led to make his suggestion because of the then current interpretation of Bosch's late grisaille painting as representing the prodigal son, this should be reconsidered in light of the studies of A. Pigler and of Lotte Brand Philip in "Astrology and Hieronymus Bosch" and "The Peddler of Hieronymus Bosch: A Study in Detection." These indicate that the painting does not portray the legendary prodigal, but an itinerant peddler. In the background of the painting there is a tree on which are a little owl and an inverted tit, just as in the Ghent work. In her interpretive decoding of "The Peddler," Mrs. Philip made no mention of either of these birds. Pigler was the first to advance the "Peddler" interpretation, which was enlarged upon with additional evidence and commentary by Mrs. Philip and by K. Seligmann, "Hieronymus Bosch: 'The Peddler.'" This interpretation was not accepted by Tolnay (Hieronymus Bosch).

13. Francis Klingender, *Animals in Art and Thought to the End of the Middle Ages*, p. 230; Spanish National Library, Madrid (Beatus MS. B.31; f. 194v).

14. T. H. White, *The Bestiary*, p. 53.

15. *Iheronimus Bosch*, p. 96.

16. Ibid, p. 31–32.

Figure 112. Detail of cock and fox from figure 108, Hieronymus Bosch's *Saint Jerome in Penitence*. Ghent: Musée des Beaux-Arts. Copyright A.C.L.

Figure 113. Detail of ducks from figure 108, Hieronymus Bosch's *Saint Jerome in Penitence*. Ghent: Musée des Beaux-Arts. Copyright A.C.L.

them is similarly vague. Dirk Bax seems to be the only author who has even mentioned the presence of these ducks in this painting, and it is not clear if he noticed the four minute ducklings or only the larger adults.[17] However, he did not attempt to interpret their significance, although he considered a number of the creatures (unspecified) in this painting as allusions to the vice of "unchastity."

This little duck family, hidden away from easy notice, may seem like a bit of discursive naturalism, but actually does have a meaning: it is a reference to the vanity of earthly effort, even of life itself. The argument behind this connotation is unfortunately a little complicated and can only be explained by going back to a Greek legend, mentioned in Homer's Odyssey, relating to Penelope, of whom the duck became a symbol, and after whom Linnaeus gave the widgeon its scientific name, *Anas penelope*, in the mid-eighteenth century.

After Penelope, wife of Ulysses, had been separated from her husband for many years because of his absence in the Trojan War, and when it seemed doubtful that he was still alive, she was importuned by a number of ardent suitors. Penelope wanted to postpone making a decision, still hoping for her husband's return. At the time, she was working on a large robe for the funeral canopy of her father-in-law, Laertes, and promised her suitors that she would decide upon one of them only when the robe was finished. Every day she worked at the robe, but each night she undid all she had done during the day, and, of course, the robe was never completed. This gave rise to the term "Penelope's web," an expression signifying something continually in process but never achieving completion, and it also caused the word "Penelope" to come into use as a general term for a virtuous wife. However, inasmuch as the whole family of ducks, not merely the mother, is shown in the painting, another meaning also applies. This goes even further, and suggests the futility of reproduction in view of the inevitable finality of death.

Penelope was likened to, and became an allegory of, the concept of Mother Nature, with her loom, "unravelling by night all that she weaves by day, and so working in vain into infinity."[18] The duck (not necessarily the widgeon) was used as a symbol of Penelope, because it was a bird that breeds in the marsh, a habitat untamed by man, and described as a "place of swift breeding and swift dying"—a place full of ever-present, hidden dangers, where death undoes the effect of reproduction, a place of marked and sudden seasonal changes. Wilhelm Fränger first brought out the connection of the duck-Penelope concept in his study of another of Hieronymus Bosch's paintings, *Garden of Earthly Delights*. In that work the duck involved is a mallard, not a widgeon, and it is not shown as breeding (with a family) or even in a marshy pond, as called for in the argument underlying its use as a symbol of Penelope. By contrast, the ducks in the present painting are precisely oriented to the specifications of the legend.

It was noted earlier that the specific identification of the duck is not too important. The reason for this is that the Greeks had another word, *penelops*, which they used for a duck without regard to the Penelope story, and which has never been identified with certainty to species. It is quite possible, even probable, that the similarity in the two names helped to bring them together in mythology. Likewise, it may be that Linnaeus

17. *Ontcijfering van Jeroen Bosch*, p. 215. It may be noted that more recently James Snyder (*Bosch in Perspective*, p. 7) concluded that the little ponds and spots with marsh vegetation in some of Bosch's pictures represent the "watery matrix for conception," and that the birds in them are associated with the ideas of lust and fertility. Snyder does not mention either of the two "Jerome" paintings, and his statement that the birds in these ponds are usually greatly inflated in size certainly does not fit the ducks in the Ghent work. The connotation of the pond itself is not contrary to Snyder's interpretation.

18. Fränger, pp. 132–33; also Wertheim Aymes, p. 44.

was aware of *penelops* and of *Penelope* and used the latter name because of the uncertainty about the former.

The rendition Bosch has given us, showing the male duck in the light (safe) area of the pond, while the female and her four young are in the dark (dangerous) part of the marsh-bordered water, stresses the implication of the futility of reproduction ending inevitably in death, more rapidly perhaps for the mother and the ducklings than for the relatively free, less tied-down male—and this suggests the greater futility of life itself.

While the interpretation advanced here does fit the content and nature of this painting, I cannot demonstrate that Bosch was aware of the Penelope legend, either by himself or through any friend or adviser. Bosch lived and worked away from the larger cultural centers, although his town, 's-Hertogenbosch, was neither small nor provincial, but so little is known of his life that it is hardly possible to guess the breadth or the limitations of his intellectual horizon. At the same time it must be admitted that even an artist capable of the pictorial originality and daring that characterizes Bosch's entire output could not have invented so rich and eccentric a visual language. He must have built it on a basis of concepts and ideas that have not yet been rediscovered to any extent. The studies of Jurgis Baltrusaitis have indicated that some of Bosch's fantastic motifs can be traced back to medieval miniature manuscript illuminations.[19] Because his studies were limited to purely fantastic figures, there is nothing in Baltrusaitis's work immediately pertinent to the duck of the Penelope symbolism, but his material does suggest that Bosch was familiar with a number of medieval visual allegories. It seems unlikely that the artist would have deliberately introduced the little family of ducks in his work if no relevant significance were involved. Further, the general notion of the eventual futility of reproduction suggested by the duck-Penelope icon, and also the concept of Penelope as the virtuous wife, both fit in with the fact that Jerome argued strongly for continence, in his writings and preachings. So well do these concepts agree with the Jerome theme that it seems safe to credit Bosch with some knowledge of the meanings implied by the ducks and their pertinence in this painting.

Mention has been made of what Combe called a "strange cucurbit, an emblem of alchemic heresy." While this identification seems justified, it may be noted that a somewhat similar, but very differently colored gourd is shown growing to the left of the meditating Baptist in another of Bosch's works, *Saint John the Baptist in the Wilderness* (Madrid: Museo Lazaro Galdiano). Combe reminds us of Bosch's constant recourse to alchemic symbolism, and further specifies that "one of the alchemic postulates is the sexual basis of the development of creation as a whole." The gourd here is broken and empty, a gourd that can no longer be productive. This, in turn, supports the concept of the futility of reproduction, and even of life itself, that is suggested by the family of ducks.

To the right of the ducks, between the pond and Jerome's cardinal's hat, is a hollow tree stump. Barely discernible, slightly protruding from a large hole in its front side, is the head of a dark woodpecker, its sharp bill pointed upward to the right (fig. 114). This woodpecker is not specifically identifiable, because so little of it is visible, and that little is in the shadow of the tree cavity. Thus, it is possible only to suggest its meaning

19. *Le Moyen Âge fantastique*, 1955.

here. In medieval symbolism the woodpecker, as an enemy of insects and "worms" hidden beneath the bark of trees, was a figure of Christ, who wages unending war on the hidden forces of evil.[20] As is so frequently the case with symbols, the same figure, the woodpecker, has at times been used for a diametrically opposite meaning as a visual reference to "anti-Christ," attacking the Tree of Life.

To the right, on a thin twig branching off from a lower portion of the stump, perches a small sparrowlike bird, identifiable as a chaffinch, *Fringilla coelebs* (fig. 114). This is a bird that has seldom been used in religious art, and is one for which I have found no pertinent antecedent legend or folklore. However, its Latin name, *coelebs*, suggests its meaning. The name *coelebs* refers to celibacy, which may be a reflection of Saint Jerome's interest in, and arguments for, celibacy, not only as it affected the story of the Holy Family, as in his famous tract *Adversus Helvidium*, but also as a general practice. It must be admitted that this is only a matter of inference from the bird's name, but this clearly did not originate without reason and must have been derived from earlier knowledge or legend. In the case of the bird's Latin (scientific) name there is documentation. It was believed that the two sexes of the chaffinch lived in separate flocks during their long nonbreeding season, and this "celibacy," even if only seasonal, was the reason why, in his own words, Linnaeus deliberately selected *coelebs* for the little bird's specific name.[21]

Chaffinches occur in a few other religious paintings, not as symbolic creatures but as additional birds among others in such themes as Giotto's *Saint Francis Preaching to the Birds* (Assisi) and Pisanello's *Vision of Saint Eustace* (London).

To the right of the owl, hanging upside down from a small branch of the dead tree stump, is an accurately depicted coal tit, *Parus ater* (fig. 111). Combe misidentified this bird, and also a blue tit in Bosch's *Garden of Earthly Pleasures*, as woodpeckers, and interpreted them accordingly.[22] The coal tit, as well as other species of tits, the blue tit and the great tit, were used very seldom in religious art. All three species shared the connotation of "fertility." Thus, in Filippino Lippi's *Madonna and Child with Saint Jerome and Saint Dominic*, in the National Gallery, London, there is a blue tit in the upper part of the painting "flying to its nest of waiting young ones."[23]

As already mentioned, the titmouse in the Ghent "Jerome" is in an inverted position, as are also the blue tits in two other paintings by Bosch, *Garden of Earthly Delights*, and *The Peddler*. While this upside down posture is one that is very frequently assumed by these birds in their normal feeding behavior, it is possibly significant that it was just this particular inverted position that appealed to Bosch as one more aspect of the topsy-turvy world of his visions. "The Peddler" theme illustrates the toilsome and disheartening passage through the futile and dismal experience of living, a concept not dissimilar to Jerome's pessimistic attitude.

The occurrence in *The Peddler* and in the Ghent painting of the owl and the tit in such closely similar relationship to each other may help to correlate some of the ideas expressed in each. Wertheim Aymes[24] considered the tit in Bosch's art to be symbolic of uncertain, chaotic, fluttering thought, which becomes more understandable in the Jerome context

20. Fränger, p. 63.

21. Alfred Newton, *A Dictionary of Birds*, p. 82, fn.; Linnaeus, *Systema natura*, 10th ed., vol. 1, p. 179.

22. *Iheronimus Bosch*, p. 63.

23. William Norton Howe, *Animal Life in Italian Painting*, p. 44.

24. *Hieronymus Bosch*, p. 41.

Figure 114. Detail of chaffinch from figure 108, Hieronymus Bosch's *Saint Jerome in Penitence*. Ghent: Musée des Beaux-Arts. Copyright A.C.L.

Figure 115. Detail of heron from figure 108, Hieronymus Bosch's *Saint Jerome in Penitence*. Ghent: Musée des Beaux-Arts. Copyright A.C.L.

wherein is stressed the futility or vanity of reproduction, shown here as a disoriented (inverted) concept. In *The Peddler*, which he considered to be "The Prodigal Son," Wertheim Aymes found the tit, fluttering between mental decisions, to express the general disinclination of man to start on the narrow but definite road to heaven.

There are five other creatures in the Ghent painting. In the right background, about halfway up on the right edge of the picture, is a tree with two birds. A woodpecker can be made out on the right side of the trunk and a whitish heron is standing on the ground a little behind (deeper into the background) and to the left of the base of the tree (fig. 115). These can be distinguished by carefully examining the original painting, but can barely be seen in the photograph. The woodpecker is not completely dark, as is the bird whose head appears in the hole in the tree stump near the lower-right corner of the picture, but has black and white marks and a little red on the head, as in the spotted woodpeckers of the genus *Dendrocopos*. It is probably the lesser spotted woodpecker, *Dendrocopos minor* (there are three closely similar species in western Europe), but the figure is so tiny and sketchy that specific identification is uncertain. Fortunately, another lesser spotted woodpecker of greater size and more certain recognition is perched on the stone tablet immediately above Jerome's head. The implication of these woodpeckers is like that of the darker one already discussed.

The stone on which this woodpecker is perched has been likened by Tolnay to the "tablet of the law" in the story of Moses,[25] but this seems very uncertain. No inscription can be distinguished on it. Tolnay also suggested that the large broken object to the left of it is a bucranium, or ox skull. This seems to me still more uncertain, since it is so broken as to be quite unrecognizable.

The tiny figure of the heron (a fairly sizable bird in reality) to the left of the tree seems to be a reference, albeit a faint one because of its small size and inconspicuousness, to the ideas of penitence and righteousness, suggested by Millard Meiss for the much larger figure of a gray heron in Giovanni Bellini's *Saint Francis*, in the Frick Collection, New York.[26] There was an old, widespread legend that the heron was very constant in its diet, and could not be enticed by strange food. This caused it to be likened to the true believer, who spurned alien doctrine. As Edward Payson Evans expressed it, the heron never touches carrion "nor does it fly from place to place but abides in one spot, dwelling there where it finds suitable food. So the righteous do not care for the corrupt things of this world . . . neither do they wander hither and thither after false doctrine."[27] In the legend no distinction was made between different kinds of herons, of which there are several species in Europe. The fact that Bosch's heron is white, like an egret, whereas Bellini used the larger, gray heron, *Ardea cinerea*, is not important. It may be that the artist chose to make his heron white to suggest "purity" or merely to make it a little more visible in the shadowy background. A similar white heron also occurs in Bosch's other version of *Saint Jerome in Penitence*, in Venice, where it is much more conspicuous, about halfway between Jerome and his lion.

In another depiction of the same theme, attributed to the school of Hieronymus Bosch (Bruges: Musée Communal), there is a small heron in the background, which is still another species, a bittern. In this painting, the right panel of a triptych, the central panel of which represents the "Ordeal of Job," and the left "The Temptation of Saint Anthony," Jerome is shown in loose, red robes, kneeling before a crucifix and holding a stone in his right hand, a more usual figure of the penitent Jerome. There is no lion, but there are two snakes, two small finches, and an unidentifiable creature with two or more long spines on its back, possibly intended to be a porcupine or a hedgehog, recalling somewhat the so-called porcupine in Mansueti's *Saint Jerome in the Wilderness*, formerly in the collection of Arthur Hughes, London.

The other two birds in the Ghent painting are not identifiable, and, because of that, are not subject to meaningful comment. One of them, barely discernible, is a dark silhouette at the lower edge of the pond just above and to the right of the sleeping fox. In fact, it can only be guessed that it is a bird. The other is unmistakably a bird, although not identifiable to any known species. It is perched on a thin branch extending to the right from the crown of the curious, bulbous-trunked tree at the upper-left corner of the painting, and is facing the crown of the tree, which supports a bulky open nest containing one white egg, presumably belonging to this bird. Unfortunately, the nest, unnatural in its represen-

25. Tolnay, p. 36.

26. *Giovanni Bellini's St. Francis in the Frick Collection*, pp. 22–23.

27. *Animal Symbolism in Ecclesiastical Architecture*, p. 148.

tation, provides no clue as to the identity of the bird. In its rather long-tailed and fairly long-billed outline it is somewhat similar to a bird seen through the opening of Jerome's grotto home in Bosch's other "Jerome" painting (Venice). It is also slightly like another bird in the right panel of Bosch's "Saint Anthony" triptych in Lisbon. In its form and proportions the latter bird suggests a bee-eater (*Merops*), but is certainly not a portrayal of the one European species (or, for that matter, of any other) of this group of birds.

This completes the amazing fauna of the Ghent picture. Aside from the two unidentifiable birds, meanings can be found for all the other creatures in it. The lion is Jerome's "emblem," here reduced from a powerful beast of prey to just an identifying label; the lizards echo the saint as seekers after salvation, their need for which is emphasized by their unusually dark (evil) coloration; the owl represents the evil that makes repentance necessary; the pair of widgeon and their young, the chaffinch and the inverted coal tit lend visual support to Jerome's judgment of the futility of reproduction and even of life itself; the female duck suggests virtue and continence; the fox and the cock illustrate the perils that accompany the passage through life; the white heron shows the steadfast path of life of the faithful; and the three woodpeckers the ceaseless war waged by the forces of good against the evil hidden beneath the surface of things. In two of the three cases the forces of good are minute and difficult to see; this is in keeping with Bosch's moralistic attitude. Erwin Panofsky concluded that Bosch was "not so much a heretic as one of those extreme moralists who, obsessed with what they fight, are haunted, not unpleasurably, by visions of unheard-of obscenities, perversions and tortures."[28] Bosch tended to emphasize the ills and the troubles, the errors and the dangers of this world, but even so he refrained from introducing into either of his penitent Jerome pictures such symbols of evil as snakes and scorpions. Both of these were widely used in the Jerome context by other artists; snakes were included in the Bosch school painting in Bruges.

The entire assemblage of faunal symbols in the Ghent painting occurs in the darker, tense, lower portion of the picture, the area that is the setting for Jerome's abandonment to utter penitence. By contrast, the bright and sunny landscape of bucolic peace in the upper part of the painting is free of symbols. Where all is good and serene there is no need of them.

In Bosch's second version of the theme of the penitent Jerome, the central panel of the *Altarpiece of the Hermits*, in the Doge's Palace, Venice (fig. 109), we find a very different conception. For one thing, this panel is not alone, as is the one in Ghent, which, so far as is known, apparently was not part of a triptych. The Venice "Saint Jerome" is flanked by two penitent ascetics, Saint Anthony on the left and Saint Giles on the right. The three panels are mutually independent, although connected by the theme of penitence. There is some continuity in the background landscape of the Jerome and Giles panels, while that of the Anthony panel is in violent contrast to the others.

In this altarpiece Jerome is shown kneeling before a crucifix, but he is erect, not recumbent as in the other; his very erectness is accentuated by his most unnaturally tall stature. In this instance Bosch has exaggerated the saint's height more than in the Ghent panel, and more than might be

28. *Early Netherlandish Painting*, p. 357.

apparent at first glance because of the kneeling position. The elongation of the figure is as extreme as one finds in the works of El Greco (for example, his *Saint Jerome in Penitence* in the National Gallery of Art, Washington, fig. 79). Only occasionally have other artists given Jerome such tall stature (as did Macrino d'Alba in *Madonna and Child Enthroned with Saints*, in the Sabauda Gallery, Turin).

Saint Jerome is not shown praying in this picture; he holds no stone with which to beat himself; and his expression and his gestures suggest not so much an attitude of repentance as an attempt to probe into his own mind or conscience for a solution to what is troubling him. Tolnay seems to have found the correct interpretation in Jerome's own writings.[29] He considers that the saint is not so much a penitent as one who is attempting to evaluate and to reconcile the conflicting thoughts that caused him so much distress in his contemplations. The curious setting of the picture, combining classical ruins, bits of pagan idolatry and sun worship, mingled with Christian symbols, seems to be a reflection of Jerome's dual love of the classical authors and of the Bible.

According to Tolnay, and also to Carl Linfert,[30] this introspective searching of the saint's contradictory interests and visions explains why the setting is full of signs of the nonspiritual world and its many heresies, mingled with other concepts. Thus, Jerome is kneeling before a little crucifix placed in the ruins of a classical pagan chapel, the curved outer wall of which, to the saint's right, is decorated with a frieze depicting "Judith with the Head of Holofernes," a biblical, nonclassical story of a type of deliverance from conflicting drives that might be compared with what the perplexed Jerome is seeking for himself in this picture (fig. 116). Furthermore, Judith was, at times, considered a prefiguration of Mary.

Unlike the Ghent "Jerome," this picture has a number of unreal, mythical creatures, some of which, like the fighting reptilians in the lower-right foreground (fig. 117) and the curious skeleton near the lower-left corner, are quite conspicuous. Of the relatively realistic animals in it, four are also found in the other: the lion, the dark lizard, the white heron, and the little owl. Jerome's lion is quite similar to the one in the Ghent work, except that it is turned around, facing into the picture, not toward the beholder. In both, the lion is bending down; in both it is on the left side of the panel, small in size, thin, and relatively long-legged.

The lizard is difficult to detect; it is very small and is shown from behind, but with its head turned to the right (which helps to make it identifiable); it is immediately above the skeleton in the lower-left foreground and is silhouetted against the pale ground area. The dark lizard, so similar to the more clearly rendered ones in the other painting, must have the same underlying significance, although with lesser emphasis—a seeker after the light of salvation following a life of error. That it is reduced is in keeping with the fact that in this painting salvation is not the immediate goal as it is in the other. Here salvation can be sought only after Jerome's doubts are settled.

There are two other indistinct "creatures" in the Venice picture that may also be lizards. Again, they are small and are partly hidden; the painting's poor state of preservation further obscures them. One creature, of which only the tail and hind legs are visible, is disappearing into

29. *Hieronymus Bosch*, p. 37.

30. *Hieronymus Bosch: The Paintings*, p. 115.

Figure 116. Detail of the Judith frieze from figure 109, Hieronymus Bosch's *Saint Jerome in Penitence*. Venice: Doge's Palace.

Figure 117. Detail of fighting reptiles, skeleton, and frog (in hole near base of column) from figure 109, Hieronymus Bosch's *Saint Jerome in Penitence*. Venice: Doge's Palace.

the leaning hollow stump near the lower-left corner of the picture; its tail is hanging down to the right from the open top of the stump. The other is only inferential, hardly demonstrable as a lizard. Its head alone is visible below the left edge of Jerome's cardinal's hat. The only reason for even suggesting that this dark spot, intruding onto the pale stone on

Figure 118. Detail of heron, lion, magpie, and deer from figure 109, Hieronymus Bosch's *Saint Jerome in Penitence*. Venice: Doge's Palace.

which the hat is lying, is a lizard is that it seems to have a contrastingly light eye spot, similar to the one, already described, in the lower-left part of the painting. Also, the shape of the dark creature would not be unnatural for a lizard.

The white heron (fig. 118), standing about midway between Jerome and his lion, to the left of the opening of the saint's little grotto, is more conspicuous than it is in the Ghent version. Its meaning here is presumably the same: the steadfast way of life of the faithful. In this instance, it may be that Jerome's opposing dual interests in the pagan classics and in Holy Scripture were thought to have interfered with such a steadfastness, and it is partly to achieve this that he is shown searching his inner self.

The owl is very small and inconspicuous, indeed it is not too readily recognizable as such, because it is part of the crumbling, painted decoration on the sloping, curved arm of the little ruined classical chapel, to the left of Jerome's hat (fig. 116). Immediately below it is painted a beehive made of a wicker basket, into which a crawling man has disappeared down to his waist. Above the owl are painted some unidentifiable flying birds. The owl attacked by flying birds was a well-known medieval allusion to the persecution of the Jews, who, like the owl that symbolizes them, preferred to remain in the dark of pre-Christian dogma rather than to accept the new light, to the vexation of the birds of the light. The man delving head first into the beehive is one of those pictorializations that has two opposing meanings. It is a visual reference to the errors of those who abandon everything for the pleasures, the sweet seductions (honey), of this world[31], but, to a lesser extent, it is also an allusion to the whole-hearted seeker after the Good. The argument behind this is that in the Middle Ages a colony of bees and their hive were

31. Evans, p. 5.

described by ecclesiastics as an example, especially to the friars and nuns, of an ideal life of true communal industry and cenobitic chastity. The bee was also used occasionally as a symbol of Resurrection. The risen Christ was referred to as *apis aetherea*, or heavenly bee, in a sermon by Peter of Capua.[32] The first meaning, a reference to the moral blindness of the seeker after pleasure, is quite in keeping with the willful blindness of the owl, shunning the light brought into the world by the Messiah.

The only other decoration on this ruin is a relief of a man attempting to tame or to capture a unicorn. This is an example of a hopeless quest or a vain desire. In the legends of the unicorn it is emphasized that no hunter was able to capture one alive unless he had the help of a young virgin. The hunter would deck a chaste maiden with beautiful trinkets and ornaments and seat her in a solitary glade in a forest frequented by the unicorn, and leave her there. On seeing the lovely virgin the unicorn would run to her, lay its head on her lap, and, feeling secure, would quickly fall asleep, whereupon the hunter would quietly return and capture the prized beast.[33] The unicorn was, thus, a "lover of chastity," and as T. H. White found in a twelfth-century Latin bestiary, the unicorn was also a visual reference to Christ.[34] That ancient account likens the unicorn running to lay its head in the lap of a virgin to the fact that "by the sole will of the Father," Jesus "came down into the virgin womb for our salvation." This old bestiary adds further that Jesus was called a spiritual unicorn; that one psalm noted that He was loved like the "Son of the Unicorns"; and that the one horn of the unicorn signifies Christ's statement, "I and the Father are One."

To recapitulate, the ruined classical chapel where Jerome kneels in his dilemma has three bits of decoration: the Judith and Holofernes frieze depicting an act of deliverance; the owl and the honey-seeking man, symbolic of willful blindness, tempered, it is true, by a secondary allusion to the zealous search for the Good; and the unicorn illustrating the futile attempt to tame the animal force that can only be conquered by chastity. All of these concepts bear directly on the Jerome theme. Each of them must have been deliberately selected by the artist when creating the composition, and it should not surprise us that they prove to be pertinent and mutually supportive. Individually and collectively, they are not classical and are not particularly germane to a classical, pre-Christian chapel, but they are to the Christianized use of what was left of the ruins of the old pagan edifice.

To continue with the fauna of this picture, we may note a long-tailed bird perched above and to the right of Jerome's head. This is a paroquet, a small, long-tailed parrot, but not identifiable to any known species. Bosch could have had only limited opportunities to see living parrots, and he had to improvise his bird. During the Middle Ages the parrot was used as a sign of the virgin birth of Christ. As may be seen from the account in the Bestiary section (p. 280 ff.), parrots were introduced into a fair number of pictures of Saint Jerome, who was one of the earliest and staunchest supporters of the concept of the perpetual virginity of Mary.

Behind Jerome there is an opening to his grotto in the hill, and through it two birds may be made out. One is merely a small silhouette clinging to the left wall of the far end of the opening. By its shape and pose it may be identified as a woodpecker, a bird we have already met in the

32. Louis Charbonneau-Lassay, *Le Bestiaire du Christ*, pp. 515–16.

33. Evans, p. 95.

34. *The Bestiary*, p. 21; Odell Shepard, *The Lore of the Unicorn*; Klaus Günther, *Das Einhorn*.

Ghent "Saint Jerome." The other is perched on a narrow branch in the middle of the opening. It is not identifiable, but seems similar to the un-identifiable bird near the upper-left corner of the Ghent painting.

In the lower-left portion of the Venice picture is a truncated column on which is depicted a sun worshipper (fig. 117). Near the base of the swollen lower part of the column is a hole in which may be discerned what seems to be a frog (possibly, but not likely, a lizard with its head raised; only the head and forelimbs of the creature are visible). The frog was a creature associated with evil and disaster. One of the plagues visited upon Egypt was a shower of frogs (Exodus 8). R. Holbrook traced Dante's use of the frog in this sense back to Rabanus Maurus, and added that the little amphibians came to symbolize heretics.[35] In this sense the frog would be "at home" in the pagan column devoted to such a heresy as sun and star worship. On the other hand, because of the sudden reappearance of frogs in the spring after a long winter's absence, they were at times looked upon as symbols of Resurrection in the same way, but not as frequently, as were swallows and other harbingers of spring.[36] Because of the curious suspension of logic in allegorical thinking, the frog, as a symbol of rebirth, came to be also a sex symbol.[37]

Below and to the left of the base of the column are two animals, neither of which is identifiable, yet they seem not purely mythical. The one to the right, a thin, elongated wormlike creature with many short legs, looks like a millipede, but thinner and less flattened. Millipedes, like other "worms" of the early bestiaries, were supposed to generate directly from decayed meat, or wood, or earth, in which respect they were occasionally mentioned as resembling scorpions, but without the venomous sting of the latter.

The other animal, to the left and close to the edge of the painting, is a hemispherical, banded or spotted buglike creature with six pairs of legs (no real insect has more than three) and with large eyes—possibly intended to be the cimex found in the bestiary translated by White—a buglike organism said to have a very offensive odor and to be born from decaying meat.[38] This latter creature is much like the so-called scarab as drawn by Dürer in the illustrations he made for his friend Willibald Pirckheimer's translation of the *Hieroglyphica* of Horapollo. Dürer's sketch shows a somewhat flatter, less convexly arched, and more elongated oval body form with seven pairs of legs, a most unnatural and quite surprising figure, especially in light of Dürer's keen interest in natural history. As described by Horapollo,[39] the male scarab makes a round ball of cow dung and, rolling it from east to west, it "faces the east, so as to give it the shape of the world, for the world is borne from the east to the west. Then burying this ball, it leaves it in the ground for twenty-eight days, during which time the moon traverses the twelve signs of the zodiac. Remaining here, the beetle is brought to birth. And on the twenty-ninth day, when it breaks the ball open, it rolls into the water. For it considers this day to be the conjunction of the moon and the sun, as well as of the birth of the world." This close correlation of the birth of the scarab with zodiacal events makes one wonder if, in Bosch's painting, it may be a continuation of the sun and star worship depicted on the column nearby. But, as in so many of Bosch's uses of creatures, we do not know how well he knew the legends about them that we have gradu-

35. *Dante and the Animal Kingdom*, pp. 211–14.

36. Charbonneau-Lassay, p. 819–28.

37. Wertheim Aymes, p. 83.

38. White, p. 194.

39. George Boas, *The Hieroglyphics of Horapollo*, p. 62.

ally come to know from literary sources that may or may not have been available to him.

In the lower foreground, near the bottom of the picture and to the left of the artist's signature, are two fighting reptiles, much larger than the lizards and not so dark in color, but too small to be taken for dragons. The vanquished one is lying on its back, while the other is trampling on its stomach and biting its left hind leg. To the left of them is a skeleton of another of the same kind of creature. That it is the same is shown by its peculiar skull, with the elongated snout like that of the victorious reptile in the fight to the right. The presence of this skeleton calls to mind a touch in Rembrandt's engraving of 1634, in which a skull of a small mammal or reptile is lying in the lower-right corner of the picture, and at which the saint's lion is gazing. Reptiles usually were looked upon as sinister, basically evil creatures, although the sun (salvation)-seeking lizard was an exception. These unidentifiable reptiles might best be described as signs of evil, while the loser of the battle on the right and the skeletal remains of the one on the left clearly denote death.

A most unexpected animal figure, an unidentifiable, medium-sized mammal that might be a fawn or a doe, appears upside down on the rock behind and below (from the viewer's eye, in front and below) the lion. To see it clearly, it is necessary to turn the picture (or a photograph) upside down; then the animal approximates a pose of running toward the picture edge. Right side up, it practically disappears as a shadowy area on the rock. It may be intended to be a dead creature that the lion has killed for its next meal. That this is not an idle thought is borne out by the fact that in a few paintings of Jerome in penitence the saint's lion is shown in the act of eating another animal: a deer (hind-quarter only shown) in one picture by an anonymous sixteenth-century Netherlandish artist (Brussels) and a gray rabbit in another, attributed to Isenbrandt, in the Hermitage, Leningrad (fig. 72).

This completes the survey of the meaningful fauna of this painting. There are still other animals present in the distant background of no, or relatively little, interest as far as the mood and the iconographic message of the painting are concerned. In the far background in the upper half of the picture, Bosch has included a small group of deer, a little above the lion. One deer is partly hidden behind the left edge of the hill in which Jerome's grotto lies, only its hind legs and body being visible. On its rump perches a bird, apparently intended to be a magpie. This is a natural enough occurrence for a number of kinds of birds, and shows that the artist was very observant. While the magpie here is probably merely a bit of discursive naturalism, it does have a traditional, but vague, association with the concept of death, particularly of the gallows. In *The Peddler*, Bosch placed a magpie on the gallowslike wooden gate at right, and a painting by Pieter Brueghel is titled *The Magpie on the Gallows*. In his discussion of the magpie, K. Seligmann considers the bird to stand for the frailty of human decisions, apparently on the old assumption that white stands for purity and good, and black for the opposite, so that the combination of both in the magpie produces a state of uncertainty.[40] Further, Jacob Grimm records that there is an old Flemish legend that the magpie was "ver Ave" ("frau Ave," in common speech), and that there still lingers a trace of magpie worship, usually in the form of food

40. Seligmann cites as his ultimate source the thirteenth-century German epic poet Wolfram von Eschenbach, who discussed the magpie in the introduction to his *Parzifal*. There, the magpie paradigm is explained as follows: The white man is the knightly ideal, the black man stands for moral wavering, while the combined black and white man (as the colors are combined in the magpie) fights doubt and overcomes it. Apparently Seligmann was less certain of the outcome than was Wolfram.

offerings tied in the branches, because the chattering of the bird tended to warn people of the approach of a wolf.[41] This legend may also have been in Bosch's mind when he decided to include the magpie in this painting. Both in *Saint Jerome in Penitence* and in *The Peddler*, the magpie is a small item in the background, not apt to be noted by the casual viewer. It would seem that the most that can be said of its role in the "Jerome" picture is that it can be no more than a faint reference to the theme of death that plays such a part in the painting as a whole.

There is still another, quite unidentifiable creature in this painting, deeper in the background to the right of Jerome's hill—possibly a doe or a horse or an ass. To complete this survey, a few very minute pale birds may be noted beyond and to the left of Jerome's hill; they are too vague and small to be identifiable or interpretable.

In this picture, as in the Ghent version, we have now seen that iconographic reasons may be adduced for the presence of the various kinds of creatures included in it, and that, even without explicit documentary evidence as to the artist's intention, or that of possible iconographic advisers, we may have confidence in the validity and in the general applicability of our explanatory suggestions. There are far too many of them to be merely coincidences.

The two paintings stress different thoughts about Jerome and serve to evoke different moods. In so doing they depend in common on such creatures as the lion, deer, lizard, heron, woodpecker, and owl; they differ in their other faunal symbols—paroquet, unicorn, reptilians, frog, scarab (or cimex), and millipede in the Venice panel; cock, fox, duck, chaffinch and tit, in the Ghent one. In neither of these works are any of the animals included without meaning: these pictures are not the result of "menagerie-mindedness" in the sense that are Mansueti's crowded Bergamo (fig. 36) and London pictures of Saint Jerome. The creatures that Bosch included in his versions of the theme give us some of the all too few firm insights into what would otherwise remain inscrutable daydreams of the artist. Otto Benesch[42] was impressed with Bosch's knowledge of, and use of, the compilations of animals, demonic or otherwise, in the medieval bestiaries and in the writings of their subsequent commentators, a corpus of material that had already been issued in book form in Bosch's time. Benesch rightly stated that Bosch was both a naturalist and a visionary.

41. *Teutonic Mythology*, p. 675.

42. "Hieronymous Bosch and the Thinking of the Middle Ages," in *Collected Writings*, vol. 2, pp. 26, 35.

Antonello da Messina's "Saint Jerome in His Study"

Antonello da Messina's justly famous painting, *Saint Jerome in His Study*, in the National Gallery, London (fig. 119), has been assumed by most recent authors to have been inspired by a lost work of Jan van Eyck, a triptych created for Battista Lomellini, and acquired around 1445 or shortly afterward by Alfonso V of Aragon. The pertinent part of van Eyck's triptych was one of the lateral panels on which was painted Jerome in his study chamber. The central panel showed the Annunciation, and the other lateral one Saint John the Baptist. On the shutters were painted Giovanni Battista Lomellini and his wife, Jeronima Lomellini. All that is known of the triptych is the 1455 description by Bartolommeo Fazio, which is too slight and sketchy to be of much help iconographically.[1] It is doubtful that André Chastel intended the definiteness his words convey when he wrote that Antonello's painting was an "imitation" of the lost van Eyck,[2] a picture that is also generally credited as the source from which Colantonio patterned his well-known work (fig. 1) in Naples. If Antonello's and Colantonio's paintings are indeed derivatives from the same lost van Eyck, they show by their great divergence from each other that their original source of inspiration could only have given both of them the idea of a book-lined study setting in which to place the saint. Fazio's description of the lost van Eyck mentions no lion in the picture. There *is* a lion in the Detroit painting of the same theme by van Eyck. The lion in this case was probably painted by Petrus Christus, possibly as his own contribution or else in accordance with a design or instruction of van Eyck. All that Fazio tells us about the lost painting is that Jerome was very lifelike, and the library was executed with marvelous skill. If one steps but a short distance from it, Fazio explains, the setting gives the impression of receding inwardly and of displaying entire books, whose headings need only to be approached to be readable.

Beyond this meager information it is not possible to reconstruct the lost van Eyck. Any such attempt is complicated by the fact that the painting was supposed to have influenced not only Colantonio and Antonello, but also at least two of the manuscript illuminators who were

1. *Bartholomaei facii de viris illustribus*, pp. 46–47. This has been conveniently reprinted in Erwin Panofsky, *Early Netherlandish Painting* (paperback ed., vol. 1, n. 7 to p. 2).

2. *The Age of Humanism*, p. 317.

working at the time in Naples for the Aragonese court under Alfonso V. In their resulting pictures these artists transformed Jerome into Seneca in one case, and into Cyril of Alexandria in the other.[3]

The action depicted in the Antonello and the Colantonio versions of Jerome in his study could hardly be more different. Antonello presents us with the saint quietly reading at his desk; his lion is small and is far off in the background to the right, not in the study alcove itself. Colantonio's very large lion is in the central part of the picture plane, having the thorn removed from its foot by Jerome, who has left his scholarly work to attend to the animal's distress. Furthermore, in Antonello's painting, "Jerome" seems definitely to be a portrait, although of whom is not known, while in Colantonio's work there is no suggestion of a particular individual as a model for the saint. The thought that Antonello's Jerome is a portrait, probably of a prominent ecclesiastic, is entirely in keeping with van Eyck's earlier action in his picture of Cardinal Albergati as Saint Jerome, now in Detroit.[4] The portrayal of a noted churchman as his patron saint was a recognized, privileged method for a prelate of importance to approach that saint and thereby to absorb some of his qualities, as well as to secure his blessings. It was not, as a cynic might think, an imposition on the part of an ambitious churchman to have himself depicted in this guise.[5] It is not known if van Eyck's lost work was also a portrait, but the surviving painting is sufficient, in itself, to have established a respectable precedent for Antonello.

The fact that in his other painting of Saint Jerome (Reggio Calabria) Antonello has given the saint the more traditional long-bearded appearance further supports the thought that in his London picture he was portraying an actual person as Jerome.

Whoever the sitter may have been, he is shown reading, not writing, agreeing in this detail with van Eyck's Albergati-Jerome. As Hall has noted, in the early iconography of the saint in his study, Jerome, if not treating the lion's paw, is usually shown writing, in keeping with his reputation as one of the most prolific of the early Christian authors.[6] In the case of the Detroit van Eyck, there was reason for showing Jerome reading rather than writing, namely that Cardinal Albergati, who is portrayed as the saint, was not noted for his literary efforts. It seems that Antonello followed the van Eyckian model in this respect as he did in painting Jerome beardless, not with a long beard as in Colantonio's picture. Parenthetically, it must be admitted that we do not know the pose or the state of Jerome's beard in the lost van Eyck and can only go by the painting in Detroit, and in that one the artist was portraying the appearance of Albergati, who was a beardless man. This last consideration could also apply to Antonello and his presumed model.

Another striking difference between Colantonio's and Antonello's pictures is the array of genre, but yet symbolic, items that the latter has placed in the near foreground, at the very bottom of the painting—a peacock, a partridge, and a bowl, while at the edge of Jerome's cubicle he has placed potted plants, and, at the extreme left, a cat. Colantonio included none of these items, but restricted himself to the large figures of the saint and the lion against a background of a book-lined study. Curiously enough, he did add a very inconspicuous mouse in the lower-right part of the picture. In both paintings, and possibly also in the lost van

3. The translation is from Fazio's statement as reported by Roberto Weiss in "Some van Eyckian Illuminations from Italy," p. 320. Weiss's study is also the source of the information about the work of the two manuscript illuminators who altered their versions from Jerome to Seneca and to Cyril of Alexandria, respectively.

4. Edwin Hall's study of the Detroit picture ("Cardinal Albergati, Saint Jerome, and the Detroit van Eyck") has established the fact that the figure of Jerome is indeed a portrait of Cardinal Albergati and that, conversely, the Vienna portrait and the Dresden silverprint drawing, formerly considered to represent Albergati, do not portray this churchman. See also Hall's "More about the Detroit van Eyck," pp. 181–201.

5. Edgar Wind, "Studies in Allegorical Portraiture," pp. 152–53; F. Oswald, "Die Darstellungen des Hl. Hieronymus beim Meister dés Bartholomaüsaltares," pp. 342–46.

6. "More about the Detroit Van Eyck," p. 21. Professor Hall's suggestion that a creative scholar would be shown writing rather than reading may be too sweeping. Erasmus of Rotterdam, certainly a famous and voluminous author, was often portrayed either reading or simply meditating with his hands resting on a book.

7. Melito, "De Avibus," in Pitra, *Analecta novissima spicilegii solesmensis*, p. 510.

8. Edward MacCurdy, *The Notebooks of Leonardo da Vinci*, pp. 1077, 1082. Renate Jungblut (*Hieronymus Darstellung und Verehrung eines Kirchenvaters*, p. 69) connects Antonello's use of the peacock as a symbol of immortality with Konrad von Megenberg's statement that the flesh of this bird is incorruptible. However, the immortality symbolism was very ancient and widely known; it was not first presented, but merely repeated, in Megenberg's book. It seems doubtful that Antonello would have known, or would have been able to use, a book written in German.

9. Wolfgang Stechow (*Northern Renaissance Art 1400–1600*, p. 30) translated Marcantonio Michiel's description to read: "A peacock, a partridge, and a shaving basin are carefully portrayed." George C. Williamson (*Anonimo*, p. 115) called it a "barber's basin." It seems to me that this identification is needlessly prosaic, as such a household utensil as a bowl would serve in more than one capacity, and as a "bowl" would be more appropriate in a painting of Jerome than would a bowl explicitly designated for shaving. On the other hand, it must be recognized that a person of the first half of the sixteenth century, such as Michiel, may have had reason for thinking that this particular bowl was of the type used by barbers chiefly, if not exclusively.

Eyck, if we may judge by the Detroit version of the same theme by the same master, it may be noted that one of the most frequently used symbols of transience, the skull, or death's head, is absent. Another of the usual signs of the transitory nature of life on earth, the hourglass, is present in the van Eyck and the Colantonio, but absent in the Antonello picture. In general, it may be said that Antonello's Jerome is more involved with lasting, and less with transitory, concepts than either of its assumed forerunners. This is in keeping with its placement of the saint's study inside a church, and also with the prominent place in the lower foreground given to the peacock, symbol of, among other things, Immortality. Also, the partridge to the left of the peacock fits in with the calm, assured serenity, the utter lack of conflicting feelings, in Antonello's painting. The partridge was said, in old legends, to make a practice of going to the nests of other birds and stealing their eggs, supposedly out of envy, and then taking them back to its own nest, where it hatched them. In this sense, the partridge was a despoiler of homes and families, and was likened to Satan, even by Jerome himself, who wrote "*Clamavit perdix, congregavit quae non peperit*" ("called partridge; it gathers what it has not bred").[7] However, the legend of the egg-stealing partridge had been extended by a concluding statement to the effect that the young birds, on hatching, left the partridge and returned to their true mother. This caused Antonello's great contemporary, Leonardo da Vinci, to consider the partridge a symbol of the Eventual Triumph of Truth,[8] and it is probably in this sense that the bird appears here.

It may be noted that the partridge and the peacock shared the old meaning of *Luxuria*. Jerome's long period of penitence in the wilderness was a flight from *Luxuria* and worldliness, although, from his own account, he was not wholly freed thereby from lecherous dreams and visions. The ideas of Pride and of Immortality were expressed by the peacock. Antonello has here painted this bird with its resplendent train of feathers shut, not opened in a fan of gorgeous color, as it would have been if it were meant to stress Pride and Vainglory particularly. It seems that Immortality was the thought intended to be conveyed, another example of the permanent, as opposed to the transitory, nature of the painting's message.

The peacock is facing an empty bowl. This has been called a shaving basin, a precise identification that may or may not be true.[9] If true, it would be a curious choice for even an unimaginative artist, as Antonello is said to have been, to place along with the symbolic partridge and peacock. If it is a shaving basin one cannot help but wonder if it bears any connection with the fact that Jerome is beardless in this picture. The one point about it that is obvious is that it is empty, a fact that tempts the beholder to wonder if some indication of the emptiness of worldly things is here suggested. However, Antonello's thought cannot be said to be known.

The setting in Antonello's painting is unique. The scholar-saint is sitting in an open "room," two walls of which are absent, thus making it, in effect, an open alcove on a raised platform. This structure, in turn, is inside a large, Gothic, churchlike building, which continues far to the rear on either side, and above it. The whole is viewed through a simulated architectural portal. Purely from an iconographic angle the setting is so unusual that it causes one to wonder if Antonello may have had in mind anything other than to create an opportunity to indulge his interest in, and to exhibit his mastery of, problems of lighting and perspective. As a fairly recent arrival in Venice, with its large and active group of rival, local painters of high competence, Antonello may well have given some thought to creating such an opportunity to show his particular talents. With so prosaic and factually minded a painter as Antonello such a question is apt to be particularly pertinent. Thus, in his short history of Italian art, Frank Jewett Mather, Jr., noted that no such a discerning eye as Antonello's "had as yet applied itself to the problems of painting . . . in his rare interiors, such as the St. Jerome in his Study . . . he announced new perfections in lighting, modelling and perspective. . . . Antonello's work imposes itself primarily by its mere intensity of existence. It has no charm and no especial emotion."[10] Similarly, Berenson concluded that Antonello was not an imaginative artist, but was more interested in extracting and presenting the physical rather than the symbolic significance of things.[11]

The opinions of two such scholars as Mather and Berenson suggest caution in attempting to "interpret" Antonello's possible intentions. The only writer who has found even a rough parallel to the curious setting of Jerome's study is Anna Strümpell, who thought it not very different from the way in which Saint Anne's delivery room is placed in an aisle of a church in Altdorfer's painting, *The Birth of Mary*, in the Alte Pinakothek, Munich.[12]

Antonello's work is outstanding among the early Italian attempts to combine the idea of the humanist with that of the ecclesiastic in the Jerome theme. His placement of the saint's study as an open space on a low platform in a churchlike building suggests that the artist was not inclined to stress the humanist at the expense of the church father, and with Italian logic and tradition made the scene of the scholar's labors merely a somewhat elevated area in a church, an area set apart from the usual functional space of the church, but still within it. Strümpell notes that what she considered to be Netherlandish influence, especially the accessory items such as the peacock, partridge, cat, plants, combined with the Italian elements, set Antonello's picture apart from earlier Italian renditions of the subject, including Colantonio's. She stresses the conviction that the Netherlandish additions to the old churchly tradition are unmistakable and pronounced, and she goes on to specify that Jerome lacks a halo (present in Colantonio's picture; absent in the Detroit van Eyck), and that the lion, moving about in the far background "in the manner of Flemish genre" has here shed any possible symbolic meaning. This last is unclear, as the lion is merely the saint's animal companion, and, in most cases, is nothing more than that. Strümpell's listing of the peacock and partridge as "Netherlandish" items is misleading. I have found only one Flemish and no Dutch paintings of the Jerome cycle containing either of these birds. Aside from Patinir's *Saint Jerome in the Wilderness* (New York: Metropolitan Museum), the peacock has been found only in Venetian "Jeromes" (Antonello, Bastiani follower, Gentile Bellini, and Bartolomeo Montagna), and the partridge also only in Venetian ones (Antonello, Basaiti, Catena, Cima da Conegliano, Mansueti, Palma Vecchio) and in a few pictures by the German, Lucas Cranach.

10. *A History of Italian Painting*, p. 347.

11. *Venetian Painting in America: The Fifteenth Century*, p. 33.

12. "Hieronymus im Gehäuse," p. 191. Strümpell compared Antonello's picture with Altdorfer's *The Birth of Mary*, in the Alte Pinakothek, Munich. In the latter, the curtains on two adjacent sides of Saint Anne's bed are competely open. This arrangement produces a visual effect comparable to the absence of walls on two sides of Jerome's study room in Antonello's painting. Otherwise the two have little in common, other than that they are both "sites" placed inside church structures. Antonello's painting is, of course, considerably earlier, and it seems improbable that it was known to Altdorfer.

The partridges in Cranach's paintings are a different kind, the gray partridge, *Perdix cinerea*, whereas those in all the Venetian works are the red-legged, or chukar partridge, *Alectoris* (two species). They are here considered as alternative identifications of the legendary "partridge," although they are very different zoologically.

The cat, resting placidly near the left end of the edge of the floor of Jerome's cubicle, is unique, at least in the thousand or so pictures and sculptures of the Jerome theme examined in the course of the present study. It is, however, not a very important addition, either pictorially or symbolically. When dealing with so unemotional and precise an artist as Antonello, his great qualities as a painter notwithstanding, one is almost inclined to accept the cat as a factual part of an everyday domestic menage, and to think no more about it. One feels that Antonello may have included it in just that way. I think that André Chastel's suggestion that in Antonello's picture Jerome is a "Baudelairian *savant austére* guarded by a somnolent lion in the role of a cat"[13] is erroneous, not only because the cat could hardly qualify as a lion, but also because the lion is included in the painting—off in the far-right background. Inasmuch as artists in the fifteenth century were not wholly free in their work, and ecclesiastics, either directly or through their influence on the decisions of the parishioner clients, had something to say in the choice of what was to be included and what left out in a painting, we should at least mention that the cat did have a number of symbolic connotations that are not out of place in a religious picture such as this.

The domestic house cat represented the attributes of the family and forebears of the Virgin, of the plain, unassuming Judaean maiden who was destined to be transformed and elevated by divine choice.[14] The fact that no other instances of the inclusion of the cat in the pictorial ambience of the Jerome cycle have come to hand suggests that its significance to that theme was tangential or slight at best. However, insofar as the cat may refer to the Virgin, it is of interest as a pictorial device, independent of, but parallel to, the occasional inclusion of a lioness with the lion of Saint Jerome (see p. 253 ff.), a disguised reference to the Virgin. In the case of the lioness-Mary symbol, however, I have found what seem to be valid reasons for using it in connection with Jerome (see p. 261 ff.), but the cat as an allusion to the Virgin seems uncalled for in the saint's study. The cat was also an old, but relatively seldom used symbol of Heresy, because its ability to see in the dark likened it to those in touch with the evil spirits of darkness.[15] This cat, however, comfortably reposing in Antonello's picture, seemingly completely at home in the saint's study, hardly suggests the latter theme.

One last meaning sometimes claimed for the figure of a cat is that of "Choleric Savagery." In his discussion of Dürer's great engraving, *The Fall of Man*, Ivan Fenyö noted the presence of four animals, each of which he considered as symbolizing one of the four temperaments: the hare for "sanguine sensuousness," the ox for "phlegmatic sloth," the stag for "melancholy," and the cat for "choleric savagery."[16] How valid Fenyö's interpretations may be is uncertain, and it may be pointed out that he seems to have overlooked some other animals in the same engraving—the mouse near Adam's right foot and the parrot immediately

13. *The Age of Humanism*, p. 83.

14. M. Oldfield Howey, *The Cat in the Mysteries of Religion and Magic.*

15. Saint Jerome was much concerned with the problem of heresy and how to combat it. Mariana Monteiro (*The Life of Saint Jerome*, pp. 190–206) describes how Satan persecuted the saint in the wilderness by sending to him argumentative heretics, who intruded on his meditations and harassed him.

16. *Albrecht Dürer*, p. 34.

to the left of Adam's head, to say nothing of the snake with the apple in its mouth. While it seems farfetched to see choleric savagery in Antonello's house pet, it must be admitted that the pose and the somnolent attitude of the cat in the Dürer engraving and in the Antonello painting are quite similar.

Antonello's painting is a serene, calm rendition of its theme, quite free of any conflict between ideas of transience on the one hand, and of eternity on the other. It is a picture in which the painter, with his characteristic focus on the realistic, physical existence of the things he was depicting, has not allowed judgments or emotion to intrude. Besides being of great aesthetic quality and a lasting delight to the eye, Antonello's work is an important historical document attesting to the onset of Flemish influence in Italian painting of the last quarter of the fifteenth century, and is an early and superb example of "interior" painting. In this respect it is the foremost Italian rival to the van Eyck of the same theme.

Francesco di Giorgio's Bronze Relief

The magnificent bronze relief of *Saint Jerome in Penitence* by Francesco di Giorgio (fig. 120), in the National Gallery of Art, Washington, poses something of a problem. It is unusually enlivened with animals, eleven of them, of nine kinds—far more creatures than may be found in all but a small number of paintings of the same subject; yet, because of its dark patina, black lacquer over dark brown bronze, and because of its monochromatism, it has a disturbing obscurity that makes it very difficult to discern much of what it contains. If it had been created some centuries earlier, at a time when faith was more literal and complete, the relief's veiled inclusions might be assumed to reflect the conviction that the all-seeing eye of God was on the artist, who dared not omit anything. By the late fifteenth century this compulsion appears to have lessened, giving the artist more freedom of choice. This leaves us with the thought that such a relief was probably designed to be looked at very closely, not viewed at a distance like a painting hanging on a wall, and that on such close inspection its contents would emerge and reward the viewer for his effort. However, it seems almost as though the artist had given himself free rein to indulge his fancy with needless, discursive inclusions. This becomes clearer if we compare it with another bronze relief of the same theme, more or less contemporary, or only slightly later in date, and also exhibited in the National Gallery of Art, Washington, a work by an unidentified Paduan sculptor of the early sixteenth century (fig. 121). Here the background is certainly not devoid of detail, but it is much less crowded and it attempts to present fewer levels of pictorial depth. These factors combine to make its contents much easier to decipher. Francesco di Giorgio's relief is as crowded with details as are some of his most cluttered paintings.

Something of the difficulty of making out its contents is revealed in the published descriptions of this piece. Adolfo Venturi's well-known appreciation of it is really more an attempt to describe the mood evoked by the plaque than a factual listing of its contents: a fantastic, poetical landscape with a background of rugged mountains and with a cold stream of water, "from a northern sea" (hardly in keeping with the known geography of Jerome's wilderness retreat in Chalcis, southeast of Antioch!).[1] Selwyn Brinton's account also suggests, possibly based on Venturi's earlier description, the feeling of "wintry desolation, of rocks pointed to forms of ice or crystal,"[2] but the only thing in the composition that might be considered wintry is the fact that the prominent tree to the left, on which the crucifix is hung, is bare. This, however, is not a

1. "Francesco di Giorgio Martini scultore," p. 213; *L'arte e San Girolamo*, p. 169.

2. *Francesco di Giorgio Martini of Siena*, p. 46.

Figure 120. Francesco di Giorgio, *Saint Jerome in Penitence*. Washington: National Gallery of Art; Samuel H. Kress Collection.

Figure 121. *Saint Jerome in Penitence*, Paduan (?), early sixteenth century. Washington: National Gallery of Art; Samuel H. Kress Collection.

sign of winter. It is, rather, a dead tree, signifying, especially with its appended crucifix, "life through death," the future life that can be approached only through the death of the present one. I discussed this concept in the chapter on Lucas Cranach, where I pointed out that the dead tree, more often only a dead tree stump, is practically a pictorial attribute of Saint Jerome.

In Francesco di Giorgio's bronze, we may stress the lack of a suggestion of winter, as there actually are a good number of well-foliaged trees along the far shore of the stream, and on the very pinnacle of the rocky background to the right. Brinton describes the scene in a way that shows how hidden from his gaze some of its contents remained: "Life seems absent here; only serpents and scorpions crawl over the rocks; even the lion, his traditional companion, is hardly visible." He goes on to stress the desolation of Jerome's wilderness solitude.

Figure 122. Detail of lion from figure 120, Francesco di Giorgio's *Saint Jerome in Penitence*. Washington: National Gallery of Art; Samuel H. Kress Collection.

Repeated exposures to the original, and innumerable scrutinies of photographs of this relief, give me a feeling of the loneliness of the scene depicted, but not one particularly of winter or of cold. Venturi and Brinton both mention the surface of the relief, especially the part to the left of Jerome, as catching and reflecting little points of light, but to me, at least, these are more suggestive of background foliage than of wintry desolation. John Pope-Hennessy also noted the leafy tangles out of which rise the broken arches of the ruined building at the left.[3] Aside from personal reaction to the mood of the piece, the fact remains that in this moving relief the sculptor has included many faunal elements, some of which are interpretable as symbolically pertinent to the theme, while others are less obvious in their significance.

Jerome's lion, remarkably small and inconspicuous for a sizable object in the front plane of the plaque, is immediately in front of the saint's right foot (fig. 122). It is shown in the act of drinking from the stream, a naturalistic pose, superficially without suggestive significance. However, Johann von Neumarkt, in his emotional praise of Jerome, wrote that the latter was the pure water from which humanity could slake its thirst, as the lion is doing here.[4] A similar action is represented by the stag in the lower-right background, but there the action is more explicitly meaningful. The stag drinking from a stream was an old pictorial reference to the human soul seeking salvation from the waters of the true religion, but

3. *Renaissance Bronzes from the Samuel H. Kress Collection*, p. 26.

4. "Schriften Johanns von Neumarkt," in J. Klapper, *Vom Mittelalter zur Reformation*, vol. 6, p. 17.

Figure 123. Detail of scorpion and tortoise from figure 120, Francesco di Giorgio's *Saint Jerome in Penitence*. Washington: National Gallery of Art; Samuel H. Kress Collection.

this emblem was restricted to the stag, and could not be assumed to be applicable to a drinking lion or other beast.

Between the lion and Jerome's left foot is a scorpion, as large as the lion is small, while to the right of the foot are a small tortoise and a lizard (fig. 123), and still further to the right a snake. All of these creatures—the scorpion, tortoise, and snake—are essentially evil in their implications. The tortoise was actually considered by Jerome himself as a symbol of heresy. He wrote that it was a heretical creature of the gravest errors, and one that preferred to live in disgrace in scum and filth like that of a pig sty. The lizard, on the contrary, is a salvation-seeking creature, and, in a very symbolic sense, is a parallel to the penitent Jerome. It is shown moving away from the tortoise. To avoid repetition it need only be said that the legend of the "sun lizard" is given fully elsewhere (pp. 268–69).[5]

A scops owl is perched on a projecting ledge of the ruined arch to the left of, and slightly above, Jerome's head (fig. 124). As the bird of darkness by its own will, and as a symbol of the Jews, who preferred to remain in pre-Christian gloom rather than to avail themselves of the new light suddenly brought to the world, the owl is here, symbolically, akin to the tortoise. It should be noted, in considering the present use of these two animal symbols, that both the owl and the tortoise are far from usual in renditions of the theme of Jerome in penitence. The owl I have found in only twelve cases, including this one (see p. 274 ff.), and the tortoise in only four other versions, three Italian, one painting, one drawing, and one engraving, and one German painting (see p. 300). Even the "menagerie-minded" painters of the Bellini-Mansueti-Bastiani group seldom thought to include the tortoise in their renditions. I have found this creature in only a single painting by any of them—the Mansueti portrayal of Jerome literally crowded by his faunal companions, formerly in the

5. Edward Payson Evans, *Animal Symbolism in Ecclesiastical Architecture*, p. 94.

Figure 124. Detail of owl from figure 120, Francesco di Giorgio's *Saint Jerome in Penitence*. Washington: National Gallery of Art; Samuel H. Kress Collection.

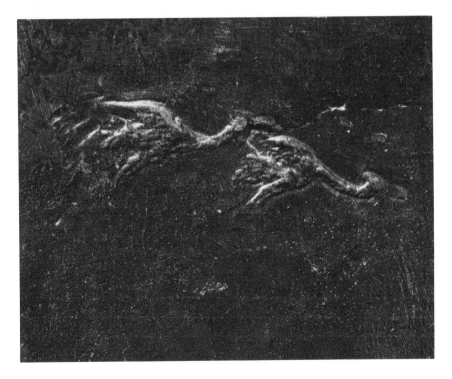

Figure 125. Detail of porphyrios from figure 120, Francesco di Giorgio's *Saint Jerome in Penitence*. Washington: National Gallery of Art; Samuel H. Kress Collection.

collection of Arthur Hughes, London, and in one drawing by Jacopo Bellini (fig. 53).

Two birds flying across the sky in the upper-middle background (fig. 125) pose some serious problems for convincing ornithological identification, as they are not sufficiently accurately done for any of the possible interpretations. Venturi called them falaghe, or moorhens,[6] but this is

6. *L'arte e San Girolamo*, p. 169.

7. Inasmuch as the possibility of these two flying birds being swans has been raised, it may be noted that the swan had little direct, symbolic pertinence to the Jerome story. Its chief meaning was Purity (not too different from Chastity) because of its snowy plumage; and it also came to denote, from the sweetness of its dying notes (which are quite apocryphal), the "swan song" of legend, something of the happy anticipation of the future life by pious martyrs. I know of no other version of the Jerome theme that contains, in a meaningful way, either the purple gallinule or the swan. In a painting of *Saint Jerome in Penitence*, attributed to Bastiani (Brescia), there are two swans in a pond in the mid-background, but they seem to be merely a bit of decorative detail used to enliven that part of the picture, and are not connected with the penitent figure in the foreground.

The two birds in Francesco di Giorgio's relief do have broad, heavy bills, and short, dense and squarish occipital crests much like the swans in many Leda paintings, where there can be no question as to the kind of bird intended. Still more pertinent, in light of their identical authorship, these two flying birds agree in these details with the two large wood and stucco relief sculptures of standing

only an approximation, or an identification by elimination of other possibilities. However, they do have long, gangling legs with long toes; long, stout, and somewhat rounded bills; short wings; a peculiar appearance of a round "cheek" area around the eyes with a fairly definite perimeter; and what seems to be a difficult, almost awkward, flight. In all these respects they more closely resemble, not the common moorhen, to which Venturi referred them, but the related, larger, purple gallinule, *Porphyrio porphyrio*; more so than cranes or swans, with both of which they have been identified in the past. They are little more than impressionistic, but if an identification is desired, this is the most likely. It would seem that Venturi may have had an ornithologist advise him when he referred to them as moorhens, and that his own unfamiliarity with birds may have caused him to think the term "falaghe" covered both the smaller moorhen and its larger, brighter-colored relative, the porphyrio. The latter creature was, moreover, definitely connected in symbolism with *Pudicitia*, or Chastity (as in Alciati's emblem xlvii, fig. 126), a theme certainly not unconnected with Saint Jerome, who argued at length, and repeatedly, against sexual relations, and who was, from his own words, much troubled with the discrepancy between his convictions and his desires in this matter. A similarly uncertain, but possible, porphyrio occurs in Jacopo della Quercia's relief, *The Sacrifice of Noah* (Bologna: San Petronio), among other creatures coming out of the ark after the deluge. An engraving by Adrian Collaert, a plate from the *Avium Vivae Icones*, now in the Victoria and Albert Museum, London, shows the physical characteristics of the porphyrio as visualized by a naturalist-artist a little over a century after Francesco di Giorgio's time (fig. 127).[7]

Two other large wading birds, with much longer and slenderer bills, long necks, and long legs, are standing at the edge of the stream, behind, and to the right of Jerome's left leg (fig. 128). These were termed pelicans by Pope-Hennessy, but they certainly look much more like storks; or, less likely, cranes or heron.[8] Pope-Hennessy's identification may have been influenced by the fact that literally dozens of Italian artists, when painting the legendary "pelican in her piety," feeding her offspring with the blood from her own breast, often at the top of the cross in pictures of the Crucifixion, made birds that resemble egrets or other herons far more than they do real pelicans. Yet, Pisanello, Piero di Cosimo, and a number of other painters did produce naturalistically acceptable pelicans, which shows that these birds were known to those artists who wanted to portray them correctly. I cannot help but conclude that in this relief Francesco di Giorgio reveals a sufficient interest in natural-history forms that he could easily have made these two birds more pelicanlike had that been his intention. These two are long-legged birds; pelicans are short-legged; these two have long, narrow bills with no large gular pouch hanging below the mandible, as is markedly present in the wide-billed pelican. I consider them to be storks, even though they have one unnatural feature—marked protuberances on the backs of their heads (which would be equally unnatural in pelicans or herons). Parenthetically, it may be mentioned that in many old European pictures, herons, cranes, and storks are frequently so similarly rendered as to make their identifications hardly better than tentative.

The stork was used as a symbol of Filial Devotion. I know of only two

Figure 127. Adrian Collaert, *Porphyrio*. Plate from *Avium Vivae Icones*. London: Victoria and Albert Museum.

Figure 128. Detail of cranes from figure 120, Francesco di Giorgio's *Saint Jerome in Penitence*. Washington: National Gallery of Art; Samuel H. Kress Collection.

paintings of Saint Jerome that contain (one in each) an accurately rendered, clearly identifiable white stork. One of these, by Lucas Cranach the Elder (Innsbruck), has the stork in the middle background, not closely connected, compositionally, with the penitent saint, whose other animals (lion, beaver, tortoise, birds with human faces, and so forth) are much closer to him. The other painting (present whereabouts unknown), by Pier Francesco Sacchi, is not simply of Jerome in penitence, but includes him along with Saint Anthony Abbot and another elderly, unidentified saint, and shows a white stork in the remote background. In this instance the stork cannot be said to be more connected with any one or another of the saints involved.

swans, one at either end of Francesco di Giorgia's cassone painting of *The Triumph of Chastity* in the J. Paul Getty Collection, Malibu, California, correctly identified and described in Burton B. Fredericksen's detailed 1969 study. However, they differ from swans in their long, thin legs, which support the porphyrio identification. The squarish occipital crests are unnatural for either the swan or the purple gallinule.

8. See note 3 above.

As Pope-Hennessy correctly concluded, the birds at the edge of the stream and those flying across in the sky are not regular elements in the iconography of Jerome. Their presence in this relief can only be due to the whim of the artist; the two at the water's edge are so inconspicuous that they could not have been introduced merely to fill a space with something of interest, as might have been the case with the two flying birds. As an expression of the artist's freedom of choice of what to put in and where and how to do it, this great relief bears out Pope-Hennessy's judgment of it as the most personal and most fully carried out of Francesco di Giorgio's works in this medium.

Finally, to complete the list of animals in this relief, there is an antlered deer, a stag, bending down to drink from the stream, immediately to the right, and behind, Jerome's left knee. The symbolic significance of this figure has already been discussed. The small size of the stag is disturbing, since it is not placed far behind the two storks, but it is much smaller than they are. As noted in the case of the lion and the scorpion, relative size seems to have been of little interest in this otherwise highly naturalistic composition. The deer is a frequent associate of Jerome in art in Florentine, Sienese, Venetian, Ferrarese, Veronese, and German paintings and in a few Florentine sculptures, such as that attributed to Rossellino (fig. 51), and in a free version of that work, attributed to Giovanni della Robbia.

I have mentioned the difficulty of identifying some of the animals because of their unnatural, or merely suggestive, modeling. This indistinctness of form is even more true in what one would normally expect to be carefully delineated, even if small in size: the body of Christ on the little crucifix. If the crucifix in the present bronze were looked at apart from the rest of the relief, it is not at all certain that it could be recognized for what it is! Also, the penitent Jerome is usually shown holding a stone in his right hand, with which he beats his breast in self-inflicted punishment. In the case of this relief, the stone is very small, hardly more than a pebble. Here again we find the curious disregard for relative size already noted in some of the creatures present in this fascinating work.

Francesco di Giorgio's *Saint Jerome in Penitence* is of interest in that it transcribes into relief sculpture the type of pictorial treatment otherwise found in paintings. As far as its use of symbolism is concerned, it is the only instance in which I have found the purple gallinule, one of the extremely few cases in which the tortoise and the stork are present, and one of the relatively few works utilizing the figure of an owl. Further, it conveys the impression that the artist was, for his time and place, widely conversant with a variety of kinds of animals, but that he was an artist to whom mere naturalistic accuracy was a secondary matter, as shown by his lack of concern with literal verisimilitude in their presentation. His interest in animals may well have been stimulated by his earliest datable commission, an illumination for a copy of the manuscript *De Animalibus* of Albertus Magnus.

Tura's "Saint Jerome in Penitence"

An unusually emotional painting, the *Saint Jerome in Penitence* by Cosimo Tura (frontispiece) presents some iconographic peculiarities that have been overlooked, or at least, left unstudied and undescribed until now. The figure of the penitent Jerome, kneeling on his right leg, his left one bent at the knee, is shown with a stone in his upraised right hand as if about to strike his chest. The figure is in front of a gnarled and twisted large tree, behind which, in the distance to the right, may be seen two men in similarly orant poses, possibly the donors of the painting to the chapel for which it was intended. Behind them a rocky precipice rises to a flat grassy area in the far distance, on which may be discerned a number of cows, one with a sucking calf, tended by a seated herdsman leaning against the pier of a fantastic rocky arch, through which the landscape continues out of sight. To the left of the great tree behind Jerome is a steep, barren mountain of rock on which is a ledgelike, winding, narrow trail along which two monks are walking toward a building, the one in front with a long-handled maddock over his shoulder, the other driving a cow ahead of him. Some other monks may be made out directly in front of the tall arched door of their building in the far distance.

The painting was originally considerably larger; it is known that in its complete state it included at upper left the little figure of Christ crucified, now in the Brera, Milan (figs. 129, 130). The size of the entire painting in its original condition has been estimated to have been one and a half times as high and about twice as wide as the fragment now in London.[1] This would have reduced the figure of the penitent saint to more reasonable proportions for the picture, which, in the fragmentary state, it completely dominates, and would also have placed it compositionally to one side, as is usual in depictions of this theme.

The intensity of feeling expressed by Tura's figure of the saint was something new in the iconography of Jerome at the time it was created. I have compared it with hundreds of others and have found only one, by Hieronymus Bosch (fig. 108), that is emotionally more intense. The emphasis in Bosch's rendition lies in the completely abject penitence of the figure, while in Tura's painting the emphasis is on urgency of response. Two other versions that approach Tura's work most closely in their emotional intensity are the very unfinished one by Leonardo da

1. Eberhard Ruhmer, *Tura, Paintings and Drawings*, p. 42.

Figure 129. Cosimo Tura, *Christ Crucified*. Milan: Pinacoteca di Brera.

Figure 130. Cosimo Tura, Original relationship of *Saint Jerome in Penitence* and *Christ Crucified*, before cutting (*frontispiece* and figure 129).

Vinci, in the Vatican (fig. 48), where the pose of the saint is somewhat similar to Tura's, but, as noted by Werner Meinhof,[2] even more like that in the drawing by Pollaiuolo; in the derivative engraving by Florentine Anonymous Fine Manner (fig. 131); and in the similarly unfinished painting by El Greco (fig. 79) in the National Gallery of Art, Washington. The Leonardo painting is dated by recent students as about 1481,[3] almost identical in time with Tura's painting (about 1477 to 1481), while the El Greco is, of course, much later, 1610 to 1614. Neither of these two, both by artists of greater fame than our Ferrarese master, conveys the sense of frenzied rush, the almost irrepressible feeling of urgency with which Tura's saint appeals for divine benediction, for some sign of assurance that his long penitence has been found acceptable.

In a remarkable description of Cosimo Tura's painting, Adolfo Venturi wrote that Jerome, no longer the silent, contemplative, scholarly saint of

2. "Leonardo's Hieronymus," pp. 101–24.

3. J. Castelfranco, *The Paintings of Leonardo da Vinci*, p. 59.

Figure 131. Florentine Anonymous Fine Manner, ca. 1480–1500, *Saint Jerome in Penitence*. Washington: National Gallery of Art; Rosenwald Collection.

so many other renditions, seems to have just rushed out to the edge of the woods with a frenzied outcry.[4] The assumed outcry is accompanied by the violence of Jerome's gesture, the force of which, in turn, is accentuated by an intense gleam inflaming the orant figure, placed, for dramatic pictorial effect, in front of the contorted and twisted trunk of a great tree, forming the arch of a grottolike background.

In Leonardo's version the face of the saint is a masterful expression of spiritual yearning, probing greater psychological depths, but without the immediacy and insistence of Tura's Jerome. It is a finer and subtler conception than Tura's, but its primary focus is different, more pleading for an eventual response than beseeching an immediate one. El Greco's saint is more a "type" of religious fervor than a depiction of any identifiable portion of that state of being.

In Tura's painting the faunal companions of Jerome are four in number, not counting some cows in the far background. All four of them pose some special considerations, and all reveal the very original mental-

4. *L'arte e San Girolamo*, p. 88.

ity of their painter. The first and, in pictures of Jerome, the most usual of them, is the lion (fig. 132). William Norton Howe described it as hanging its head in "a most dejected attitude."[5] This is accurate, but insufficient. Merely to state, as Howe did, that the lion looks dejected is to miss the real point of this particular rendition. It seems as though Tura has here seized upon the moment in the legend of Jerome's lion when the beast is most contrite—the time when it was accused (falsely) by the monks of having killed and eaten the ass it was assigned to guard. The pose of the beast, with its head hanging down, suggests that it may be, like Jerome himself, a penitent figure. Unlike other versions of the theme, Tura has shown the lion in precisely the same psychological state as the saint, whose attribute it is. The two are astonishingly exact reflections of each other's position. What Tura has done is to take an attribute and to instill into it the meaning of the figure it stands for; in his treatment the lion is not just an identifying label for Jerome, but for Jerome in penitence.

The lion is not very well drawn; its legs are too long, raising the body too high off the ground, but its slightly upturned gaze with a down-bent head leaves it not only its usual self as an attribute of Saint Jerome, who is also looking upward, but helps to incorporate it into the scene and the action of the painting to a remarkable degree. It is a small detail, but one that only an original, alert, and perceptive artistic personality would have designed.

Tura was not alone in having attempted to present the lion as reflecting the emotional state of Jerome. In his discussion of Andrea del Castagno's fresco, *The Trinity with Saints Jerome, Paula, and Eustochium*, in the church of Santissima Annunziata in Florence (fig. 133), Millard Meiss was led to observe that the lion's rolling eyes and gaping mouth convey the feeling that the beast is deeply agitated by the sight of the blood from Jerome's bruised breast on the stone in his hand directly over the animal's head.[6] A case such as this, created wholly independently by an unrelated artist, supports the validity of the thought that Tura was similarly using the saint's faithful lion as a mirror echoing the exact emotional state of its master.

The second animal that concerns us is the owl (fig. 134) in the upper-right corner of the picture, and in its claws it holds the third animal, a frog. The owl, without restricting it to a particular species (of which there are eight kinds in Italy), has many symbolic connotations. One is that of Solitude, and in this sense the owl may appear in pictures of hermits, especially when shown in the privacy of prayer. Another old, classical meaning is Wisdom, and here again the owl could be a fitting companion to Saint Jerome, the most learned of the early Church Fathers. However, the commonest significance of the owl in religious art was as a symbol of "those who dwell in darkness," quite the opposite of wisdom.

Repeated observation and prolonged study of Tura's painting, both in the original and in photographs, has convinced me that Tura has attempted to recapture into his version of the figure of an owl more than a trace of its old, classical concept of Prophetic Wisdom. In order to corroborate and substantiate this conviction I must go into great detail

Figure 132. Detail of lion from frontispiece, Cosimo Tura's *Saint Jerome in Penitence*. London: The National Gallery.

5. *Animal Life in Italian Painting*, pp. 56–57.

6. *The Great Age of Fresco: Discoveries, Recoveries, and Survivals*, p. 153; and *The Great Age of Fresco: Giotto to Pontormo*, p. 160.

Figure 133. Andrea del Castagno, *The Trinity with Saints Jerome, Paula, and Eustochium*. Florence: SS. Annunziata.

Figure 134. Detail of owl from frontispiece, Cosimo Tura's *Saint Jerome in Penitence*. London: The National Gallery.

because, so far as I know, this is the only instance where the owl has been so used in the Jerome context.

Because the owl in religious art was so largely a symbol of evil, of the old law, of the inability to see or to stand the light, and, by inference, of the Jews, who shunned the new radiance that accompanied the advent of the Messiah, it is necessary to document the fact that its other, ancient and favorable meanings *did* persist through the Middle Ages and the early Renaissance, and were, thus, available to the unconventional and original mind of an artist like Cosimo Tura. As a matter of fact, these implications have persisted right down to the present time. In order to show the widespread awareness of these meanings across the centuries, the individual bits of evidence chosen for inclusion here have been picked deliberately from a wide variety of sources. In order to avoid needless duplication, it may be well to mention that the more "ordinary" symbolic usages of owls in European art are presented in the Bestiary.

We may begin here with a usage of the owl in art made not too far from Ferrara and within a few decades after Tura's painting. A medal in honor of Giovanni Bellini by Camelio (b. ca. 1455–60; d. 1537), the master of the dies of the Venetian mint, bears on its obverse a profile of the great artist, while on its reverse it shows an owl, earless as in Tura's picture, and above it are the words *virtutis et ingenii* ("virtue and ability"),[7] a phrase that can hardly be looked upon except in a clearly favorable connotation.

In the 1591 edition of Alciati's famous emblem book, we find (emblem xix) the figure of an earless owl, fairly like the one used by Tura, on a shield hanging from a branch of a tree (fig. 135).[8] The title of this emblem is *Prudens magis quam loquax*, which may be rendered in English as "prudent rather than loquacious," recalling and anticipating the epigram of Francis Bacon, of 1597, "Discretion of speech is more than eloquence." The explanation for the emblem, given toward the end of Alciati's book, begins with the significant words "Noctua Minervae sacra" ("owl sacred to Minerva"). The connection of the owl with *prudens* and with Minerva is also reflected in the old French proverb *Minerve est la Prudence, et Venus la Beaute*, cited by Jean Seznec.[9] Furthermore, in his study of the birds of the Latin poets, E. W. Martin quotes a poem entitled "The Owl," by the nineteenth-century American W. H. C. Hosmer, of interest here as a later echo of the "owl on the shield" motif used by Alciati, as well as the age-old recognition of the owl's ability to see in the dark.

His image flamed out on the terrible shield
That Pallas up-bore when arrayed for the field,
An Emblem that Wisdom, when others are blind,
Clear-sighted, a path through the darkness will find.[10]

In his survey of zoological mythology, Angelo de Gubernatis concluded that although the owl was primarily a bird of sinister meaning, even in classical times, it was sacred to Athena, the goddess of wisdom, and that this connection sprang from the thought that Athena, with her superior, prophetic wisdom, could, like the owl, see in the darkness.[11] De Gubernatis adds that from this the owl of Athena passed into common use as a proverbial figure, the common expressions of which, even today,

NOCTVA *Cecropiis insignia praestat Athenis,*
Inter aues sani noctua consilij.
Armifera merito obsequiis sacrata Minerua,
Garrula quo cornix cesserat antè loco.

Matu.

Figure 135. *Prudens magis quam loquax*, after Alciati's emblem xix.

7. Medal no. 146 in G. F. Hill and G. Pollard, *Renaissance Medals from the Samuel H. Kress Collection of the National Gallery of Art.*

8. Alciati, *Emblematum flumen abundans*, p. 36, emblem xix; also p. 168.

9. *The Survival of the Pagan Gods*, p. 86.

10. *The Birds of the Latin Poets*, p. 155.

11. *Zoological Mythology*, vol. 2, p. 247.

are to be found in such phrases as "wise as an owl" or in the description of someone as a "wise old owl."

The owl has been used in an old emblem entitled *Nox illuminatio mea.* ("The Night is My Illumination"). It so happens that in this emblem,[12] the owl represented is an eared, or scops owl, the one kind of owl usually associated with the sinister qualities of darkness, and not the little owl, the bird of prophetic wisdom. This indicates how extensively all owls were considered interchangeable in allegorical usage (fig. 136).

From classical sources the connection of the owl with prophetic wisdom found its way into the Arthurian legends, in which Merlin, the royal magician, was sometimes described as having an owl perched on his shoulder,[13] and, as a result, in medieval Europe the owl was looked upon as the companion of seers and alchemists.

Further evidence of medieval acceptance of the owl as a favorable, if sober, symbolic figure, is afforded by the late twelfth-century English poem "The Owl and the Nightingale," one of the outstanding works of Middle English literature. In its long (almost 2,000 lines) discourse, the two birds discuss many and diverse topics, and while scholars disagree on precise interpretations of the characters of the birds they agree that they stand for human attitudes toward life—the nightingale, on the whole, representing the happy, joyous approach, and the owl the serious, more sober one. As pointed out by N. D. Hinton, one of the most important of the topics they discuss is man's attitude toward religion: should it be "penitential" or "celebratory"?[14] Throughout the length of this poem the owl defends the church, the clergy, and the serious attitude toward life, in marked contrast to the nightingale, which reflects the easy, un-thinking acceptance of the joys and pleasures of the present world with-out much concern for the future.

To be serious and to be mindful of the future life, and of the moral values and religious concepts involved, is surely not to be equated merely with death and funereal matters, and certainly not with evil. It may be noted that in his brief account of the owl and the nightingale, Hinton used the very words "penitential or celebratory" in describing their re-spective attitudes toward religion. The owl as a spokesman for the peni-tential attitude is certainly most fitting as a companion to Jerome in penitence.

A very different medieval attempt to bring Minerva, the goddess of whom the little owl was the attribute, into the context of Christian thought, took place in the chapter house at Noyon in 1296, when a figure of Minerva was surrounded by an inscription, *Ave Maria gratia plena,* obviously equating, by substitution, Minerva (or Athena) with Mary.[15] It is true that the owl is not mentioned as being either present or absent in this figure, but in their transformation and survival in medieval Chris-tian thought and art, the pagan deities often carried their symbols with them. The entrance of Minerva into the imagery of Mary at least pro-vided an acceptable entrance for her symbolic owl as well.

Sir Philip Sidney, in "A Remedy for Love," revealed the favorable connotation of the owl, when he wrote

O you virtuous owle
The wise Minerva's only fowle.

Figure 136. *Nox illuminatio mea.* Em-blem from Jacobus Boschius, *Sym-bolographia,* 1701.

12. Jacobus Boschius, *Symbolographia: sive de arte symbolica*; illus. in Heinrich Schwarz and Volker Plagemann "Eule," col. 298.

13. M. L. Grossman and J. Hamlet, *Birds of Prey of the World*, p. 841.

14. "The Owl and the Nightingale," *New Catholic Encyclopedia*, vol. 10, p. 841.

15. Jean Seznec, *The Survival of the Pagan Gods*, p. 105, fn.

Another indication of the connection of the owl with favorable meanings may be sensed in the fact that one of the common folk names of the barn owl, which is the owl used by Tura, in all the German-speaking countries was "Kirch-Eule"; and in French areas, "chouette des eglises"; in England, "church owl." This is clearly the basis for our illustration (fig. 137), taken from Buffon's celebrated compedium on the natural history of birds of 1770,[16] which shows the owl perched on an architectural adornment of a church spire. This species of owl was known to nest in the sheltered, seldom intruded upon, openings in church belfries and spires. From this it came to have not only a connotation referring to the church, but also a reputation as a bird seen or heard at funerals in the churchyard cemeteries. Buffon described it as a funereal bird of church cemeteries, living in the church towers. Thus, a mid-nineteenth-century English "parson-naturalist," the Reverend F. O. Morris, without referring to Buffon, wrote of the barn owl, "this bird, a 'high churchman' is almost proverbially attached to the Church within whose sacred precincts it finds a sanctuary, as others have done in former ages."[17]

To go back to Renaissance England, M. L. Grossman and J. Hamlet noted that the "bishop of Norwich" (Joseph Hall, bishop from 1641 to 1656) tried in vain to understand why the ancients regarded the owl as sacred, except for its admittedly singular perspicuity, and went on to explain that during the darkness of the nocturnal hours, when most other creatures are supposedly unable to see well, the owl has an inward source of light, which enables it to discern even the smallest objects to its own advantage.[18]

As Joseph Hall himself put it, "he is truly wise, who sees by a light of his own; when the rest of the world sit in an ignorant and confused darkness; unable to apprehend any truth, save by the helps of an outward illumination."[19] My reason for mentioning this is that it is still another indication of the owl as a sign of wisdom, a creature with an inner source of light.

There is, as we have now seen, ample evidence that the owl continuously retained its favorable, as well as its sinister meanings, from classical times to the present. While it is true that the latter implications were the ones usually read into, or out of, the owl symbol, the fact still remains that the connotations of prophetic wisdom, of a serious, thoughtful attitude toward life and religion, were available to be used and be given new emphasis by an artist, especially since this stress did not necessarily exclude the funereal and evil suggestions associated with the bird.

To strengthen the case for the suggestion that Tura reinstilled into his owl some of its old classical allusion to prophetic wisdom, without necessarily eliminating its usual antithetical meanings, we may compare Tura's bird with another rendition of the identical species of owl in a Hispano-Flemish painting of about the same period. As an unusually clearly oriented symbol of doom, and of the old law, in the form of a barn owl, we may single out the one perched on the ruined wall in the left background of Juan de Flandes's painting, *The Nativity*, in the National Gallery of Art, Washington (fig. 138). The new light, the anticipatory glory that came upon the earth with the birth of Christ, is almost literally depicted in the radiance in the sky of the upper-right background close to, but

Figure 137. *Barn owl*. From Buffon, *Histoire naturelle des oiseaux*, vol. 2, Paris, 1790.

16. G. L. L. Comte de Buffon, *Histoire Naturelle des Oiseaux*, vol. 2, pl. xii.

17. *A History of British Birds*, vol. 1, p. 169, pl. 1.

18. *Birds of Prey of the World*, p. 841.

19. *The Works of Joseph Hall*, vol. 12, p. 10.

Figure 138. Juan de Flandes, *The Nativity*. Washington: National Gallery of Art; Samuel H. Kress Collection.

sharply demarcated from, the darkness of the antecedent era to the left, in the midst of which the owl is perched, embodying to the full its dire and dismal tidings.

Tura's rendition of the appearance of the barn owl is of a kind that was not only accepted and repeated in Alciati's emblem book, but, even in Buffon's great work (fig. 137), where the interest was purely zoological. Indeed, the close correspondence between Tura's bird and the figure used by Buffon, with very definite species identification, serves to prove that the barn owl, and no other, was the kind Tura depicted. Tura's lightening and whitening of the barn owl is in keeping with its favorable rather than its unfavorable connotations, and one cannot help but wonder if this emphasis on the "church" or "white" owl, as contrasted with the funereal bird of woe may not have permeated European culture sufficiently over the next two centuries to have caused a fine naturalist like Buffon to have looked upon his artist's illustration of the bird as satisfactory for inclusion in a zoological encyclopedic compendium.

Tura improvised on his owl and what he did was to make it conspicuously lighter and brighter. Insofar as it is a symbol of Wisdom, such an owl could only represent a more refulgent wisdom. Venturi sensed the intensity of Tura's pictorialization correctly when he referred to the bird as an incandescent owl, a living lamp ("incandescente forma di un gufo, lampada vivida").[20] This would be a graceful reference to the light brought to the people generally by Jerome's great accomplishment, the translation of the Scriptures from Hebrew and Greek into Latin—the standard, Latin Bible. As we shall see, this recognition of Saint Jerome's outstanding achievement is further symbolized elsewhere in the painting as well, and this fact serves to corroborate the unusual luminosity of the owl. Tura's owl has not only come out of the darkness behind it, but has become a source of light in itself. It has left the gloom that prevailed before the coming of the Messiah and reflects the new light that is abroad in the world. It is actually partly lighted on the left side by the radiance from the apparition of the crucified Christ (in the Brera, Milan). All this makes it seem to refer particularly to Jerome's part in making that new light available. In this connection, the statement attributed to the bishop of Norwich that the owl has "an inward source of light" seems in keeping with Venturi's description of Tura's owl as a "living lamp."

Not only is Tura's owl bright and light beyond all other owls in such paintings, but it is depicted in a totally new and unique capacity. It has just caught a frog, which it is holding in its claws. In the *Physiologus*, the frog was the symbol of those who snatch at the fleeting pleasures of this world and give no thought to the next. As such, it came to represent mundane or worldy things as opposed to spiritual ones. To show the enhanced wisdom of the world (the luminous owl) with its successful, recent capture of worldliness (the frog) is yet another tribute to the value of Jerome's long labors. It may be recalled that Jerome himself wrote in one of his letters to Heliodorus (Epistle XIV): "You are too pleasure-loving, brother, if you wish to rejoice in this world and hereafter to reign with Christ." This is the main implication in the frog and in the fact that it is shown caught by the owl. For further frog lore see the account of this batrachian in the Bestiary (p. 217).

The fourth and last creature that Tura introduced into this painting is

20. *L'arte e San Girolamo*, p. 88.

one of exceeding rarity in religious art, not only in the art of Renaissance Italy, but of all Europe. As a matter of fact, it has been found in only three paintings, two by Tura, and one, a miserable transcript of the bird in an altarpiece by Pietro di Domenico,[21] who must have seen it in one or the other of Tura's paintings. Near the left side of Tura's London picture, about half-way up, on a stub projecting from the large tree trunk, is a little-known European bird, the wall creeper, *Tichodroma muraria* of the zoologists, the "picchio muraiolo" or "cerzia muraiola" of the Italians, a bird primarily of northern Europe, south to the Alps and related mountainous areas of Austria and northern Italy (fig. 139). The few writers who have noted the presence of this bird in their discussions of Tura's painting have all misidentified it. J. A. Crowe and G. B. Cavalcaselle called it a woodpecker, as did also Emma Gurney Salter; William Norton Howe erroneously called it a bird "of the bee-eater family."[22] The bird is very readily identified; it is the only small European bird of a soft-gray color above, white on the throat, and dark gray on the underside of the body, and with a large amount of very bright red on the upper sides of the wings. This red color is prominently exposed during flight, strikingly edged by the broad black tips of the feathers, the outermost flight feathers having white spots on the black areas, but when the bird is at rest the red remains visible chiefly as a narrow lengthwise band on the otherwise black wings. The wall creeper has a long, narrow bill with which it searches for its food in crevices in the rocks and the stone walls over which it climbs. In short, it is a very distinctive bird, not easily mistaken for any other, but it is a bird known to relatively few people.

It would seem that Tura may well have watched a wall creeper at times or even may have had a living or a recently killed one as a model when he made his painting, as his rendition of it is so accurate. The astonishing verisimilitude of this representation calls for some comment. It is further evidence of Tura's accuracy that he has depicted the wall creeper in its winter plumage (the chin and throat feathers of this bird are black in the summer, white in the winter plumage), and it is only in winter that the bird would occur in his area of Italy, and only occasionally at that. The illustration (fig. 140) from Charles Robert Bree's work on European birds[23] was selected because it shows the wall creeper in winter plumage, and in a pose fairly similar to that of Tura's bird. When we consider that Tura was not nearly so meticulously accurate in his rendition of the barn owl one cannot help but think that in the case of the wall creeper he must have had a special interest in making it so naturalistically correct that it would be perfectly identifiable to anyone who looked at the painting.

The thought behind the inclusion of the wall creeper in this painting is as follows: the bright red in its wings, first of all, serves to connect the bird with the hat and other emblems of the cardinalate with which Saint Jerome was so frequently depicted, as in this particular instance. The red is continued in the cover of the open book on the ground beneath the bird; inasmuch as this red-bound volume represents the Latin Bible, the Vulgate, Jerome's great life work, this visual agreement in color would seem as indicative of a mutual connection. The red color would also, traditionally, invoke the idea of Sacrifice, and, consequently, of the Passion of Christ. That this connection is not farfetched will be apparent if

Figure 139. Detail of wall creeper from frontispiece, Cosimo Tura's *Saint Jerome in Penitence*. London: The National Gallery.

Figure 140. *Wall Creeper.* From Charles Robert Bree, *A History of the Birds of Europe, Not Observed in the British Isles*, London, 1875–1876.

21. *Nativity with Saints Galganus and Martin* in Pinacoteca Nazionale, Siena.

22. Crowe and Cavalcaselle, *A New History of Painting in Italy from the II to the XVI Century*, vol. 1, p. 518; Salter, *Nature in Italian Art*, p. 96; Howe, *Animal Life in Italian Painting*, p. 56.

23. *A History of the Birds of Europe, Not Observed in the British Isles*, vol. 3, p. 158.

we recall that in the original, uncut painting the apparition of the crucified Christ was in the sky almost directly above the bird.

However, there is still another reason for the inclusion of the bird in this picture. There was an old belief, still current at least as late as the middle of the eighteenth century, to the effect that the wall creeper inhabited old and neglected cemeteries in preference to other places, and that it frequently laid its eggs and raised its young in human skulls. It is, actually, a bird that nests in holes or crannies in and between the rocks, and its common English name, wall creeper, the Italian "picchio muraiolo," or the German "Mauerläufer" or "Mauerspecht," are all quite descriptive of its way of life. Inasmuch as crumbling tombs, gravestones, and so forth, appeal to it as much as do stone fences and rock walls, it may, indeed, often be seen around cemeteries. Also, it is true that in Tura's time people did visit churchyard cemeteries, while they seldom indulged in walks in wild or rugged places, and therefore they would have been more apt to see the wall creeper in these guarded, safe, park-like areas than elsewhere. All this would tend to connect the bird in their minds with cemeteries; agreeing in this respect with the barn owl, or "church" owl.

The belief that the wall creeper used human skulls as nesting places led to the thought that each generation of these birds, hatching out of skulls, was, in effect, an example of life emerging from the dead, and this might readily have caused the wall creeper to be connected with the concept of Resurrection. It is suggestive that in a mid-eighteenth-century German work on natural history, G. H. Kramer tells the story of the bird using human crania as repositories for its eggs, adding that the common names applied to it by the local people are "todtvogel," or "death bird," as well as "Mauerspecht," or "wall-pecker."[24] The name "death bird" is chiefly based on the fact that the little bird frequents tombs and gravestones. Inasmuch as common names generally are not adopted into the vernacular until the underlying reasons are not only well known but long accepted, it would seem that the connection between the wall creeper and death must have been well established. This is further borne out by the fact that there was also a French name for this bird, "oiseau des cimetières," and an Italian name, "picch de la mort," with precisely the same connotation. The Italian country folk went even further and applied to the wall creeper names as evocative of religious significance as "usel de la Trinita," "Madoneta," and "osel della Madona."[25]

In France the wall creeper was also called "papillon" ("butterfly"), because the fluttering of its wings as it climbed about caused it to show a flash of red with each move, like the wings of a colorful butterfly.[26] This nomenclatural agreement readily caused the wall creeper to assume the connotation of the butterfly, an old and well-known symbol of Resurrection: the caterpillar was the earthly life, the cocoon the tomb, and the beautiful butterfly that emerged from the tomb was the glorious future life.

It must be stressed that I have been unable to find any documentary references beyond the mere local names themselves. Yet such names could not have come into popular use without antecedent legends or adages as their bases. The natural history literature provides no help in this area. Konrad von Megenberg, author of the earliest work of this

24. *Elenchus vegetabilium et animalium per austriam inferiorem observatum*, p. 336.

25. Ettore Arrigoni degli Oddi, *Ornitologia Italiana*, pp. 185–86.

26. Eugène Rolland, *Faune populaire de la France*, vol. 2, pp. 80–81.

type in the German language, a century earlier than Tura, did not even know of the bird. Konrad Gesner, writing two centuries earlier than Kramer, and less than one century after Tura painted his wall creeper, did not know of the supposed habits of the bird.[27] He wrote almost nothing about the wall creeper other than a very brief description of its appearance. Aldrovandus was similarly noncommunicative, and similarly confined his remarks to a description of the plumage and to the geographical range of the bird. It would have been welcome and pertinent to our present discussion if Gesner or Aldrovandus had made some mention of the story, but their silence is not to be taken as suggestive that it was more recent in origin. Purely literary sources are also completely devoid of wall creeper lore. The bird is not mentioned in the two great literary repositories of late medieval Italian culture—the works of Petrarch and Dante. Neither is it mentioned by Ariosto whom Tura may have known personally in Ferrara. I mention him, not as a "source," but as a conveyor and reflector of local legends, as Ariosto was only an infant when Tura's *Saint Jerome* was painted, and he did not actually come to live in Ferrara until considerably later.

The absence of old legends about the wall creeper, other than the story of its inhabiting old cemeteries and nesting in human crania, is further corroborated by the fact that so inclusive a survey of old animal folklore as O. Keller's compendium makes no mention of it except to assure the reader that it is not the same bird as the blue rock thrush, *Monticola cyanea*, of which a short account is given.[28]

The inclusion in this painting of an unusual bird like the wall creeper may well reflect the fact that in quite a number of the cultural centers in fifteenth-century Italy, and especially in that of the Estensian court of Ferrara, there was a lively and increasingly active interest in the various kinds of animal life. These interests were particularly pronounced with respect to the rarer creatures, those that were seldom seen and usually not available, and especially those exotic beasts that were brought in occasionally as a result of the far-ranging mercantile enterprises and diplomatic maneuverings of the time. In Ferrara this interest developed to a very high degree a few decades after the date of Tura's *Saint Jerome* under the impetus and the patronage of Duke Alfonso I d'Este, but it was well established considerably before his time. Duke Alfonso's avid curiosity about animals is amply documented. As a single instance, on one occasion he went so far as to send a message to his agent in Venice to commission Titian to paint a portrait of a gazelle he had heard was in the possession of a Venetian merchant, Giovanni Cornaro, and which he had not been able to see for himself.[29]

In the lower-left corner of Tura's painting are two books (fig. 141), one lying on the ground, the other on top of it. Because of Jerome's scholarly activity he is often shown with one or more books, even in pictures of him in the wilderness. Here, however, we come upon a new iconographic detail. The upper of the two books is open, but without any physical support. In other words, it is a perpetually open book, and as such it would seem to be a visual reference to the value and effect of the saint's great life work in producing the Vulgate. As already mentioned in the discussion of the owl, the saint's work had the effect of opening permanently to a much wider audience the text of the Scriptures,

27. *Historia animalium*, p. 683.

28. *Die Antike Tierwelt*, vol. 2, p. 80 fn.

29. Fern R. Shapley, "Giovanni Bellini and Cornaro's Gazelle," pp. 27–30.

Figure 141. Detail of the saint's books from frontispiece, Cosimo Tura's *Saint Jerome in Penitence*. London: The National Gallery.

previously inaccessible (the closed book below it) save to the small handful of scholars who were able to read it in the Hebrew or Greek text. In practically all other pictures of Saint Jerome in which an open book appears, it is shown leaning against some support or is being held open by the fingers of the saint; that is, its open condition is directly understandable as a physical fact. Tura has here created a simple but effective improvement over such a prosaic reference to Jerome's great contribution to the dissemination of religious thought.

The binding of the book is red, an obvious reference to its author, who in the art of the Renaissance was often shown as a cardinal, even though that office was not created until long after Jerome's time.[30] As Erwin Panofsky pointed out, the "myth" that Jerome was ever made a cardinal was born in the Middle Ages and was accepted by succeeding centuries.[31]

It seems that the open book, shedding the light of its contents on a far greater audience than its predecessor (the closed book) is further evidence of the same trend of thought that caused Tura to change his owl from a bird of darkness into a living lamp.

While the juxtaposition of the open book and the closed one, indeed the superimposition of the former on the latter, in Tura's painting is clearly meaningful, and is used to good effect, the idea of the self-opened book may not have been wholly novel with this artist. In Domenico Ghirlandajo's fresco in the Ognissanti, in Florence (fig. 84), there is a similar book lying on the table, its upper cover raised without visible explanation or support. The fact that Ghirlandajo also made use of the motif might imply a general awareness of the idea, in towns as far apart as Florence and Ferrara. Ghirlandajo's painting is dated 1480 and is therefore almost contemporaneous with, or at most a very few years later than, Tura's work. There is no reason to suppose that the duplication of the open book motif was a copy by Ghirlandajo from Tura, as neither apparently spent any time in the town, or in the company, of the other. If Tura was not the inventor of the motif—and he may well have been—at least he was alert to its possibilities, and he utilized it effectively.

30. G. Kaftal, *Iconography of the Saints in Tuscan Painting*, p. 537.

31. "A Letter to St. Jerome: A Note on the Relationship between Petrus Christus and Jan van Eyck," p. 106.

Another aspect of the emotional intensity of this painting may be noted. In most pictures of Saint Jerome in penitence, he is shown looking at a small crucifix, either held in his hand or propped up against a rock or branch of a tree. Tura was not satisfied with so tame or stereotyped a concept, and depicted his saint praying to a mystical, celestial vision of the crucified Christ; an inner religious experience of a much profounder psychological nature. The importance the artist gave to the idea, as opposed to the factual nature of the revelation is further stressed by the omission of the cross itself from the apparition of the crucified Christ. This, in itself, reveals the intellectual selectivity of the artist. It is in close agreement with Eberhard Ruhmer's conclusion that Tura's saints attempt to convey a complete expression of their inner problems, with an almost pietistic fervor and esotericism, in keeping with which the traditional attributes, signs, and symbols are invested with more intense and heightened meanings.[32]

Celestial apparitions of the crucified Christ are found chiefly in paintings dealing with the stigmatization of the saint, most frequently Francis. As an instance particularly pertinent to our present study, it may be noted that in Jacopo del Sellaio's *Saint Jerome and Saint Francis* in the El Paso Museum of Art (fig. 40), Jerome is shown kneeling before a small crucifix, while Francis, in the upper-right background, is receiving the stigmata from an apparition of one in the sky. The highly personal selectivity shown by Tura in his elimination of the cross, and of its supporting seraphim or wings, is shown very clearly by comparison with Sellaio's version. It brings out Tura's emphasis on the introspective nature of his Jerome. While it is true that in its original condition the painting extended further to the left than does the part now in London, it seems unlikely that there would have been another, ordinary crucifix somewhere in the lower portion now missing. Saint Jerome's gaze is certainly toward the upper part, where the Brera fragment was originally.

Tura's knowledgeable selection of symbolic items to be included in this painting also extended to the plants he depicted. The plant with whorled leaves on an erect stem, growing immediately behind the books, and to the right and slightly behind the saint, may be another indirect reference to the color of the cardinalate already mentioned. It is the common madder, *Rubia tinctorum*, the very plant of which the rhizomes or root stalks were used as the source of the red dye known as "madder" or "turkey red." A practicing artist, such as Cosimo Tura, would probably have been familiar with the botanical and mineral sources of the pigments of his profession, and it seems, therefore, that his inclusion of this particular plant may well have been deliberate. This would be, in effect, a case of disguised symbolism (of Jerome as cardinal) in the same sense that Ingvar Bergström showed a pharmaceutical jar labeled "Tyriaca" to be a reference to Christ as Healer in van Eyck's Detroit painting of *Saint Jerome in His Study*.[33]

The low plants growing on the rocks are European ivy, called by the botanists *Hederoma muralis*, or wall ivy. Symbolically, ivy has been identified with the idea of immortality, which is one of the reasons it is used extensively on gravestones and on church walls. Because it remains green throughout the year, it conveys a suggestion of fidelity and eternal life, and from the way in which it clings to the rocks and walls, it also alludes

32. *Tura, Paintings and Drawings*, p. 6.

33. "Medicina, Fons et Scrinium," pp. 5–7.

to the concept of strong attachment. This ivy occurs in a *Saint Jerome* (fig. 22) by Giovanni Bellini, and in many other Italian paintings, including Leonardo's *Madonna of the Rocks*.

In looking back over all we have found in this painting, we may ask if it seems probable that Tura could have had in his own mind all that we have come to have in ours, and if these various symbolic items would have been meaningful, even intelligible, to his audience. I think the answer to both questions is largely in the affirmative. As Ruhmer found from his study of all the extant works of the artist, of his life and his surroundings, Tura was a cultivated man, who delighted in using unusual and even novel iconographic items. He was much given to incorporating in his pictures little-known Latin quotations, and mysterious ciphers. During the quattrocento, allegory and symbolism were taken more seriously at the Estensian court of Ferrara than in most cultural centers in Italy. Poets, dramatists, and artists attached to the ducal court there were all equally devoted to delving into, and improvising upon, the whole genre of allegory. Ruhmer found evidence pointing to the conclusion that in Ferrara this interest in allegory gave each person an opportunity to show and to utilize his knowledge and acumen, to be unconventional and even deliberately complicated and obscure, and to put before his audience puzzles, rebuses and enigmas to test their ability. Ruhmer writes that these allegorical riddles were well received, and that the intellectuals of the court took them as a challenge and worked on these hidden references and allusions as a cultivated pastime.[34]

In this connection, Ruhmer noted the heightened meanings in Tura's use of even relatively traditional symbols and attributes, and concluded that while the alert and inquiring mind of the artist was apparently acquainted with the usual sources and meanings, Tura avoided mere conventionality and grasped at new or seldom used means of instilling new vitality and even new meanings in the pictorial language of allusion. My present findings bear this out, and in a field so fraught with the dangers of subjective analysis it is reassuring to find such agreement. In his use of the wall creeper, the "luminous" owl, the penitent lion, and the frog, Tura is unique among painters of the Jerome theme.

34. In his study of the Estensian court (*Ferrara: The Style of a Renaissance Despotism*, pp. 234–36), Werner L. Gundersheimer found that the art of Ferrara was largely conceived by, and intended for, the learned members of the court, who amused themselves with recondite classical allusions, completely mysterious (even, at times, fabricated) allegories, and enigmatic emblems. This is portrayed in Torquato Tasso's play *Il re torrismondo*. In one scene a group of the principal characters are gathered about a mysterious emblem, and all attempt to guess its meaning. That they are unable to do so is presented in such a casual manner as to suggest that this was not unusual. It was the occasion for learned discourse and not the need for a satisfying explanation that engendered this type of social entertainment.

The Bestiary

By definition a bestiary is a collection of moralized animal tales, a combination of natural history, legend, and mythology, oriented to convey ulterior meanings. The word "animal" is used here in its biological sense, to include all forms of life that are not plants. As may be seen from the pages that follow, the total fauna associated in art with the Saint Jerome story includes a large number of kinds of mammals, birds, reptiles, amphibians, arthropods (scorpions, crustaceans, and insects), and even mollusks (snails). These are taken up, one at a time, to describe the symbolic meanings they were intended to express, and also to note in which renditions of the Jerome cycle, and by which artists, they were so employed. In other words, their use is charted in terms of place as well as of time, in terms of frequency or rarity, and this charting is presented with relation to pertinent temporal and regional knowledge and tradition.

A word of caution, already given in the preface, may be repeated here. When we find that pertinent meanings were expressed symbolically by a given kind of animal, or that a certain creature was connected with an event or a place or an object in the legend of the saint with whom it is shown, this does not necessarily prove that the artist involved knew of this particular relevance. He may have included the animal merely because he had seen it in older pictures of the same subject. However, this still does imply that there was local, contemporaneous or antecedent, intentional use of the creature involved. All we can do is to outline the ideas—real, legendary, and allegorical—that brought these animals into association with the Jerome story and thereby made them available to the artists. It is too much to expect that each and every one of these creatures should have been "presented" or "explained" in local, contemporary documents. Where such do occur, whether in the sermons of the clerics or the ballads of the troubadours, in letters or in commentaries on church literature, or in the various versions of the *Physiologus* and its derivative bestiaries, these records are, of course, very pertinent and important in our current "reading" of these animals.

In a few cases, particularly of animals that were used rarely, or even only once, in works of art, the symbolism involved is discussed at length in the six chapters devoted to individual artists. To avoid duplication, the treatment of these creatures is abbreviated in this Bestiary, but page references indicate where the fuller presentations are to be found.

I have also omitted such creatures as the ass and the camel, because these are animals whose presence was required by the Jerome story (the ass was supposed to be guarded by the lion, and the caravan of camels was eventually brought back to the monastery by the saint's faithful lion). These are "real," not symbolic, animals in the Hieronymite legend. It may be noted that there is a picture which, by itself, is a seeming exception. In a painting of *Saint Jerome in Penitence* by, or attributed to,

Jacopo Bassano, in Ponce, Puerto Rico, the ass is present, and its presence in such a scene is not only uncalled for, but meaningless, inasmuch as the usual lion is absent. It is not known if the painting has been cut, but its composition does not suggest that. It seems that what we have here is an incomplete version of two other similar paintings by Bassano of Jerome in penitence, one in the Alte Pinakothek, Munich, and one in the Fitz-william Museum, Cambridge. In both of these the lion is present and the ass as well, but the latter beast is faggot-laden, thereby explaining its presence as illustrating a part of the Jerome lion legend, although this incident was not part of the saint's penitential experience. In the version in Ponce only the head and front of the ass are shown, making it impossible to say if the beast is supposed to be carrying a load of wood, but it would seem probable that the picture was based on one or both of the other two. In other words, the ass in this painting is not a symbolic beast, merely an unthinking repetition of part of an earlier version in which the animal is understandable, even if somewhat misplaced.[1]

Also not included in the following accounts are unidentifiable creatures, particularly small birds and inadequately rendered insects that cannot be identified with reasonable certainty. In the case of the small birds it may be recalled that any of them could be a winged symbol of the soul, the part of man that is not earth-bound. Beyond this, those birds that have even a speck of red in their plumage may have been intended to be one of the "small birds of the Passion of Christ," that is, one of the little sympathetic birds that tried to extract the spines from the brow of the thorn-crowned Jesus and whose plumage became bloodstained as a result. The European robin and the goldfinch are the species usually so recorded (see the accounts of these two). There is nothing to be gained by assuming that other birds—so inaccurately depicted as to defy identification—are pseudo-robins or pseudo-goldfinches. The highly inaccurately drawn insects in a few paintings, such as pictures by Altdorfer and Andrea di Giusto, are even less intepretable, and are best left without comment.

1. A third version of this composition is in the collection of Dr. Ernesto Suardo, Chiudno, Bergamo. I have seen no reproduction of the painting, so I cannot say if the lion is present or if the ass is similar to the one in the version in Ponce.

The Ant

Ants have been noted in only one rendition of "Saint Jerome in Penitence," a small predella painting by Carlo Crivelli (fig. 35), below his *Madonna della Rondine* in the National Gallery, London. In it there are a dozen or more ants crawling about the base of the tree to the left of the kneeling saint, and two of them are crawling up the trunk toward Jerome's cardinal's hat. They are too crudely done to invite any attempt at specific identification.

The apparent meaning of the ant is derived from the statement in the Bible advising man to "Go to the ant, thou sluggard; consider her ways and be wise";[2] the ant was considered an industrious creature with some provident thought for its welfare, storing up food in the summer to last it through the barren winter months ahead. It cannot be demonstrated that Crivelli had in mind any meaning close to the Jerome theme, but one might see in the ant a parallel to the penitence of the saint, the insect trying to assure itself of sustenance in the time to come, and Jerome seeking salvation for his future condition. This suggestion is enhanced by the fact that in a twelfth-century Latin bestiary, T. H. White found the statement that provident people, like ants, take themselves to where they may expect to get their future reward.[3] Further, it is said that when an ant stores grain in its nest it divides the seeds into two sections so that one may be saved if disaster should overtake the other. The moral derived from this is that man should divide the words of the Scriptures similarly and should discriminate between the spiritual and the carnal meanings involved, for, as "the Apostle observes . . . the latter kills but the spirit gives life." In the *Fiori di Virtu* the ant is given as the symbol of prudence ("prudenza").[4] The providential nature of the ant was mentioned by Aristotle, Aelian, Pliny, and other classical writers, and, in Christian theological literature, by Saint Augustine.[5]

2. Proverbs 6: 6–8; 30: 25.

3. T. H. White, *The Bestiary*, pp. 96–98; also Wehrhahn-Stauch in Engelbert Kirschbaum et al., *Lexikon der Christlichen Ikonographie*, vol. 1, cols. 110–111.

4. Otto Lehmann-Brockhaus, "Tierdarstellung der Fiori di Virtu," p. 13.

5. Saint Augustine, "Enarratia in Psalmum lxvi," in Migne, *Patrologia Latina*, vol. 36, col. 804. "Non est imitatus formicam: non sibi collegit grana, cum aestes esset (Prov. vi, 6, et xxx, 25)." Also, Saint Basil, in his Homily ix on the Hexaemeron (English edition of 1965, p. 138) mentions the industriousness of the ant.

The Badger

What probably was intended to be two badgers occur in Gentile Bellini's *Saint Jerome in the Wilderness* (fig. 26) in Toledo, Ohio. They are on the rocky ledge immediately above Jerome's grotto. While lacking the clear-cut dark and light pattern so well brought out in the badgers in Sodoma's *Life of Saint Benedict*, in Monte Oliveto, for example, there is a suggestion of darker and lighter areas in the heads and upper part of the backs of the two. It may be mentioned that in his description of Lucas Cranach's Berlin paintings of Cardinal Albrecht of Brandenburg as Saint Jerome, Edwin Redslob refers to a badger (Dachs),[6] but the animal in that painting is really a beaver.

The two badgers in Gentile Bellini's painting are in the background, relatively far removed from Jerome, and probably have no particular allegorical connotation. The artist liked to include animals and enjoyed drawing them, as may be seen from his numerous sketches preserved in Paris and London; thus, his inclusion of them in this work is possibly nothing but a reflection of this interest.

6. *Gemäldegalerie Berlin-Dahlem, Ehemals Kaiser-Friedrich-Museum*, pp. 210–11.

The Bear

This beast figures rarely in the iconography of Saint Jerome. It has been noted in one sculpture and five pictures (paintings, woodcuts, and engravings), and has been described as being present in two others that I have not been able to examine. All are of "Saint Jerome in Penitence," and all are by Italian artists: Carlo Crivelli (formerly in Spiridon Coll., Berlin; not listed by Berenson, not seen by me); Filarete attribution (fig. 81); Filippino Lippi, (fig. 142); Mansueti (fig. 36); Mansueti's studio; Italian engraving ca. 1480–1500 (Hind, no. 85); Domenico Campagnola (fig. 56); and a painting attributed "possibly" to Girolamo di Giovanni da Camerino (not listed by Berenson, not seen by me).

In the two Mansueti paintings and in the fifteenth-century engraving, the bear is present, but is not doing anything. In the Filippino Lippi the bear is on a rocky hill to the left side of the background with only its front half or so visible, and it is looking down in confrontation with Jerome's lion, which is growling angrily at it (fig. 143). This confronta-

Figure 143. Detail of bear and lion from figure 142, Filippino Lippi's *Madonna and Child with Jerome and Dominic*. London: The National Gallery.

Figure 142. Filippino Lippi, *Madonna and Child with Jerome and Dominic*. London: The National Gallery.

7. *One Hundred Details from Pictures in the National Gallery*, p. xxii.

8. Jacob Grimm, *Teutonic Mythology*, pp. 667–68.

9. Sermon clxxix; cited in Edward Payson Evans, *Animal Symbolism in Ecclesiastical Architecture*, p. 88.

10. The bear licking its cubs into shape is described by Aristotle (ed. and trans. J. A. Smith and W. D. Ross, vol. 4, p. 580) and by Pliny (trans. H. Rackhan, vol. 3, p. 91).

11. This is described and illustrated in a fifteenth-century French Book of Hours in the John Rylands Library, Manchester (Latin MS. 164, f. 246v, ca. 1460); also reproduced in Francis Klingender, *Animals in Art and Thought to the End of the Middle Ages*, p. 457. There are numerous variations of the theme of the spiritual power of different saints causing originally feral and ferocious beasts to become docile and to submit passively to penal tasks in atonement for their real or supposed crimes.

12. First published and illustrated by John Beckwith, *The Adoration of the Magi in Whalebone*. Klingender (pp. 314–15) pointed out that the "beast-fight" motif illustrates the relationship of the symbolic animals to the sacred personages figured in the main scene above them, but this is by no means evident.

13. *Iconologia de Cesare Ripa accresciuta dell'Abate Cesare Orlandi*, vol. 4, p. 72.

14. Edward MacCurdy, *The Notebooks of Leonardo da Vinci*, p. 1075. The bear as a sign of anger is older than Leonardo; it occurs in the *Fiori di Virtu*, chap. 12 (Lehmann-Brockhaus, p. 9). The use of the bear in the religion of antiquity has been described in detail by J. J. Bachofen, *Der Baer in der Religion des Altertums*.

15. Leon Gautier, *Oeuvres poetiques d'Adam de Saint-Victor*, 3d ed., p. 46.

16. A possible, but uncertain, use of the bear as a "reformed creature" occurs in a fresco by Bartolo di Fredi, *Saint Francis Receiving the Stigmata* (Lucignano: S. Francesco). In this painting a bear is shown drinking from the same tub or trough as a deer. Since the drinking deer was a frequently used reference to the human soul thirsting for the waters of the true religion, the bear, thus similarly engaged, may be also a seeker after sal-

tion is similar to the one between a wolf (or jackal?) on a ledge looking down at a dragon in a drawing of *Saint Jerome in the Wilderness* by Jacopo Bellini (fig. 54). Kenneth Clark commented on this to the effect that the serious nature of their commissions often forced Renaissance artists to include much "fantasy and invention" in the backgrounds where they did not interfere with, or detract from, the main purpose of the picture.[7] This overlooks the possible significance the incident may have had originally, and to which I shall return. In the engraving the head and shoulders of a bear are appearing from behind a rock, not too unlike the positioning given this animal in Filippino's picture. In the Campagnola the lion and the bear are fighting, closely locked in hostile embrace, standing semierect on their hind legs while Jerome watches them from across a swiftly flowing stream. The bear is readily identifiable as such by its lack of a long tail, conspicuously present in the lion. It is headed away from the observer, its head thus hidden, and is therefore not otherwise diagnostic. In the painting attributed to Girolamo di Giovanni da Camerino, a bear is said to be licking its paw behind and to the right of the saint. In the bronze relief attributed to Filarete, a snarling bear's head protrudes from behind a rock to the left of the kneeling Jerome; it is between two lions' heads and is balanced by a wolf's head on the saint's right side. Filarete may have gotten the idea of the bear and lion combination from Filippino Lippi's painting, *Madonna and Child with Jerome and Dominic* (fig. 142). In this picture the bear, only the front part of which is visible, is in angry confrontation with Jerome's lion.

The bear and the lion had in common some very similar legends, which suggests that they may have been looked upon at times as similar in a symbolic sense. (In Teutonic mythology, both the bear and the lion were regarded as "King of the Beasts.")[8] Saint Augustine wrote that the two animals typify the devil, "who is figured in these beasts, because the bear's strength is in its paw and the lion's in its mouth."[9] This might help to explain why the bear is licking its paw in the painting attributed to Girolamo di Giovanni da Camerino: Jerome's penitence has blunted (hurt) the power (paw) of the devil (bear). However, this is only a suggestion; no documentation for it has been found.

Both animals were also believed to bring forth their young in a formless state, sometimes said to be even lifeless, and three days later to lick them into proper form.[10] This matter of giving a proper, new shape was likened loosely to the idea that Christianity reforms and gives new life to those whom it gathers into its fold. The three-day interval was likened by theologians to the same period between the entombment and the resurrection of Christ, Who then took on new "form."

Just as in the Jerome story when the lion, accused by the monks of having killed and eaten the ass it was assigned to guard, was ordered to take its place as a daily bearer of faggots, so a similar tale grew up about the bear. In the legend of Saint Claude, Bishop of Besançon, a bear was harnessed to a cart and was forced to draw it in place of an ox it had killed, and was berated explicitly by the saint for its misdeed.[11] In the story of Saint Gall the bear is generally depicted as carrying a log of wood, not too dissimilar from Jerome's lion laden with firewood. Even the incident of the saint removing a thorn or a splinter from a lion's foot in the Jerome story has been repeated with a bear in the legend of Saint

Aventine of Troyes. We must be aware that in the logic of allegory similarity in events or appearances was often taken as suggesting connotative identity.

The fight between the bear and the lion depicted in Campagnola's woodcut also had earlier, antecedent usage. Thus, for example, in a late eleventh-century English whalebone carving of the "Adoration of the Magi," in the Victoria and Albert Museum, London, there is a predella-like frieze below the main scene, and in it a lion is shown attacking a bear.[12]

The evil connotation of the bear is further shown in an emblem of Malvagita or Wickedness, in Cesare Ripa's *Iconologia*,[13] which shows a woman standing with a knife in her right hand and a tightly closed purse in her left, and with a peacock to her right and a bear to her left. In his bestiary Leonardo da Vinci considered the bear to be a symbol of anger.[14] His argument is as follows: when the bear attempts to rob a beehive of its honey it gets stung by many of the bees. Maddened with pain and unable to get at each of its tormentors, the beast rushes madly to avenge itself on any creature it encounters, and finally throws itself on the ground vainly trying to rid itself of the irate bees with its wildly beating feet. Still another use of the bear as a symbol of evil and of cruelty occurs in the Bible (Daniel 7:5), where the beast is used as a sign of the corruptness of Persia. In Adam of Saint-Victor's hymn for Easter beginning "Zyma vetus expurgetur," and recounting the symbolic references to the prefiguration of Christ in the Old Testament, the bear, *ursus*, stands for evil in the persons of the Roman Emperor Vespasian and his son Titus, who set out to destroy Jerusalem.[15]

In the "Jerome Altar" by J. Cornelisz, in Vienna, the upper part of the saint's throne has two carved figures; on the left side is a monkey looking at what may be a cardinal's hat, or a basin (!), and on the right side is a chained bear, which is possibly a "tamed" or "reformed" beast of evil.[16]

vation. It is true that in pictures of the drinking stag the water is usually shown as a stream, not in a container. Bartolo's picture is illustrated in Berenson, *Italian Pictures of the Renaissance: Central Italian and Northern Italian Schools*, fig. 406.

The Beaver

The beaver is a rarity in the iconography of Saint Jerome. So far as I know it occurs in only three paintings, all by the same artist, Lucas Cranach the Elder. In all three pictures there are many other kinds of animals as well. It is strange that the beaver should have been introduced into the Jerome orbit by only one artist, and not consistently by him (in only three out of nine pictures of Jerome). Cranach's pertinent pictures and usages of animals are more fully discussed in the chapter devoted to that artist.

The absence of the beaver from the many hundreds of Italian renditions of the Jerome story may be due to the fact that the animal does not occur in nature south of the Alps, and so was not a creature the Italian artists had many occasions to see. Also, it was barely mentioned among the many animal similes in early, medieval, Italian verse or literature. M. S. Garver found that most of these animal references stemmed from the songs and ballads of the troubadours, and not from the bestiaries.[17] The beaver was discussed in the latter, but hardly in the former, and so it probably seldom entered into thought or conversation in Italian centers.

17. "Sources of the Beast Similes in the Italian Lyric of the Thirteenth Century," pp. 276–300.

When it did, it was as an exotic, but not an unknown, creature. Dante made some slight mention of the beaver, and an unidentified Lombard artist close to Giovannino de Grassi made a beautiful and accurate drawing of it, as did also Petrus Candidus.[18] Leonardo da Vinci repeated the ancient classical legend of the beaver's self-castration and emphasized its moralized interpretation as a symbol of Peace in his bestiary; Ariosto, considerably later, included in his *Orlando Furioso* a reference to the beaver's reputed mode of fishing with its tail.[19] However, these literary instances were merely occasional references by the erudite; by and large the beaver appears to have played little part in the stock of animal lore available to the artists of Italy.

There were two legends concerning the beaver, both of ancient origin. The more important of the two originated from the idea that the genitals of this animal were considered to be of great medicinal value (the drug derived therefrom was called "castoreum," after the Latin name of the beaver, *castor*), and the demand for this material caused hunters to pursue the beaver regularly. (Actually, the drug castoreum was made, not from the genitals, but from subcutaneous glands situated near the anus.) This legend tells us that when the beaver found itself hard pressed by its pursuers, unable to escape, it would bite off its testicles and leave them for the hunters, who then would have no further interest in pursuing it, and would let the self-castrated animal escape. The legend was further elaborated to the effect that thereafter the beaver, when again menaced by hunters, would raise its rear end to show them that its prized genitals were gone; this would cause its pursuers to abandon the chase and leave it alone.

The act of self-castration (the very word, of course, comes from *castor*, or beaver) was later moralized to signify deliberate cutting off of Lasciviousness and Vice in order to attain Spiritual Peace (hence Leonardo's use of the beaver as an emblem of Peace). The beaver thereby became the sign of the holy man who cast off the temptations and sins of corporeal existence to live in spiritual peace. The hunter was likened to the Devil, who pursues the potential sinner, but who, on seeing that the object of his chase is free of evil (already castrated) and cannot be induced to sin, grudgingly departs in a state of confusion, leaving the holy man alone from then on.

According to the second, less important legend of the beaver, the animal would stand on the edge of the stream or river, when it wanted to catch fish, and dangle its broad, fat tail in the water as a lure. This is the legend repeated by Dante, and also, later, by Ariosto.

The first legend was reported by Juvenal, and was also included in Aelian's *De natura animalium*; in Asiatic literature, it appears in the Indo-Aryan *Avesta*. In the latter, the beaver was considered to be sacred and inviolable, an emblem of the moon (the chaste Diana) in accord with the popular opinion regarding it as a eunuch (*castor a castrando*), similar to the statement in Juvenal. The story is also to be found in the writings of Apuleius and Pliny, among classical authors, and in Rabanus Maurus, Isidore of Seville, the author of an old German edition of the *Physiologus*,[20] and a fifth-century version of the same work attributed to Saint Ambrose, to mention only a few of the medieval writers.

A medieval, twelfth-century bestiary, written in 1121 by an Anglo-

18. Dante, *Inferno*, xvii, 21–22; leaf 13 of the famous Giovannino sketchbook in the civic library of Bergamo; illus. in Raimond van Marle, *The Development of the Italian Schools of Painting*, vol. 7, p. 94; also in *Taccuino de disegni di Giovannino de Grassi*, facs. ed., 1961; Petrus Candidus, *De omnium animantium naturis*, 1460, MS. Vaticano Urbinato Latino 276; illus. in A. C. Crombie, *Medieval and Early Modern Science*, vol. 1, pl. xviii.

19. MacCurdy, p. 1075; Mario Praz, *Studies in Seventeenth-century Imagery*, p. 208.

20. Friedrich Maurer, *Der Altdeutsche Physiologus*.

Norman poet, Philippe de Thaun, and translated by Thomas Wright, informs us that

Castor is the name of a beast which we call beaver; it becomes castrated voluntarily, for which cause it has its name; its genitories are good, as the Bestiary says,—to put in medicine; listen how the castor effects its end.—When a man hunts it, and approaches to take it,—it bites off its genitories when it knows not what to do,—throws them to him, then flies away;—the hunter takes them, for they are what he wants,—then lets the beast alone, which is of so remarkable a character,—if he hunts it again, it comes before him,—shows its hind part, and makes him a sign—that it is castrated, he would hunt it for nothing. Keep in remembrance that this is a great signification.

The castor signifies in this life the holy man,—who deserts luxury and the sins which he did;—he leaves it to the Devil, who, on that account, hunts him about;—when the Devil has tempted and proved the holy man,—and can find no evil in him, then he lets him be,—and the man lives with God, as the writing shows;—and such is the significance of the castor, without doubt.[21]

In his translation of a twelfth-century Latin bestiary, T. H. White adds a little more of the medieval interpretation of the self-preserving action of the pursued beaver.

Hence every man who inclines toward the commandment of God and who wants to live chastely, must cut off from himself all vices, all motions of lewdness, and must cast them from him in the Devil's face. Thereupon the Devil, seeing him to have nothing of his own about him, goes away from him confused. That man truly lives in God and is not captured by the Devil who says: 'I shall persevere and attain these things.'[22]

White adds that according to Sir Thomas Browne, the origin of the legend "was probably Hieroglyphicall, which after became Mythologicall unto the Greeks and so set down by Aesop, and by process of tradition stole into a totall verity."[23]

Louis Réau concluded that the beaver, along with the bee, the elephant, and the unicorn, was one of a number of emblems of Chastity.[24]

Two variant thoughts stemming from this story may be mentioned. In my discussion of the lioness as a possible symbol of Mary (p. 253 ff.), the early impact on mid-quattrocento Italian thought of the *Hieroglyphica* of Horapollo is described. In the edition of this work by George Boas, there is the statement that when the Egyptian priests wished "to depict a man prevented from committing suicide they drew a beaver. For that animal when hunted, bites off his testicles and throws them at the hunter . . . who then pursues it no further."[25] As Boas mentioned, the beaver is one of only three animals listed by Horapollo that are non-Egyptian in their natural occurrence, the other two being the elephant and the bear.

Concerning the same legend, Edward Payson Evans commented on Konrad von Würzburg's odd and far-fetched comparison when he "commends to princes the prudence of the beaver, which saves its life by voluntarily depriving itself of what is dearest to it; he thereby intends to inculcate the virtue of liberality freely exercised for the public weal, and without stint of self-sacrifice."[26]

In his commentary on Horapollo, Karl Giehlow concluded that the beaver stood for three things: men, who by their own mutilation, en-

21. Thomas Wright, *Popular Treatises on Science Wrtten during the Middle Ages in Anglo-Saxon, Anglo-Norman, and English*, p. 94.

22. T. H. White, *The Bestiary*, p. 29.

23. Thomas Browne, *Pseudodoxia Epidemica*.

24. *Iconographie de l'art chrétien*, p. 101.

25. George Boas, *The Hieroglyphics of Horapollo*, p. 99.

26. Edward Payson Evans, *Animal Symbolism in Ecclesiastical Architecture*, pp. 138–39.

27. "Die Hieroglyphenkunde des Humanismus in der Allegorie der Renaissance," p. 219.

28. "Medicina, Fons et Scrinium: A Study in Van Eyckian Symbolism and Its Influence in Italian Art," pp. 1–20.

29. Salvador de Moya, "Biblioteca Geneologica Latina," p. 66.

30. Arthur Charles Fox-Davies, *A Complete Guide to Heraldry*.

31. Kirschbaum et al., vol. 1, col. 289.

32. Florence Turner McCulloch, *Medieval and French Bestiaries*, p. 95. The widespread knowledge of the self-castration legend is reflected in its appearance in the writings of Bartholomew Anglicus (xviii), of Pliny (vii, 30, 47), of Aldrovandus (pp. 285–86), and in the emblems of Alciati (cli) and of Camerarius (xciii). In the *Fiori di Virtu* the beaver (castoro) signifies peace (pace), as shown by Lehmann-Brockhaus, p. 9.

To my knowledge the beaver never was used in the iconography of Origen, the one great churchman for whom the animal would seem to be a particularly appropriate symbol. This great thinker of the early Eastern Church actually did to himself what the beaver was believed to have done in the legend and, "by an act more irrevocable than a monastic vow, put from him mortal bridals." (H. O. Taylor, *The Medieval Mind*, vol. 1, p. 349.) The idea of self-castration was not new with Origen: Matthew (19:12) wrote, " there be eunuchs which have made themselves eunuchs for the kingdom of heaven's sake," but Origen's case was the most famous. Emile Mâle (*Religious Art from the Twelfth to the Eighteenth Century*, p. 45) mentioned the beaver as one of several creatures discussed in the bestiaries that never were used in medieval art. He wrote that these early artists made no direct use of bestiaries as "sources," but knew only those

Figure 144. *Perseverando*. From Camerarius, *Symbolorum et emblematum centuriae quatuor*, 1677.

dured life-long injury; men who arrived at excellence through mutilation; and men who, by their ruse or deceit of mutilation, are exiled or banished from others not so guilty.[27]

The fact that the beaver's genitals were believed to contain a substance of great medicinal value would undoubtedly have been known by, and of interest to, Lucas Cranach, who was, among his other activities, a leading apothecary in his hometown, and, as such, probably had castoreum in his usual stock of available remedies. Such a curative, medicinal concept is to be found in the use in art of "Christ as Healer," and even of "Christ as a Chemist" (in the sense of an apothecary), as in the stained-glass window of 1630, now in the Schweizerisches Landesmuseum, Zürich; and, to take a particularly well-studied specific instance immediately pertinent to the Jerome theme, the jar of *Tyriaca* in van Eyck's *Saint Jerome in his Study*, in Detroit, so well described by Ingvar Bergström.[28]

The beaver also was used to signify Perseverance, because of its industry in gnawing down small trees for use in building its dams and houses (fig. 144). Also, its judgment in the matter of self-castration, as a step toward spiritual peace, caused it to become an emblem of intelligence. These two traits were obviously favorable in spiritual as well as in mundane affairs, and their illustration by the beaver goes back to old Latin sources.[29] The beaver was also used in heraldry: it was the sole figure in the arms of the German city of Biberach (literally beaver brook in German), where it was shown rampant, wearing a crown. Another heraldic figure of a beaver shows the animal with a large tusk on either mandible projecting upward above the sides of the creature's face, and its tail forked (!) with three folds on each side.[30] Father Engelbert Kirschbaum and his colleagues mention still other symbolic uses of beaver teeth in connection with the general concept of *Concordantia caritatis*, the dearly bought peace, including such seemingly unrelated topics as the "Circumcision of Christ," the "Bearing of the Cross," and the "Cure of Dropsy."[31]

In medieval French bestiaries the beaver is sometimes portrayed as a doglike animal, often in extremely contorted poses, as might be expected of an animal supposedly in the act of self-castration.[32]

animal legends that had been selected from these writings early in the twelfth century by Honorius of Autun, whose book *Speculum ecclesiae* (reprinted in Migne, *Patrologia Latina*, vol. 172, 1895) was used by countless clerics in their sermons. It was from this that the animal legends reached the artists and their clients, and Honorius did not include the legend of the beaver.

One further comment on the non-use of the beaver: in spite of its name the animal was never employed as a reference to Castor, the twin of Pollux, in the story of Leda and the Swan.

The Cat

The cat has been found in only one version of the Jerome theme, Antonello da Messina's *Saint Jerome in His Study* in London (fig. 119). Its possible meanings are discussed in the chapter on that important painting (pp. 162–63). The standard reference on the uses and implications of the cat in religious thought and in magic is M. Oldfield Hower's *The Cat in the Mysteries of Religion and Magic*, but this offers nothing directly pertinent to the Jerome story.

The Chaffinch

This familiar little bird of Europe is seldom used allegorically, but it does occur at least once in a picture of the Jerome story. In Hieronymus Bosch's painting of *Saint Jerome in Penitence* in Ghent, there is a chaffinch perched on a twig in the lower-right corner of the picture (fig. 114). As stated in the discussion of that painting (p. 146), there seem to be no old legends or tales of the chaffinch, but when, in the eighteenth century, Linnaeus coined the official scientific name for this bird, *Fringilla coelebs*, he chose the specific appellation *coelebs* (celibate) because of the belief that the two sexes remained apart, in separate flocks, except for the breeding season. The English common name, chaffinch, or finch of the chaff, refers to the straw in the manager at the Nativity. The connection between celibacy and the natal bed of chaff points to the legendary role of Joseph in the biblical story of the birth of Christ. Names applied to objects such as small birds were not chosen at random; they were based on antecedent connotations. As Jerome was much concerned with the matter of celibacy, the little chaffinch is not out of place in a picture of that saint,[33] but I know of no documents connecting the two.

33. Alfred Newton, *A Dictionary of Birds*, p. 82, fn.

The Cheetah
(and the Leopard
and the Panther)

The cheetah, or hunting leopard, and the true leopard are interchangeable so far as their use in religious art is concerned. The former is more frequent in Christian art, probably because it was more often seen in Europe as a semitame beast kept by nobles for the chase. Europe received many such hunting cheetahs from India, where there had long been a custom of using them in this capacity.[34] The true leopard is much less adaptable to domestication. The cheetah is smaller and slenderer, with considerably longer legs than the leopard, and is generally considered the fleetest of all predatory mammals. The cheetah may also be recognized by the fact that its spots are solid black, whereas those of the leopard are grouped in small rosettes with no black in the center; also, the cheetah has a wavy black line extending from the corner of the eyes across the face to the mouth.

Cheetahs have been noted in five paintings of Jerome, all of the saint in penitence; a leopard in only one. Those with cheetahs are: a painting attributed to Jacopo Bellini;[35] one attributed to Civerchio (fig. 42), in which no fewer than three of these animals may be made out in the background far from the kneeling Jerome; one attributed to Angelo Maccagnino; one by Giovanni Mansueti (fig. 36), in which two cheetahs are quietly resting on the ground near the saint's red hat; and a mid-fifteenth-century Ferrarese picture (Longhi, pl. 36). The one instance in which leopards have been identified is Carpaccio's *Meditation on the Passion of Christ* (fig. 32). In this fine painting there are two leopards, one stalking a deer and one with a deer it has already caught. Saint Jerome sits at the left and Job at the right, meditating on the seated figure of the dead Christ between them. None of the animals in this picture, which is full of them, pertain particularly to Jerome, except the saint's lion. The main theme of the painting has to do with what Jerome and Job are meditating about, not with themselves.[36]

The cheetah (and the leopard), as fierce beasts of prey, are evil creatures. Horapollo wrote that the Egyptians used the leopard as a sign of a man who has dwelt in evil, but has so concealed his own evil that even his own friends were unaware of it.[37] Like all of Horapollo's "explanations," this one also passed into the common pool of allegorical data available to artists. Leonardo da Vinci, calling the cheetah the panther of Africa, related a different aspect of its hidden evil: the spots on the cheetah are said to so fascinate other animals by their beauty that they would remain near it if it were not for the terror inspired by its cruel face.[38] The cheetah accordingly manages to hide its face, and then, as other animals draw closer, it suddenly seizes the nearest one, killing and eating it immediately.

While the cheetah, leopard, or panther, was an evil creature, it also was invested with noble qualities, even assuming a Christ-like role. According to this version, the animal sleeps for three days after a good meal, and, on awakening, emits what has been described variously as a loud belch or a sweet, ringing sound. This is accompanied by a sweet-smelling breath that attracts all animals except the dragon, which flees and hides in terror. In a twelfth-century Latin bestiary we are told that the "true Panther, Our Lord Jesus Christ" saved us from the power of the dragon (evil).[39] The cheetah (and its alter egos, the leopard, the pard, and the panther)

34. Evidence of the availability of cheetahs for observation by Italian artists is shown by very good drawings of these animals by an anonymous Lombard artist, ca. 1400; in Joan Barclay Lloyd, *African Animals in Renaissance Literature and Art*, p. 60.

35. This painting, not listed by Berenson, was in the Viezzoli Collection, Genoa. A photograph of it, filed under Jacopo Bellini, is in the set of I Tatti photographic archives, University of California at Los Angeles.

36. Frederick Hartt, "Carpaccio's Meditation on the Passion," pp. 25–35. See also Louis Charbonneau-Lassay, *Le Bestiaire du Christ*, pp. 279–93.

37. Boas, p. 105.

38. MacCurdy, pp. 1087–88.

39. White, pp. 13–17.

plays a minor role in the Jerome theme.[40] Jacopo Bellini and Giovanni Mansueti were both fond of painting animals, with or without reference to the content of the picture. In the painting attributed to Civerchio, emphasis is laid on the disagreeable or dangerous nature of Jerome's wilderness retreat. He is pictured with his lion (looking at him with an almost pitying smile), a skull grinning at him, and in the area surrounding the saint there are no fewer than ten snakes, three cheetahs, three dragons, and an eagle. The Ferrarese picture also conveys, but to a much lesser degree, the unpleasant associates of the desert locale—the lion, a cheetah, and a snake.

Berchorius, on the other hand, considered the panther a symbol of Christ as well as of Mary.[41] It may be noted that Berchorius believed the various colors present on the panther's body to represent various virtues, the black markings referring to *poenitatium* and *humilitatem*. These two, in particular, seem suggestive of a facet of panther lore pertinent to Saint Jerome.

The Cock

Aside from a single painting, *Saint Jerome in Penitence* by Hieronymus Bosch, in Ghent (fig. 108), the cock has not been found in the Jerome context. Even there, it is a very minor item, hidden in the dark at the very bottom of the picture, where its meaning is involved with that of the fox nearby rather than directed toward the saint.

That the cock may have had some pertinence to Jerome, even if it did not come to figure in the art that developed around him, is suggested in a late-twelfth-century work by Alexander Neckam. In this book we are told that the cock was emblematical of the Doctors of the Church (of whom Jerome was one), perhaps because cocks crowed early.[42] The use of the cock as a sign of a churchman is further suggested by G. R. Owst, who mentions that the medieval English Archbishop Peckham referred to nonpreaching bishops as "cocks which neither crow nor generate."[43]

The Crab

The crab, or *Cancer*, has been found in only a single rendition of "Saint Jerome in the Wilderness," a small bronze pax, attributed to Filarete (fig. 81). The crab, minute in size in this already small bronze, may be made out at lower left, just above the head of the snake and below that of the bear.

Symbolically, the crab is a creature of evil, standing for deceit, cruelty, and greed, and is, thus, fittingly placed near the serpent and the scorpion in Filarete's relief. The connection between the crab, the scorpion, and the snake is furthered by the fact that there was an old legend, cited by Isidore of Seville in his account of the transformations of various animals, that scorpions were said to be generated from crabs,[44] while the crab was sometimes believed to produce a substance that acted as an antidote for the venom of the toad or of the serpent.[45] Further, in his translation of a Latin bestiary, T. H. White tells us that the crab, when it wants to devour an oyster, is understandably afraid to insert its claws between the

40. Saint Jerome (in Migne, *Patrologia Latina*, vol. 24, col. 742, and vol. 25, col. 530) considered the leopard an evil creature.

41. *Reductorium morale super totam Bibliam*, vol. 2, p. 706.

42. *De naturis rerum*, p. 120.

43. *Preaching in Medieval England*, p. 39; Klingender, p. 529. Further information on the symbolism of the cock, not particularly oriented to Jerome's story, is brought together in the writings of Eugen Fehrle and of Gerardus van der Leeuw.

44. Klingender (p. 164) notes that in Isidore's brief chapter, "De transformatis" (in Migne, *Patrologia Latina*, vol. 82, cols. 423 ff.), various "insects" generated from corpses are listed: bees from cattle, scarabs from horses, locusts from mules, and scorpions from crabs. Klingender suggests that Isidore probably took these from Pliny, where, indeed, the crab-scorpion transformation is noted.

45. Angelo de Gubernatis, *Zoological Mythology*, vol. 2, p. 359. In the English

version of this work the substance manufactured by the crab is said to be an antidote for the venom of the toad, while in the French edition it is the snake, not the toad. It may be that it was considered a general antidote for "reptilian" poisons.

46. White, pp. 210-12, 215.

47. Wilhelm Molsdorf, *Christliche Symbolik der Mittelalterischen Kunst*, p. 224.

heavy upper and lower shells, lest they snap shut with a firm and lasting grip. To obviate this danger, the crab, on finding an oyster with its shell somewhat open, tosses in a small stone. This prevents the mollusk from closing its shell, and only then does the marauding crab reach in with its claws and tear out the soft flesh it desires.[46]

The bestiarist moralizes on this story as follows:

Now is not that just like Men—those corrupt creatures who follow the habit of the crab, creep into the practise of unnatural trickery and eke out the weakness of their real powers by a sort of cunning! They join deceit to cruelty and are fed upon the distress of others. Do you, therefore, be content with your own things and do not seek the injury of your neighbors to support you. . . . Let us then devote ourselves to acquiring merit and to maintaining what is wholesome, not to the cheating of another's innocence. Let it be left to us to make use of the marine example in perfecting our own well-being, not in the undoing of our neighbor.

In medieval art the crab is said to have been used as a symbol of inconstancy, along with several other creatures, such as the ostrich and the monkey,[47] but it seems that its occurrence in this role was quite infrequent.

In sum, while the crab is not symbolically out of place in the Jerome context, its limited use shows that it was not an important element of Hieronymite iconography.

The Crane

The crane (based on the European crane, *Grus grus*) is of little importance in the Jerome context and rarely occurs in this connection. I have found it in only three paintings, and even in them its identification is to some extent an interpretation. In old paintings cranes, herons, and storks were often so indifferently rendered that their identification is fraught with uncertainty.

What appears to be a crane (wrongly identified in the "literature" as a flamingo![48]) occurs in Carlo Crivelli's little London predella of *Saint Jerome in Penitence* (fig. 35). The identification is based on the fact that the bird has too short a bill for a heron, more like that of a crane, and also has the bunched up, curved feathers on the rump characteristic of cranes in art. It is shown wading in the stream at the lower-left corner of the picture.

A flying group of nine cranes appears in the dusky sky at the top of Cranach's *Saint Jerome in Penitence* in Innsbruck (fig. 94). As mentioned in my discussion of this painting (pp. 125-26), a flying crane, or a flying group of cranes, assumed a meaning of a "man seeking higher things," a readily moralized concept. This arose from Horapollo's statement that this was the intent of the ancient Egyptian crane hieroglyph,[49] a statement that was known and respected in southern Germany in Cranach's time. In a picture of Jerome in penitence there is a possible parallel between the saint's desire for redemption and the crane as one who seeks higher things.

The third picture is Marco Zoppo's *Saint Jerome in Penitence* (Baltimore, fig. 64). At the very bottom of this painting are four whitish

48. William Norton Howe, *Animal Life in Italian Painting*, p. 86.

49. Boas, p. 107.

"cranes" in as many different poses, feeding in the water. One of them shows the curled, bunched up, rump feathers that lead me to call them cranes rather than herons. They are much lighter in color than is Crivelli's rather grayish crane. The flying flock of cranes in the Cranach picture are less certain in identification, but I have decided, with some goodwill, to let them stand as cranes, since this is what the present owner, the Tiroler Landesmuseum, calls them. As far as their actual drawing goes, they are only "probable" cranes.

The crane was an old symbol of Vigilance or Loyalty,[50] and as such was often portrayed as standing on one leg with the other bent at right angle near the body, which is not the case with Crivelli's version. The concepts of vigilance or loyalty, while of general applicability to most saints, were not connected particularly with Jerome personally. All that may be said of them is that they are not out of place here.

Saint Jerome wrote that cranes formed into a Y-shaped flock when flying,[51] which is what they are doing in Cranach's Innsbruck painting. The account of the crane in Konrad von Megenberg's *Buch der Natur*, a work known to Cranach, cites this reference to the flight formation of the bird as coming from the writings of Jerome and Saint Ambrose.

50. Hans Martin von Erffa, "Grus vigilans," pp. 286–309. In many renditions of the crane as a symbol of Vigilance (*Grus vigilans*), it is shown holding a stone in its raised foot. One of the old explanations for this was that if the crane became sleepy it would drop the stone, which then, falling onto its other foot, would wake up the bird again.

51. Epistle cxxv, *Ad rusticum monachum*, in F. A. Wright, *Select Letters of St. Jerome*, p. 422.

The Deer

Deer of at least three kinds, the red deer (*Cervus*), the fallow deer (*Dama*), and the roebuck (*Capreolus*), and a possible fourth, the gazelle (*Gazella*), have been found in connection with the Jerome theme. In many cases, where the deer are without antlers, as in the doe or the fawn, they cannot be identified satisfactorily, because artists were prone to overlook relative size or precise coloration. In some renditions, the animal is too crudely done for specific identification. In all, deer have been noted in forty-three paintings, graphics, or carvings of "Saint Jerome in the Wilderness" by some thirty-three different artists. Aside from a few paintings by Lucas Cranach the Elder (Berlin, Innsbruck, Sarasota, Zollikon), one by Hieronymus Bosch (Venice), one by an anonymous sixteenth-century Netherlandish painter (Richter Archives), and an engraving by Pieter Brueghel, all the others were done by Italian artists: Basaiti (Budapest); Basaiti school (fig. 145); Gentile Bellini (fig. 26); Giovanni Bellini (Florence); Jacopo Bellini (three drawings, two in the Louvre, one in the British Museum, figs. 53–55); Bono da Ferrara (fig. 62); Carpaccio (three pictures: Venice [fig. 31], New York [fig. 32], Zara); Cima (one in Harewood House, York; one in Venice); Carlo Crivelli (London, fig. 35); Battista Dossi; Ferrarese, fifteenth century (Richter Archives 252:I:30); Filippo da Verona; Florentine Anonymous Fine Manner (fig. 131); Francesco di Giorgio bronze relief (fig. 120); Giraldi; Italian engraving, ca. 1460–1470 (Hind, no. 38); Mansueti (Bergamo, fig. 36); Bartolomeo Montagna (Bergamo, fig. 37); Moretto attribution; Pisanello follower (fig. 63); Giovanni della Robbia attribution; Rossellino attribution (fig. 51); Sano di Pietro (Paris, fig. 146); Sellaio (three pictures: El Paso [fig. 40], Paris, Sarasota); and Antonio Vivarini (London).

Figure 145. Basaiti school, *Saint Jerome in Penitence*. Budapest: Musée Hongrois des Beaux-Arts.

There is no reason for assuming any symbolic differences in the various kinds of deer with the one exception of the roebuck. This species of deer was well known in Europe because of its monogamous habits, in contrast to the polygamous breeding of the red deer and the fallow deer. Thus, in Cranach's Berlin picture of Cardinal Albrecht as Saint Jerome (fig. 102), there is a roebuck very close to the seated saint, whereas the red deer are in the far background. As mentioned in my discussion of that painting (pp. 129–31), it may be that the relative continence of the roebuck was behind the artist's decision to place it close to the ardent

Figure 146. Sano di Pietro, *Legend of Saint Jerome*. Paris: Musée du Louvre.

advocate of abstinence. In his Sarasota picture (fig. 104), Cranach even brought the roebuck into Jerome's study chamber, a setting where deer otherwise were not included. This special meaning attached to the roebuck cannot be assumed in the relatively few pictures in which a few Italian artists have included it (Basaiti school, Jacopo Bellini, Pisanello follower, and one of Sellaio's numerous Jeromes, now in El Paso).

The stag, or hart, the antlered male of the red deer, was an ancient symbol of the human soul thirsting for salvation, and as such was frequently pictured in the act of drinking from a stream, an image derived from Psalm 42:1, which states, "As the hart panteth after the water brooks, so panteth my soul after thee, O God." Correlated with this concept, we find a sixteenth-century emblem depicting a doe looking up toward the sun, and with it a motto reading *Mens intenta deo* ("Mind intent on [seeking] God").[52] There was also an emblem of the stag with its head lowered, not to the water but to sparsely vegetated earth, bearing the motto *Multi sunt vocati, pauci vero electi* ("Many are called, but few are chosen"),[53] a figure repeated in the background of the engraving by Florentine Anonymous Fine Manner (fig. 131) of Jerome in penitence. Hunter-sportsmen of southern Germany in the sixteenth and seventeenth centuries sometimes used the antlers, the trophies of the chase, from which to fashion chandeliers, as indeed we find in Cranach's Sarasota picture of *Saint Jerome in His Study* (fig. 104).

In most pictures where deer, often a small herd of them, are shown in the Jerome context, they are in the background as denizens of wild places, to convey the nature of the site chosen by the saint for his period of penitence.

Other meanings associated with the deer were such antithetical concepts as longevity on the one hand, and men preoccupied with thoughts of their own impending burial, on the other, and also with the idea of blind flight from danger.[54] The last named concept may be associated with the fleeing stag in Carpaccio's painting of *Saint Jerome Leading the Lion to the Monastery* (fig. 31). The stag was also used as a visual reference to the sense of hearing, particularly in north European pictures of the five senses.[55]

52. A. Henkel and A. Schöne, *Emblemata*, cols. 468–69, from Joachim Camerarius, *Symbolorum et emblematum centuriae quatuor*.

53. Henkel and Schöne, col. 468; also Nicolaus Reusner, *Emblemata Nicolai Reusneri*. Still older sources for this are Matthew 20:16 and H. Rackham, *Pliny, Natural History*, vol. 8, p. 14.

54. Karl Giehlow, "Die Hieroglyphenkunde des Humanismus in der Allegorie der Renaissance," p. 220; also P. Gerlach in Kirschbaum et al., vol. 2, cols. 286–90.

55. Seymour Slive (*Frans Hals*, p. 79) refers to such uses of the stag by the Dutch painters Jan Saenredam and Jacob Backer. Volkman Kellermann ("Der Hirsch") has discussed the many ideas associated with the deer; also Beryl Rowland, *Animals with Human Faces*, pp. 94–101.

The Dog

The dog, so frequently included in other subjects of religious art, is absent from all but a very few pictures of the Jerome cycle. In fact, out of more than a thousand representations of this saint, dogs have been noted in only four: Cranach's *Saint Jerome in His Study* (Darmstadt, fig. 103), Dürer's great engraving of 1514 of the same subject (fig. 83), Mansueti's *Saint Jerome in the Wilderness* (Bergamo, fig. 36), and Crivelli's little London predella of *Saint Jerome in the Wilderness* (fig. 35). The dog is shown sitting and awake in the Cranach and Mansueti pictures, curled up and asleep in those by Dürer and Crivelli.

The introduction of the dog in pictures of Jerome in his study stems from a pictorial tradition perhaps first illustrated in Altichiero's painting of Petrarch, in Padua. With the advance of the cult of humanism, the early scholar-saints of the Church were considered similar to the great writers, and in art were given their booklined settings and other accompaniments, including the little dog. Erwin Panofsky was convinced that "given the basic affinity between such 'studio' portraits of individual men of letters and the representations of saints, it was under the influence of the 'personalized' portrayals that Dürer included the . . . dog in his famous engraving of St. Jerome in which this charming little animal, undocumented by hagiological tradition, is shown in 'peaceful coexistence' with the well documented lion. . . . St. Jerome's little dog rightfully belongs not to him but to Petrarch and other less saintly *hommes de lettres*."[56]

The inferences to be drawn from Dürer's unique dog and lion combination are developed elsewhere (p. 101 ff.). In connection with the thought there expressed that the sleeping dog represented "blind loyalty" or "blind faith," it may be noted that in one of his famous "table talks" Martin Luther made the derogatory statement that birds, dogs, and babies all display a simple and unsophisticated faith.[57] In Cranach's Darmstadt picture it is not possible to sense the profound feeling evident in Dürer's engraving. Mansueti's use of the dog, unfortunately, is like most of the rest of his inclusions—quite meaningless. I am afraid that the same is true, to a lesser degree, of Carlo Crivelli's lavish use of animals in his predella panel, much as I would like to "read" Crivelli more sympathetically.[58]

The dog was a very old and widely used symbol of Loyalty or Fidelity.[59]

The Dove

The dove is hardly involved in the Jerome story in art, but it may be mentioned here because it was included in one painting of the saint, by the late fifteenth-century German painter, Michael Pacher. This picture is one of a series of four panels forming the *Altar-piece of the Church Fathers*, now in the Alte Pinakothek, Munich. Each presents one of the four Fathers—Jerome, Augustine, Gregory, and Ambrose. A white dove is flying down toward each, obviously as a visual reference to the "divine inspiration" that enabled each to do his work for the Church. The dove, therefore, is not a creature peculiar to Jerome; often it is an attribute of Gregory in art, usually hovering near his ear. Unlike the traditional white dove of the Holy Spirit, these doves have no halos.

Doves not white in color, and hence, not divine messengers, may occur

56. Letter of November 15, 1960, in H. van de Waal, "Hommage au Professor Panofsky," p. 261.

57. Roland H. Bainton, *Studies on the Reformation*, pp. 67–74.

58. As an example of the inaccuracies regarding animals in some of the literature of paintings it may be mentioned that Crivelli's sleeping dog is referred to by Crowe and Cavalcaselle (*A History of Painting in North Italy*, vol. 1, p. 94, fn. 1) as a "lioness with her cub."

59. Vital Huhn, "Löwe und Hund als Symbole des Rechts," pp. 1–63; also Alciati (emblem cliv), Camerarius (lxiii), Ripa ("Fidelita"), Joseph Maria von Radowitz ("Devisen und Mottos des spätern Mittelalters," p. 339), and others.

in a few other pictures, but in no case can the bird in question be identified definitely as such. It is safer, therefore, not to consider them as such. The turtle dove, an old symbol of conjugal fidelity, and which might, therefore, seem more amenable to the trend of Jerome's moralizings, has not been found in any pictures of the saint.

The extensive role of the dove in religious art, other than with particular reference to Saint Jerome, has been discussed by many writers, among whom may be named Georg Weicker and F. Sühling.

The Dragon

The dragon, a purely imaginary creature, was widely believed in and was always considered a most dangerous and evil animal. It was a symbol of Satan, following Saint Augustine's pronouncement that the devil is a lion because of his rage and a dragon because of his wiles. The popular image of a dragon was a lizardlike reptilian of great size, often given batlike wings, powerful feet with sharp claws, occasionally with horns, and often with heavy armorlike scales. In European art the dragon is seldom the creature belching fire and smoke of ancient Chinese tradition, and is found associated primarily with certain saints who overcame the dangers of evil, such as George of Cappadocia, Margaret of Antioch, Philip, Sylvester, the Archangel Michael, and, more pertinent to our present study, Jerome. The connection between the dragon and Saint Jerome is usually in scenes of him in penitence in the wilderness. However, much as one might anticipate that the dragon would have been used by artists to express the element of danger in their depictions of Jerome's desolate wilderness settings, the fact is that only four artists, all Italian and all of the fifteenth century, have been found to have made such use of the beast. There is, however, one very early (fourteenth-century) manuscript illumination (fig. 147), an Initial, that shows the saint with a dragon. The context of this picture is not clear, as it has no identifiable "setting." This is the only time a dragon has been found with Jerome, other than in the wilderness.

The pertinent works are as follows: Jacopo Bellini, one painting in Verona (fig. 29) and four outline drawings, two in the Louvre and two in the British Museum (figs. 53–55); Civerchio attribution, one painting (fig. 42); Carlo Crivelli, one predella painting (fig. 35); Rossellino attribution, one marble relief (fig. 51).

Another work may be mentioned here, although it is unclear if the dragon involved is supposed to relate in any way to Jerome. In Paris Bordone's *Saint Jerome in a Landscape* (fig. 58), there is a winged dragon, in the far background, from which a man is fleeing. This seems unrelated to the penitent saint in the foreground.

The dragons in the foregoing works are not all alike; some are wyverns, having one pair of legs and a pair of small wings. In a drawing by Jacopo Bellini, in the Louvre (fig. 53), there are two dragons, one of them a wyvern, but the other with two pairs of legs as well as a pair of wings. One of the dragons in the painting attributed to Civerchio (the one at the extreme left side of the picture) is almost a crocodile, lacking wings and not revealing its legs as it lies curled on the ground; a second one, to the right of the verticle pole of the crucifix, is also wingless, but has assumed a most uncrocodilian pose, erect on its two legs with its body

Figure 147. *Jerome and Dragon*, Italian, early fourteenth century. Oxford: Bodleian Library, MS. Canon Bibl. Lat. 49, f. 1.

raised well off the ground in a curve more horizontal than vertical; the third dragon, much farther into the background, has small wings and is a typical wyvern, which the other two are not.

All of these dragons are references to the dangers Jerome encountered in the wilderness, but in none of these works is the dragon attacking or even remotely threatening the saint; they are merely there. In one of the Jacopo Bellini drawings, there is a crouched dragon at the base of a steep slope hissing at a wolf or jackal that is looking down at it from the top of of the hill. In no instance does Jerome seem particularly aware of the proximity to him of any of these dragons.

Millard Meiss observed that dangerous, predatory beasts, such as dragons, were used by Jacopo Bellini in his wilderness scenes around the penitent Jerome, but that they tend to disappear from later versions of the theme.[60] In Giovanni Bellini's relatively tame and benign landscapes, these beasts are replaced by rabbits and deer; the same is true for the painters of his immediate circle—Cima, Titian, and others.

While they are not positively identifiable as dragons, mention may be made of two smallish, fighting reptilians in Hieronymus Bosch's *Saint Jerome in Penitence* in Venice (fig. 109). It is a little surprising that the dragon seems to have made no appeal to an artist like Bosch, who could have done so much with it in his nightmarish visions.

60. For a compendium of dragon meanings, most of which are not directly pertinent to Jerome, see Charbonneau-Lassay, pp. 391–401, and Lieselotte Stauch, "Drache," cols. 342–66.

The Duck

In religious iconography the duck is quite unimportant, although it did have attached to it at times the concept of constancy and of adoration, as exemplified by reverential genuflection.[61] The idea of constancy[62] was an outgrowth of the duck's use as a symbol of Penelope, the paragon of the "virtuous wife," as explained in the chapter on *Saint Jerome in Penitence* by Hieronymus Bosch (p. 144). Bosch's painting is the only instance to my knowledge in which the duck has been employed symbolically in the Jerome context. The Penelope, or "faithful wife," connotation of the duck may contain in it some vestige of the archaic "mother duck" symbolism described by Werner Danckert ("Mutter Ente"), but this is hardly demonstrable.

Ducks (not readily identifiable to species) occur in a small number of other paintings of the saint, but in them they have no particular, discernible connotation. The instances of their occurrence are as follows: Gentile Bellini, *Saint Jerome in Penitence* (Toledo, Ohio, fig. 26); Jacopo Bellini attribution, *Saint Jerome in Penitence*, which contains three birds, either white ducks or swans (scale is no help here) in the water in the lower-right part of the composition; Bosch, *Saint Jerome in Penitence* (Ghent, fig. 108); Diana, *Saint Jerome in Penitence* (Middlebury, Vt.); Marco Meloni, *Saint Jerome in Penitence* (formerly in Silberman Coll., Vienna); Perugino, *Crucifixion with Saint Jerome and Saint Christopher* (Rome); and Piero di Cosimo, drawing of *Saint Jerome in Penitence* (New York).[63]

In all of these the ducks are used merely as casual bits of naturalism, as they swim about on little ponds or streams—except in the Gentile Bellini, where they are on the dry ground.

61. Herbert Friedmann, "Two Paintings by Botticelli in the Kress Collection," p. 120.

62. McCulloch, p. 113.

63. Jacob Bean and Felice Stampfle, *Drawings from New York Collections: I. The Italian Renaissance*, p. 20, no. 4.

The Eagle (and the Falcon and the Hawk)

Eagles, falcons, and hawks are unfortunately not represented with specifically identifiable certainty in the fourteen Jerome pictures in which they have been noted. On the whole, when they convey an impression of large size they are probably eagles; when they seem small or without particularly fierce expressions, they are probably hawks or falcons. Actually, the terms are not sharply defined in common usage. One of the factors that increases the difficulty in distinguishing between the birds is the general disregard for relative size on the part of many of the artists who created the paintings. It is still less possible to tell falcons from hawks; in the usage of those terms in ornithology, falcons tend to be swifter fliers with narrower, more pointed wings, their other distinguishing characteristics not being externally visible generally. So similar are they in art that I would hesitate to distinguish one from the other except in armorial designs where the official wording might tend to identify them explicitly.

The fourteen pictures containing one or more of these birds are all of "Saint Jerome in Penitence," as follows:

Basaiti (Budapest); Basaiti school (fig. 145); three paintings by Giovani Bellini (Washington [fig. 22], London, Florence); a drawing by Jacopo Bellini (fig. 53); two paintings by Cima (London, York); Civerchio attribution (fig. 42); Cranach (fig. 94); Crivelli (fig. 35); Mansueti (fig. 36); Ferrarese, fifteenth century (fig. 148); and a German fifteenth-

Figure 148. *Saint Jerome in Penitence*, Ferrarese, fifteenth century. Washington: National Gallery of Art; A. W. Mellon Collection.

century etching (Schreiber, no. 1535). To these may be added an early-sixteenth-century Brussels tapestry in the San Ildefonso Museum. In the sky, far above and behind the kneeling Jerome, a falcon is attacking a heron, a motif that occurs in a few other pictures, such as Domenico Veneziano's *Adoration of the Magi* (Berlin: Staatliche Museen) and Carpaccio's *Young Knight in Landscape* (Lugano: Rohoncz Collection). In the tapestry, there is a second falcon flying away from the combatants. It is not clear if the fighting falcon and heron have any meaningful relationship to the penitent Jerome in the lower foreground. The motif of an aerial encounter between a falcon and a heron is used to illustrate an emblem titled *Exitus in dubio est* ("the result is in doubt")[64]—not a thought particularly pertinent to either the Adoration of the Magi or to Jerome in penitence.

Bearing in mind the lack of certainty as to the distinction between eagles, falcons, and hawks, it may be said that the birds in the following pictures are "eagles": the Jacopo Bellini (two eagles; the one on a rocky hill top is eating a rabbit it has killed, the other, near the extreme right side of the drawing, is perched with its wings slightly opened as if it had just alighted); Crivelli (one eagle perched on the top of the vertical post of the crucifix); Cranach; and Mansueti. The eagle in the Crivelli predella has a slightly vulturelike profile, but is not to be interpreted as such, although this has been done at least once.[65] The one in the Cranach picture is very heavily, almost stockily, built, and may possibly have been given this appearance to conform to the similarly proportioned harpies next to it. The harpies are greenish in color, the eagle is brownish.

The eagles in the Jacopo Bellini drawing call for some comment, as an ancient Greek tale provides what may be a pertinent classical precedent for them. A Greek coin of about 410 B.C. shows two eagles feeding on a hare. In *Agamemnon*, Aeschylus has Calchas, the soothsayer, interpret this scene as Agamemnon and Menelaus destroying the Trojans, who, by their fecundity, were looked upon as a present and future menace to the Greeks, and had, therefore, to be destroyed. The two Greek princes were, thus, like the eagles, symbols of imperial virtue.[66]

The birds in the other pictures listed above seem to be "hawks" rather than "eagles." They differ among themselves in coloration. Thus, in the Giovanni Bellini in Washington and in the Cima in London they are very dark, almost blackish above, and whitish below; in the Giovanni Bellini picture in Florence and the Ferrarese one in Washington, they are pale brown and more slender; none are identifiable to definite species. The bird in the picture attributed to Civerchio could be either an eagle or a hawk, but it would be pointless to guess.

The eagle, among other creatures, was used as a symbol of Mary, perhaps not very frequently, but with the massive authority of Albertus Magnus behind the practice. He created such a universal symbolism for Mary in his prodigious *Opera omnium*[67] that to modern readers the force of each item may seem less convincing than if each were isolated, but to the composite mentality of the ecclesiastics, who were the formulators and perpetuators of much of symbolic thought and usage, each seemed to support and strengthen the others. Henry Osborn Taylor succinctly expressed the scope of the praise Albertus lavished on the figure of the Virgin: "There is here a whole mythology and a universal

64. Reproduced in Henkel and Schöne, col. 785, after Camerarius.

65. Howe, p. 86

66. Rowland, p. 90.

67. Vol. 20, p. 451.

68. *The Medieval Mind*, vol. 2, p. 461.

69. Boas, p. 96.

70. MacCurdy, pp. 1076–80.

71. *The Bestiary*, p. 138.

72. Wehrhahn-Stauch in Kirschbaum et al., vol. 1, cols. 70–76. Also Charbonneau-Lassay, pp. 71–87; Anselm Salzer, *Die Sinnbilder und Beiworten Mariens in der deutschen Literatur und lateinischer Hymnenpoesie des Mittelalters*, pp. 43–44.

73. Klementine Lipffert, *Symbol-Fibel*, pp. 29–30.

symbolism. Symbolically, Mary is everything imaginable."[68] Albertus wrote: "Maria aquila, quoniam aquila regina volucrum et Maria regina angelorum, contemplativorum et virginum, quae in nido suo, id est, in corde posuit ametystum, videlicet fidem, qua concepit filium dei" ("the eagle symbolizes Mary, for just as the eagle is queen of birds, so Mary is queen of angels, contemplatives, and virgins. She has placed in her nest, which is her heart, an amethyst, that is, faith, with which she conceived the Son of God"). Albertus then goes on to say that the eagle is also a symbol of Christ: "aquila ceteras aves praecellit . . . id est, filiu sui . . ." ("the eagle surpasses the rest of the birds . . . it is Her Son").

The eagle, as a symbol of Christ, was also a Christianized adaptation of its ancient, classical connotation of deity and of royalty. In addition, the eagle represented the messenger of Jove, and, at times, even Jove or Jupiter, as in illustrations of the Ganymede theme. Horapollo informs us that the ancient Egyptian priests used the figure of a hawk when they wished to suggest a king living in retirement and showing no compassion to sinners.[69] With some goodwill, this might possibly be construed as pertinent to Jerome, not as a king but as a "leader," in penitence in the desert (retired from the world of men) and as one whose vitriolic tongue and pen gave little mercy to those whom he considered in error. We have mentioned that in Jacopo Bellini's drawing one eagle is eating a rabbit; inasmuch as the rabbit, or hare, was a symbol of desire, a carnal inclination that Jerome would have condemned, it is conceivable that the eagle there might partake of the nature of the unforgiving, repentant hermit. This is uncertain, but it is possible that Jacopo Bellini might have used the eagle in such an avenging sense.

On the other hand (symbolism is full of "other handedness"), Leonardo da Vinci in his bestiary considered that the eagle stood for magnanimity, because of a legend that it always left some of its prey for lesser birds unable to forage for themselves.[70] And T. H. White, in his bestiary translation, found the accipiter or hawk to have great courage in a small body, and also to be a stern trainer of its young.[71] The eagle was a symbol of the virtuous as well as of the guilty;[72] the falcon was said to be also a symbol of death.[73]

Leonardo also suggested the falcon as an emblem of pride, since, because of its innate haughtiness, it desires to reign alone, and often the falcon is said to be so prideful as to attack even the eagle.

As may be seen, few of all these meanings are especially pertinent to Saint Jerome, and this may account for the relative scarcity of these birds in pictures of any part of his story.

The Fly

The fly has been noted in three pictures of Saint Jerome: Francesco Benaglio's standing figure of the saint (fig. 149); Sano di Pietro's *Saint Jerome in the Wilderness* (fig. 41); and the Joos van Cleve workshop *Saint Jerome in His Study* (Princeton). In the first picture the fly is on Jerome's cloak, just below his left shoulder; in the second it is on a rock at the extreme lower-right corner of the picture, much larger than it would be in nature; in the third it is on the human skull in the saint's

Figure 149. Francesco Benaglio, *Saint Jerome*. Washington: National Gallery of Art; Samuel H. Kress Collection.

chamber. The motif of the fly on a death's head is not uncommon; it often is merely an inconspicuous, additional *memento mori*.[74]

Benaglio's picture is an odd one for Jerome. As Fern R. Shapley correctly noted, were it not for the fact that the artist has painted the name "SS. Hieronymus" at the bottom of the panel, it could easily be taken to represent Saint Anthony Abbot;[75] the usual symbols of Jerome—the lion and the cardinal's hat—are missing, and the crutch is similar to the one usually associated with Anthony Abbot.

The fly was a symbol of the bringers of disease, and also of Beelzebub, the deity of the Philistine city of Ekron. Beel, or Baal, is a name commonly applied to a Semitic local deity;[76] Zebub is a name that appears in the Bible, meaning flies.[77] Jerome was probably aware of the general connection, in the popular mind, of flies with filth and disease, but this is not suggested in Benaglio's picture. We are left with the thought, unsatisfactory as it is in some respects, that all the artist did in depicting the fly on the saint's garb was to repeat an old painter's trick to show how clever, how naturalistically accurate, he could be when he so desired. As Panofsky noted, the illusionistic use of the fly goes back to classical antiquity.[78] In the Narcissus chapter of his *Imagines*, Philostratus described just such an incident of a painter "enamored of verisimilitude."

In the panel by Sano di Pietro, the creatures around the penitent Jerome—three snakes, two scorpions, and a "cimex"-like "insect,"—are all of evil implication. So is the fly, but the reason for its placement far off to the right can only be surmised. It is possible that Sano could not have placed it near the other creatures and still kept it visible without violating relative scale to an unreasonable extent. By placing it off by itself, he could avoid this direct comparison by the viewer. This is, however, purely a surmise; relative scale was frequently ignored by painters.

A. Pigler has interpreted the painted fly as an amulet against the multitude of living flies;[79] in other words, as a talisman against the diseases and death associated with these insects. Pigler gives an admittedly incomplete list of paintings that have one or more flies in them; none of them are of Saint Jerome.

Flies were considered a nuisance in religious services, and in the middle ages the *flabellum* was used to prevent these annoying insects from molesting the celebrant of Mass.

Obviously, the fly is of little direct importance in the iconography of Jerome.

The Fox

A readily identifiable fox occurs in only one version of the Saint Jerome theme, the painting of the saint in penitence by Hieronymus Bosch, in Ghent. The fox, curled up as if asleep, is small and is hidden in the dark at the bottom of the picture (fig. 112) near a figure of a cock. As explained in the discussion of this painting (p. 142), the fox is here a symbol of deceit and of the devil, waiting for the unwary cock to come close enough for the fox to seize it.

The only other instance of an animal that might be thought to have been intended as a fox (and this is uncertain) is in a marble relief by

74. Erwin Panofsky, *Early Netherlandish Painting* (1958 ed.), pp. 488–89.

75. *Paintings from the Samuel H. Kress Collection*, p. 10.

76. William L. Wardle, "Beelzebub," in Encyclopaedia Britannica, ed. 14, vol. 3, p. 313.

77. It is mentioned in Isaiah 7:18; Eccles. 10:1.

78. *Early Netherlandish Painting*, pp. 488–89.

79. In "La Mouche-peinte: Un talisman" (p. 61), A. Pigler writes: "En connaissance des legendes enumerées, l'hypothèse selon laquelle sur les tableux figurant dans la liste la mouche peinte fut appliquée pour servir de talisman contre la multitude de mouches vivants, ne semble pas trop osée."

Mino da Fiesole in the Museo d'Art Industriel, Rome. The possible fox is very faintly carved and is walking off to the right edge of the plaque below, and to the right of the base of Jerome's crucifix. In the area to the right of the crucifix are four long, faintly indicated snakes, and near the base of the crucifix is seated what may have been intended to be the saint's lion, looking up to the figure on the cross, but it could easily pass for a sketchy outline of a small dog in a baying attitude. Finally, to complete the list of oddities, there is a remarkably apelike face peering out of a hole in the ground immediately below the base of the cross. In such a company of uncertainties, the fox, if such it be, is relatively well done.

Anna Jameson identified the sleeping dog in Dürer's 1514 engraving of *Saint Jerome in His Study* as a fox, and wrote that this animal was a symbol of the wisdom or acuteness of the saint![80] This is quite erroneous both in identification and in interpretation. In the old bestiaries the fox was a sign of the devil, with his sly, deceitful ways. In his notebooks Leonardo da Vinci repeated the old story of the fox feigning death, lying with its mouth open and its tongue hanging out, until the curious magpies or jackdaws come close to peck at the tongue, whereupon it suddenly snaps its jaws and bites off their heads.[81]

The fox is obviously of little direct importance in the iconography of Jerome.

80. *Sacred and Legendary Art*, p. 291.

81. MacCurdy, p. 1077; Camerarius (lv, lvi).

The Frog

The frog was rarely included in renditions of the Jerome cycle, but it has been noted in seven pictures of Jerome in penitence, and in one sculptural decoration (not demonstrably connected with Jerome alone), as follows:

Bastiani school (fig. 145), a painting quite full of animals of several kinds in which two frogs occur at the edge of the water in the background; in the Gentile Bellini painting (Toledo, Ohio, fig. 26), the frog is somewhat blurred and indistinct, in the lower-right foreground; in the Bosch (Venice), a frog is in the base of a hollow column decorated with sun worship and other pagan (sinful) themes (see p. 154; fig. 109); an engraving by Master P. W. of Cologne has a frog on the ground near the lion in the lower-right corner; in Parenzano's *Christ Bearing the Cross*, with Jerome in penitence on the right and Augustine in prayer on the left, a lion, a frog, and two snakes are near the kneeling Jerome; in a painting by Romanino (Brescia), Jerome's lion is looking at a frog at bottom center; in Tura's painting (frontispiece), the frog is caught in the talons in the owl; and Anton Pilgrim's pulpit of the Church Fathers (Vienna, St. Stephen's Cathedral, fig. 150) is reached by winding stairs whose balustrade is covered with carved frogs in single file, but toward the top the frogs are replaced by lizards and snakes. Anton Macku informs us that the frogs, as inhabitants of the swampy areas, appear only on the lower half of the flat surface of the balustrade. There are lizards and snakes in the upper part, and an alert dog is at the very end. Inasmuch as all four of the Church Fathers are represented by half-length figures on the sides of the pulpit, it is not possible to say if the procession

Figure 150. Anton Pilgram, balustrade, pulpit of the Church Fathers. Vienna: St. Stephen's Cathedral. Photo by Wolfgang Feil, Innsbruck.

of the frogs, lizards, and snakes is meant to be connected more with one or another of these men. Macku merely refers to the frogs as symbols of evil.[82]

During the long, but intermittent, use of the frog in religious art, it has usually been an evil creature; but it did have other connotations as well. Where the toad was distinguished from the frog, that creature was even more of a wicked, sinful animal. However, the reappearance of frogs in the ponds in the spring, with their constant noise, made them, like the swallows, signs of spring and symbols of the Resurrection, quite a turnabout from the usual implication of Vice and of Satan.[83] Pliny noted that frogs died in the winter and were born again in the spring. Angelo de Gubernatis added that Christ was resurrected amid the noise of, among other things, the croaking of frogs announcing the coming summer.[84] The frog as a resurrection symbol, "resurrectio carnis," has been described by Nicolaus Reusner, who wrote, "vere nova remeat sub bruma

82. "Zur Symbolik an Pilgrams Kanzel des Wiener Stephansdomes."

83. Charbonneau-Lassay, pp. 819–28.

84. *Zoological Mythology*, vol. 2, p. 373.

rana sepulta; mortuus in vitam sic redit alter homo" ("truly, the frog buried under a (deep) winter returns; thus the dead human being will return to life as another human being").[85]

A frog and a butterfly, both obviously as symbols of resurrection, occur below the figure of Saint Francis in the Master of Saint Serverin's *Stigmatization of Saint Francis* in the Wallraf-Richartz Museum, Cologne.

In connection with the "Resurrection" meaning, the frog became a sexual symbol as well, related to the stork (the bird of birth), and was sometimes considered an attendant, or servant, of Gabriel.[86]

In its more usual, evil meanings, the frog was a reminder that one of the plagues visited upon Egypt was a shower of frogs (Exodus 8). Dante went so far as to liken frogs to heretics,[87] and, in one of his "table talks," Martin Luther considered frogs as signs of his Catholic opponents.[88] This may have been based on the old statement (Apocalypse 16:13) that spirits of devils in the form of frogs issued from the mouths of false prophets.

An early sixteenth-century Netherlandish artist, Colijn de Coter, in a painting of "The Damned," from a *Last Judgment* (Cologne Museum), placed a frog on the right breast of a nude woman standing in flames with various demons and other lost souls around her.

Frogs also figured in emblems as deformed, defective, or brazenly impudent men.[89]

In its connection with the story of Saint Jerome the frog is basically a creature of evil, but its connection and its use are slight.

85. *Emblemata Nicolai Reusner.*

86. Wertheim Aymes, *Hieronymus Bosch*, p. 83.

87. R. Holbrook, *Dante and the Animal Kingdom*, pp. 211–14. In his discussion of the nature of Dante's usage, Holbrook implies that the source in this case goes back to Rabanus Maurus.

88. Bainton, p. 67.

89. Giehlow, p. 219.

The Genet

The genet, a southern European catlike carnivore, the *Genetta genetta* of the zoologists, has been found in only two paintings of the Jerome cycle: Jacopo Bellini's *Saint Jerome in Penitence* in Verona (fig. 29) and Carpaccio's *Burial of Saint Jerome* in Venice. In the first picture the genet is near the lower-right corner, just above (behind) the dragon; in the second it is tethered to a palm tree in the background. In another picture of Carpaccio's Jerome series, *Jerome Leading the Lion Back to the Monastery*, there is an animal that has, at times, been mentioned as a genet, but which seems to me, poorly drawn as it is in this picture, just as likely, if not more so, to be an otter! (See p. 272.)

The genet apparently has no definite symbolic meaning, and is merely an element of the dangerous fauna of the saint's wilderness retreat, an aspect of the desolate area emphasized more by such early Renaissance artists as Jacopo Bellini than by later painters.

It may be mentioned that the rendition of Bellini's beast is not so good as to make the identification more than "probable." There are two other spotted cats that have to be considered, the civet and the serval. The large ears Jacopo has given his animal would tend to rule out the civet, and the generally dusky color in which the spots are somewhat concealed suggests the genet rather than the serval.

The Goldfinch

This colorful and familiar bird of Europe was a very frequently used symbol of the Passion of Christ and of the Resurrection in hundreds devotional paintings. In the early years of the Renaissance it became a substitute version of the classical "charadrius," and as such was much employed as an antiplague symbol in art.[90] Inasmuch as Saint Jerome was deeply concerned with the religious meanings it encompassed, the goldfinch is certainly not out of place with him.

One of the reasons the goldfinch came to symbolize the Passion of Christ was that it has some red feathers on the sides of its head, which caused it to be identified as one of the small birds that tried to extract the thorns from the brow of Christ and became stained by His blood. In the *Legenda aurea*, Jerome's sanctity is explained, "per puritatem et sanguine tinctus per dominicae passionis meditatione" ("through his purity and on account of his being tinged by blood through meditation of the Passion of our Lord.").[91] This suggests a great symbolic affinity between Jerome and the goldfinch, but the little bird did not enter into the saint's iconography to any great extent. It has been noted in only seven paintings, much less than one percent of all pictures dealing with Jerome. The seven are:

Altdorfer's *Saint Jerome in Penitence* (fig. 76), in which there are two goldfinches near the pool in the lower-right corner, one of them drinking from it; Carpaccio's *Meditation on the Passion of Christ* (fig. 32), but here, the goldfinch does not refer especially to Jerome, seated at the left side of the painting, but to the main theme of the composition; Joos van Cleve workshop's *Saint Jerome in His Study* (Cambridge, Mass.) has the goldfinch in a small cage in the upper part of the picture (any small bird in a cage symbolized the soul confined in the body, a meaning additional to the specific connotation of the goldfinch); Dürer's *Saint Jerome in the Wilderness* (Raveningham Hall); Filippo da Verona's *Saint Jerome in the Wilderness*; Pier Francesco Sacchi's *Saint Jerome, Saint Martin and the Beggar, and Saint Anthony Abbot*; and Sellaio's *Saint Jerome in Penitence* (Paris), which is the only one of Sellaio's many versions of this theme that includes a goldfinch—evidence that the artist felt no direct or demanding pertinence of the bird to the subject.

It has been mentioned that the little goldfinch came to "absorb" the connotation of spiritual judge and of resurrection from the "charadrius" of classical legend. Saint Jerome was aware of the legend, since he wrote of it in his commentaries on Aelian.[92] It would be convenient to assume that this might "explain" the presence of the goldfinch in these pictures, but we have no real evidence that the artists involved connected that bird with its ancient predecessor in its symbolic content. However, van Cleve's inclusion of a caged goldfinch in his Cambridge picture may suggest such knowledge. For a comparable, but wholly independent example, although dealing with a different saint, we may recall Bartolome Bermejo's *Saint Isidore of Seville* in Chicago.[93]

90. Friedmann, *The Symbolic Goldfinch*, esp. pp. 7–35.

91. Jacobus de Voragine, *Legend aurea* (Graesse ed.), p. 653.

92. Aldrovandus, vol. 3, bk. 20, chap. 76, pp. 536–37.

93. Friedmann, "Bartolome Bermejo's 'Episcopal Saint,'" esp. pp. 9–12. For a fuller discussion of the caged bird motif, not necessarily a goldfinch, see Ingvar Bergström, "Den fångne fågeln."

The guineafowl, the *Numida meleagris* of the ornithologists, is an African bird that was known to the Romans and was introduced into Europe as a semidomestic fowl in the sixteenth century from Guinea in western Africa, whence its common name. It was considered unusual enough to be included among other live creatures presented around 1516 by King Emmanuel of Portugal to Pope Leo X.[94] Emmanuel may have gotten the guineafowl from western Africa in the course of his missionary enterprises there. However, in spite of the assumed West African source of the birds, the old Italian name for them was "gallina de faraone," or "Pharaoh's chicken," which suggested an Egyptian source, or possibly a subsequent reinterpretation of the bird as something connected with the ever mysterious, and significant, ancient culture of Egypt.

The guineafowl has been noted in only six pictures of the Jerome cycle, all by Venetian artists: Basaiti, *Saint Jerome in the Wilderness* (Baltimore); Gentile Bellini, *Saint Jerome in Penitence* (fig. 26); Carpaccio, *Meditation on the Passion of Christ* (fig. 32); Catena, *Saint Jerome in the Wilderness* (fig. 151); Catena, *Saint Jerome in His Study*

The Guineafowl

94. Howe, p. 78, fn.

Figure 151. Vincenzo Catena, *Saint Jerome in the Wilderness*. Baltimore: Walters Art Gallery.

(Frankfurt am Main); and Mansueti, *Saint Jerome in the Wilderness* (formerly in Arthur Hughes Coll.).

Guineafowl occur in a fair number of other religious paintings, again chiefly by Venetian artists, but the loci of their appearance give no clue as to their special meaning (if any). The bird was equated symbolically by Millard Meiss with the gray heron in Giovanni Bellini's *Saint Francis* in the Frick Collection, New York.[95] The heron was correctly interpreted as conveying the idea of righteousness, and possibly of penitence, and the equation would suggest that these connotations also applied to the guineafowl—but no documentation in support of this was there given, or is known to me.

In connection with the Catena picture in Baltimore, it may be noted that in another, quite similar work (London) the guineafowl is replaced by a partridge, which suggests a possible similarity in symbolism. The partridge (see p. 282 ff.) was a symbol of the devil, in Jerome's own words, and later was modified into an emblem of the "ultimate triumph of truth."

The guineafowl is of little direct importance in the iconography of Jerome, a conclusion in keeping with the absence of special meanings associated with the bird, as reported by Joan Barclay Lloyd.[96]

The Harpy

Of all the hundreds of artists who depicted parts of the Jerome story, only one, Lucas Cranach the Elder, brought the harpy into the Hieronymite iconography, and he did so only once, in one out of the nine renditions (paintings and graphics) he made of that theme, a painting in the Tiroler Landesmuseum, in Innsbruck (fig. 94). As noted in the chapter on this artist, Cranach knew of the harpy through his awareness of Konrad von Megenberg's *Das Buch der Natur*.

Harpies are a legacy of ancient Hellenic mythology: cruel, rapacious, eaglelike birds with human heads. In Greek literature and art, and, by derivation, in Latin literature, harpies were sirens with women's faces and voices, luring with their singing such mariners as came their way; the best known being Ulysses and his crew in Homer's *Odyssey*. Once the harpies had succeeded in capturing their victims they starved them cruelly and eventually destroyed them. They were malicious, selfish, and destructive, with no redeeming virtues whatever. Still, Virgil was content merely to describe them as birds with women's faces, with no comment on the nature of their characters.[97]

The evil connotation of the harpies persisted for many centuries. Thus, Isidore of Seville, writing in the seventh century, informs us that the church considered them as harlots, as symbols of worldly enticement luring their victims away from the paths of rectitude and proper conduct.[98] It was not until about half a millennium later that they became changed into contrite mourners repenting their earlier crimes. Examples of this surprisingly altered conception of them in late medieval literature are the accounts given in such completely unconnected works as John Gower's *Confessio Amantis* in fourteenth-century England and Konrad von Megenberg's *Das Buch der Natur* in fifteenth-century Germany. It is a remarkable instance of a reversal of meaning in an icon borrowed by

95. *Giovanni Bellini's St. Francis in the Frick Collection*, pp. 22–23.

96. *African Animals in Renaissance Literature and Art*.

97. *Aeneid* 3. (trans. C. Day Lewis, 1961), pp. 210 ff.

98. *Originum sive etymologiarum*, bk. 20, pp. xi, 3, 31.

one civilization from an earlier one that in Christian usage the harpies became symbols of remorse and repentance for their cruel and bestial acts. This transformation, recounted in considerable detail by Ferdinand Piper, went even further: the harpies eventually becoming symbols of penitent Christian souls that had been cleansed and purified through baptism.[99]

In the writings of the Christian moralizers the ancient Homeric story was reinterpreted. In their commentaries the figure of Ulysses tied to the mast (by his own command to prevent him from following the enticing sirens) was considered as a variant version of Christ on the cross; the ship was the church and the earwax that plugged the ears of the crew to save them from hearing the temptation of the harpies' songs was a symbol of the Scriptures, protecting them from the lust of the flesh, portrayed by the harpies, as told in the *Speculum ecclesiae* of Honorius of Autun, especially the "Dominica in Septuagesima."[100] Honorius informs us that the harpies were three in number (there are three large birds, only two of which have human faces, in Cranach's Innsbruch picture), that they all had the faces of women (only one in Cranach's painting), and the wings and sharp, cruel talons of powerful birds of prey. They lived on a little island, which Honorius explains represented the scene of earthly joy and pleasure, constantly disturbed by pain, just as the island's shore was ever menaced by the erosive action of surf and waves. The surrounding sea, according to Honorius, represented his own tempestuous time with its stormy restlessness caused by unceasing winds of trial and hardship.

In Cranach's picture, the harpies as symbols of penitence are not out of place with the figure of Jerome, although they seem a little contrived in this connection, as if they were there as a vague reference to the saint's old interest in classical literature, as well as his more immediate concern with redemption.

While the figure of the harpy came to European Christian art from classical sources, the ancient Greeks were not alone in having such a creature. Thus, in an old Egyptian papyrus of unknown period, there is an outline sketch of Ani and his wife Tuta, standing on the roof of their tomb, each shown as a large bird with, respectively, a male and a female human head.[101] In ancient Egyptian art, much earlier than Greek and Roman usage, birds with human heads—harpies in form but not in spirit —were merely "soul-birds," as in the carved relief from the tomb of Amen-em-eret at Memphis (now in the Egyptian Museum, Munich). In a sense, it may be said that the harpies began as innocently as they ended, but they had a long period of wickedness in classical and early medieval culture. The harpies in medieval Islamic art are quite different, in aspect and in connotation, having crowns and necklaces and diadems of pearls, and usually with spirally curled volutes at the ends of their wings.[102]

99. Piper (*Mythologie und Symbolik der christlichen Kunst von der ältesten Zeit bis ins sechzehnte Jahrhundert*, p. 385) credits the use of the harpy as a symbol of the soul saved through baptism to a certain Abbe Voisin.

100. In Migne, *Patrologia Latina*, vol. 172, col. 855-57. Rowland (p. 140) gives a convenient summary of this material.

101. Illustrated in White, p. 25-27; source not indicated.

102. Eva Baer, *Sphinxes and Harpies in Medieval Islamic Art*.

The Hawfinch

This thick-billed finch, the *Coccothraustes* of the ornithologists, or what looks like a fair attempt to represent one, occurs in a single painting including Saint Jerome, by a minor sixteenth-century Lombard arist, Pier Francesco Sacchi. The picture, *Saint Jerome, Saint Martin and the Beggar, and Saint Anthony Abbot*, in Berlin, shows Jerome seated at an improvised table, quill in hand, with his head turned to the right to talk to Anthony Abbot, while on the ground near him are a lion, a snake, a goldfinch, and a probable hawfinch.

So far as I know, the hawfinch carried no particular symbolic meaning; any small bird could be a symbol of the soul, but this alone would hardly qualify it for a meaningful place in the faunal iconography of Jerome.

The Heron

As noted under "crane," it is often very difficult to distinguish between herons, cranes, and storks in old paintings, especially in ones in which a long-legged, long-necked, and long-billed wading bird is pictured in the background as a small, distant object. Three kinds of herons have been used in European religious art: the large gray heron, *Ardea cinerea*; the white egret, *Casmerodius albus*; and the least bittern, *Ixobrychus minutus*. Of these, the latter two occur within the Jerome context; the egret occurs in two paintings by Hieronymus Bosch (Ghent and Venice, figs. 108, 109), in one by a member of Bastiani's studio, and in an early sixteenth-century Brussels tapestry (San Ildefonso Museum). The bittern occurs only once, in a painting by the "school of Bosch" (Bruges). In Perugino's *Crucifixion with Saint Jerome and Saint Christopher*, there are two small herons near Christopher. It is not clear if they are thematically attached to him or to Jerome.

Herons are of slight pertinence to the Jerome theme, as may be sensed from their scarcity in the art built up around him. As mentioned in the chapter on the two penitent Jeromes by Bosch (p. 148), the heron was supposed to be very constant in its diet and not easily tempted by strange foods, a legend that permitted a moralized interpretation as a faithful believer who paid no attention to alien teachings.[103] In this symbolic capacity the heron is not out of place with Jerome, who had his own problems with discarding his love of classic, pagan Roman authors, and concentrating on the texts of the Scriptures. This meaning of one "steadfast in the correct path," is roughly in agreement with Meiss's interpretation of the gray heron in Bellini's *Saint Francis* as referring to the souls of the elect or to ideas of righteousness or penitence.[104]

The Hoopoe

The hoopoe, with its prominent crest and its bright brick-orange and black plumage, is one of the most strikingly patterned of European birds, and is, consequently, readily identified in art even though some artists took considerable liberties when depicting it. It figures but slightly in the Jerome context, where it has been noted in only five pictures—four paintings and one engraving: Cranach's *Saint Jerome in Penitence* (Innsbruck, fig. 94), in which the artist, who was interested in natural history, nevertheless improvised his hoopoe to the extent of giving it pendulous wattles, which the real bird does not have, and placing it high up in a tree, while in reality it is largely terrestrial; Cornelius Cort's engraving of Jerome in a landscape, said to be after Titian; Diana's penitent Jerome (Middlebury, Vt.), in which it is not really clear if the bird, perched on a rail fence near the water, is meant to be a hoopoe or a kingfisher, but I

103. Evans, *Animal Symbolism*, p. 148.

104. *Giovanni Bellini's St. Francis in the Frick Collection*.

105. *Etimologias*, bk. 12, chap. 7, p. 66.

106. White, pp. 131, 150.

107. Aelian, *De natura animalium*, XVI; iii, 23; x, 16. See also W. Houghton, *Gleanings from the Natural History of the Ancients*, pp. 207–10.

"place" it as a hoopoe because of the large size of its crest and because it seems to have bands of lighter and darker color on its folded wings and body; Marco Meloni's *Saint Jerome in Penitence* (Vienna); and Bartolomeo Montagna's *Saint Jerome in Meditation* (Bergamo, fig. 37).

The hoopoe is a bird of contrary legendary implications, not all seemingly pertinent to its occurrence in the iconography of Jerome, but which may be outlined briefly. The bird was believed to be most unclean, nesting in filth, in human ordure, and even in graves, where, according to Saint Isidore of Seville, it associates with the demons inhabiting such places.[105] Isidore called it *avis spurcissima*, a most filthy bird, and noted that Jerome had said the same of it centuries earlier. In his thirteenth-century bestiary, Guillaume le Clerc of Normandy called it *un oisel vilaine* for the same reason. In reality, the hoopoe nests in holes in the ground or in tree stumps, where its nest does become fouled because the hoopoe seems to lack the habit, common to many other species, of removing the excrement of the nestlings. Its reputation as a filthy creature goes back to Aristotle, Aelian, and Pliny, all of whom commented on it as a bird that makes its nest of ordure. In his translation of a twelfth-century Latin bestiary, T. H. White noted that the anonymous author claimed that the Greeks named the bird *Upupa* "because it lines its nest with human dung. The filthy creature feeds on stinking excrement. He lives on this in graves. . . . If anybody smears himself with the blood of this bird on his way to bed, he will have nightmares about suffocating devils."[106] The bestiarist does not, however, attempt to explain how the name *Upupa* was supposed to stem from the Greek. However, when Linnaeus, in the middle of the eighteenth century, established his code of zoological nomenclature, he took over the Greek *Upupa* as the generic name of the bird, whose complete name was given as *Upupa epops*.

On the other and brighter side of the picture, the hoopoe was an old symbol of filial devotion and gratitude, a concept that Aelian and other early writers claimed to trace from Egyptian sources.[107] In his translation of Horapollo's *Hieroglyphica*, Boas calls the Egyptian bird of gratitude, "which is really the hoopoe," a stork, "because the Renaissance translators so interpreted it and because the stork was in the sixteenth-century emblem-literature a symbol of filial piety. . . . The gratitude of the hoopoe and the stork is also reported by the Physiologus and by Aelian . . . which shows pretty clearly that little distinction was made between the two birds. Cf. Artemidorus, Oneirocriticon, II, 20."[108]

This alternative identification utilizing two completely dissimilar birds as equally valid interpretations shows how far from naturalistic reality symbolism may carry us. The stork, a black and white wading bird with long legs, bill, and neck, stands as many feet high as the brightly plumaged hoopoe, with short neck and legs, stands inches tall. Of both, the legend relates that when the parents become old and feeble and unable to take care of themselves, their grown offspring, remembering their own youth, feed and preen their aging progenitors. Albertus Magnus states explicitly that when an old hoopoe becomes blind its young anoint its eyes with the herb that opens shut places, and in this way it recovers its sight.[109] Leonardo da Vinci goes even further and informs us that "the virtue of gratitude is said to be found especially in the birds called hoopoes, which being conscious of the benefits they have received

108. Boas, p. 50

109. The most detailed and revealing account of the hoopoe is to be found in Guillaume le Clerc's bestiary, originally written in 1210–1211, translated by George C. Druce. Lines 821–70 are as follows:
"The hoopoe is a horrid bird,
Its nest is not nice and clean
But is made of mud and filth.
But of a very good nature are
The little birds, which are born to it;
For when their parents are grown so old
That they have lost all their strength
For flying and for seeing,
Then their children succour them.
When they see them grown so old
They tear out with their beaks
Their old feathers unceasingly,
Then they warm them soothingly
And cherish them in like manner
As these had done to them before
Until they are restored and fresh
And their sight made clear again
And their feathers well grown.
When they have thus restored them
Well may their children say:
Good father, good mother dear,
Just as in like manner
You have bestowed great care
On us and on our sustenance,
As recompense for such service
Now have we devoted ourselves to you
And rendered kindness for kindness
So that there is nothing misreckoned."

The moral then is given as follows:

"My masters, since this creature,
Which by nature has no reasoning power,
Acts in the way which I have told you,
In what parlous state a man must be,
Who is fully possessed of reason
And who takes no heed to his ways.
Alas, in what evil hour was he born
Who dishonours father and mother,
When he sees them before his eyes
Sick and feeble and old
And yet has no care or thought for them!
How evil a nature has a man
Who has understanding
And hates his father and his mother
And slanders them quite wrongfully.
It were fit that he die violent death!
For God commanded in the law,
Which we must keep faithfully,
That a man should honour father and mother,
And that he should serve and keep them;
And promised that he shall die the death
Who curseth his father or his mother."

from father and mother in life and nourishment, when they see these becoming old make a nest for them and cherish them and feed them, plucking out their old and shabby feathers with their beaks, and by means of certain herbs restoring their sight, so that they return to a state of prosperity."[110] The whole, and somewhat involved, corpus of hoopoe lore has been conveniently brought together by Warren R. Dawson,[111] while the totally dissimilar natural history of the bird has been summarized and well illustrated in a little monograph by Hans Münch.[112]

As far as the Jerome story is concerned, both the hoopoe and the stork are of minor significance, and both were seldom included by artists. Jerome's penitence does have in it concepts of "filial piety" and devotion, but there is little real connection between these thoughts and those expressed in the hoopoe story. The bird has been looked upon as an antithetical emblem to the "paradise bird," the symbolic representation of the contemplative life of piety.[113]

The hoopoe is a Mediterranean-African species; in Europe it occurs chiefly in southern areas from Spain and southern France to Italy, Greece, and Turkey. In Italy it is sometimes called "the little cock of March," is thought to announce the advent of spring, and is also supposed to possess the virtue of divining secrets.[114]

110. MacCurdy, p. 1075.

111. "The Lore of the Hoopoe," pp. 126–142.

112. *Der Wiedehopf.*

113. Charbonneau-Lassay, pp. 428–30.

114. Angelo de Gubernatis, vol. 2, p. 230.

The Jackal

115. It is so identified by Victor Goloubew, *Les Dessins de Jacopo Bellini au Louvre et au British Museum*, pl. xxi.

In one drawing by Jacopo Bellini of Jerome in penitence (Paris, fig. 54), an animal that has been termed a jackal,[115] but might just as readily be looked upon as a wolf, is on a rocky pile looking down at a dragon, which is snarling up at it. The jackal was not found in Europe, but was known to Europeans from Africa, and, so far as I know, had no specific symbolic meaning. It is present in Bellini's drawing merely as one of the dangerous beasts inhabiting the penitent saint's desert home. This is the only instance found of its occurrence in the iconography of Jerome. (*See also* Wolf, pp. 304–5.)

The Jay

The jay, *Garrulus glandarius*, a common and familiar bird of Europe, occurs in only a small number of pictures involving Saint Jerome, and, in them, it is not always close to Jerome either spatially or meaningfully. The six pictures are as follows: Cranach's *Saint Jerome in Penitence* (Innsbruck, fig. 94), in which the jay is hidden in the foliage of a tree top near the upper-left corner of the painting; Andrea di Giusto, *Saint Jerome in the Wilderness* (Montreal, fig. 43); Cornelius Cort, engraving after Titian, of *Saint Jerome in a Landscape*, in which the jay is perched over the entrance to the opening of the little rocky grotto to the left; Romanino, *Madonna and Child with Saint James Major and Saint Jerome* (Atlanta, fig. 152); and two paintings by Sellaio of the penitent Jerome (Paris and Sarasota), in both of which the jay is in flight in the upper part of the picture. Flying jays appear in the sky in numerous paintings of other saints—especially Saint John the Baptist and Saint Francis of Assisi, so the bird was not strictly connected symbolically only with Jerome.

One of the oldest legends about the jay is that the blue feathers on the

Figure 152. Girolamo Romanino, *Madonna and Child with Saint James Major and Saint Jerome*. Atlanta: High Museum of Art; Samuel H. Kress Collection.

wings are luminescent and shine so brightly in the dark that the course of the bird's wanderings can be followed by the glowing of its plumage. The concept of the jay as a source of light makes one wonder if this may have recommended it as suitable for the iconography of the saints mentioned above; if so, however, no one seems to have taken the trouble to record the fact. Precedence for such argument is indicated by the reference of Saint Isidore of Seville to the jay as a creature that sheds light on the road,[116] an idea he took over from Pliny, who informs us that in "the Hercynian forest of Germany we have heard there are strange birds whose feathers shine like fire in the night."[117]

This legend is repeated in the twelfth-century bestiary translated by T. H. White;[118] and is echoed in a much later poem by Robert Chester titled "Love's Martyr," which, as edited by Grosart, goes as follows:

The gentle birds called the faire Hircinie,
Taking the name of that place where they breed,
Within the night they shine so gloriously
That mans astonished senses they do feed:
For in the dark being cast within the way
Gives light unto the man that goes astray. [119]

116. *Etimologias*, bk. 12, p. 310.

117. Arthur Rackam, *Pliny, Natural History*, vol. 10, p. 132.

118. White, p. 130.

119. Percy Ansell Robin, *Animal Lore in English Literature*, pp. 171–72.

According to an old French legend, the jay was the bird which, by its cries, betrayed the presence of Jesus in the Garden of Olives, and in atonement for this treachery it has suffered apoplectic strokes every Friday since then.[120] However, the legend goes on to add that the jay is an omen or a foreboding of good times to come! Just how these two contradictory meanings are to be combined is not explained. Albertus Magnus credited the jay with the ability to imitate other voices, including that of man, which may be connected with the French legend of its betraying calls.[121] Albertus also wrote that the jay sometimes becomes so enraged that it hangs itself on a branched tree, and so dies. There is nothing that connects this excess of feeling with its penal apoplexy, but one cannot help but wonder if these two are somehow connected in a legend not yet rediscovered.

Further implication of evil in the jay is given by the fourteenth-century English poet John Gower, whose poem *Vox clamantis* reflects the panic he felt at the uprising of the peasants in 1381. In it one character, Wat Tyler, in the form of a jay, addresses the rebellious beasts, urging them to allow honor, law, and virtue to perish, "Arson, murder, and rapine reign, until the jay is slain."[122]

The jay was singled out in Italian folklore because of its great fondness for acorns; its common Italian name, ghiandaia, and its German equivalent Eichen-häher, or Nuss-häher, refer to this diet. This fondness for such food is connected with the jay's supposedly great ability to learn. Pliny wrote that people deny that some pies (magpies) are able to learn, "save those belonging to the group which feed on acorns. . . . The jay is said to live more on acorns than any other bird."[123]

To recapitulate, the jay did have implications of being a source of light, and of being able to learn, two positive virtues that could make it symbolically suitable in the iconography of Jerome, but only in a rather mild, corroborative way. This lack of direct applicability, together with its scarcity in the Jerome ambience, points to its being of only slight importance in this connection.

The most detailed and realistically accurate jay in any painting including Jerome is in Romanino's fine altarpiece (fig. 152). In his catalogue of the Kress Collection in Atlanta, Wilhelm E. Suida erroneously referred to the bird as a pigeon.[124]

120. These legends are cited, without reference to source, by Eugene Rolland, *Faune populaire de France*, vol. 10, p. 8.

121. In A. Borgnet's edition of *Animalium*, vol. 12, p. 489.

122. Klingender, p. 373.

123. Cited by A. H. Evans in his edition of Turner's opus of 1544, the earliest book on birds by an Englishman.

124. *Italian Paintings and Northern Sculpture from the Samuel H. Kress Collection*, p. 35.

The Kingfisher

The kingfisher is included in this Bestiary solely on the strength of a description of a picture once attributed to Cima in which it is written that near the orant figure of Saint Jerome there are a number of creatures —a stag, two partridges, a lizard, and one kingfisher—on a rocky ledge by a pool, and a second one flying off with a fish in its bill.[125] So far as I have been able to trace this painting, formerly (1912) in the collection of Major Kennard, in London, it is probably the same as one now attributed to Basaiti in the Budapest Museum of Fine Arts. The photograph supplied by that institution does not show the birds clearly enough for certain identification, but they may be kingfishers. No other identifiable or inferential kingfishers have been noted in Hieronymite art.[126]

The kingfisher was identified in legend with the fabled bird halcyon—the "halcyon" (or kingfisher) days when the seas were so calm and peaceful that these birds nested on the quiet waves. Inasmuch as peacefulness—*tranquillitas*—is a concept deeply involved in the theme of "Saint Jerome in His Study," it is puzzling that the kingfisher was not used as a symbol in any representation of that theme. The halcyon bird might have been expected to play a similar role in connection with pictures of Jerome in meditation or in prayer, but, aside from the one painting mentioned above, it has not been found in them. The halcyon was also connected with the story of the Pleiades, a disguised reference to which (not involving kingfishers, however) occurs in two pictures of "Jerome in His Study" by Lucas Cranach (see p. 130).

Otherwise, the absence of the kingfisher from the iconography of Jerome can only suggest that it was little connected by the artists and their advisers with the story of the saint. There is, therefore, no need to review here the great mass of literature about the halcyon, or alcyone. It seems that the inclusion of two kingfishers in one relatively minor Venetian painting was hardly more than a reflection of current interest in the world of nature.[127]

125. Howe, p. 82. While this author probably knew the little European kingfisher, and may well have been correct in his identification, his book is so full of zoological errors that by itself it cannot be taken as proof. The photograph, although not too clear in this detail, does seem to corroborate his statement.

126. See, however, the remarks under "Hoopoe" on a painting attributed to Diana.

127. Charbonneau-Lassay (pp. 556–57) notes the kingfisher as a symbol of Christ and His Church. Lipffert (p. 27) considers this bird to be a symbol of the Resurrection, but gives no documentation.

The Lion

The lion occurs in the great majority (more than three-quarters) of all paintings, graphics, and sculptures representing Saint Jerome in the wilderness, either meditating, reading, or praying in his penitential solitude. It also occurs in more than half of all renditions of the saint in his study chamber. The beast is to be found in many, if not the majority, of representations of Jerome's last communion and of his death, as well as in more than half of other compositions in which Jerome is shown, either by himself as a formal, hieratic figure of a great Church Father, or as one of the attendant, lateral figures in conventional altarpieces, especially in those created after the first years of the fifteenth century. In his pioneering survey, Adolfo Venturi commented on the absence of lions in trecento paintings of Saint Jerome,[128] but we may now reappraise that statement in the light of present knowledge, which has increased greatly since Venturi's time. The lion is certainly far from numerous in these early paintings, but it is to be found in not a few of them. Thus, we may note at least two early Veneto-Byzantine pictures of Jerome extracting the thorn from the lion's paw, one in the National Gallery, London, and one in the David and Albert Smart Gallery, Chicago (fig. 19), and these suggest a still earlier, as yet undiscovered, probably wholly Byzantine model as a source. Further, we may cite a polyptych by Jacopino da Bologna in the picture gallery of Bologna; in its extreme right panel Jerome is shown removing the thorn from the lion's foot. Another early Bolognese triptych, *Madonna and Child with Saints* by Simone dei Crocifissi (fig. 153), also shows Jerome similarly engaged.

Although the first great impetus to portray Jerome with his lion arose in Bologna, the idea was not wholly local. There were statues of the saint

128. *L'arte e San Girolamo.*

Figure 153. Simone dei Crocifissi, Jerome with the lion, a detail from *Madonna and Child with Saints.* Athens: University of Georgia, Georgia Museum of Art; Kress Study Collection.

with his lion in Germany and France early in the fourteenth century, and in Italy the idea quickly spread. In the third quarter of the fourteenth century, Giovanni del Biondo painted a large standing figure of Saint Jerome with his lion at his feet (Florence, high altar of Santa Croce). The early marble relief of *Saint Jerome in His Study* (extracting the thorn from the lion's paw) by Jacopo della Quercia (fig. 18) is said to have been derived from a still earlier predella relief by an unidentified Sienese sculptor, now in the cathedral of Siena. The list of trecento versions of Jerome with his lion could be extended, but these may suffice to show that the inclusion of the lion was far from unknown prior to 1400. Emil Mâle went so far as to write that the saint could hardly be imagined without his lion, "the faithful companion the Middle Ages had given him in his solitude."[129]

In his book on Saint Jerome (written about 1342) that started the popularity of the saint in art, Giovanni Andrea said that he wanted him to be shown with his tame lion. The fact that the lion was absent more often than present in paintings of Jerome done in the second half of the fourteenth century suggests that Andrea's work took some time to make its impact felt. Actually, in trecento Italian art the Jerome theme was relatively uncommon, with or without the lion. In the many hundreds of paintings produced in that century in Venice and its immediate surroundings, listed and illustrated by Rodolfo Palluchini,[130] there are only four of Jerome as a formal, standing figure of a Doctor of the Church, only one of him seated in his study, and a single instance of him extracting the thorn from the lion's foot. The last is the Veneto-Byzantine London picture already mentioned. One of the others, the *Saint Jerome in His Study* by Tomaso da Modena (hardly a Venetian painter), includes a lion (fig. 11). Palluchini does not mention the same artist's *Jerome Healing the Lion*. The other paintings he lists are four full-length Jeromes with no lions, by Jacobello Alburegno, Nicoletto Semitecolo, Lorenzo Veneziano, and Jacobello di Bonomo.

The pictorial composition of "Saint Jerome in the Wilderness," showing the saint either quietly sitting, reading, meditating, or in the act of penitence, kneeling in prayer and beating his chest with a stone in front of a crucifix, appeared for the first time in Florence in the early years of the quattrocento. Artists were quick to incorporate the lion in their renditions of this topic. As noted earlier, Millard Meiss has suggested that this theme was probably inspired by the penitential hermits of the Order of Hermits of Saint Jerome.[131] The theme achieved much popularity and became even more widely acclaimed in Venice and northern Italy than in Tuscany, but continued to be in demand there as well, as shown by the large number of quattrocento Florentine and Sienese versions.

The story that brought the lion into the Jerome theme, as presented in the *Legenda aurea*, and its source, the similar tale of Saint Gerasimus in the *Pratum spirituale*, has been given fully in the introductory chapter (pp. 21–22). It is strange that the vast number of reproductions in various art media give a somewhat erroneous transcript of the legend. In the great majority of those that show the incident of the actual extraction of the thorn from the lion's foot, it is Jerome who is doing it, although the legend clearly states that when the lion came limping to the monastery, Jerome calmly waited for it to come closer, and then ordered his frightened monks to be unafraid and to wash the beast's paw, see what was wrong with it, and heal its injury. To have Jerome, rather than one of his assistants, remove the thorn simplified the representation of the incident, but that in itself does not explain the change. It may be that the advent into art of this incident stemmed first, not from the *Legenda aurea*, but

129. *Religious Art from the Twelfth to the Eighteenth Century*, pp. 191–92.

130. *La pittura Veneziana del trecento.*

131. *The Great Age of Fresco*, p. 153.

Figure 154. Nicolás Francés, *Saint Jerome in His Study*. Dublin: National Gallery of Ireland.

from *Hieronymianus* by Giovanni Andrea, who was intent on giving Jerome the credit for the incident and for having artists show him with his tamed lion.

What seems to be one of the rare "correct" representations of the story as given in the *Legenda aurea* is a painting by the Spanish artist Nicolás Francés of *Saint Jerome in His Study*, in Dublin (fig. 154). The saint is shown seated at his table, writing and dictating to three monks. In

Figure 155. *Jerome Legend*, Flemish, fifteenth century. New York: The Pierpont Morgan Library, M. 675.

the lower-left corner of the picture the lion is holding up its paw to another monk, apparently for his attention. Strangely enough, in the catalogue description of this painting, the action has been described as showing one of Jerome's assistants about to take blood from the wound in the beast's foot to use instead of ink in his work as a scribe—a surprising and, so far as I know, unwarranted interpretation, even though given as "according to the legend."[132]

A parallel composition, a painting by an anonymous fifteenth-century French artist, shows a youthful monk extracting the thorn from the lion's foot in the foreground of the picture, while an elderly Jerome sits at a table in the center background, dictating to three monks. This painting is known to me only from a photograph in the Richter Archives (no. 304A:V:95). Another, less certain rendition, by Filippo Lippi, in Altenburg, is discussed in the account of the lioness (p. 253).

The story in the *Legenda aurea* ends with the lion bringing the robber merchants and their caravan and the ass to the monastery. This caused the lion to be restored to its former good grace, and even the penitent thieves were forgiven by Saint Jerome. A version of this episode appears in an early Flemish manuscript illumination (fig. 155). At right in this picture we see the lion, a load of faggots still bound to its body, bringing the ass, the thieves, and their camels to Jerome, who is standing at the door of his monastery. The beast here has ridiculously large and semi-human ears, an indication that the unknown limner had probably never seen a real lion. In a French illumination (fig. 10), there is a quaint, faggot-laden lion with a white-bearded monk. This can hardly be Jerome, who is shown immediately above, on the same sheet, as a thin, beardless penitent appearing before Christ the Judge, with a background of angels, some of them carrying bundles of rods with which to flog him.

132. National Gallery of Ireland, *Centenary Exhibition, 1864-1964* (1964), p. 16, no. 8.

Figure 156. *Legenda aurea*, French, ca. 1300. San Marino, Calif.: Henry E. Huntington Library, HM 3027, f. 136.

Still another illustration of the lion as a bearer of wood before the return of the stolen ass occurs in a painting by the brothers Lorenzo and Jacopo Salimbeni da Sanseverino, at one time in the collection of Dr. Gustav Arens, Vienna.[133] The theme is quite infrequent in art, however.

Inasmuch as the great popularity of the *Legenda aurea* in the late Middle Ages throughout much of western Europe did much to make the Jerome-lion legend widely known, it is interesting to find that, while mentioned in the text, the lion is not included in a miniature illumination in a very early copy of this work. This precious manuscript, done in Paris about 1300, merely shows Jerome and one of his monks standing looking at an ass laden with firewood, but with no guarding lion (fig. 156).

The original legend, concerning Saint Gerasimus, was a little different, chiefly in that it described the daily load of the ass as water from the Jordan, not firewood. This is worth noting, because in a few pictures, as in Baldung's woodcut and in Cranach's Innsbruck painting, Jerome's lion is taking water (drinking) from a stream. This is, however, not the only, or possibly even the primary, thought expressed by the drinking lion. In his eulogistic statements about Saint Jerome, Johann von Neumarkt wrote that the saint was the clear, pure water from whose flow ailing humanity could slake its thirst, a text that may be behind the renditions of Jerome in which his lion is shown drinking.[134]

The lion legend, once transferred to Jerome, is sufficient to explain the ubiquitous lion in renditions of this saint. The transference was, itself, expedited by the fact that the lion was earlier a general symbol of those who retire from the world to the desert, as well as of all who vigil at night, because of the ancient idea that lions keep their eyes open even when asleep. A different, but less likely and unsupported story has been suggested for the inclusion of the lion in the Jerome context. Anna Jameson wrote that the lion was adopted as Jerome's symbol because of his fervid, fiery nature and because of his sojourn in the wilderness, and that it was only later that the legend invented to explain the symbol came to include the incident of the thorn removal.[135]

In her study of the thorn-extraction incident, Grete Ring pointed out that the story was early invested with a moralized lesson.[136] In the *Gesta Romanorum* (tale 104), the thorn-crippled lion was likened to the erring human race, the thorn being considered a symbol of original sin, which, in turn, was drawn out by the redeeming qualities of baptism! In this version of the legend the person involved, while apparently based on Jerome, was transformed into a knightly hero, who is presented to the reader as an agent for the cure of error. This moralized version lends itself to the conclusion that just as Jerome's kind act freed the lion from pain, so too his writings and preachings helped free the human soul from sin. This thought has been explored further by William S. Heckscher, starting with the old, classical sculptures of a youth pulling a spine out of his foot, and going on to the later, moralized, Christian examples of similar healing acts.[137]

The splinter or thorn extraction has figured in the stories of other saints. Aninas, a hermit saint, was said to have lived in a cave with two lions, one of which he similarly treated for a thorn embedded in its foot. Still other, relatively slightly known saints—Mammas, Macarius, John

133. Illustrated in E. Sandberg Vavala, "Story of Jerome: Predella Attributed to the Brothers Salimbeni of San Severino," pp. 95–97.

134. In Joseph Klapper, *Vom Mittelalter bis zur Reformation*, p. 17. Neumarkt's concept that Jerome was the pure water from which mankind could slake its spiritual thirst may not have been unconnected with the fact that at one time a painting of *The Fountain of Living Water*, now lost, hung in the chapel of Saint Jerome in the cathedral of Palencia, Spain. An old supposed copy of this painting was for years in the Hieronymite convent of Our Lady of Parrel, near Segovia (now in the Prado, no. 1511).

135. *Sacred and Legendary Art*, pp. 288–89.

136. "St. Jerome Extracting the Thorn from the Lion's Foot," p. 189.

137. "Dornauszieher," cols. 289–99.

the Silentiary, and Theophanes—are also connected in their legends with lions. The case of Saint Mark is quite different, as his lion was a winged creature, and there is no story that Mark ever extracted a thorn from its foot. Nevertheless, occasionally Jerome and Mark were connected in the minds, or in the eyes, of the unlettered, and were confused or even mistaken for each other because of their lions.[138] Justus Bier noted that in Germany Jerome's lion stemmed historically from the apocalyptic lion of Saint Mark,[139] as is revealed in a relief on the sandstone pulpit in the parish church of Karlstadt, carved in 1523 by an unknown pupil of Tilmann Riemenschneider. In this sculpture Jerome is shown writing on a crude lectern set in an arid, rocky landscape, while at his feet his lion, squatting comfortably, has long, pointed wings extending vertically from its shoulders (fig. 157). Another, similar example may be found in the decorations of the pulpit of the Stadtpfarrkirche in Bozen, carved in 1513–1514.

In support of Bier's contention, it may be noted that occasionally the four Latin Church Fathers were paralleled with the four Evangelists, and that the symbols of the latter were at times bestowed on the former in early Christian art.[140] This may have served to connect Jerome graphically with Saint Mark and his winged lion. Ring has suggested that a medieval scribe, "seeing a picture of Jerome and his animal companion, and not knowing the context, but remembering that the saint had lived for a long time in the desert, the residence of wild beasts, may have invented the fable on the authority of the picture,"[141] but this seems unlikely.

As might readily be anticipated, in the vast number of representations of the Jerome theme there is infinite variety in the size, pose, placement, and degree of naturalistic accuracy in the rendition of the lion by different artists, and even by the same artist in different paintings. Inasmuch as the beast was so closely connected with Jerome that it became an identifying attribute of the saint, there was little or no need in most instances for further symbolic connotation. This is true regardless of the particular rendition in most cases; whether the lion was shown as placid or snarling, quietly lying on the ground or rearing on its hind legs, alert or somnolent.

It is true that the artist either included a lion (usually) or did not, and while the lion portrayed was merely the attribute of Jerome, the fact remains, nevertheless, that the prominence, the size, and the particular pose given to the lion must have been the result of a deliberate decision in the creation of each picture. It so happens that a good number of artists produced many versions of the saint's story, and in no case is there a stereotyped "ready made" lion in all the paintings by the same artist. Bartolomeo di Giovanni, Basaiti, Bastiani, the Bellinis, Catena, Cranach, Dürer, Lotto, Lucas van Leyden, Mantegna, Montagna, Perugino, Sano di Pietro, Sellaio, Titian, and Veronese are only a few of the prominent artists who created numerous pictures of "Saint Jerome in the Wilderness" or "Saint Jerome in His Study." Although they did not invariably include the lion in all their paintings, they did in most of them, and in these the placement, the action, and the pose given the animal vary greatly. It would be foolhardy to attempt to interpret or to read into these diverse renditions particular meanings in most cases, but there are a few that do appear to call for special comment.

138. Ansgar Pöllmann, "Von der Entwicklung des Hieronymus-Typus in der älteren Kunst," p. 501.

139. "Riemenschneider's St. Jerome and Other Works in Alabaster," p. 228. The confusion between Mark and Jerome appears occasionally in a few other pictures, as, for example, the engraving by Crispin van de Passe, titled *Saint Marcus*. If this were untitled it would most probably be assumed to represent "Saint Jerome in His Study," because in it the lion is wingless, and the whole composition seems to derive from Dürer's 1514 masterpiece. No such confusion seems likely in the case of Donato Bragadin's painting *The Lion of Saint Mark between Saint Jerome and Saint Augustine*, in the Palazzo Ducale, Venice, although at first glance one may wonder if the winged lion, here without Mark, may have been intended as Jerome's faithful beast.

140. Karl Künstle, *Ikonographie der christlichen Kunst*, vol. 2, pp. 299–307.

141. "St. Jerome Extracting the Thorn from the Lion's Foot," p. 189.

Figure 157. Riemenschneider follower, *Saint Jerome with a Winged Lion*, 1523. Karlstadt: Parish Church.

Thus, in the chapter on Cosimo Tura's *Saint Jerome in Penitence*, the lion was found to echo the depth of the saint's emotional state (p. 176), and a similar agreement was noted by Meiss in Castagno's fresco, *The Trinity with Saints Jerome, Paula and Eustochium*, in Florence.[142] Further, in Dürer's great engraving of *Saint Jerome in His Study*, the spatially juxtaposed lion and dog may reflect, as suggested (pp. 108–9), the artist's deep desire for a peaceful settlement of the opposing thoughts of the Reformation and the papacy.

Another painting in which the lion may have more than its usual meaning is Jan van Eyck's picture of *Saint Jerome in His Study* (fig. 16)

142. *The Great Age of Fresco*, p. 153.

in the Detroit Institute of Arts. This famous and much discussed work has recently been "read" in persuasive detail by Edwin Hall, who showed that the picture is much concerned with explicit dating by its meticulous rendition of the astrolabe depending from the book shelf in the saint's study.[143] Professor Hall has suggested that the lion may be also a reference to the zodiacal constellation Leo, in addition to its usual role as Jerome's faithful attendant. That this may, indeed, be the case is suggested by the fact that the zodiacal Leo corresponds exactly with the date on the abbreviated astrolabe, on which lack of space forced the artist to omit the zodiacal scale.

To return to the brief list of artists who painted many pictures of the Jerome cycle with widely differing renditions of lions, the first name may be taken as an example. Bartolomeo di Giovanni made at least five such paintings. In some the lion is merely posed near the feet of Jerome, doing nothing in particular, but in one, in the Yale University Art Gallery, the beast is shown actually holding a book open in its front paws (fig. 158). In still another, in the Florentine Academy, the lion is behind Jerome, some distance away from him.

In seven paintings of "Saint Jerome in the Wilderness" by Giovanni Bellini, with greater or lesser studio assistance, the lion is included, but in two others it is left out. In two pictures similar enough so that one (Escorial) has been described as derivative from the other (Brera), Titian showed the lion peacefully somnolent in one and angrily growling in the other. In a third painting (Lugano), Titian repeated the sleeping lion.

The same tendency to treat the lion differently in different renditions is also encountered in sculpture. Alessandro Vittoria, for example, did two full-length standing marble Jeromes for two churches in Venice. In one, S. Maria dei Frari, the reclining lion at the saint's feet has its head raised, looking up at Jerome; in the other, in SS. Giovanni e Paolo, the lion appears to be asleep.

Just as each pose and each placement of the lion resulted from a deliberate decision on the part of the artist, so too must have been the complete omission of the animal in other pictures. Thus Ghirlandajo's famous fresco of *Saint Jerome in His Study* in Florence (fig. 84) is generally assumed to have been influenced by, if not patterned after, the little panel by van Eyck, now in Detroit, but Ghirlandajo has not included the lion, although his "source" has it prominently displayed in the lower part of the painting.

In pictures in which the lion is not included it is unusual to find any other animals with Saint Jerome. There are exceptions to this rule, however. In a painting attributed to Masaccio, with studio assistance, especially by Andrea di Giusto, there is no lion but there are a number of noxious "insects" and a scorpion near the kneeling Jerome. In Domenico di Michelino's painting of the saint in the desert (fig. 159) there are two snakes and a scorpion, but no lion; in a work by Luini in the Kunsthistorisches Museum, Vienna (no. 583), there is a scorpion and a lizard, but no lion; in a late fifteenth-century picture by an unidentified Ferrarese master, presently in the picture gallery of Bologna, Jerome is accompanied by a snake, but has no lion; in a painting by Sano di Pietro in the Louvre (fig. 146), the penitent saint is surrounded by a varied fauna:

143. "More about the Detroit Van Eyck," pp. 181–201. I am indebted to Professor Hall for calling to my attention the lion as the zodiacal Leo, and for his gracious permission to mention it here.

Figure 158. Bartolomeo di Giovanni, *Saint Jerome in Penitence*. New Haven: Yale University Art Gallery; University Purchase from James Jackson Jarves.

three snakes, two scorpions, one large unidentifiable, somewhat "buglike" creature with six or more pairs of legs (!), while off to the side, behind Jerome, are two deer and one unnaturally large fly on a rock, but no lion; in Catena's *Saint Jerome in His Study* in Frankfurt, there is a guineafowl, but no lion.

In a few paintings the lion is included but is hardly visible, almost as if there was such a certainty that Jerome would be identifiable without the

Figure 159. Domenico di Michelino, *Saint Jerome in the Wilderness*. Dallas Museum of Fine Arts; Samuel H. Kress Collection.

lion that the artist took strange liberties with the beast. Thus, in a painting of the *Madonna and Child with Saint Jerome and Saint John the Baptist*, attributed to Giulio Campi, in Agram (Zagreb), only the front feet of the lion are visible; the rest of the animal is ostensibly behind Jerome. In a picture of *Saint Jerome in Penitence* by Dosso Dossi, in Vienna (fig. 160), the lion is behind the seated saint, moving away to the left, with its head actually out of the picture. Again, in Lucas van Leyden's *Saint Jerome in Penitence* in Berlin (fig. 73), the lion is walking behind a tree that hides its head and front legs. These renditions can only have been deliberately designed to hide the lion partially while yet including it.

At times the lion was made very large compared to the figure of Jerome, as in Colantonio's painting in Naples (fig. 1), in Bastiani's Milan picture (fig. 30), in Domenichino's famous *Last Communion of Saint Jerome* in the Vatican, and in Raffaellino del Garbo's altarpiece in San Francisco (fig. 161).

In some other pictures the lion is extremely small, as if it were included merely as an identifying tag, as in, for example, Sano di Pietro's *Saint Jerome in Penitence* in Siena, in Tura's *Madonna and Child with Saint Jerome and Saint Apollonia* in Ajaccio, and in a painting attributed to Guercino in the Los Angeles County Museum of Art (fig. 162). In the last work, the lion is only faintly indicated in the background at the extreme right.

The degree of naturalistic verisimilitude in the depiction of the lion varies with the knowledge and competence of the artist. Lions were available in menageries for artists to observe if they so desired, even as early as the thirteenth century, when Villard de Honnecourt made his famous drawing, which he proudly informs us was done "from the life." On the other hand, many artists did not go to such effort, and contented themselves with looking at earlier pictures or at the innumerable carvings of lions so common in medieval monuments and church decorations. Thus, the beast is given a ridiculously long tail in the French Gold Scroll Master's mid-fifteenth-century manuscript illumination (fig. 163), in which, to complete the unnatural depiction, the tail is terminally bifurcated into two graceful curls of hair! An artist much interested in animals, Lucas Cranach took liberties with the lion. In some of his pictures Cranach gave the beast accurate short, upright, triangular ears, but in one painting of the penitent Jerome, now in Innsbruck (fig. 94), he either gave it long drooping ears like a beagle or allowed the long hair of its mane to give this appearance.

Many artists were tempted to study living lions and have left us sketches of them; such artists as Pisanello, Giovannino de Grassi, the Bellinis, Dürer, and Titian come to mind immediately, and these are by no means all. Because the real animals were available for study and observation throughout the time span covered by the painters of the Jerome cycle, and because these numerous and diverse artists reacted, not as members of a progressively more accurate set of practitioners but on purely individual degrees of interest, it is not possible to sense a steady growth of zoological knowledge in the chronology of their pictures. The lion was so well known to people generally, including, of course, the artists, that the historian of zoological observation finds no indices of

Figure 160. Dosso Dossi, *Saint Jerome in Penitence*. Vienna: Kunsthistorisches Museum.

Figure 161. Raffaelino del Garbo, *Madonna Enthroned with Saints and Angels*. San Francisco: M. H. De Young Memorial Museum; Samuel H. Kress Collection.

advancing knowledge in the many renditions of the lion. As concrete evidence of the availability of living lions for ready observation in quattrocento and cinquecento Italy, we may mention that in his notebooks Leonardo da Vinci wrote that in Florence "there are always from twenty-five to thirty of them."[144]

In pictures showing the lion in a resting pose, sitting or crouching, the eyes may be wide open or so nearly closed as to suggest somnolence. Somnolent lions occur in pictures by such diverse artists as Dürer, Titian,

Figure 164. Master of the Saint Lucy Legend attribution, *Saint Jerome and His Lion*, late fifteenth century. Los Angeles County Museum of Art; gift of Anna Bing Arnold.

Figure 162. Guercino, *Saint Jerome in Penitence*. Los Angeles County Museum of Art.

Figure 163. French Gold Scroll Master, ca. 1450. *Jerome in His Study*. San Marino, Calif.: Henry E. Huntington Library, HM 1125, f.147.

Figure 165. Ulocrino, *Saint Jerome and the Lion*. Washington: National Gallery of Art; Samuel H. Kress Collection.

Ridolfo Ghirlandajo, and Sellaio. Whether resting or not, the lion is usually close to Jerome. In a few paintings, however, the lion is placed at a considerable distance from the saint. Thus, in Antonello da Messina's London picture of the saint in his study the lion is far off in the right background, walking toward the frontal plane of the picture. This led Anna Strümpell to conclude that here the lion had shed all symbolic meanings and was merely moving about in the background in the "manner of Flemish genre."

In pictures showing Jerome extracting the thorn, it is usually from the lion's right front foot, but in some cases it is the left one. Colantonio's picture in Naples (fig. 1) is such an instance; another not depicting the actual extraction of the thorn is the right-wing panel of a late-fifteenth-century Flemish triptych attributed to the Master of the Saint Lucy Legend (fig. 164). In sculpture, instances of this sort are a bronze plaquette attributed to Ulocrino (fig. 165) and a marble relief by Jacopo della Quercia (fig. 18). In stained glass, the incident of the thorn in the lion's left foot is shown in a window of Ulm cathedral, designed by Peter Hemmel of Anlau, a fifteenth-century German artist.

So far as I know, a work by Jacopino da Bologna is the earliest Italian attempt to depict the thorn extraction. Erwin Panofsky wrote that it was

144. MacCurdy, p. 1130.

145. *Early Netherlandish Painting* (1958), vol. 1, pp. 249, 458.

146. "St. Jerome Extracting the Thorn from the Lion's Foot," p. 189.

147. *Art in Medieval France*, p. 82.

148. The scene of the extraction of the thorn from the lion's paw has been noted in the following works of art, listed here alphabetically by artist or period without regard to chronology, geography, or medium employed. Johannes Andreas; Antoniazzo Romano; Austrian, fifteenth century (seven works: Tripp, p. 88; Hajos, p. 34; Vienna: University Art Museum; two in Hajos, p. 35; *Très Belles Heures*, Turin; *Belles Heures d'Ailly*, f. 186v); Belbello da Pavia; Bicci di Lorenzo; Bugatti; Colantonio (fig. 1); Cologne Master, ca. 1470; English, early fifteenth century (fig. 197); Enzola; Ferrarese (Bisogni, fig. 45; Hind [1938], vol. 4, pl. 422); Flemish, fifteenth century (Pierpont Morgan Library, MS. 46); Fra Diamante and Filippo Lippi (fig. 47); Frankentaler School; French manuscript illuminations (ca. 1415, Pierpont Morgan Library MS. 866, f. 144v; ca. 1430–1435, Pierpont Morgan Library, MS. 46); late fifteenth century, Bodleian Library, MS. Queen's College 305, f. 220); German, fifteenth century (Ring, fig. 7; fig. 166; Frankfurt); Giambono attribution; Giovanni di Paolo attribution; Juan Gomez; Benozzo Gozzoli; Hemmel d'Andlau; fifteenth-century stained glass (Ulm Cathedral); Jacopino da Bologna; Jacopo della Quercia (fig. 18); Pietro Lianori; Jean de Limbourg; Lombard School, fifteenth century (fig. 167); Zanobi Macchiavelli; Matteo di Giovanni; Hans Memling (three works); Mino da Fiesole; Neapolitan, fifteenth century; Ottaviano Nelli; Netherlands, sixteenth century; Pellegrino (fig. 168); Pesellino; Pinturicchio; Riemenschneider (two sculptures); Sano di Pietro (fig. 41); Sienese, late fourteenth century; Simone dei Crocefissi (fig. 153); Tomaso da Modena; van der Weyden (two paintings, including fig. 67); Venetian, fourteenth century; Veneto Byzantine (two paintings, including fig. 19).

Rogier van der Weyden who "if not invented, at least reformulated and popularized the subject of St. Jerome compassionately extracting the thorn from the foot of his faithful lion,"[145] as in his Detroit painting published by Grete Ring.[146] Panofsky did, however, give a number of references to pre-Rogerian instances in northern European art of what he termed "Jerome's excursion into the domain of veterinary surgery," but he did not extend these to include Italian art. Jacopino's painting was done several decades earlier. Another Bolognese altarpiece, *The Madonna and Child with Saints*, by Simone dei Crocifissi (fig. 153), shows a similar action; it, too, is earlier than van der Weyden. Obviously, two such minor masters as Jacopino and Simone did not exert much influence on the course of Italian painting during the last quarter of the trecento or the early decades of the following century. That they both depicted Jerome's act of mercy toward the lion may have been a result of the presence in Bologna of Giovanni Andrea, whose enthusiasm for Jerome and for his representation in art gave the original impetus to the eventual flood of Hieronymite paintings and carvings.

An unusual iconographic treatment of the lion is to be seen in a polychromed sculpture of about 1490, *Madonna and Child with Saint Leonard and Saint Jerome* by Hans Klocker. Jerome's lion has no thorn in its raised right front paw, but it does have a ring around its "ankle," possibly a suggestion of its status as a tamed, domestic animal.

Although the rendition by Jacopino da Bologna, mentioned above, is the earliest one found by an Italian artist and is actually earlier than any of the Flemish ones, a still earlier rendering, a twelfth-century French sculpture of this subject in the capital of the portal of the Abbey Church in Autun is mentioned by Joan Evans.[147] I have not noted any other attempts to portray the thorn extraction between this one and Jacopino's.

The incident has, of course, been represented many times, although the number is relatively small when compared to the total of potentially "suitable" compositions in which Jerome and the lion are merely shown together. Fewer than 10 percent of all such cases show the actual thorn removal.[148]

In a small number of paintings the lion is shown eating another animal. Thus, in a picture attributed to Isenbrandt, in the Hermitage (fig. 72), it is eating a gray rabbit. In an anonymous sixteenth-century Netherlandish picture (Brussels, Musées Royaux des Beaux-Arts, no. 979a), the lion is shown gnawing on the hind quarter of a deer (identification as deer is based on its cloven hoof, thus eliminating any possibility of its being the ass, the death of which had been falsely blamed on the lion in the old legend). In one picture, by Jacopo Bertucci (Paris: Louvre), the lion is gnawing on a bone, probably of a deer, whose other inedible remains (two cloven hooves) are lying on the ground nearby. In some other instances, such as Battista Dossi's *Saint Jerome in Penitence* in the Louvre, and in *Saint Jerome in his Study* attributed to Jorge Ingles, in the Valladolid Museum, the identity of the animal being eaten cannot be made out.

In some altarpieces, especially those composed of multiple panels, there is an attempt to portray the various parts of the lion story. Thus, in the Valladolid picture, originally the central part of a large retable from La Mejorada, there are several incidents involving the lion in the small,

Figure 166. *Saint Jerome in His Study*, German (Upper Rhine), ca. 1470. Washington: National Gallery of Art; Rosenwald Collection.

lateral panels, including one showing Jerome extracting the thorn from the lion's paw, and another showing the lion driving, or guarding, laden camels into the monastery. In the central panel, where the lion is devouring the leg of an animal, Jerome is shown writing, not noticing the lion. Three small figures of attendant monks at the lower left of the panel also seem oblivious to the lion and its action.

In the *Jerome Altar* by Jacob Cornelisz (fig. 169), the lion actually appears in four places. In the central panel, where Jerome is enthroned in cardinal's garb, the lion is standing at his feet with its right front paw, pierced by a thorny branch, raised toward the saint's right hand; in the

Figure 167. *Jerome and the Lion*, Lombard school, fifteenth century. Bergamo: Accademia Carrara.

Figure 168. Aretusi Pellegrino, *Jerome Legend*. Modena: S. Pietro.

Figure 169. Jacob Cornelisz, *Jerome Altar*. Vienna: Kunsthistorisches Museum.

background, to Jerome's right, the saint is shown, in small scale, in penitence, while the lion is bending down to drink at a stream; in the background, to the enthroned Jerome's left, the lion is guarding a camel and an ass on their way to the monastery; and below the large figure of Jerome on his throne the lion is shown being laden with firewood, as the legend informs us was its punishment after the ass had been stolen.

A Flemish painting, a pair of grisaille panels by Jan Gossaert (fig. 71), studied by Sadja Herzog, also illustrates several parts of the lion-Jerome legend. In the foreground of the right panel the lion is sitting beside the penitent saint; it appears again in the background of both panels—in the right, with its injured paw in the saint's left hand, and in the left, with the laden ass it was delegated to protect. In an early sixteenth-century Brussels tapestry (San Ildefonso Museum), the lion occurs twice: behind the kneeling Jerome and in the background, where the saint appears to be extracting the thorn from its foot.

At times, the background episode appears to have been intended, but then omitted, leaving the lion without a direct explanation. An example is a Florentine engraving, done about 1460 to 1470, showing, in the foreground, Jerome in penitence with his faithful lion nearby.[149] If one looks carefully at this work, one can just make out, in the upper-left background, the tail end of another lion going up the hill and out of the picture limits. The explanation of this curious situation would seem to be that the engraver had seen pictures of the penitent saint in which various episodes of the lion legend were included as small details in the background. In this particular engraving, the episode of the lion guarding, bringing up the rear, of the laden-ass or camel caravan on its way back to the monastery would fit the situation, if we were to assume that the episode was stopped short by the picture's edge. If the engraving had originally extended further up, and was cut off, the result we have here could have been produced. That either this actually transpired or that the artist merely stopped abruptly when he came to the edge is equally possible. We know from many paintings in which animals are truncated by the picture's edge that this would not necessarily have disturbed the artist.

In the majority of paintings or graphics of the Jerome theme the artists were satisfied merely to include the saint's lion near him, without attempting to depict various parts of the beast's legend. In those instances in which several parts of the story are portrayed, the lion necessarily appears in each, but there is only one lion in each episode.

An iconographically somewhat enigmatic bronze relief of *Saint Jerome in Penitence*, attributed to Filarete (fig. 81), does have two lions, both probably meant to be males, as both are given indications of manes. Only their heads are visible (frontally); there are also a bear and a wolf whose profiled heads are shown, one on either side of the kneeling Jerome. This combination of two lions, a bear, and a wolf, as well as a snake in the lower-left corner, is unique in the approximately 1,100 versions of the Jerome theme studied in the present connection. This uniqueness, in turn, suggests that the artist accepted motifs from various sources and thereby produced an unusual assemblage of creatures in the saint's wilderness surroundings.

At this point mention may be made of a small group of paintings and

149. Illustrated in Hind, vol. 2, pl. 39.

engravings with what I consider to be confused, even conflated, iconography. The "source" artists involved are Bernardino Passeri and Girolamo Muziano; the "derivative" ones, whose engravings are based on these two, are Cornelis Cort and Johann Sadeler. Inasmuch as the engravings are probably better known than the paintings, we may begin with them. In each of two sheets by Cort, generally assumed to represent Saint Jerome, there are, not one, but two, lions. The first of these (fig. 170), representing the body of Saint Jerome supported by the angels, is based on a painting by Bernardino Passeri, in the J. H. Beckmann Collection, Bremen. In it two lions are digging in the ground at the bottom of the picture. The dead saint has no identifying attributes, and the story depicted fits either Saint Onuphrius or Saint Paul the Hermit, but not Saint Jerome. The legends of the first two inform us that when each died in the wilderness two lions came and dug graves for their bodies. Jerome, on the contrary, died in his monastery, and his normal obsequies have been depicted by numerous artists, as, for example, by Carpaccio (Venice). In another version of his painting (fig. 171), Passeri placed the two digging lions, not at the bottom of the picture but halfway up on the left side, and he introduced, in the lower-right corner, below the dead saint's left hand, a crucifix, a book, and a cardinal's hat, objects that support the identification of the figure as Jerome. In Passeri's paintings, as in Cort's engraving, one of the lions is a male, the other a female. As an example of "correct" iconographic employment of two grave-digging lions, we may take Sebastiano and Marco Ricci's *Death of Saint Paul the Hermit* (University of Kansas Study Collection, Lawrence). Not only does this picture have the two lions, but the saint's body is supported by two angels, much as in Passeri's painting. The Ricci picture includes Anthony Abbot kneeling beside the dying hermit saint.

The other engraving by Cort (fig. 172), based on a design by Girolamo Muziano, shows the saint, nude to the waist, his hands clasped in ecstasy close to his bearded chin, gazing yearningly at a crucifix, while two male lions walk into the picture's middle background from the right, the one in front turning its head to look back at its companion. The saint is devoid of Jerome's usual attributes (stone, crucifix, cardinal's hat) and is similar to the figure in the first engraving. Near him, however, are a human skull and three books, which do lend support to his identification as Jerome. This sheet is one of a series of seven prints of "comtemplative saints in landscapes" by Cort,[150] all based on compositions by Muziano. In this series there is another print of Saint Jerome meditating in the wilderness, which contains only the saint's usual single lion.

In making his engravings Cort did not invent the idea of two lions but carefully copied them from his sources, Passeri and Muziano.[151] The Muziano picture was also engraved by Johann Sadeler, exactly as by Cort. However, the Passeri original and Cort's version of it, are hardly to be considered as "normal" representations of Saint Jerome, and the Muziano picture, on which Cort's other "Jerome" engraving with two lions was based, had the lions, but no saint! ("Un dessin à la plume, bistre, le paysage *sans le saint, avec deux lions.*") In short, the engraver faithfully copied Muziano's picture and then added to it the figure of the saint with his books and his death's head. This makes one wonder if he was aware of the iconographic conflation he was creating. Cort made a

150. A. R. Turner (*The Vision of Landscape in Renaissance Italy*, pp. 117–18) writes that there were six prints of contemplative saints in extensive landscape settings. Bierens de Haan (*L'Oeuvre gravé de Cornelius Cort*, pp. 121–22) lists seven, two of which he calls Saint Jerome; the others, Saints Eustace, Francis, John the Baptist, Onuphrius, and Mary Magdalene.

151. Bierens de Haan (fig. 38, opp. p. 143) reproduces Passeri's *Le Corps de St. Jerôme soutenu par des anges*, which is in the collection of J. H. Beckmann, Bremen. It shows the two lions as they appear in Cort's engraving (reversed). In his description of the Muziano, on which Cort based his other engraving containing two lions, Bierens de Haan writes: "Un tableau de Muziano, en sens inverse, avec quelques changements, à la Pinacothèque de Bologna" and "Un dessin à la plume, bistre, le paysage sans le saint, avec deux lions, à Milan (coll. Dubini)." In other words, there are two works by Muziano, a painting of Jerome (with one lion at his feet) in Bologna, and a pen drawing of a landscape, with two lions, but no saint, in the Dubini Collection, Milan. What Cort (and also Sadeler) did was to transpose the Bologna figure of Jerome (and his crucifix) into the Milan landscape, leaving out the lion lying at the saint's feet in the Bologna original. The resulting composition and the Bologna Muziano original are reproduced together on one page in Ugo da Como's *Girolamo Muziano*, with a single, mutually applicable title, *L'anacoreta prediletto* (*The Beloved Anchorite*). The figure of the saint is the same in both. Ugo Procacci ("Una 'vita' in edita del Muziano"), merely mentions the list of Muziano's designs used by Cort, but does not discuss their iconographic details or deviations.

Figure 170. Cornelis Cort, *Saint Jerome Sustained by Three Angels*. New York: Metropolitan Museum of Art; Harris Brisbane Dick Fund, 1953.

Figure 171. Bernardino Passeri, *Death of Saint Jerome*. Cambridge, Mass.: Fogg Art Museum; gift of Professor and Mrs. John Tucker Murray.

good number of other engravings of Saint Jerome, with a single lion in each, after compositions by Caraglio, Parmigianino, Muziano, Titian, Neroni, and Jacopo Palma the Younger. These are all readily identifiable as Jerome, and pose no iconographic problems. For convenience, references to pictures with dubious or conflated "Jeromes" are listed as "Jerome (?)" in the Appendix.

One further iconographic conflation may be blamed on Cort. In an engraving titled by Ugo da Como as *Saint Jerome after Muziano*, a lamb is curled up near Jerome's feet in place of the saint's usual lion.[152] This

152. Ugo da Como, *Girolamo Muziano*, p. 103.

Figure 172. Cornelis Cort, *Saint Jerome*, 1573 (after Muziano). New York: Metropolitan Museum of Art; gift of George Hallman, Whittelsey Fund, 1959.

creature, of course, is usually associated with John the Baptist, never with Jerome. Indeed, if we look at Sadeler's engraving of *Saint John after Muziano*, we find the same lamb, in the same pose, in the same place.[153] In this picture Saint John is bearded and aged (which may have caused him to look like Jerome to Cort), but he holds a slender rod, from which hangs a narrow streamer bearing the words, typical of the Baptist, *Ecc[e] agnus dei* ("Behold the lamb of God"). It seems likely that Cort may have realized, belatedly, when transposing John into Jerome, that the animal with the latter should be a lion rather than a lamb, because when he completed it, he drew its right hind foot (the only foot showing), not with a small cloven hoof as in Muziano's and Sadeler's "Saint John," but with a suggestion of leonine toes and claws! Inasmuch as the lamb here is a copyist's error, that animal is not included in this Bestiary.

153. Ibid, p. 108.

A puzzling iconographic use occurs in a small number of renditions of the "Saint Jerome in the Wilderness" theme, in which the saint is associated with two lions, one male, the other usually a female, and, in some instances, even additional lions, in renditions without separate episodes represented in the background to account for the extra animals.[154]

The total number of such instances, fifteen in all, not counting duplicate or derivative versions, are few enough to list and to discuss individually.

The seven paintings are: Filippo Lippi (Altenburg); a close copy by the pseudo Pier Francesco Fiorentino (fig. 173); Jacopo del Sellaio (fig. 174); Marco Ricci (Rome); Titian attribution (fig. 175), which is possibly the same as a picture now attributed to Domenico Campagnola in the Norton Simon Collection, Los Angeles (fig. 176), or else the latter is a derivative from a "lost" Titian (and there is also a woodcut copy by Boldrini); Jan van Hemessen attribution; and Roelandt Savery (fig. 177).

The four sculptures are by Desiderio da Settignano (fig. 45, and a recently published very similar version in the Michael Hall Collection, New York); Antonio Rossellino attribution (fig. 51); Austrian, early sixteenth century, a panel from a carved altarpiece, in Vienna; and a Filarete attribution relief in which there are two lions (heads only showing), a bear's head, and a wolf's head, as well as a snake. Both lions seem to be males; at least both have indications of manes (fig. 81). This piece has been discussed in the section on the lion.

The three drawings are all by Jacopo Bellini, two of them in the Louvre, one in the British Museum (fig. 53, 54, 55), and finally, there is an engraving by Florentine Anonymous Fine Manner, ca. 1480–1500 (fig. 131). We do not include here a group of iconographically conflated pictures by Cort, Muziano, Passeri, and Sadeler, as these are discussed elsewhere (p. 248 ff.).

Of these fifteen works, nine are from the mid-fifteenth century. Two paintings, two sculptures, and one engraving are Florentine; three drawings are Venetian; and one sculpture is Roman. The six others are later, two of them Flemish, three Venetian, and one Austrian.

In the following discussion, the premise is that the basic explanation behind the inclusion of the lioness or extra lion must be sought in the

The Lioness: An Iconological Problem

154. The presence of a lioness with Jerome's lion in a small number of works of art had gone largely unnoticed in the literature until after the first draft of this study was completed, but since then Rudolf Wittkower ("Desiderio da Settignano's 'St. Jerome in the Desert,'" pp. 7–37) has published a careful study of one of the most important and beautiful examples, the marble relief by Desiderio da Settignano (fig. 45), the very piece that first alerted my attention to this problem. In the course of his paper, Wittkower also mentioned several of the other pieces, all of which I had also found and studied, and all of which are discussed here. I am very glad, and considerably fortified, to have a study by a scholar of such eminence to cite, and am gratified by our general agreement. However, additional information has suggested to me an origin and significance behind the introduction of the lioness with the lion of Jerome, unsuspected by Wittkower.

Apparently the presence of the lioness with the lion had been noted prior to Wittkower's paper only by Father Pöllmann (p. 473) and by Leo Planiscig (*Desiderio da Settignano*, p. 16).

173

Figure 173. Pseudo Pier Francesco Fiorentino, *Saint Jerome and Saint Francis.* Bergamo: Accademia Carrara.

Figure 174. Jacopo del Sellaio, *Saint Jerome in Penitence.* Present whereabouts unknown. Photograph courtesy I Tatti, Florence.

Figure 175. Titian attribution, *Saint Jerome in the Wilderness.* Formerly in the W. J. Davies Collection.

174

175

Figure 176. Domenico Campagnola, *Saint Jerome in the Wilderness*. Los Angeles: The Norton Simon Foundation.

Figure 177. Roelandt Savery, *Landscape with Saint Jerome and Lions*. Bonn: Rheinisches Landesmuseum.

early fifteenth-century works, because there is always the possibility, even the probability, that the artists who created the later ones could have gotten their ideas from the earlier renditions as "sources" without knowing or caring about their particular possible connotations. We may, therefore, simplify this discussion by referring to the notes these later examples, with such comment as may be necessary.[155]

155. These later examples, which do not contribute basically to the problem of the original meaning of the lioness or of the extra lion, are nevertheless worth mentioning in some detail at this point. The first is a painting by Roelandt Savery (1576–1639), a Flemish painter of landscapes literally teeming with animals. This picture (fig. 177) shows the kneeling, praying saint relegated to the far background of the composition, where he appears as a small and quite inconspicuous figure, while the left foreground is devoted to the depiction of a group of no fewer than seven lions. The multiplicity of lions in this part of the painting has nothing to do with Jerome, who actually has his regular lion close to him. It is possible that the penitent eremite was put in to make the picture more readily disposable, although the general tendency of northern art at that time and place was to crowd the foreground with still life and genre incidents, while the religious motifs were placed in the far background. By current practices Savery's picture could be titled more accurately, "Lions in a Landscape with Saint Jerome in the Background."

The second picture is a triptych in the Musée du Petit Palais, Paris, by Jan Sanders van Hemessen (1500–ca. 1566). The central panel depicts the martyrdom of Saint Sebastian; the left one, Saint Roch with his dog and an angel; and the right panel shows a completely nude, fairly elderly, bearded man seated in a rocky landscape with two lions at his feet. This figure has been assumed to be Saint Jerome, possibly because of the lions—but it shows little in common with other portrayals of that saint. He is not reading, writing, praying, or rapt in meditation. He holds a rosary in his right hand, while his left rests on a walking stick. There is no stone in his hand, and no crucifix or book or skull or any other symbol of transience in the picture. The figure is not emotionally tense, as in El Greco's similarly completely nude Jerome (fig. 79). It is futile to compare it with at least six other pictures of Saint Jerome by van Hemessen (two in Vienna, one each

in Modena, Genoa, Parma, and Prague), because in them the saint is clothed and is a half-length figure, without any lion. The Petit Palais painting may not even represent Jerome. A possible alternative interpretation might be Onuphrius or Paul the Hermit, since in the story of each of these saints two lions dug their graves. Onuphrius is the more likely, because he was usually shown entirely nude. Another reason for doubting that van Hemessen's figure is Jerome is that most altarpieces involving both Saint Roch and Saint Sebastian were offerings against the plague. Jerome appears to have been absent from antiplague iconography, even though he was one of the saints most frequently included in a great variety of other altarpieces.

The early sixteenth-century Austrian carved polyptych shows, in one of its panels, Jerome kneeling before a crucifix, while behind him are two lions and one lioness, resting quietly on the ground. There is here no doubt that the saint is Jerome; the extra lion and lioness are difficult to account for unless the unknown artist had seen Jacopo Bellini's sketches, or some of the fifteenth-century Florentine works discussed on p. 258, or, more probably, a lost "Titian" painting, which also included two male lions with one lioness.

The two late Venetian paintings are: one by Marco Ricci, in the Corsini Gallery, Rome (not illustrated, as the photograph shows very little), and one, formerly in the W. J. Davies Collection (fig. 175), where it was attributed to Titian, and another version (possibly the same), formerly in the Davies Collection and now in Los Angeles, Norton Simon Foundation Collection, where it is attributed to Domenico Campagnola (fig. 176). It is possible that this work is actually a copy of a now lost Titian, given tentative status by H. Tietze (*Titian*, fig. 324), in a discussion of a woodcut of the same composition made by Boldrini around 1565.

In the Boldrini-Campagnola-Titian composition, Saint Jerome is kneeling before a crucifix at the right side of the picture, a small figure in the far background of an

extensive landscape, while three lions occupy much of the rest, one male lion asleep near the center of the bottom of the picture, a lioness above it, watching the saint, and a second male lion at the lower-left corner behind (to the left of) a tree, with its head looking away to the left.

The inclusion of two extra lions, one male and one female, in this design of Titian's seems to be traceable to the sketches of his precursor, Jacopo Bellini. It is true that in those of his paintings that have come down to us, Jacopo never included more than one lion in any picture of Jerome, but in at least three of his drawings of the same subject there is a lioness as well as a lion. Trained in the Bellini studio, Titian may well have seen these spontaneous creations of the venerable Jacopo and carried with him for many years some memory of them. If, as Tietze suggested, the "lost" original painting by Titian was a relatively late work, painted around the middle of the sixteenth century, the time lapse would have been more than enough to permit errors of memory. What he was apt to recall was that Jacopo had included many animals, including multiple lions, in some of his designs for "Saint Jerome in the Wilderness." If anything, this picture shows a more retentive memory of the sketches than we find in the paintings of Mansueti, who took over the Jacopo Bellini "menagerie-mindedness" with more enthusiasm than judgment.

Marco Ricci, living and working in Venice, could easily have known the Titian composition and the copies of it, so it is not impossible that his own painting may be to some degree derivative. In Ricci's picture, Jerome is again a rather small figure unobtrusively placed in the lower-right portion of a fairly extensive landscape, while the two lions are at lower left, nearer the front of the picture plane. One of them is in full profile, and is looking back to the second, whose face only is visible, but which is following closely the first lion. The second of the two lions seems to be a female, since it is not heavily maned.

156. Alessandro da Morrona, *Pisa illustrata nelle arti del disegno*.

157. Hind and Morrona agreed in considering that the subject of the engraving they attribute to Finiguerra was "almost certainly based on Antonio Pollaiuolo, and is closely related to a drawing of his in the Uffizi." However, the Pollaiuolo drawing of the penitent saint is a reversed image of the later engraving, and, furthermore, it contains but a single lion, shown in the act of eating, but definitely not attacking anything, let alone a lioness.

Morrona thought the engraving reproduced a painting, since lost, known to have been in the Capella Maggiore of the Campo Santo in Pisa. The fact that a harbor with two ships is shown in the left background bears out the suggestion of Pisa, because it was a port, whereas Florence was not. In Pollaiuolo's drawing there are four ships in the harbor. It may be mentioned that in Jacopo Bellini's silver-point drawing, in London, there are two ships, a wreck of one to the left and another in good condition to the right. Unfortunately, we do not know what Bellini may have meant by the inclusion of these vessels, but in his sketch they need hardly refer to Pisa, because his own city, Venice, was a still greater and more important seaport. This cannot help but raise some doubt as to whether the ships in the engraving are necessarily a reference to Pisa and not simply a "memory" of the Bellini sketch.

To return to the Pollaiuolo drawing, Hind further informs us that apart from the lost picture, formerly in the Campo Santo, another work relevant to the engraving is a fresco, in San Domenico, Pistoia, of Saint Jerome, discussed by Procacci ("Opera sconosciute d'arte toscana") and, more recently, tentatively attributed to Ridolfo Ghirlandajo by Berenson (*Italian Pictures of the Renaissance: Florentine School*, p. 73), but earlier thought by Hind to be "directly inspired by Pollaiuolo, if not by his hand." However this may be, the pertinence of this painting to the "Finiguerra" engraving seems a little remote. The figure of "Saint Jerome in Penitence" was so frequent in the art of the period that not too much may be inferred from similarities between any two of them, especially when they also present differences.

As already mentioned, I know of no real documentation, verbal or pictorial,

The eight quattrocento Florentine and Venetian versions of "Jerome in the Wilderness" are the core of the problem. In all but one of these there are two lions, one male and one female. The fact that five of these were produced in the mid-fifteenth century in Florence alone leads us to assume that the lioness figure must have meant something there, even though a much greater number of representations of Jerome in the wilderness, with but a single lion apiece, were created in the same place, at the same time, and, in some cases, by the same artists.

The Venetian pictures with two lions apiece, a male and a female, are three spontaneous, outline sketches by Jacopo Bellini, and one woodcut by Domenico Campagnola. The three Bellini drawings are contemporaneous with the mid-fifteenth-century Florentine works.

Of the five Florentine works, only one has three lions (one male, two females); the others have one lion and one lioness in each. The presence of three of these animals in the engraving does seem to connect it with the sketches by Jacopo Bellini, and also, as a possible "source," with the later Titian-Campagnola-Boldrini composition, but the lions are very differently activated in it. In the Florentine Anonymous Fine Manner engraving (fig. 131), Jerome is in the extreme right foreground, kneeling before a crucifix, with one lioness resting just below and a little to the left of him, looking away from the saint, over its shoulder, to the other two lions. These are most remarkable: the male lion is shown attacking and biting a lioness, whose wide open, snarling mouth is turned toward its attacker. This calls to mind the account given by Pliny of the lion chastising the lioness for her adultery with the leopard. This story must have been well known in Italy at the time this anonymous engraving was made, as at least five quattrocento printings of Pliny's works were issued by presses in Venice, Rome, and Parma, to say nothing of reissues in other countries. Furthermore, the tale of the lion punishing the adulterous lioness had been moralized in the *Gesta Romanorum*; the lion was there a symbol of Christ, and the lioness of the erring soul requiring correction.

In his discussion of the engraving, attributed by him to Finiguerra, Arthur Hind cited Alessandro da Morrona to the effect that the fighting lion and lioness might be explained as a reference to the subjugation of Pisa by Florence. I can only assume Morrona had some evidence for this suggestion, but I have not been able to find it.[156] The figure of a lion was much used in the heraldry and the arms of Florence, but I have found no explicit reference to a lioness in those of the rival state of Pisa. Even if Morrona's suggestion is accepted, Pliny's old tale might still be an "ultimate source" theme behind the composition. It might be that, in the language of allegory, Pisa, like the lioness of Pliny, had erred and deserved to be punished. Even if this were part of the concept behind the composition, it would not explain the presence of the other, noncombatant lioness in the anonymous engraving. This is the animal that connects the engraving with the other Florentine works of its period. The attacked lioness is obviously a particular item added to this one piece.[157]

There is one further iconographic zoological detail in the engraving that contributes to our understanding of the composition. At the extreme left, about half-way up the picture, is a stag with its head bent down and its ears lowered. The stag bending down to drink from a stream was an old icon of the "soul thirsting for the life-giving water of the true religion," but the stag bending its head, not to water but to the earth, semiarid or only sparsely covered with edible vegetation, occurs in old emblems where it is used to illustrate the motto *Multi sunt vocati, pauci vero electi* ("Many are called, but few are chosen").[158] We must remember that during his penitence Jerome, from his own statements, was yearning for forgiveness and acceptance; he wanted desperately to be one of the *electi*. The inclusion of the stag in just this pose suggests that the anonymous artist was alert to the current usage of animal symbolism, and this gives us reason to ask about his trinity of lions.

In a woodcut by Domenico Campagnola (fig. 176), a lion is shown attacking a bear with such force as to cause Saint Jerome, at the far left side of the picture, to lean forward to watch the fight. Hans Tietze and E. Tietze-Conrat called this composition *Saint Jerome with the Fighting Lions*, as did also Emil Galichon,[159] but the animal the lion is fighting cannot be a lioness (for one thing, it lacks the long tail characteristic of that animal). In fact, it is a bear with a very short tail or almost none. It is possible that Campagnola may have seen an early (ca. 1400) drawing by an unknown Veronese artist of two lionesses "at play," in fairly similar, but less serious-looking poses, now in the British Museum,[160] but, if so, he converted the beasts into a male lion and a bear. William Norton Howe correctly identified the two animals in his mention of this woodcut.[161] The observant Anna Jameson mentioned an engraving of *Saint Jerome in Penitence*, after Titian, "a superb landscape, in which are seen a lion and a lioness prowling in the wilderness, while the saint is doing penance in the foreground."[162] I have not been able to identify this work, unless it is possibly the same as the Boldrini design or the Cort engraving mentioned earlier.

This leads me to the sculpture by Desiderio da Settignano (fig. 45) and to the one attributed to Rossellino (fig. 51), the paintings by Filippo Lippi (with a copy by the pseudo Pier Francesco Fiorentino) and the one by Jacopo Sellaio. In the Desiderio relief, Jerome is kneeling at right, facing the crucifix to the left of the plaque. The lion is facing him and appears to be growling, frightening the monk behind Jerome, who is about to flee from the scene. Ansgar Pöllmann, Leo Planiscig, and Rudolf Wittkower are the only writers who noticed that the monk's terror was due to the approach of a pair of lions, not just a single one.[163] The second animal, a lioness, is shown as if coming from behind a hill to the left; only her head is visible, immediately behind the lion and immediately above its tail. The lioness is looking at the terrified monk, but is not growling at him, as its mouth is closed.

Planiscig seems to have been the first critic to suggest that Desiderio's composition may have been derived from pictorial rather than sculptural sources. John Pope-Hennessy tentatively suggested the paintings of Filippo Lippi, done between 1450 and 1460, a suggestion accepted by Wittkower.[164] Inasmuch as the Desiderio relief has been dated as "about 1461,"[165] this would seem like an immediate, contemporary source.

However, Filippo's Altenburg painting is so different in its composition as to make one wonder if it could have been the source. The fact that in it only the head of the lioness is present may have led Wittkower to agree that Filippo's picture did serve in this capacity and was the first

to support Morrona's suggestion that a reference to the conflict between Florence and Pisa is involved. At the same time it does not seem likely that his interpretation was advanced without some reason. It would imply that in this engraving Jerome's faithful lion had assumed a second, temporary function. It is possible that here the lion may be both Jerome's faithful beast and also a symbol of Florence, but this is not at all certain.

The recumbent lioness, with its head turned to look over its shoulder, is a reversed image of a similar one in Lorenzo Ghiberti's relief of the *Story of Noah*, one of the panels in the second pair of bronze doors he made for the Florentine baptistery. Inasmuch as the engraving is said to be derived from one or more designs by Antonio Pollaiuolo, the fact that the latter served as an assistant to Ghiberti for some time adds to the plausibility of this lioness being a Ghibertian motif passed down through Pollaiuolo to the anonymous engraver.

158. The expression *Multi sunt vocati, pauci vero electi* is one that occurs in one of Jerome's letters to Eustochium (Epistle xxii; F. A. Wright, *Select Letters of St. Jerome*, p. 102), wherein he praises virginity at length, ending by saying that one who "perseveres to the end will be saved; for many are called, but few are chosen." It also occurs in the Gospel of St. Matthew 20:16, from which source Jerome probably copied it.

159. Tietze and Tietze-Conrat, "Domenico Campagnola's Graphic Art," p. 459; Galichon, "Domenico Campagnola," p. 547.

160. Illustrated in A. E. Popham and Philip Pouncey, *Italian Drawings in the British Museum*, pl. cc/xvii.

161. *Animal Life in Italian Painting*, p. 44, fn.

162. *Sacred and Legendary Art*, p. 294.

163. Planiscig, *Desiderio da Settignano*, p. 16; Wittkower, "Desiderio da Settignano's 'St. Jerome in the Desert,'" p. 29.

164. Pope-Hennessy, *Italian Renaissance Sculpture*, pp. 303–4.

165. National Gallery of Art, *Summary Catalogue of European Paintings and Sculptures*, p. 152.

in which the "lioness graces the scene." Whether this painting was done in the decade assumed by Pope-Hennessy is uncertain. Filippo's only other version of the Jerome-lion story known to have been executed in the last years of that decade shows the saint removing the thorn from the lion's paw, and there is no lioness in it and no fleeing monk.

The sculpture attributed to Rossellino (fig. 51) is quite different from the Desiderio relief. In it Jerome's lion is standing behind the kneeling saint, looking out at the viewer from the lower-left corner of the composition. The lioness is behind the rocky hill above and behind the lion, and is looking to the left, its mouth somewhat opened.

A third Florentine relief has been described as containing an extra lion. Allan Marquand wrote of a marble altarpiece by Giovanni della Robbia in the church of San Medardo, in Arcevia, near Ancona, that the third panel of the predella contains "St. Jerome and his lions."[166] In a later book Marquand suggested that this work was designed by Giovanni, but actually carried out by one of his collaborators, probably his brother Fra Mattia.[167] In it there is something behind the seated figure of Jerome, whose usual lion is in front of him with its paw on his lap, but it is not possible to tell if the indistinct modelling behind him represents another lion or not.[168]

In the Sellaio painting (fig. 174) the lion is standing at the base of the crucifix looking at Jerome; the lioness is reclining behind the crucifix, and is also looking toward the saint. It is the only one out of seventeen versions of the "Jerome in Penitence" theme by Sellaio that contains a lioness as well as a lion. Inasmuch as Sellaio appears to have been relatively unoriginal, imitating, or at least drawing upon, the works of such contemporary Florentines as Filippino Lippi, Ghirlandajo, and Botticelli, it is possible that he had seen the relief by Desiderio and imitated it as Wittkower suggested.

The picture by Filippo Lippi and its close copy by pseudo Pier Francesco Fiorentino may be considered as one. It differs from all the foregoing in that it includes not only the penitent Jerome, but also, in the foreground, a large figure of a monk, who holds out his left hand to the lion in the lower-right corner of the picture. The lion is sitting with its right front paw raised and its mouth open. Immediately to its right the head of a lioness appears from an opening below the stone slab that serves as the penitent Jerome's "altar table" on which are a human skull and two limb bones.[169]

The youthful-looking monk in the lower foreground has been called Saint Francis in the literature,[170] but Robert Oertel considered it to represent Jerome at a younger age than the penitent figure in the background; this is essentially what Wittkower also suggested. It seems that Oertel assumed the monk was reaching out to remove the thorn from the lion's paw, although there is no visible thorn in the beast's foot. The picture is not as explicitly interpretable as one might wish. The young monk reaching to the lion is wearing a Franciscan habit, and may be Saint Francis. As this saint was famed for his friendliness and sympathy toward all creation, his gesture to the lion may be one of mere friendship and not of surgical assistance. There are a good number of paintings by, for example, such artists as Botticini, Palmezzano, and Sellaio, that combine Jerome in penitence with Saint Francis, but in these the latter is

166. *Giovanni della Robbia*, pp. 54–55.

167. *The Brothers of Giovanni della Robbia*, pp. 8–10.

168. The work is from the late fifteenth century, some decades later than the Desiderio and Rossellino pieces, and may be to some extent a reflection of their influence. That this may be the case is suggested by the fact that in a terra-cotta relief, figured in the 1918 sales catalogue of the Bardini Collection, where it was attributed to Giovanni della Robbia and called a copy of Rossellino's piece in the same collection, the lion (there is only one) is behind Jerome. In other words, in this piece the lion is where the uncertain "object" is in the San Medardo predella, the photograph of which is too poor and uninforming to be worth reproducing here.

169. Robert Oertel (*Frühe Italianische Malerei in Altenburg*, p. 146) thought the lioness was merely a reflection of the lion in a spring below Jerome's makeshift altar. But this cannot be; it is a lioness, not a lion, and its mouth is closed whereas that of the lion is open. It is clearly not a mirror image.

170. Berenson, *Italian Pictures of the Renaissance: Florentine School*, p. 111.

shown receiving the stigmata and is always a smaller figure in the background, sometimes quite far back. In Filippo's picture the opposite is the case, which peculiarity may cause some question as to who the monk may be, if he is not Saint Francis.

One further thought may be expressed about this picture. In the original version of the legend in the *Legenda aurea*, Jerome did not extract the thorn from the lion's foot, but bade one of his monks to do so. It is conceivable, therefore, that in this painting Filippo may have made a rarely accurate picture of the incident. This would identify the young monk as one of Jerome's assistants, not as a more youthful Jerome.

These few sculptures and paintings, each with a lioness as well as a lion, and all created at a time and in a town that turned out a much larger number of renditions of the same subject with but a single lion in each, cause one to ask if there may have been any new concept, any new source of ideas and of the means of expressing them in visual terms, that came into the intellectual climate of Florentine art circles in the second quarter of the fifteenth century. That even a small number of artists, working independently, made a few such renditions shows that such a composition was iconographically acceptable in that community at that time. To be more precise, we may ask if there was any such source that might have been responsible for the introduction of the lioness in these few works, and that, at the same time, was sufficiently restricted in its influence so that it did not affect the great majority of current productions of the Jerome-lion legend.

Indeed, there *was* such a "new" source that fits these seemingly contradictory requirements. It was known only to a small group of scholars, the humanists gathered in the Medicean court, and by them it may have been imparted only to a few people, which could explain its restricted influence on the art of its immediate period. This new source of ideas and of their graphic representation was the *Hieroglyphica* of Horapollo Niliacus.[171]

The *Hieroglyphica* was the work of an obscure, otherwise unknown Alexandrian writer, whose real name is lost. The text was supposed to have been translated from Egyptian into Greek by "Philippus," who is otherwise also unknown. The important thing about the work is that it claimed to explain, in simple, undocumented statements, the content and meanings of the hieroglyphic symbols used in the carvings of ancient Egypt. It was welcomed with enthusiasm by the humanists in Florence, who had already been convinced that much wisdom and knowledge was implied in the mysterious and undecipherable markings scratched on the surface of obelisks and other ancient Egyptian monuments. There was conviction that anything coming from Egypt was significant and meaningful, even if the meaning was unknown or unknowable.

Suddenly, with the advent of Horapollo's work, there was a "key" to these intriguing mysteries from the land of the pharaohs. As Jean Seznec trenchantly put it, "Everyone believed that a real discovery had been made. In reality, all that Horapollo did was to sanction the mistaken view of hieroglyphics which had arisen by way of Apuleius, Plutarch, and Plotinus—namely, that they formed an ensemble of rebuses designed to make religious precepts incomprehensible to the profane. Later, Marsilio Ficino and his circle showed the greatest enthusiasm for this little trea-

171. George Boas's translation of Horapollo's book, with notes and commentary, is the version that has been used in this study. While not casting doubt as to its influence on the thought and the art of mid-quattrocento Florence, it is only proper to state that it is not possible to demonstrate that Horapollo's work was definitely the "source" behind such details as an occasional lioness in a few renditions of the Jerome theme. The best we may hope to achieve is to suggest its seminal function; it is more a suggestion than a firm iconological interpretation.

tise, which so admirably confirmed their theories. Naturally they supposed that the great minds of Greece had been initiated into these Egyptian 'mysteries'—which, in their turn, were of course one more prefiguration of the teachings of Christ."[172]

In a commentary on the passage in Plotinus in which hieroglyphics were described as Platonic ideas rendered in graphic form, Ficino wrote as follows: "The Egyptian priests, when they wished to signify divine things, did not use letters, but whole figures of plants, trees, and animals: for God doubtless has a knowledge of things which is not complex discursive thought about its subject, but is, as it were, the simple and steadfast form of it. Your thought of time, for instance, is manifold and mobile, maintaining that time is speedy and by a sort of revolution joins the beginning to the end. . . . The Egyptians comprehend this whole discourse in one stable image, painting a winged serpent, holding its tail in its mouth. Other things are represented in similar images, as Horus describes."[173]

There were four copies of the manuscript of Horapollo in the Medicean library in Florence in the fifteenth century; one of them may have been acquired as early as 1419, from Cristoforo de Buondelmonti, a Florentine monk, who obtained a Greek manuscript of the *Hieroglyphica* in the Aegean island of Andros in that year and brought it back to Florence. In other words, Horapollo's work, with its readily credited, although undocumented, explanations of Egyptian hieroglyphs, was available and was studied by the members of the Medicean academy for some time prior to the creation of the few sculptures and paintings showing Jerome with a lioness as well as a lion.

It is known, from the studies of Karl Giehlow,[174] that the *Hieroglyphica* rapidly became increasingly influential in the formulation and expression of concepts in art and in thought. As its influence extended north of the Alps we find that in the early years of the sixteenth century, in Germany, no less an artist than Albrecht Dürer was commissioned by Maximilian to illustrate Pirckheimer's similarly commissioned translation of Horapollo's work, so respected had it become in the eyes of the reigning monarch. In Florence, in the fifteenth century, according to Boas, "not only had vision taken on in the thought of the Florentine Academy an almost mystical importance, but the habit of seeing symbols in what most people thought of as literality had become second nature to its members."[175]

The point of immediate interest to our present problem is that Horapollo informs us that when the Egyptian priests "wish to indicate a woman who has conceived once, they draw a lioness. For the lioness is never pregnant twice."[176] This suggests the Virgin Mary as the most obvious "subject" implicit in the Christianized use of the visual form of a lioness in religious art.

This is merely a suggestion, requiring independent sources to support it. The idea of Mary as a lioness was not new at the time Horapollo was first studied in Florence. Anselm Salzer noted that Mary had been mentioned explicitly as the "lion's mother" by Epiphanius, Basil, Bochart, and Berchorius, and, through the statement of the last named, by Isidore of Seville.[177] Of these authors, all but Bochart are earlier than the mid-fifteenth century, and could, therefore, have predisposed the Medicean

172. *The Survival of the Pagan Gods*, p. 100.

173. Boas, *The Hieroglyphics of Horapollo*, p. 28.

174. "Die Hieroglyphenkunde des Humanismus in der Allegorie der Renaissance," p. 221.

175. *The Hieroplyphics of Horapollo*, p. 24.

176. Ibid, p. 103.

177. *Die Sinnbilder und Beiworte Mariens in der deutschen Literatur*, pp. 25, 55, 538.

humanists into considering Horapollo's statement about the lioness as applying to the Virgin Mary. Berchorius made a direct comparison of the lioness and Mary when he wrote: "Leaena filios suas diligit et pro eis se opponit contra insidias venatorum, ut dicit Isidorus. Sic beata virgo pro sibi devotis contra diabolum pugnat et eas valde diligit atque fovet" ("a lioness loves her young and braves for them the snares of the hunters, as we read in Isidore. Likewise, the Blessed Virgin battles the devil for her devotees and loves and cherishes them greatly").[178] The Horapollonian idea of the single conception furnished one more important similarity between the lioness and the Virgin Mary; it was an additional character common to both suddenly brought to the attention of scholars in Florence.

Horapollo was neither alone nor the first to state that the lioness cannot conceive a second time. Herodotus not only made the same statement but attempted to justify it with what he probably considered a valid explanation. He wrote that the lioness "brings forth young but once in her lifetime, and then a single cub; she cannot possibly conceive again, since she loses her womb at the same time that she drops her young. The reason of this is that as soon as the cub begins to stir inside the dam, his claws, which are sharper than those of any other animal, scratch the womb; as the time goes on, and he grows bigger, he tears it more and more; so that at last, when the birth comes, there is not a morsel in the whole womb that is sound."[179]

While it is interesting to find that Herodotus had anticipated Horapollo in this matter, it cannot be assumed that the statement by the great Greek historian had much influence on the later thinking of either the ecclesiastical scholars or the Medicean humanists, because both of these groups relied heavily on Aristotle as their chief classical source for matters relating to natural history. Aristotle rightly and explicitly rejected what Herodotus had written, saying that the story "about the lioness discharging her womb in the act of parturition is a pure fable, and was merely invented to account for the scarcity of the animal."[180] However, when Horapollo's text was first studied with uncritical enthusiasm, the old account of Herodotus may well have been remembered as a corroborative statement from respected antiquity. Still, Horapollo's statement, with or without that of Herodotus, would have been corroborated and probably strengthened by the fact that so revered a church figure as Saint Basil had written a similar statement to the effect that the lioness becomes the mother of scarcely a single lion: *leaena vis unius leonis mater efficitur*.[181] The fact that the lion was already a long-established symbol for Christ made it understandable for the lioness to assume the connotation of His Mother.[182]

The creation in Venice at about the same time of three sketches by Jacopo Bellini (figs. 53–55), each containing a lioness as well as a lion, would seem also to have been a result of the influence of Horapollo's text. This work was known and respected in Venice, as the first printed version of the *Hieroglyphica* was issued in that city by Aldus Manutius in 1505. Still earlier, as noted by Seznec, it had inspired a chapter of Leon Battista Alberti's *De re aedificatoria* and had greatly influenced the illustrations of Francesco Colonna's *Hypnerotomachia Poliphili*. It is also possible that when Jacopo Bellini went to Florence in his youth, about

178. Reductorium morale super totam Bibliam, I. 10, c. 58; II. 691.

179. *The History of Herodotus*, trans. G. Rawlinson, p. 186.

180. *Historia animalium*, trans. D. W. Thompson, p. 574.

181. Homily ix on the Hexaemeron: The Creation of Animals in *Exegetic Homilies*, trans. Sister Agnes Clare Way, p. 143.

182. A. N. Didron, *Christian Iconography*, vol. 1, p. 341.

183. *The Development of the Italian Schools of Painting*, vol. 17, p. 129.

184. Jerome's treatise "Against Helvidius" was translated into English by John N. Hritzu in *The Fathers of the Church*, vol. 53, pp. 11–43.

185. John Hand (*Joos van Cleve and the Saint Jerome in the Norton Gallery and School of Art*, unpaginated, 9th column of text) has stressed still other types of iconographic evidence elucidating the very close connection between Jerome and the concept of the perpetual virginity of Mary. He mentions especially the white madonna lily, a preeminent symbol of Her virginity, placed in Jerome's study in the picture by the Boucicaut Master; the stoppered carafe, metal ewer, basin, and the clean white towel, "distinct references to the purity and virginity of Mary" in van Cleve's *Saint Jerome in His Study* (Cambridge, Mass). He further notes that this artist used these objects as Maryological symbols in his *Annunciation* (New York: Metropolitan Museum) and that they were included as well in the Merode triptych by the Master of Flemalle, in the same museum, and he suggests that Jerome's ideological alliance with Maryology was furthered by his early and continuing defense of the Immaculate Conception and, hence, of Mary's virginity, and also by his insistence upon personal celibacy and chastity. This last factor in his personal attitude has also been stressed in E. P. Burke's discussion of Jerome as a spiritual director (in F. X. Murphy, *A Monument to Saint Jerome*, pp. 155–63).

In his analysis of the iconography of van Eyck's Detroit painting, of *Saint Jerome in His Study*, Bergström ("Medicina, Fons et Scrinium," p. 14) was led to write as follows: "It seems a somewhat strange idea to include symbols which are normally appropriate for representations of the Holy Virgin in a picture of one of the fathers of the Church, and it demands some explanation. The symbols are all connected with the great mystery of the virginal birth of the incarnate word. It may be suggested van Eyck justly regarded Saint Jerome as particularly closely connected with the *verbum* in a special way because of his Latin translation of the Bible, the famous *versio vulgata*." Hand accepts this, and it seems plausible enough to me also; it is another line of connection between Jerome and

the middle of the quattrocento, he may have become acquainted with Horapollo's work. Jacopo was said to have been of an alert and curious temperament, and is thought to have found the teachings and ideas of the humanists congenial to his own tastes and inclinations.

These three sketches were not his only spontaneous designs for pictures of "Jerome in the Wilderness." In the same sketch books, now divided between the British Museum and the Louvre, are two other designs of the same theme that contain a lion in each, but no lioness. None of these outline sketches was used as a design for any of Jacopo's paintings that have come down to us, although Raimond van Marle did suggest that in two of them there are details that might conceivably be looked upon as bits used later in the paintings.[183] The drawings do tell us that Jacopo spent much time playing with the theme of Jerome in the wilderness. To that extent they are revealing of his familiarity with the iconographic acceptability of the lioness in the Jerome theme.

The lioness as a possible symbol of Mary was introduced into religious art only a few times, and then only in connection with Saint Jerome. Far from raising a seemingly unanswerable question as to why the Jerome theme should be singled out for such embellishment, this usage actually clarifies the iconography of the lioness-Mary figure. That it was possibly considered as a valid sign of the Virgin is enhanced by the fact that this would have supplied good reason for its inclusion precisely and exclusively in the Hieronymite context. Not only was the saint connected in the popular mind, through legend and art, with the lion, but also, early in his career, Jerome had ardently defended the concept of the perpetual virginity of Mary in the thesis *Adversus Helvidium*.[184] In this he argued at length against the statements of Helvidius, who had claimed that Mary had borne children to Joseph. Jerome's view, which won the acceptance and support of Pope Damasus, and which, in subsequent centuries, was even more widely upheld, argued that the presumed siblings of Jesus were children neither of Mary by Joseph nor of Joseph by an earlier marriage, but of another Mary, wife of Cleophas or Alphaeus, and said to have been a sister of the Virgin. It followed from this argument that the Virgin had, therefore, conceived only once, and that once, not by Joseph, but by divine power through the Holy Spirit. Jerome was the earliest and foremost of the champions of the concept of the perpetual virginity of Mary. If any saint provided the proper ambience for association in art with the lioness-Mary icon it was Jerome.[185]

Again, it must be kept in mind that while this icon seems to be something that grew out of Horapollo's text, that it seems to "fit" the otherwise puzzling production of the few works where the penitent Jerome has a lioness with him as well as a lion, this is all that can be said for it with any assurance. I know of no proof that Horapollo's text was the stimulus that it seems to have been.

It need only be repeated, in support of the foregoing argument, that in each of the mid-fifteenth-century works discussed, and even in the later Venetian painting by Marco Ricci, the additional lion is a female, not another male. This cannot be looked upon as mere coincidence; it can only imply that the lioness as an object added to the Jerome theme—and to that theme only—must have been meaningful and that this meaning

Figure 178. Domenichino, *Saint Jerome in a Landscape*. Glasgow Art Gallery.

must have had a bearing on, or a relation to, the story and life of that saint.

The fact that the lioness was seldom used is paralleled by the even more infrequent introduction of another symbol, also involving the Virgin, into a very few pictures of "Saint Jerome in His Study." In these the motivating reason was similar to that outlined for the lioness—the saint's long and ardent defense of the concept of the "perpetual virginity of Mary." In these instances we find in Jerome's study the apple, symbol of original sin, and a jar or ewer of medicinal antidotes for that evil. These, in turn, are symbols of the healing power of the Virgin, particularly of the Virgin bearing within Her the incarnate Christ. Whereas the lioness appears to have been used solely in connection with the Jerome story, the apple and the antidote were more often employed in pictures of the Annunciation than of the scholar-saint, but their occasional transfer to pictures of the latter reflects his great attachment to the cult of Mary.

It is not to detract from the particular pertinence of the lioness-Mary icon to the story of Jerome to suggest that its very limited use in art may have been due to the fact that the lioness, as a creature, was associated too firmly with concepts of ferocity to be readily adaptable as a visible the basic tenets of Maryological thought. However, it must be admitted, as I hope I have expressed in the discussion of the lioness as a possible symbol of Mary, that real proof still is lacking.

Crowe and Cavalcaselle (*A History of Painting in North Italy*, vol. 1, p. 94, fn. 1) mention a lioness with her cub in the cave in the background of Carlo Crivelli's predella picture of *Saint Jerome in Penitence* in London. In reality, however, there is only one animal—and it is a sleeping dog! (fig. 35). In one of his paintings of *Saint Jerome in the Wilderness*, now in the Glasgow Art Gallery (fig. 178), Domenichino painted a lioness instead of a lion. I can only assume that this may have been a "slip" on his part, as in his other versions the artist painted a lion. At least I know of no evidence that Domenichino knew, or cared very much about, the symbolic distinction between the lion and the lioness.

Figure 179. Paul Lautensack, *Annunciation*. Present whereabouts unknown; formerly in Hospital Church of Grimmenthal. Illustration from Friedrich Rudolphi, *Gotha Diplomatica*, 1717.

186. Wittkower, p. 29.

187. Evans, pp. 101–2. The Lautensack picture, reproduced in F. Rudolphi, *Gotha Diplomatica* (opp. p. 310), has been made available to me in a photograph from that book (fig. 179) through the kind cooperation of the Joseph Regenstein Library of the University of Chicago. It is certainly not an "Annunciation," as Evans briefly called it, in the usual form, but rather a conglomeration of images pertinent to the mystery of the divine Motherhood of Mary—images stemming from biblical sources, from hymns, and from the lays of the medieval troubadours. Inasmuch as it is an almost unknown picture, now lost as well, and iconographically highly peculiar, it may be discussed here at some length, especially since it contains the "Maria Leo" of immediate interest to the present study.

The textual caption above the woodcut reproduction in Rudolphi's book reads "Abbildung der Altar Tafel in der Hospital Kirche zu Grimmenthal; Oder der Neuen Walfarth im 'Ämte Masifeld'" ("Illustration of the Altar Panel in the Hospital Church of Grimmenthal, Or the New Pilgrimage (Church) in the Do-

"sign" for the kind and gentle Virgin. Something of this seems to have been in Wittkower's mind when he wrote that Desiderio's lioness is a kind of "counterpart to the acolyte, and one might even argue that she is perhaps meant to illustrate the curbing of fear in the beast by the magic attention of the God-inspired man."[186] In Desiderio's beautiful relief everything seems to be so thoroughly planned that the lioness cannot be looked upon except as a meaningful addition. That there were other uses of the lioness-Mary emblem is shown by the fact that in a painting attributed to Paul Lautensak (Paul von Bamberg), formerly in the Hospital Church at Grimmenthal, now lost (fig. 179), there was a lion breathing over two motionless whelps, with above it the words *Maria Leo*.[187] It may be recalled that other seemingly "unlikely" allegorical

main of Masifeld"). In Hans Vollmer's continuation of the standard Thieme Becker series (vol. 22, p. 463), the picture is referred to as *Heiligendarstellung, Hortus Conclusus,* or *Sacred Personages in the Closed Garden*.

The angel Gabriel, definitely identified by the words *Angelus Gabrielis* immediately over his head, is blowing a slender trumpet held in his left hand, and is holding in his right hand a spear and a leash attached to two dogs, the inscriptions on the collars of which may be read as *Pax* ("peace") and *Justitia* ("justice"). These

dogs are close upon the heels of two others, not on the leash, which are pursuing a unicorn that has reached the seated Mary and is about to lay its head on Her lap. The unicorn was a symbol of chastity; its head on the Virgin's lap was likened to the immaculately conceived Christ Child in Her womb (see p. 153). Over Mary's halo are the words *Maria unicornis*; at Her feet is a plant, next to which, immediately below Her, are the words *Virgo Jessia florida* ("Virgin, Flower of Jesse," the ancestral lineage of Mary). In the upper-right background

Moses is shown kneeling before the burning bush, from the top of which God extends His right hand in benediction; this has the wording *Rub, Moysis*, while in the empty sky above appear the words *Maria aquila* ("Mary Eagle"), an expression that may be traced back to Albertus Magnus (*Opera omnium*, vol. 20, p. 451), who used those exact words "Maria aquila," a symbolism treated in more detail here in the Bestiary account of the eagle. Not shown in the painting, the eagle was also a symbol of Christ, of majesty, and of nobility. In the patristic literature Mary is sometimes called *nidus dei* ("nest of God"). Thus, to quote Albertus Magnus again (p. 272), "nidus columbae, id est, receptaculum spiritus sancti, qui sicut columba, descendit in Christum" ("the nest of the dove, the receptacle of the Holy Spirit, which, like the dove, descended into Christ").

To the right of Gabriel is a lion breathing over its inert whelps; above it, the interpretive label *Maria leo* ("Mary Lion."). This is, of course, the detail of immediate pertinence to our present study, as evidence of meanings expressed by the lion and of their bearing on the lioness as a sign of Mary. The lion was believed to erase its tracks with its tail as it walked, to sleep with its eyes open, and to revive, or to give life to, its dormant cubs three days after birth. Thus, it was likened to Christ, Who concealed the traces of His divinity when He assumed human form, Who never closed His eyes to kindness and compassion, and Who was raised from the dead three days after His entombment. The lion is sometimes shown in art together with another symbol of Christ's sacrifice, the pelican feeding its young with its blood from its own breast, the so-called "pelican in its piety" figure. This group is actually present in the Grimmenthal picture; it also appears in other compositions including the lion, as in stained-glass windows at Freiburg and in the church of St. Etienne, at Bruges (Rowland, p. 119). The figure of the pelican at its nest with its young is related to the concept of Mary as the *nidus dei*, and, its avian form also partly suggests a sign of the eagle *Aquila*. We may note that the figure of an eagle at its nest with its young, practically a superimposition of the eagle on the more usual "pelican," occurs in a sixteenth-century emblem titled *Amor Filiorum* ("love of offspring"), illustrated in Henkel and Schöne, col. 813, from Florentius Schoonhovius, *Emblemata* no. 50. This emblem

also involves something of the phoenix in its ornithological composite, as the nest is shown in flames.

To the right of the lion is an orant man before a gate bearing the words *Porta Coeli* ("Gate of Heaven"), above which rises the figure of the Almighty, His right hand raised in benediction, His left holding the sphere surmounted by the Cross. A crescent moon is to His left (viewer's right) with the words *Pulcra ut Luna*, and the sun to His right, appropriately titled *Clara ut Sol*, to the immediate right of which we find the words *Maria phoenix* with the eight-pointed star, *Stella maris*, to its right. On the ground immediately before the kneeling man is a stretched hide labeled *Vellus Gideonis*, ("fleece of Gideon"). This is, of course, a story taken from the Bible (Judges 6:36–40), the point of which is that the fleece became a Divine sign of assured success. When Gideon was about to begin his military campaign to free the Israelites from the oppression of the Midianites, he asked God for a sign of His assistance, saying, "Behold, I will put a fleece of wool on the floor; and if the dew be on the fleece only, and it be dry upon all the earth besides, then shall I know that Thou wilt save Israel by mine hand, as Thou hast said."

Still other unusual items are also included in this exceptional composition, but we have mentioned enough of them to emphasize the multiplicity of Marias in the "text" of this picture: *Maria aquila* in the upper right near the Moses incident and the *altare aureum* ("golden altar")and the depiction of the pelican and its young; *Maria phoenix* ("Mary arisen"), *Maria unicornis* ("Mary, the Immaculate"); *Maria leo* ("Mary, Lion, the lifegiver"); the lion breathing life into its young being comparable to the role of the Word in the conception of Christ). The whole action of the picture takes place behind a wall, the gate of which bears the words *Hortus conclusus*, ("closed garden"), an old and widely used symbol of the purity of Mary in Her protected life. Actually, just to the left of Her face is a little circle, a polished circular mirror disc, with a face on it, possibly a reflection of Mary's, and around its border are the words *Speculum sine macula* ("mirror, or image, without stain"), an obvious reference to the Immaculate Conception, a theme still further suggested by the immediately adjacent fountain, the "Fountain of Life" mentioned in the Song of Solomon (4:12, 15), another image used

to express the purity and immaculateness of Mary. As if this were not enough, the artist has added, just behind the unicorn, between it and the pursuing dogs, a flowering lilylike (or iris?) plant with the words *sicut lilium inter spina* ("as a lily among thorns")!

The items included in this altarpiece may be divided into two groups as far as their symbolic orientation is concerned. One group, the fleece of Gideon and the figure of Moses listening to the voice of God, refers to divine guidance; indeed, the tale of Gideon and his fleece has been looked upon as a prediction of the later divine guidance associated with the figure of the angel Gabriel, namely the virgin birth he announced to Mary. The other group includes the various Marias and the story of the unicorn. All are references to the perpetual purity and virginity of Mary, divinely selected for this role. The general emphasis of so many of the items in this picture on this one theme confirms the thought that the lion—the Maria leo—is similarly oriented symbolically to this concept.

A welcome corroboration of this overall interpretation is to be found in Salzer's book (esp. pp. 12–58). While no mention is made of the Grimmenthal altarpiece, Salzer discusses so many of the items included in it that it seems he may well have known it. However, his studies were not of art but of the literature that lay behind the visual renditions. Thus, he mentions and gives references to "sources" in medieval Latin hymns, in the *Physiologus*, and in the songs of the itinerant medieval minstrels, for each of the following images that occur in the Grimmenthal painting: the Moses incident (pp. 12,. 35), the fleece of Gideon (pp. 40–42), the unicorn (pp. 44–50), the lion (pp. 54–57), and the pelican (p. 58). He notes that Mary was mentioned explicitly as the "lion's mother" by Epiphanius, Basil, Bochart, and Berchorius. The last named (vol. 2, p. 691) made a direct comparison between the lioness and Mary, as noted earlier. In the *Speculum historiale* ("Mirror of History") portion of the great thirteenth-century compendium of Vincent of Beauvais, the *Speculum majus*, the Virgin Mary is explicitly typified by the burning bush and by the fleece of Gideon, among other symbols (Taylor, *The Medieval Mind*, vol. 2, p. 110). Identical symbolism is present also in hymns written for the festival of the Assumption, and for Christmas, by the slightly earlier (twelfth-century) Adam of Saint-Victor. Thus, in a Christmas hymn, one stanza reads:

"Frondem, florem, nucem sicca
Virgo profert, et pudica
  Virgo Dei Filium.
Fert coelestem vellus rorem
Creatura creatorem,
  Creaturae pretium."

The fourth line, "a fleece bears heavenly dew," is an obvious reference to the fleece of Gideon as a sign of the Virgin as the mother of Christ. The entire poem is given in Gautier, *Oeuvres poetiques d'Adam de Saint-Victor*, p. 10.

188. A Katzenellenbogen, *Allegories of the Virtues and Vices in Mediaeval Art*, pp. 38–39; Suida, *A Catalogue of Paintings in the John and Mable Ringling Museum of Art*, p. 7.

189. "Icones Symbolicae: The Visual Image in Neo-Platonic Thought," pp. 172–73.

190. *Renaissance and Renascences in Western Art*, p. 178.

usages have been found in the iconography of religious art. A case in point is that of the allegories of the Virtues shown in the act of crucifying Christ in order to prove themselves at His death.[188]

At the same time it must be realized that in general, in Neo-Platonic thought, the symbolic implication of an object was not explicitly represented by the symbol, but was somehow incorporated and embodied in its otherwise unlikely form. As E. H. Gombrich interpreted Ficino's doctrine of the use of such symbols, there is no possibility of a completely rational elucidation because it is basically an irrational mode of thinking.[189] Furthermore, the distinction between the symbol as a representational object and its use in the act of symbolizing is always somewhat imprecise; inconsistency is part of its inevitable nature. It is only within the terms and conditions of this mental system, devoid of sharp, crisp definitions, that the acceptance and use of hieroglyphs and other pictorial symbols can be appreciated. Gombrich reminds us that "the gravity with which the casuistry of the emblem and the device was discussed by otherwise perfectly sane and intelligent people remains an inexplicable freak of fashion unless we understand that for them a truth condensed into a visual image was somehow nearer the realm of absolute truth than one explained in words."

Erwin Panofsky considered that in spite of its enthusiastic acceptance by the Medicean humanists shortly after 1419, the *Hieroglyphica* failed to interest any artist for more than two generations.[190] This would suggest that Horapollo's book did not exert any influence until after its praise by Ficino, which could hardly have been early enough to affect Desiderio's beautiful relief. This carving, if done as thought between 1455 and 1460, would have been created while Ficino (born in 1433) was still in his twenties. Who, if anyone, may have brought Horapollo to Desiderio's attention is therefore unknown.

The Lizard

Lizards appear in renditions of "Jerome in the Wilderness" fairly often. These creatures have been noted in some twenty-six versions of the theme by the following artists: Andrea di Giusto (fig. 43); Basaiti (Budapest); Gentile Bellini (Toledo, Ohio, fig. 26); Giovanni Bellini (Washington, fig. 22, and Florence); Bermejo (Barcelona); Bosch (Ghent and Venice, figs. 108, 109); Buonconsiglio (Venice); Dürer (Raveningham Hall); Francesco di Giorgio (fig. 120); Luini (two paintings, both in Vienna); Masaccio circle or Giovanni Toscani (Princeton); Pacher (Munich); Patinir (New York); Pesellino (London; predella to altarpiece by Fra Diamante and Filippo Lippi); Pinturicchio (two pictures, in Baltimore and Perugia); Sadeler (etching, supposedly after a painting by Mostaert, which I have not found); Sassetta (Washington Crossing); Solario attribution (Bowes Museum, Barnard Castle); von Saaz (Prague); Titian (two pictures, one in Milan and one said to be a workshop version of the Brera painting, in Rome).

The lizard, based on the ancient tale in the *Physiologus*, of the "sun lizard," was a "seeker after salvation" and thus was eminently suitable as an associate of Jerome in penitence. The story, which has been mentioned in the chapter on Bosch's two pictures (p. 140), tells us that when the lizard becomes more or less blind in its old age, it crawls into a crevice in a rock or a wall facing the east, and there stretches its head to the rising sun, which restores its sight. As Edward Payson Evans repeated the implied moral, "In like manner, O man, thou who hast on the old garment, and the eyes of whose heart are obscured, seek the wall of help, and watch there until the sun of righteousness, which the prophet calls the dayspring, rises with healing power, and removes thy spiritual blindness."[191] Knowledge of this symbolism is what probably caused William Norton Howe to write of Titian's Brera picture that, "a sympathetic lizard watches St. Jerome at his self-discipline before the crucifix";[192] as otherwise it would be difficult to appraise the expression of a lizard in this way.

An outgrowth of the *Physiologus* legend is reflected in one of the emblems in Camerarius, in which a lizard illustrates the motto *Hinc redit ad vires* ("hence return to strength").[193] Heinrich Bodmer furthers the concept inherent in the original story by describing the lizard as an allegory of fidelity, loyalty, and sincerity.[194]

The lizard was at times confused with the superficially somewhat similar salamander, a creature supposed to be able to live unharmed in fire. Thus, Federico Gonzaga, Duke of Mantua (1500–1540), had a motto with a picture of *lacerta* (lizard) in the midst of flames, which read *Qvod Huic Deest, Me Torqvet* ("What this one [the lizard] lacks or knows not [i.e., the consuming flames of amorous fire] torments me"), a statement based on Aristotle's comment that the lizard is cold by nature. In this combination of lizard and salamander the creature could be suspected, in pictures of Jerome in penitence, to be an allusion to the saint, who was tormented in his stay in the wilderness by erotic visions. It cannot be stated, however, that this was intended in any one case. The lizard was mentioned in the Bible (Leviticus 11:30) as one of the unclean beasts.

Artists took considerable liberty in their renditions of lizards—from very dark, almost blackish, as in Bosch's Ghent painting, to pale green and yellow, as in the Montreal picture attributed to Andrea di Giusto.

191. *Animal Symbolism in Ecclesiastical Architecture*, p. 94.

192. *Animal Life in Italian Painting*, p. 90.

193. Camerarius, *Centuria I*, no. 86, p. 172.

194. Leonardo, p. 233.

195. This painting is in the Schlesisches Museum für Kunstgewerbe und Altertümer in Wroclaw, Poland (formerly Breslau, Germany); illustrated in E. G. Troche, *Schlesische Quellen zur Altniederländischen Malerei*, p. 129.

The Magpie

The magpie, *Pica pica*, one of the most strikingly marked of the larger common birds of Europe, had many legends about it, mostly of its thieving nature and its cleverness and intelligence, but not much of the sort that would bring it into the ambience of the Jerome story. The magpie was used very seldom in that context; in fact, only two such instances have been found in the present survey: a Silesian picture of "Saint Jerome in Penitence," dated about 1500,[195] and one painting by Hieronymus Bosch (Venice, fig. 109). In both of these works the magpie is inconspicuous and in the background; in the very far background indeed, in the Bosch picture, and on a rock behind Jerome in the anonymous Silesian painting.

The magpie was loosely associated with the idea of the conflict and uncertainty of life and death, and in this sense was pictured with the gallows, as in Brueghel's *Magpie and Gallows*, or, as in Bosch's *The Peddler*, perched on a gate that simulates a gallows. Insofar as the Jerome theme is concerned, the magpie, with its bold pattern of black and white, signifies the frailty of human decisions, with, it seems, an element of optimism about the correctness of the outcome. In the *Parzifal* of the great medieval German poet and minnesinger Wolfram von Eschenbach, a dramatic poem dealing with the conflict between faith (light) and ignorance or doubt (darkness), the white person is characterized as the knightly, ideal man; the black one symbolizes moral wavering; while the black and white person fights and overcomes doubt. The magpie, with its combination of the two colors, and with its general reputation for cleverness, is the victorious pied individual.[196] Probably also stemming from the concept of moral victory is the old Flemish use of "ver Ave" or "frau Ave" as common names for this bird.[197] The fact that this legend was Teutonic, and not known in Italy, may account for the bird's absence in Italian renditions of the Jerome story.

The Monkey

The monkey is of little importance in the iconography of Saint Jerome. It has been found in only three pictures, in each of which the kind of monkey shown is a long-tailed macaque, probably the rhesus monkey, *Macacus rhesus*, of India, a very common species and the best known of the many Old World monkeys. A species that was frequently tamed, it was often brought to Europe at a very early date. The only monkey native to Europe (today only at Gibraltar), the Barbary ape, is a larger species with practically no tail, and is definitely not the kind depicted in these renditions of Jerome. The three pictures are all of the saint in penitence: one by Jacopo Bellini (Verona, fig. 29); one by Giovanni Mansueti (Bergamo, fig. 36); and one by Marco Zoppo (Baltimore, fig. 64).

In the illustration of the Bellini, the monkey unfortunately does not show up clearly. It has been commented on by Horst Janson as a prime instance of the animal's traditional role in legend and allegory as a hypo-critical parody on man.[198] It is squatting on the ground behind the praying saint and has its front paws folded in a simulated prayerful atti-tude, "feigning the outward forms of piety but utterly lacking in the spirit of repentance." In the Mansueti the monkey is in the middle of the bottom of the painting, partly cut off by the picture's edge. In the Zoppo, there are no less than three macaques on the classical ruins at left, in as many different poses, but none seemingly involved in anything pertinent to the theme of the picture.

Janson's exhaustive study of apes and ape lore in the Middle Ages and the Renaissance makes it unnecessary to repeat here the largely un-favorable symbolism of the monkey, especially since it had little perti-

196. K. Seligmann ("Hieronymus Bosch: The Peddler," p. 100) also cites earlier references.

197. Grimm, p. 675.

198. *Apes and Ape Lore in the Middle Ages and the Renaissance.*

nence to the Jerome theme. Its place in thought and allegory is summed up in the condemnatory phrase *turpissima bestia, simillima nostri* ("most shameful beast, so similar to ourselves"), an epitome of the subhuman in man.[199]

The Mouse

The mouse occurs but once, to my knowledge, in any rendition of the Jerome story, a painting by Colantonio of the saint in his study extracting the thorn from the lion's foot (fig. 1). The mouse is in the right background, quite removed from the main action of the picture, and is small and obscure enough to escape notice by the casual viewer. Anna Jameson suggested that the mouse, looking into an empty cup, expressed the self-denial of the penitent saint,[200] but this is an unwarranted assumption. For one thing, Jerome is not shown as a penitent and is not in any form of deprivation or want, but is comfortably established in his well-ordered, book-lined study. Furthermore, the mouse is not looking into an empty cup, but is gnawing away on a little scrap of paper. Another, larger scrap lies on the floor behind and to the left of the lion, which makes one wonder why all this litter in the saint's study. The usual implication of the mouse in art is that of "destructive time, the great devourer," because of its usual relentless gnawing away on objects, as the mouse is here doing with the bit of paper. The mouse eating the paper may be a reference to the oblivion that results when records are destroyed.

It was this meaning that Panofsky rightly considered Michelangelo had in mind for the mouse he intended (but failed) to carve on his monument to Giuliano de Medici.[201] Horapollo also stated that the mouse represents destruction, but added that it also includes the concept of discrimination in its destructive effects, as it selects the best of the pieces of bread lying about: "Wherefore the judgement of the baker lies in the mouse."[202]

We know so little about Colantonio or about what details there may have been in his supposed van Eyckian model that it is unwise to suggest any special meaning for his inclusion of the mouse. In van Eyck's known works every little detail has been shown to have real meaning and reason, and it would be understandable if Colantonio might have wanted to be similarly purposeful. Possibly some further explanation of the picture may be gained from the writing on four pieces of paper that seem deliberately placed for such attention, two on the bookshelf immediately above the lion's head, one on the floor behind the lion, and one tacked on the right end of Jerome's desk, over his cardinal's hat. However, I have not been able to decipher any of them. Even these might make no reference to the mouse, which is curiously insignificant in Colantonio's picture.

Beryl Rowland has brought together much information about the symbolic connotations expressed by the figure of the mouse.[203] The little creature was not only a symbol of destructiveness (and death) but also of fertility—quite the opposite. Rowland notes that Pliny considered the mouse to be the most prolific of all known animals, that 120 mice

199. E. Panofsky, *Studies in Iconology*, p. 195.

200. *Sacred and Legendary Art*, p. 298.

201. The theme of the mouse as "destructive time" is well expressed in Panofsky's study, *The Mouse that Michelangelo Failed to Carve*.

202. Boas, p. 80.

203. *Animals with Human Faces*, pp. 127–29.

might be born to one mother. It was even believed that unborn mice still in their mother's womb were sometimes pregnant. This excessive fecundity led to the creature's becoming a sign of lechery, especially of female lechery.

As a death symbol the mouse was used to represent the souls of departed persons. As a symbol of avarice and greed the mouse was used to signify thieves, who, in their avid desire for gain, steal from others. Rowland quotes from the *Allegoria in sacram scripturam* of Rabanus Maurus as a source for this derogatory statement: "Mystice autem mures significat homines cupiditate terrena inhiantes et praedam de aliena substantia surripientes" ("mystically, mice symbolize persons who in their eager desire for mundane wealth steal their loot from another's store").

The Otter

The otter has been identified in only two pictures of the Jerome theme: Giovanni Mansueti's *Saint Jerome in Penitence* (Bergamo, fig. 36) and Vittore Carpaccio's *Saint Jerome Leading the Lion Back to the Monastery* (Venice, fig. 31). The Mansueti painting contains not only the elderly, white-bearded, kneeling figure of the penitent saint, but surrounding him a veritable menagerie, consisting of his faithful lion, a white dog, a bear, an otter, a squirrel, two rabbits, a doe, a monkey, two cheetahs, an eagle, a small owl, a small, dark, long-tailed bird with a hooked, parrotlike beak (unfortunately, not certainly identifiable), and a small, unidentifiable dark mammal only partly in the picture at the center of its lower edge. All this on a little rounded piece of land, a sharply demarcated area of the total picture! Behind and to the right is a busy scene with buildings, a church, a castle tower, a stream on which are four boatmen in two boats. Two women are doing their laundry; four ducks and six swans are swimming; and, in the area next to the stream, are numerous people, cows, sheep, dogs, and a laden ass! One has the feeling that if the picture had been larger the artist would have put still more into it. Yet, to give Mansueti the credit that is due him, Saint Jerome and the crucifix, on which his attention is fixed, dominate the scene.

The otter, quite accurately rendered, with its pale grayish head clearly differentiated from its dark brown body, and with a dark area around the eyes and at the tip of its snout, is immediately behind Jerome's feet. Like so many of the creatures in paintings of this sort, relative size is not adhered to: the otter is much smaller than the lion, but almost as large as the bear immediately below it in the painting's lower-left corner.

The otter, like many of its companions in this crowded picture, is inactive; it is just there, adding its presence as a recognizable member of Saint Jerome's excessive faunal entourage. Whether it was inserted for any special symbolic meaning is uncertain, particularly so with an artist like Mansueti, who was much given to crowding his pictures. However, since there is a possible symbolism involved, it may now be discussed.

Four kinds of mammals, superficially somewhat similar but zoologically quite distinct—the otter, the weasel (not the ermine or white winter pelage of the weasel), the mongoose, and the ichneumon—seem all to be somewhat interchangeable in an old tale originally stemming from

Egypt, where the native animal would be the ichneumon. In Europe the legend of the ichneumon was transferred to the otter and occasionally to the weasel, which beasts were known to the people there, in place of the exotic ichneumon and mongoose, which were not. In the original Egyptian tales the ichneumon was venerated because it was said to feed largely on the eggs of the crocodile. Wittkower found that it was held sacred as early as the twelfth dynasty (2000–1780 B.C.) and noted that classical authors, from Aristotle to Strabo and Pliny, described the ichneumon as a great enemy of snakes, on which it was said to feed.[204] Plutarch believed that its veneration resulted from its effective enmity toward serpents and crocodiles, and in this sense the story of the ichneumon-otter in the *Physiologus* was essentially an adaptation into Christian allegory of the preexisting Egyptian legend.

According to the legend of both the ichneumon and of its otter replacement, the animal rolled itself in the mud until it was completely covered. Then it would lie in the sun to let the mud dry and form a hard, armorlike plate protecting it. When it saw a crocodile sleeping with its mouth open, as is characteristic of these great saurians, it would enter the mouth, where its caked mud armor would protect it from the teeth of the huge reptile, which would then swallow it whole. In the warmth and moisture of the monster's stomach, the mud would soften and then the ichneumon would immediately begin to chew at the entrails of its engulfer, and, in this way, kill the beast so much larger and more powerful than itself. The victorious ichneumon would then emerge from the body of its prostrate foe.

In the ancient legends the ichneumon of the Nile was variously termed the Hydrus or Enhydrus. When the tale was taken over by the Christian moralists the crocodile became a symbol of Death and of Hell. By inference, in the logic of allegory, its enemy would assume the meaning of Christ, Who not only gave promise of eternal life, but Who also made a "Descent into Limbo," comparable to the ichneumon's or the otter's experience inside the crocodile, and where He rescued some of the lost souls present there. Edward Payson Evans put it as follows: "So our Saviour, after having put on flesh, descended into hell and carried away the souls dwelling therein; and as the otter comes forth unharmed from the belly of the crocodile, so our Lord rose from the grave on the third day, alive and uninjured. The ichneumon is fabled to slay the dragon in the same manner, and both animals are symbols of the triumph of the incarnate God over Satan."[205]

In Carpaccio's famous painting of *Saint Jerome Leading the Lion to the Monastery* (fig. 31), there are a great many kinds of animals, mostly done with considerable naturalistic accuracy—a stag, a roebuck, guineafowl, parrot, peacock, rabbit, a possible gazelle, and an otter. Guido Perocco praised these as copied from nature, and obviously studied with the passion of a naturalist ("studiati dal vero . . . con la passione del naturalista").[206] Unfortunately, he lessened the intended effect of his praise by misidentifying the otter as a beaver. The scene is one of considerable consternation: several of Jerome's monks are fleeing from the approaching lion and their disturbance is reflected in the running pose of the stag (red deer) and of the peacock. The otter is not disturbed, but is resting quietly.[207] This creature was identified years ago by William

204. "Miraculous Birds," pp. 253–57.

205. *Animal Symbolism in Ecclesiastical Architecture*, pp. 131–33.

206. *Carpaccio*, p. 108.

207. Giehlow, p. 108, in translating a passage from Horapollo's *Hieroglyphica* (book II, no. 87), informed us that the combination of otter and deer was a visual symbol of "blindly fleeing," which is what Jerome's monks are doing in Carpaccio's picture. However, Giehlow used the word "otter" inadvisedly. In German the word "otter" is used for the animal we call by that name, but it is also an old and infrequent name for the viper. The sense of Horapollo's statement clearly suggests the snake rather than the aquatic mammal. Aside from Giehlow, all other commentators on Horapollo have considered the reference to be to a viper.

208. *Animal Life in Italian Painting*, p. 78.

209. Formerly in the Liechtenstein Collection, present whereabouts unknown; illustrated in Hind, *Early Italian Engravings*, no. 86.

210. Henkel and Schöne, col. 466, write of the "Fischotter" that it is a "Tyrann, der von Wut und Raserei geschwollen ist," a seemingly extreme interpretation of its supposed habit of overeating.

For further symbolic usages, see also Charbonneau-Lassay, pp. 314–16 (mangouste-ichneumon) and p. 317 (otter); Rowland, pp. 129–30; and Camerarius (xcv).

To a very limited degree the otter was at times confused with the beaver because the two creatures are somewhat similar in size and general coloration, and both are aquatic as well as terrestrial in habit. In my discussion of the beaver I mentioned that the beavers' teeth figured in the "Cure for Dropsy," a medical connection that also enters into the story of the Hydrus, another name for the ichneumon (Kirschbaum, et al., p. 289). This confusion apparently does not affect any version of the Jerome legend in art.

Norton Howe as a genet,[208] but from a small black and white photograph it agrees much more with Mansueti's rendition of the otter.

These are the only identifiable otters I have found in connection with the Jerome theme. However, what appears to be an attempt to portray an ichneumon occurs in a single Italian engraving, of about 1480–1500, by an unidentified artist, depicting *Saint Jerome in Penitence*.[209] In this design the animal, shown drinking from a stream, is in the lower-left corner; the other animals present are the saint's usual lion and a tortoise, a rarely used symbol of evil.

The otter also had an unfavorable meaning—a despot or a tyrant swollen with rage and frenzy. This was based on a legend that the animal killed far more fish than it could use, a gluttonous creature with a lust for killing.[210] This meaning obviously does not enter into the beast's usage in its few occurrences in the Jerome context. It appears to have been of only slight use in any context.

The Owl

Three different kinds of owls have been found in renditions of the "Saint Jerome in the Wilderness" theme—the barn owl, *Tyto alba*, the "eared," or scops owl, *Otus scops*, and the "earless," little owl, *Athene noctua*. To avoid misunderstanding and possible redundant explanations, it may be said that by "eared" is meant having erectile feather tufts that project from the upper side of the head like small horns or ears; by "earless" is meant the absence of such tufts. While all three species of owls are symbolically equivalent in some respects, it is well to distinguish between them, because in other ways they do have different implications. These meanings may be clarified briefly. The owl that was the ancient Greek bird of "Wisdom," the avian sign of Minerva, or Athena, Goddess of Wisdom, was the little owl; the owl most intimately associated with the concept of "Death" was the barn owl; the scops owl was basically the bird of "Darkness." In the course of centuries all owls came to share in these sinister implications as creatures that preferred the dark and shunned the daylight. All three species are common and widely distributed throughout the art-producing countries of Europe, and all three were well known.

The barn owl was not only a bird of Death, often associated with cemeteries, particularly churchyard burial grounds, but its habit of nesting frequently in the steeples of nearby churches caused it to become known also as the "church owl" ("Kircheule" in German), and the whitish color of its breast and abdomen also gave it the name of "white owl." These two appellations opened the way for the bird to acquire a favorable connotation as a symbol of the church, without shedding its meaning of Death. The long and involved history of this ambivalent symbolism of the barn owl is gone into in detail in my discussion of Cosimo Tura's painting of *Saint Jerome in Penitence* (p. 176 ff.), where the evidence suggests that the bird has been reinfused with its favorable, but rarely expressed meanings—the only instance of its kind in the Jerome context.

Owls occur infrequently in the iconography of Saint Jerome. Originally, I had anticipated that they would prove to be much more commonly used, but after a very prolonged search I am able to report their presence in only twelve compositions, all dealing with the penitent saint in the wilderness. Only twelve instances out of a total of more than six hundred paintings, reliefs, engravings, and other graphics, and one tapestry depicting Jerome in landscapes of varying degrees of desolation or of rural verdure! One reason for anticipating a higher frequency of owls in these compositions was that one of the established meanings associated with these nocturnal birds was that of Solitude, a concept certainly germane to a portrayal of a religious eremite. It must be remembered that the idea involved in the retreat from human society, with all its faults and evils, into the seclusion of the wilderness, was to enable the anchorite to commune with spiritual, as opposed to secular, matters. Religious hermits were a group apart from the rest of mankind: they had shown a willingness to forego the amenities and the fleshpots of societal life, and to that extent had purged themselves of some of the sins and weaknesses of their fellows. It is, therefore, surprising that the owl, avian symbol of Solitude, was so rarely included in their depiction. There must have been a reason for this general exclusion of the owl—and the reason was that the bird was more generally looked upon as a sardonic, evil creature of darkness than as a favorable symbol to accompany salvation-seeking hermits. The other basically evil creatures that were more frequently included, especially snakes and scorpions, were dangerous or malicious, but not "antiethical" as were owls in their deliberate preference for the darkness as opposed to the light.

Another expectation that proved to be erroneous was that the owl, as an ancient and well-known symbol of Wisdom, would figure, as an accessory item, in pictures showing Jerome in his study chamber. This pictorial composition became a widely accepted visual image of the erudite scholar-saint, the most learned of the Church Fathers. The "Jerome in His Study" icon came to include overtones of humanism, of scholarship leaning on or growing from the ancient, classical cultures in which the owl was the avian associate of Minerva. That owls were banned from, or, at least, not included in, any of these icons, more than a hundred of which have been examined in the present study, would seem to be because of the same dominating influence that made them rarely accepted in renditions of the saint in the wilderness. Wisdom and learning were supposed to be sources of illumination and light in a world all too often unclear and dismal, but it seemed unacceptable to connect these concepts with a bird that habitually preferred the darkness to the light of day. The ecclesiastical scholars, who influenced the iconography of art, were probably well aware of the fact that the owl had an ancient and honorable association with the concept of Wisdom, but the bird's sinister implications seemed to outweigh its favorable ones in their judgment.

Mention should be made at this point of one possible exception. A manuscript illumination in the Huntington Library (HM 1807, f. 134) by an unknown French artist, made at Amiens around 1450, of "Saint Jerome in His Study," shows the saint seated in a thronelike chair with a high back, the two upper corners of which terminate in little carved figures of faunal designs. The one in the right corner resembles a scops owl, although this is not wholly clear; the other corner figure appears to be a squatting mammal.

Throughout the late Middle Ages and the Renaissance, the primary meaning associated with the owl was unquestionably that of the bird of darkness, a macabre and sinister creature. As a result, as noted earlier, the owl was frequently used as a pictorial reference to the Jews, who preferred to remain in the dark of the pre-Christian world rather than to come out into the new light brought there by the Messiah. Jerome himself defined the owl as a symbol of False Deity.[211] This derogatory consideration of owls as "unwise" creatures was enough to exclude them from pictures of Jerome as a scholar-saint. The degree to which that attitude prevailed has been described by Horst Janson, Jakob Rosenberg, and, more recently, in an exhaustive compilation of the use and the lore of owls in European art by Heinrich Schwarz and Volker Plagemann.[212]

However, as is so often the case with symbols, especially symbols that were transmitted from one culture to another with a total span of many centuries of use, the figure of the owl came to encompass, at various times and in various places, many, and even some unreconcilably opposed, meanings. The mere fact that the same avian figure could mean "Wisdom" at one time and "False Deity" at another, that it could be the bird of "Darkness" and yet be the "Illuminator of the Darkness," the bird of "Death" and of "Reflection on the Future Life" shows how versatile, how pliant, and how adjustable a symbolic element the owl has been throughout the history of European culture. Because of the multiplicity of its possible allegorical implications, and because all of these connotations persisted through the centuries, even if, in some cases, seldom coming to prominent usage, we must be prepared to find that two or more meanings may be implied in the same owl image, even if one connotation may be more immediately obvious than the others. The difficulty is usually one of interpretation, because documents are seldom available to inform us as to exactly what the artist or his clients may have had in mind in any specific case.

Schwarz and Plagemann brought together examples of owls in European art, where the bird stands for more than two dozen concepts, many of them quite similar in meaning, others quite divergent. If we add to these a smaller number not included in their compilation, we find the owl figure has served in European culture as a visual reference to the following persons, places, and ideas: amulet against the evil eye and epilepsy, Athens (a symbol identifying a city in a picture as Athens), Christ, church, culprit, darkness, death, debauchery, decoy (false lure), demonic influence, devastation, devil, discretion, disgrace, dream, drunkenness (as, for example, in Frans Hals's *Malle Babbe*, so well described by Seymour Slive in his monograph), evil, false deity (Jerome's own interpretation of the owl), foresight, Freemasonry, gluttony, godlessness, gross folly (associated, with many ramifications, in the "Eulenspiegel," or owl-and-mirror concept, and from that allowed to appear to illogical and almost farcical excesses in the whole fabric of tales developed about the Teutonic madcap, Till Eulenspiegel), hermit, Holy Spirit, ignobility, ignorance, implacable hostility, Jews (who shunned the new light of Christianity), lewdness, light in the darkness, melancholy, mischief-making (as in the Till Eulenspiegel tales), night, phlegm, prudence, moralizing reflection on the future life, Saturn, sloth, solitude, stupidity,

211. Jerome's commentary in Joel 3, in Migne, *Patrologia Latina*, vol. 25, p. 980.

212. Janson, pp. 178–84; Rosenberg, "On the Meaning of a Bosch Drawing," pp. 422–26; Schwarz and Plagemann, *Eule* (this is complete in its coverage, replete with references to the "source" literature).

the synagogue (the old law), vintage (as an omen of the vintage to come), virtue, vulgar people, wilderness, wisdom!

The twelve instances in which owls have been found in renditions of "Saint Jerome in the Wilderness" are all paintings except for one etching, one tapestry, and one bronze sculpture. This last work, apparently unique in its medium, is the magnificent relief by Francesco di Giorgio in the National Gallery of Art, Washington (fig. 120). Not only is this the sole instance of its kind that I know of as far as the owl is concerned, but it contains such a wealth of other animal life—lion, tortoise, snake, lizard, scorpion, gallinules, and storks, that it calls for detailed treatment, and is, accordingly, discussed elsewhere (p. 164 ff.).

The nine paintings of Jerome in the wilderness in which owls have been noted are two by Hieronymus Bosch, both discussed in detail on pages 137–56, and one each by Bartolomeo di Giovanni, Lucas Cranach, Ferrarese fifteenth-century master, Giovanni Mansueti, Andrea Mantegna, Pietro Perugino, and Cosimo Tura.

Bartolomeo di Giovanni painted at least four pictures of this subject, but he included an owl in only one of them, a painting now in Florence (fig. 44). This work has been listed in the literature as by an unidentified member of Filippo Lippi's studio, but is attributed to Bartolomeo by Berenson.[213] The bird in this case is a little owl, perched on a dead branch of a tree behind and above the figure of the penitent saint. Near it a swallow, symbol of Resurrection, is flying, possibly as an antithesis to the owl's dire funereal connotation. The owl is very accurately depicted.[214]

Lucas Cranach's 1502 painting of the penitent Jerome in Vienna (fig. 93) contains two birds in its upper portion, an owl and a parrot. Their presence here and in the portraits the artist painted of the noted humanist and historiographer of the University of Vienna, Dr. Johannes Cuspinian and his first wife, is taken to suggest that the Jerome picture was probably also commissioned by Cuspinian.[215] In the two portraits, Ludwig Baldass considered the owl as a symbol of the planet Saturn and of the melancholic temperament; the parrot as a symbol of the sun and of the sanguine temperament. He also believed that the two birds were included as emblematic references to the characters of the persons portrayed, as well as astrological references, the owl with the learned doctor, the parrot with his wife.[216]

Considering that Cranach is said to have been an observant naturalist, it is surprising that the owl he painted in the Jerome panel, and also in the Cuspinian portrait, is not strictly identifiable to any known species. The owl is the same in each of these two pictures, but it is an improvised owl. It is probably based on the little owl, *Athena noctua*, but Cranach has seen fit to intensify its coloration for dramatic effect, making it darker and more richly and deeply rufescent, as well as seemingly larger than it need be. It looks, especially in the Cuspinian portrait, as if the artist combined some of the features of the little owl and the short-eared owl, *Asio flammeus*, and the tawny owl, *Strix aluco*, species not otherwise found in the Jerome entourage, but he made his composite bird much darker and more heavily marked than any of these really are in nature. It seems that this may have been done to make all the more startling the

213. *Italian Pictures of the Renaissance: Florentine School*, vol. 1, p. 25.

214. Emma Gurney Salter (*Nature in Italian Art*, p. 59) suggested that Pesellino, "noted for his animal painting," may have been responsible for the owl, but I know of no evidence to support this.

215. Heinz Lüdecke, *Lucas Cranach d. Ä. in Spiegel seiner Zeit*, p. 28.

216. "Cranach's büssender Hieronymus von 1502."

Figure 180. Detail of owl from figure 66, Pietro Perugino's *Saint Jerome in Penitence*. Washington: National Gallery of Art; A. W. Mellon Collection.

glowing eyes of the essentially sinister-looking bird of ill omen. In the Jerome panel the owl is perched in a verdant tree, which would be "natural" for the little owl, but less so for the mainly terrestrial short-eared owl, a bird of relatively treeless grasslands and moist tundralike areas. The owl's significance in the Jerome panel may be inferred from its treatment in the Cuspinian portrait. In the latter it is depicted in a rapacious, predatory act, flying with its newly caught prey, a dead small bird, in its talons. This is more than merely an expression of the melancholy temperament as Baldass and Lüdecke suggested; it has this meaning, but it is also the owl as a funereal creature, associated with death. In the absence of explanatory documents it is almost pointless to ask if it means even more than this, but, in the Cuspinian portrait at least, the owl may signify "death of the soul" because the small bird it has killed and is carrying in its talons was an old symbol of the soul. In this connection it may be noted that an owl with a small dead bird in its bill occurs as a funereal symbol in a painting of an *Author with Saints* by an unknown artist of the school of Antwerp of the second half of the sixteenth century, in the archeological museum of Nivelles, Belgium.[217]

The same kind of owl, similarly intensified in its color pattern, as in Cranach's work, also appears in the picture by Hieronymus Bosch in the Musée des Beaux-Arts, Ghent (figs. 108, 111). The owl is here in the darkness in the area back of the prostrate penitent, perching on a dead branch and looking essentially sinister.

Cosimo Tura's emotionally intense *Saint Jerome in Penitence* in the National Gallery, London (frontispiece), is dealt with in detail in a separate chapter. Here it may suffice to note that the owl involved is an unnaturally large and white barn owl (church owl), and is, I am convinced, of remarkable interest as a unique embodiment of favorable, as well as unfavorable, meanings. Because it is so unusual in this respect, with features, such as the frog in its talons, unique among owls in religious art, and because it seems to have been the occasion for an original-minded artist to "recapture" past, but largely dormant, connotations, it has been necessary to document in detail the course of this role of the barn owl in allegory and symbolism in my discussion of Tura's painting (p. 176 ff.).

Giovanni Mansueti's picture of the penitent Jerome in Bergamo (fig. 36) is unusually rich in animal life, containing besides the saint's usual lion, a dog, a bear, an otter, two cheetahs, rabbits, a squirrel, a monkey, eagle, parrot, and a little owl perched on a stump behind one of the cheetahs. The owl is small, difficult to find, and probably was unimportant to the artist in any symbolic sense.

Perugino painted no fewer than twelve pictures showing Jerome in the wilderness, but only one of these contains an owl. This is the left wing (viewer's left) of the triptych in the National Gallery of Art, Washington. Here the standing figure of Jerome is looking in adoration toward the Crucifixion that occupies the central panel. A scops owl is perched on a tree high above the saint (fig. 180). Small, and in a compositional sense quite apart from Jerome, it is difficult to invest with much significance. The fact that in none of his other pictures did Perugino think to include an owl suggests that it was quite unimportant to the artist. Why he deliberately chose to depict a scops, rather than a little, or a barn owl, here cannot even be guessed. The fact that he introduced the scops owl,

217. Schwarz and Plagemann, fig. 18.

Figure 181. Andrea Mantegna, *Saint Jerome in the Wilderness*. São Paulo: Museu de Arte.

in a similar position, in his *Combat of Love and Chastity* (Louvre) suggests it meant little or nothing to him in either instance. He probably neither knew nor cared about such matters. It is known from Vasari's life of the artist that Perugino was not a religious man and did not believe in the immortality of the soul. In other words, he was not an artist who would have given much thought to shades of difference in symbolic meaning of one kind of owl or another.

The two remaining paintings of "Saint Jerome in the Wilderness" that contain owls are one by Andrea Mantegna in São Paolo (fig. 181) and one by an unidentified fifteenth-century Ferrarese master in the National Gallery of Art, Washington (fig. 148). In the Mantegna the bird is a barn owl, and is at the very top of the picture on the rocks towering above the seated figure of the meditating Jerome. The somber feeling of the whole painting suggests an equally somber significance of the funereal owl.

The other, formerly considered to be by Andrea Mantegna, but now placed as a Ferrarese painting, contains a scops, or eared, owl, as in the Perugino triptych discussed above. The owl is looking down intently at the kneeling saint and his lion. To this extent it is a participator in the content of the picture, not merely an "item" for the iconographer to catalogue, but it is hardly more than an ineloquent symbol of the need for penitence.

The one etching containing an owl is a fifteenth-century German work;[218] the tapestry, actually the only tapestry depicting the Jerome story, is an early sixteenth-century Brussels piece.[219]

The Parrot

Parrots of several kinds, only one of them zoologically identifiable to a definite species, occur infrequently in the Jerome orbit. They have been noted in nine pictures, as follows: Baptist Master (French, fifteenth century), *Saint Jerome in His Study*; Bosch, *Saint Jerome in Penitence* (Venice, fig. 109); Carpaccio, in two paintings, *Saint Jerome Leading the Lion Back to the Monastery* (Venice, fig. 31) and *Meditation on the Passion of Christ* (New York, fig. 32); Cranach, in three pictures, two of *Saint Jerome in Penitence* (Vienna and Innsbruck, figs. 92, 94), and one of *Saint Jerome in His Study* (Sarasota, fig. 104); Andrea Mantegna *Saint Jerome in the Desert* (São Paulo, fig. 181); and Bartolomeo Montagna, *Saint Jerome in Penitence* (Ottawa). In addition, there are dubious parrots, thought to be such because of their heavy, parrotlike bills, in the following paintings: Jacopo Bellini's *Saint Jerome in Penitence* (Verona, fig. 29) and Mansueti's *Saint Jerome in Penitence* (Bergamo, fig. 36). These last two are long-tailed birds, like paroquets, but are dusky-blackish in color. While there are a very few species of parrots that are black, two in Madagascar and one in New Guinea, these were not known to Europeans at the time these pictures were created, and it seems most unlikely that an artist would deliberately paint black a bird the viewer was expected to consider a parrot. The parrot in the Bosch picture in Venice is also a paroquet, and, while dusky, is less blackish, and could be expected to be recognized as such. The one in the painting by

218. Wilhelm L. Schreiber, *Handbuch der Holz und Metallschnitte des XV. Jahrhunderts*, no. 1541.

219. Tapestry Museum, La Granja de San Ildefonso, Spain (illustrated in Juan de Contreras y Lopez del Ayala, *The Escorial: The Royal Palace at La Granja de San Ildefonso*, p. 133).

the Baptist Master, where it is shown in a cage, and the one in the picture by Montagna are also paroquets. While by no means as accurate as the superb ring-necked paroquet painted by van Eyck in his *Madonna of Canon George von der Paele*, in Bruges, these parrots would seem acceptable. That there was something of a preference for long-tailed parrots (paroquets) is further evidenced by the curious, unrealistic one in Pintoricchio's little *Madonna and Child* (Honolulu Academy of Art). The common ring-necked paroquet, *Psittacula krameri*, of northeastern Africa and western Asia, had long been known as a cage bird in Europe.[220]

Carpaccio's all-red parrot, and a red one with dusky wings by Mantegna, are pure invention: no such species of parrot are known. Although one of the species of large lories in the South Pacific islands is largely red, this bird was not known to Europeans until centuries later. Cranach's green and red parrot in his Vienna picture seems to be a "carry over" from his Cuspinian portrait, in which the same bird occurs (not an ornithologically identifiable species, but a good general "version" of a green and red parrot). In Cranach's Innsbruck and Sarasota paintings the parrots are definitely identifiable as the West African gray parrot, *Psittacus erithacus*, a bird esteemed by Europeans ever since classical times, because of its unusual ability to imitate human words. This species of parrot occurs in another German painting, a *Madonna and Child with an Angel* by Hans Baldung Grien, in the Germanisches Museum, Nuremberg. Here the parrot, perched on Mary's left shoulder, has been given a greenish tone over its gray plumage, as though the artist were hesitant to accept the fact that a parrot could be gray and not green. (A wholly dark green parrot is placed on the parapet at the lower-left corner of the picture.) Somewhat later, Rubens included a correctly colored gray parrot in his group portrait, *Deborah Kip, Wife of Sir Balthasar Gerbier and Her Children*, in the National Gallery of Art, Washington. Wolfgang Stechow noted the presence of this parrot in the Rubens painting, and that the bird's emblematic connection "with the most revered representative of motherhood, the Virgin Mary, was still present in seventeenth century minds."[221]

It was its talking ability that had the curious effect of making the parrot a symbol of the Immaculate Conception. This came about because of the fact that the conception was not physical but by the Word as spoken by the angel of the Annunciation, and the Word was received through the ear.[222] The parrot as a conveyer of words, and as a bird already associated in the popular mind with the exotic Orient where the Christ story took place, and as a bird endowed with such seemingly human attributes as using words, showing affection, and using one foot as a hand in which to hold food while eating, came to be a visual sign of the Immaculate Conception. This is gone into in detail in my discussion of Cranach's use of parrots in his Jerome pictures (pp. 117, 128).

The unusual ability of the parrot, particularly the gray parrot, as a mimic of human speech was already known and praised in old Latin and Greek literature. Panofsky noted that in Franciscus de Retza's *Defensorium inviolatae virginitatis Mariae*, a work in which a great mass of pagan myths and fables are introduced as corroborations of the dogma of

220. These two paroquets are very similar in shape and proportion to a green paroquet in Giovannino de Grassi's sketchbook in the municipal library of Bergamo (MS. VII.14. f. 13ᵛ. If, as seems likely, they were based on Giovannino's sketch, it would follow that their present darker color may be due to later repainting or to deterioration of the original pigment.

221. *Peter Paul Rubens's Deborah Kip, Wife of Sir Balthaser Gerbier, and Her Children*, p. 9.

222. The traditional legend runs: "Deus per angelum loquebatur et Virgo per aurem impregnabatur" ("God spoke through the angel and the Virgin was impregnated through the ear"). In his study *Eva and Maria: Ein Antithese als Bildmotiv*, Ernst Gulden discusses further the connection of the parrot with the theme of Immaculate Conception, and also gives many bibliographical references.

the perpetual virginity of Mary, we read, "as young Julius Caesar rode through a forest a parrot addressed him with the words 'Ave Caesar,' and this is taken not only as proof of the possibility of miracles, but also as an allusion to the angelic salutation 'Ave Maria' which proclaims the Virgin Mary as the 'New Eve' . . . by the very fact that EVA, read backwards, is AVE."[223] Further, the parrot is a figure pertinent to Jerome, as the saint was one of the first and most ardent of the defenders of the concept of the perpetual virginity of Mary. Jerome's early treatise on this subject, *Adversus Helvidium*, was widely defended and had been highly regarded as part of official ecclesiastical opinion ever since Pope Damasus I.

The Partridge

Partridges of two kinds, the chukar or red-legged *Alectoris* and the gray *Perdix*, occur in the iconography of Saint Jerome. The former is found in seven paintings, all by Venetian artists: Antonello da Messina (London, fig. 119); Basaiti (Budapest); Catena (London, fig. 2); Cima, *Saint Jerome in Penitence* (Harewood House) and *Madonna dell' Arancato* (Venice, fig. 182); and Mansueti, two pictures of *Saint Jerome in the Wilderness* (Bristol and London). The gray partridge occurs in three pictures by Lucas Cranach the Elder (Darmstadt, fig. 103; Sarasota, fig. 104; and Zollikon). Of the total ten of these pictures, nine are of Jerome alone; the tenth, Cima's *Madonna dell' Arancato*, has Jerome as one of the two attendant saints, the other being Louis.

Both kinds of partridges are alike in their symbolism, and may therefore be treated together as "the partridge." The commonest meaning associated with this bird is satanic. In the writings of both Jerome and Augustine, the devil is said to assume at times the form of a partridge. Saint Anthony of Padua added that it is a deceitful, hypocritical creature, casting adulterous looks about itself.[224] A legend, traceable back to Aristotle, Aelian, Pliny, Theophrastus, and other classical authors, tells us that the partridge conceals its eggs in the dust and then carries them to a secluded spot to hatch them, even hiding the eggs from its own mate. The legend also relates that the bird has extraordinary procreative susceptibilities, so much so that if the female merely stands near the male, "while the wind is blowing from that direction, she will become impregnated. The female will conceive also from the action of the air, as the male flies above her, and very often from only hearing his voice."[225]

Coupled with this legend of excessive fecundity was another to the effect that the partridge, partly out of the desire to breed and partly out of envy, would steal eggs from the nests of other birds and take them to its own nest, and there hatch them. This supposed habit caused Jerome and others to consider it a diabolic creature, a despoiler of homes.[226] To this concept of "rearing what they had not bred" were attached two quite divergent interpretations. On the one hand, the partridge was likened to heretics, on the strength of Saint Augustine's statement (bk. 13, *Contra Fausto*, chap. ix) that heretics, like the partridge, adopt those they have not bred.[227] On the other hand, the partridge was likened to the Church in its desire to proselyte, to save souls (to adopt eggs for hatching), the act of hatching being equated with "coming into new

223. Panofsky, *Studies in Titian, Mostly Iconographic*, p. 28.

224. Angelo de Gubernatis, *Zoological Mythology*, vol. 2, p. 227, quotes Saint Anthony of Padua as follows: "Avis est dolosa et immunda et hypocritas habentes, ut dicit Petrus, oculos plenos adulterii et inacessabilis delicti signa."

225. Pliny (trans. J. Bostock and H. T. Riley), vol. 2, pp. 516–17.

226. Thus, Hugo of Folieto (*De bestiis et aliis rebus*, in Migne, *Patrologia Latina*, vol. 177, col. 49) wrote "Clamat perdix, et congregans fovet ova quae non peperit, faciens sibi non cum judicio divitias" and quoted Jerome, "In medio enim dierum suorum direlinquet cas, et in novissimus suis erit insipiens." See also Melito in J. B. Pitra, *Analecta novissima spiciligii solesmensis*, p. 510.

227. Ramiro de Pinedo, *El simbolismo en la escultura medieval española*, pp. 53–60.

Figure 182. Cima da Cone-
gliano, *Madonna dell' Arancato*. Venice: Galleria dell'
Accademia.

life." This has been presented in more detail in a study of another legend of the partridge miraculously revived after death by Saint Nicholas of Tolentino.[228]

Leonardo da Vinci repeated, in his bestiary, the story of the egg-stealing habits of the partridge, but added that after hatching, the young birds always return to their true parents.[229] Because of this he made of the partridge a sign of the "eventual triumph of truth." It is in this sense, of evil turned to good, that the partridge occurs in the Jerome context. The fact that the bird was said to conceive by the air passing from its mate, or from the sound emanating from the cock, gave rise to its use even as a symbol of the Incarnation. As Panofsky pointed out, "if a partridge bearing the motto AFFLATU FECUNDA ('fruitful by a breath of air') could illustrate the fact that the Virgin conceived by the Holy Spirit; and since the Virgin Mary, through the angelic salutation, 'conceived through the ear' (quae per aurem concepisti), the partridge could visualize the phrase AUDITA VOCE FECUNDA (fruitful by hearing a voice)."[230]

Lucas Cranach showed his knowledge of both the favorable and the unfavorable meanings inherent in the partridge. In his two versions of *Saint Jerome in His Study* the favorable connotation seems more likely, but in a painting of Jerome reading in a landscape (Zollikon) and in a drawing he made of Adam and Eve he also included two partridges, and there, as well as in some of his paintings of the *Nymph of the Fountain*, the birds stand for Luxuria, for "increase and voluptuousness."

The partridge, unlike many other creatures used symbolically, was often shown in pairs rather than by single individuals. Of the ten paintings listed at the beginning of this account, single partridges occur in four (Antonello, Catena, and the two by Mansueti), while there are two in each of five, and two adults and their brood of young in one. This brings us to still another meaning inherent in the partridge, the vice of pederasty. The legend goes back to Horapollo's "explanations" of Egyptian hieroglyphs. In his book we find that when the ancient Egyptian priests wanted to indicate pederasty they drew two partridges, as it was believed that when these fowls lose their mates they attempt intercourse without regard to heterosexuality.[231] While there is no reason to believe that homosexuality is characteristic of these birds in reality, such actions are known to occur at times in a number of kinds of birds in which the male and female resemble each other in plumage coloration and in size. Such aberrant lasciviousness is indeed an exaggerated impression of "Luxuria," so heartily condemned by Saint Jerome, and befits the partridges for their use as satanic emblems.[232]

228. Friedmann, "A Painting by Pantoja and the Legend of the Partridge of St. Nicholas of Tolentino," pp. 45-55.

229. MacCurdy, pp. 1077, 1082. In the *Fiori di Virtu*, considerably earlier than Leonardo, the partridge represents Truth (Lehman-Brockhaus, p. 16). This is anticipated even in the *Physiologus* (trans. James Carlill, p. 220), where it is stated that just as the partridge takes eggs from other birds' nests, "So does the Devil get those who are not yet strong in mind. But, when they are come to years of discretion, they begin to recognize their heavenly parents, Christ and the Apostles and Prophets, and turn themselves to them."

230. *Studies in Titian, Mostly Iconographic*, p. 30. See also C. Zircle, "Animals Impregnated by the Wind," pp. 95-130.

231. Boas, p. 106.

232. Braunfels, in Kirschbaum et al., vol. 3, col. 505, considers Cranach's use of the partridge as an extreme interpretation of its wickedness.

The Peacock

The peacock is of little importance in the iconography of Jerome, and has been noted in only five paintings, four of the saint in penitence and one of him in his study. The last is the picture by Antonello da Messina (London, fig. 119); those of the saint in penitence are by Basaiti school; Gentile Bellini (Toledo, Ohio, fig. 26); Bartolomeo Montagna (Bergamo, fig. 37); and Patinir (New York).

The general absence of the peacock from renditions of the Jerome cycle may be a reflection of the fact that its primary meaning was "pride" or "vainglory" and its secondary one "immortality." Pride hardly was compatible with penitence, the part of the saint's story in which the bird was most frequently included, but immortality (of the soul, not of the body) was, quite naturally, of concern to Jerome. In his bestiary Leonardo da Vinci wrote that the peacock ". . . always contemplating the beauty of its tail, spreading it out in the form of a wheel, and attracting . . . the attention . . ." of others to it, was more inclined to vainglory than any other creature.[233] Connected with this is the story that peacocks are ashamed of their feet. T. H. White quotes Epiphanius to the effect that when a peacock sees its feet, it "screams wildly thinking that they are not in keeping with the rest of his body."[234]

The connotation of immortality was an ancient one, enhanced by the idea that the flesh of the peacock was very hard and tough, which gave rise to the thought that it was incorruptible. Saint Augustine asked, "Who except God, the creator of all things, endowed the flesh of the dead peacock with the power of never decaying?" It is a commentary on the logic of symbolism that the idea of immortality should arise from a dead peacock rather than a living one, and that the notion of its tough flesh should erase the fact that it was long esteemed as a dish for special feasts.

As a symbol of resurrection and immortality the peacock occurs in pictures of the "Nativity" and of the "Adoration of the Christ Child." A sixteenth-century emblem bearing the motto *Certa securitas* ("assured security") shows a peahen with its chicks (fig. 106).[235] A detailed account of the uses and meanings of the peacock in early Christian art is to be found in Helmut Lother's book.[236]

233. MacCurdy, p. 1078.

234. *The Bestiary*, p. 149.

235. Henkel and Schöne, col. 810 (see, in this connection, the discussion of Lucas Cranach's Darmstadt and Sarasota pictures of "Saint Jerome in His Study" (pp. 129–36).

236. *Der Pfau in der altchristlichen Kunst.*

The Pheasant

The ring-necked pheasant seldom occurs in the iconography of Saint Jerome; it has been noted in only six paintings, three of them by Lucas Cranach, who included a single male pheasant in his Innsbruck *Saint Jerome in Penitence* (fig. 94), and a pair of these birds with their brood of chicks in each of two versions of *Saint Jerome in His Study* (Darmstadt and Sarasota, figs. 103, 104). The other pertinent pictures are Carpaccio's *Saint Jerome Leading the Lion Back to the Monastery* (Venice, fig. 31); Gentile Bellini's *Saint Jerome in Penitence* (Toledo, Ohio, fig. 26); and Pisanello follower, *Saint Jerome in the Wilderness* (London, fig. 63).

The pheasant, *Phasianus colchicus*, a bird native to western Asia, was brought to Europe very early from Asia Minor or Persia, at least as early as the campaigns of Alexander the Great (ca. 335 B.C.). Its Latin generic name *Phasianus* stems from Phasis, a river in that part of the world. The bird, being a creature of very striking beauty in its plumage, especially in the cock, and a good "sporting" bird for the hunter, and highly esteemed as a table bird, quickly attained much popularity in Europe.

Because of its obvious relationship to the peacock, also an Asiatic import into Europe, the pheasant early assumed a connotation of immortality, and, as such, was used as a sepulchral ornament in early Christian art.[237] Thus, a pair of pheasants and of doves appear on the tomb of

237. Leclercq, in F. Cabrol and H. Leclerq, *Dictionnaire d'archéologie chrétienne et de liturgie*, col. 1081.

Henchir el Msâ-Actin.[238] Aside from, but related to, the concept of "immortality," the pheasant was particularly a sign of "redemption." As such it appears in pictures of the "Adoration of the Christ Child," as, for example in the great tondo by Fra Angelico and Filippo Lippi, in the National Gallery of Art, Washington, where a pair of pheasants and a peacock are to be seen near each other. The concept of redemption makes the pheasant a suitable associate of Jerome as a penitent, hoping for just that goal, as in Cranach's Innsbruck picture, and in the ones by Gentile Bellini and by a follower of Pisanello.

The extraordinary use of a pair of pheasants with their seven or eight young, in Cranach's Darmstadt and Sarasota versions of Jerome in his study, has been fully discussed elsewhere (pp. 129–30). Here it may suffice merely to mention that this family group is a sign of Heavenly Guidance, drawn from its being a pictorial reference to the origin of the Pleiades. The pheasants and their brood are a replacement, with the added virtue of "redemption," of the hen and seven chicks that long was the most popular Germanic icon of the Pleiades.[239]

In Gentile Bellini's picture there are two adult pheasants, but this painting is so full of various creatures in purely naturally observed poses, that it seems idle to even expect a special message in the fact that there are two pheasants instead of only one.

238. Paul Gauckler, *Catalogue du Musée Alaoui*, pl. xx, no. 1, p. 18, no. 257.

239. Grimm (trans. Stallybrass, ed. 4), pp. 728–29.

The Porphyrio (or Purple Gallinule)

This bird has only an uncertain place in the Bestiary, as it is based on the "least unlikely" identification of two sketchy flying birds in Francesco di Giorgio's bronze relief of *Saint Jerome in Penitence* (fig. 120). As fully discussed in the chapter on this work, the birds are probably purple gallinules. This bird was a symbol of *Pudicitia*, or "chastity," and was used in this sense by Alciati.[240] Chastity was a virtue very much in evidence in Jerome's thoughts and writings, and its avian emblem is therefore quite fitting in his iconography, although its presence there is based on this one admittedly uncertain instance.[241]

The Rabbit (or Hare)

The rabbit (or hare), one of the best known of small mammals, both wild and semidomesticated, was long a favorite "gentle" beast, as contrasted with dangerous ones in European thought and culture. It occurs fairly often in the iconography of Saint Jerome, as may be seen from the following list of artists who have so employed it: Gentile Bellini, *Saint Jerome in Penitence* (Toledo, Ohio, fig. 26); Giovanni Bellini, *Saint Jerome Reading in the Wilderness* (Washington, fig. 22); Jacopo Bellini, *Saint Jerome in the Wilderness* (Louvre, fig. 53; London, fig. 55); Carpaccio, *Saint Jerome Leading the Lion Back to the Monastery* (Venice, fig. 31); Cima, *Madonna dell' Arancato* (Venice, fig. 182); Cranach, *Saint Jerome in His Study* (Sarasota, fig. 104) and *Cardinal Albrecht as Saint Jerome* (Berlin, fig. 102); Crivelli, *Saint Jerome in Penitence* (London, fig. 35); Girolamo dai Libri, *Nativity with Saints* (Verona); Mansueti, three pictures of *Saint Jerome in the Wilderness* (Bergamo, fig. 36; Bristol;

and London, formerly in Arthur Hughes Coll.); Isenbrandt, *Saint Jerome in Penitence* (Leningrad, fig. 72); Moretto attribution, *Saint Jerome in Penitence* (Washington, Howard University).

The rabbit was an old symbol of fecundity, and, through that, of lust, and like so many creatures whose natural defense is based on fecundity, of meekness or timidity. Thus, in his bestiary Leonardo da Vinci wrote that the rabbit is always timid, often being frightened by falling leaves in the winds of autumn.[242]

The Renaissance emblem compilers used rabbits to illustrate both fecundity and meekness. Ripa pictures *Fécondità* by a woman holding two birds, with a hen and its chicks on her lap and a rabbit with its young on the ground.[243] Camerarius used the rabbit to illustrate *Vigilandum*, or the need for watchfulness.[244] In keeping with its attribute of fecundity the rabbit also came to stand for the sanguine temperament and sensuality, as in Dürer's engraving of *Adam and Eve*, in which Eve is accompanied by a rabbit and a cat, two of the four animals that were used to symbolize the four "humors," whose peaceful relationship and balance in the human being were irrevocably disturbed by the eating of the apple in the garden of Eden.[245] A curious meaning, stemming from Horapollo's book on Egyptian hieroglyphs, is "an opening," for it tells us that when the Egyptian priests wanted to show an opening (to, or of what, is left unsaid) they used the figure of a rabbit, "for this animal always keeps its eyes open."[246] This is repeated by Giehlow without further comment,[247] but the vague, and, by itself, quite meaningless "opening" may seem possibly connected with watchfulness or timidity, where alertness and readiness to flee are so important.

As may be sensed from the above, it is not clear just what connection was intended between the rabbit and Jerome, who was neither timid nor meek, and who was opposed to sensuality and fecundity. In Isenbrandt's picture (fig. 72) the rabbit is being eaten by the saint's faithful lion, possibly a visual reference to the destruction of carnal desire by the now moralized lion. However, in the other pictures where the two animals are present, no such action between them is depicted. In the Jacopo Bellini drawing, listed above, an eagle is devouring a rabbit (fig. 53).

In five of the fourteen paintings listed, there are two rabbits, while in the others there is only a single one in each. This seems due more to the artists' love of painting nature than of any special meaning. In most cases the rabbits are white, but at times, as in the Giovanni Bellini in Washington and the Libri in Verona, one is white and one is brown. It seems dubious that any hidden meaning is involved in the latter; whiteness always has a possible connotation of purity, which would not be out of keeping with the idea of meekness, symbolized by the rabbit, but this does not imply that lack of whiteness has an opposite suggestiveness. The rabbit, as a defenseless, timid creature, came to be used as a sign of those whose hope of future safety, of salvation, was placed in their trust in the meaning inherent in the passion of Christ. Rabbits are frequently found in pictures of the Madonna and Child, where this is usually their meaning. An example is Titian's *Madonna of the Rabbit* in the Louvre. Although in a case like this, where Mary actually touches the little creature, and where, as in this picture, it is white, there may be a further sugges-

240. *Emblematum flumen abundans*, p. 55, emblem xlvii.

241. There is a fuller discussion of the purple gallinule and its symbolism in Friedmann, *Bartolome Bermejo's Episcopal Saint: A Study in Medieval Spanish Symbolism*, pp. 2–7. Also, D'Arcy W. Thompson, "On Bird and Beast in Ancient Symbolism."

242. MacCurdy, p. 1078.

243. Ripa, vol. 3, p. 37 (*Fécondità*).

244. *Centuria I*, no. 73, p. 146.

245. Panofsky, *Studies in Titian, Mostly Iconographic*, p. 28.

246. Boas, p. 73.

247. Giehlow, p. 220.

248. *Beiträge und Volkskunde zur Ikonographie des Hasen*, pp. 158–75.

tion of the control of sensuality by the Virgin purifying the symbol, but this meaning does not replace the other; it merely adds to it.

For further details about the symbolism and folklore of the rabbit, the reader may be referred to the study by Wilhelm Jesse.[248] It should be said that for our purposes in this book, the rabbit and the hare are considered as one. Actually, they are zoologically quite distinct; in fact, there are several species of each, but in art they are impossible to distinguish, and their symbolic meanings are common to both.

The Raven

The raven occurs in the iconography of Jerome only indirectly, and then only once so far as I have been able to learn. This is in a painting by Pier Francesco Sacchi of Saint Jerome, Saint Anthony Abbot, and a third, unidentified saint (present whereabouts unknown; in 1928 in the Augusto Lurati Collection, Galleria Pesaro, Milan). Here the raven, the traditional bringer of bread to Saint Anthony Abbot, is perched on a branch above and between Jerome and Anthony, who are both holding one loaf of bread between them. If Anthony had not been in the picture, the raven would probably have been absent as well. It is only because Jerome, as well as Anthony Abbot, is holding the bread, that the former may be thought to be involved with the raven through the nourishment it has brought. This may, however, be merely because of the artist's method of designing and unifying the characters in his painting.

The Robin

The robin, the small European bird *Erithacus rubecula*, not the larger American *Turdus migratorius*, has been noted in a single Hieronymite picture, *Saint Jerome in Penitence* by Lucas Cranach in Innsbruck (fig. 94). The bird is perched on a small twig over Jerome's head, silhouetted against a bare rock.

Any small bird could share the general symbolic meaning of the "soul" as contrasted with the "body," the part of man's nature that is not earthbound. Furthermore, any small bird with a touch of red or reddish-brown could be used as reference to the Passion of Christ, even receiving its telltale coloration from contact with His blood, particularly His crown of thorns.[249] Aside from this common usage, there is nothing explicit in the robin to make it more or less appropriate to the Jerome theme. It would seem that here Cranach was merely indulging his interest in depicting natural history objects and that no particular significance is to be sought in its use.

In her study of the birds of the Bible, Alice Parmelee writes that although the robin, the goldfinch, and the crossbill are not specifically mentioned in the biblical text, devout people enhanced the account of the little birds that attempted to ease Christ's sufferings by pulling the thorns from His crown, and in so doing stained themselves with His blood, by naming these species as the actual participants in the story.[250]

Dr. William S. Heckscher called my attention to the fact that the

249. Alice Parmelee, *All the Birds of the Bible*, pp. 259–60.

250. Ibid.

251. *Le Bestiaire du Christ*, pp. 533–34.

chapter on Saint Jerome (cxlvi) in the *Legenda aurea* differs in different versions. In one manuscript version, in the Duke University Library, there is the statement: "Fuit enim sanctus. . . . per puritatem et sanguine tinctus per dominicae passionis meditatione." ("He [*i.e.*, Jerome] was saintly [or a saint] on account of his purity and on account of being tinged by blood through meditation of the Passion of the Lord.") This refers to Jerome in the wilderness and may well give special connection between him and the similarly "blood-stained" robin, goldfinch, and crossbill. The robin is one of the "small birds of the Passion of Christ" mentioned by Louis Charbonneau-Lassay.[251]

The Scorpion

That the scorpion figures frequently in the iconography of Saint Jerome is not surprising when we recall that in his letter to Eustochium, describing his life in the wilderness, Jerome wrote that "scorpions and wild beasts" were his daily companions. I have noted from one to three scorpions in each of twenty-two versions of the saint in the wilderness, nineteen paintings, one drawing, and two relief sculptures, as follows: Andrea di Giusto (Montreal, fig. 43); Gentile Bellini (Toledo, Ohio, fig. 26); Jacopo Bellini (drawing, Paris, fig. 54); Botticini (London, fig. 38); Cima (Washington, fig. 33); Civerchio attribution (fig. 42); Lucas Cranach the Elder (Innsbruck, fig. 94); Carlo Crivelli (London, fig. 35); Domenico di Michelino (Dallas, fig. 159); Filarete attribution (Cambridge, fig. 81); Flemish or Lombard, seventeenth century (Turin); Francesco di Giorgio (Washington, fig. 120); Benozzo Gozzoli (Montefalco, fig. 183); Luini (two paintings, Vienna); "Masaccio" and Andrea di Giusto (Altenburg); Masaccio circle (Princeton); Perugino (Baltimore); Sano di Pietro, three paintings (New York; Paris, fig. 41; and Siena, fig. 80); Sassetta (formerly in Washington Crossing, Pennsylvania, Mrs. F. J. Mather Collection).

The scorpion was always looked upon as an evil creature; it carries a poisonous sting in its tail, which causes great pain to anyone stung by it. It was early likened to Judas, whose kiss was poisonous and treacherous, and from this the scorpion came to be used, in a malicious sense, as a symbol of the Jews, who not only refused to accept the teachings of Christ, but were hostile to Him. This iconographic use has been fully dealt with in a book-length monograph by Marcel Bulard,[252] which makes it unnecessary to go into detailed discussion here. Aside from this particular Jewish connotation, the scorpion was a symbol of evil in general, and of destructiveness. In some pictures of the Crucifixion, the scorpion, as a symbol of treachery, appears on the insignia of the Roman soldiers, but in paintings of Jerome in the wilderness, the scorpion is both a sign of the wild, dangerous setting, and of the evil forces the saint was attempting to ignore or to overcome. The scorpion also was looked upon as the "*antithèse du Scarbée*," the opposite of the scarab beetle, used by the ancient Egyptians as a symbol of immortality;[253] in other words, as a sign of death. It may be noted that Scorpio is the eighth sign of the zodiac, corresponding to the period of the human life span that lies under the threat of death. An unusual variation on the zodiacal scorpion occurs in a marble relief of an "Allegorical Portrait of Ferdinand, King of

251. *Le Scorpion, symbole du peuple juif dans l'art religieux des XIVe, XVe, XVIe siècles.*

253. Charbonneau-Lassay, pp. 908-9.

Figure 183. Benozzo Gozzoli, *Saint Jerome in Penitence*. Montefalco: S. Francesco.

Figure 184. *Morte medetur*. From Camerarius, *Symbolorum et emblematum centuriae quatuor*, 1677.

Sicily," attributed to Domenico Gagini (Los Angeles County Museum of Art). The scorpion, below a figure of Mars, is shown vertically, head downward, and from each of its front pincers hangs a small basket containing a number of oval objects—eggs (?) or fruits(?).

In his bestiary Leonardo da Vinci makes the scorpion a symbol of gluttony, cited as a particular aspect of interest in the pleasures of this world, as contrasted with the virtuous life. He informs us that if a man who has been fasting spits upon a scorpion the saliva kills it, "after the manner of abstinence from gluttony, which carries away and puts an end to the illness that proceeded from this gluttony, and opens the path to the virtues."[254] The evil connotations of the scorpion were further utilized in emblems by Camerarius, who figured this creature as an illustration for the mottoes *Procul este profani* ("stand off ye uninitiated") and *Morte medetur* ("it heals by death") (fig. 184).[255]

The scorpion and the snake were the two animals of evil that continued to be used in pictures of Jerome in the wilderness after the larger dangerous beasts, such as dragons, cheetahs, and bears, were largely replaced by harmless deer and rabbits.

As is often the case with symbols, the scorpion was also used as a reference to affluence and fortune, [256] but this usage does not seem to be involved in any of the pictures of Jerome.

The snail seldom occurs in the iconography of Jerome, and while it is symbolically pertinent, or at least not out of place there, it is not essential to the theme, which is probably why it was used so infrequently. Snails, not certainly identifiable to species, but of the somewhat convex, helical shell form, have been noted in five paintings: Filippino Lippi, *Saint Jerome in Penitence* (Florence, fig. 185); Carlo Crivelli, *Madonna and Child with Saint Sebastian and Saint Jerome* (London); Titian, two paintings of *Saint Jerome in Penitence* (Milan, fig. 59; and Paris); and Veronese attribution, *Saint Jerome in Penitence* (Chicago). In none of these is the snail prominent; it is shown either on a stone or on part of a tree trunk or branch, and is easily overlooked.

The snail has two meanings, quite divergent in themselves, neither of which is of primary importance or relevance to the Jerome story. As discussed in an earlier connection, the snail was a symbol of sloth, and of those men who, by their sluggish indifference, seem to be content to attach themselves to the things of the physical world at the expense of striving for the higher and more virtuous things of the spirit.[257] In this sense the snail may stand for the barren world in which Jerome spent his long period of penitence and from the unspiritual aspects of which he wanted to free himself, but this relevance cannot be firmly established. The snail was also looked upon as a symbol of Christ, a use that may be traced back to Tertullian,[258] who, in turn, took over and enlarged upon the pre-Christian thought expressed by the classical Delphic oracle, that the snail is a sign of those who die and rise again from the tomb,[259] and advanced the argument that the belief that the snail remained buried in the earth for the three coldest months of winter, and then came out again as the weather became warmer, was similar to the three days of the entombment of Jesus prior to His Resurrection. The fact that the snail shell has a lid, or operculum, which remains tightly shut during its burial in the earth, but which it opens when it emerges and begins to move about, was looked upon as a parallel to the raising of the cover of His tomb when Christ rose from the grave. The shell of the snail thus came to be a visual reference to the tomb from which man shall rise on the day of Redemption. The snail emerging from the shell was thus a symbol of Resurrection, and it is chiefly in this sense that the snail applies to the iconography of Jerome in penitence. E. B. Smith pointed out, further, that the use of the dome as a favored design for church architecture arose, in a sense, from this same source, that the early Christians at

The Snail

254. MacCurdy, p. 1083.

255. Camerarius, *Centuria I*, no. 74, p. 148, and *Centuria IV*, no. 95, p. 190.

256. Waldemar Déonna, "Mercure et le scorpion," pp. 614–58.

257. Friedmann, *Bartolome Bermejo's "Episcopal Saint": A Study in Medieval Spanish Symbolism*, pp. 14–16.

258. *Apologeticus*, xlviii.

259. Charbonneau-Lassay, pp. 930–31.

Figure 185. Filippino Lippi, *Saint Jerome in Penitence*. Florence: Galleria degli Uffizi.

Jerusalem associated the form of an omphalos with the domical tomb of Christ.[260]

Another concept connected with the snail, curiously similar to the "stay-at-home" meaning of the tortoise (see p. 300), which, like the snail, moves about with its shell, is expressed in a sixteenth-century emblem with the caption *Secret est à louer* ("Privacy is praiseworthy"),[261] a meaning hardly pertinent to the Jerome story, except insofar as the saint's penitence was done in the privacy of the lonely wilderness.

Angelo de Gubernatis has pointed out that in popular superstition, especially in Teutonic areas, the snail has an evil, even demoniacal, meaning.[262] In Germany children invoke the snail by the name of the funereal Saint Gertrude.[263]

Psalm 58:8 (from the King James version) refers to the snail, which was thought to devour itself gradually as it moves along: "As a snail which melteth, let every one of them pass away," probably an allusion to the slimy excretion left in the snail's passage.[264] I am indebted to Dr. William S. Heckscher for calling this to my attention.

260. *The Dome*, p. 76.

261. Henkel and Schöne, col. 616.

262. *Zoological Mythology*, vol. 2, p. 75.

263. Karl Joseph Simrock, *Handbuch der deutschen Mythologie*, p. 516, gives this as follows:
"*Kuckuck, kuckuck, Gerderut Stäk dine ver (vier?) Horns herut.*"

264. F. A. Schilder, "Die ethnologische Bedeutung der Porzellanschnecken," pp. 313-20.

The Snake

Snakes (including asps and vipers), not zoologically identifiable to particular species but varying in size and in color (usually dark), occur with great frequency in renditions of "Jerome in the Wilderness," possibly more frequently than any other creature except the saint's identifying lion and the deer. Snakes are often introduced in multiples, two or three in one picture are common, and in one case, a picture attributed to Civerchio (fig. 42), no fewer than ten snakes may be made out! Snakes are present only in pictures of Jerome in the wilderness, never in those showing him in his study. Even the one case listed below that might seem to be an exception, a painting of *Saint Jerome in His Study* by the Master of Saint Gudule, a follower of Hugo van der Goes, includes the snake only in the far background, which shows, through the open study door, the saint in penitence with his lion and a snake, as a separate part of the Jerome story. In the two pictures by Bergognone and by Paris Bordone, respectively, listed below, the snake is closer to Jerome than to the other figures in those altarpieces.

In the following list of artists who have introduced snakes into their compositions, the picture in all but three instances is of Jerome in a wilderness setting, and in these the title of the picture is not repeated here. The artists are: Altdorfer (Cologne, fig. 76); Andrea di Giusto (Montreal, fig. 43); Angelico follower (Boston); Basaiti (Budapest); Basaiti school (fig. 145); Jacopo Bellini (drawing, Paris, fig. 53); Bergognone, *Saint James, Saint Ambrose, and Saint Catherine* (Milan); Bermejo, *Pieta with Jerome and Donor* (Barcelona); Bono da Ferrara (London, fig. 62); Paris Bordone, *Sacra Conversazione* (Los Angeles, fig. 186); Bosch school (Bruges); Botticini (London, fig. 38); Aelbert Bouts (Los Angeles, fig. 69); Cima, two paintings (London, fig. 34; and Washington, fig. 33); Civerchio attribution (fig. 42); Carlo Crivelli (London, fig. 35); Domenico di Michelino (Dallas, fig. 159); Ferrarese, fifteenth century (Longhi, pl.

Figure 186. Paris Bordone, *Sacra Conversazione*. Los Angeles County Museum of Art; Paul Rodman Mabury Collection.

36); Ferrarese, late fifteenth century (Bologna); Francesco di Giorgio (bronze relief, Washington, fig. 120); Filarete attribution (fig. 81); Hugo van der Goes follower, the Master of Saint Gudule (Richter Archives, 277:IX: 1); Italian engraving, ca. 1470–90 (Hind, no. 84); Lombard School engraving (Kristeller, p. 40); Masaccio circle (Princeton); Palmezzano (Rome); Parenzano (Modena); Perugino, *Crucifixion with Saint Jerome and Saint Christopher* (Rome); Sacchi, *Saint Jerome with Saint Martin and the Beggar and Saint Anthony Abbot* (Berlin-Dahlem); Sano di Pietro, three paintings (New York; Paris, fig. 41; and Siena, fig. 80); Sassetta (Boston); Sellaio, two paintings (Sarasota and El Paso, fig. 40); Solario (Barnard Castle, Yorkshire); and Domenico Tintoretto (Rome fig. 187).

In all these pictures, save two, the snakes are merely present, but are not "involved" in any action. In the *Sacra Conversazione* by Paris Bordone the lion and the snake, both somewhat obscured in the background

behind and to the left of Jerome, are in confrontation, the lion looking
down the slope at the crawling serpent with an expression interpretable
as hostility, or, at least, of lack of amity. This may have been intended to
suggest an effort to keep evil and danger (the snake) away from the holy
personage in the main part of the painting. Similarly, in Domenico Tintoretto's *Saint Jerome in Penitence*, the lion is in the shadow beneath the
saint's crude table, and is glaring at two snakes to its left (away from the
orant Jerome).

In the Jerome context, it seems that snakes are always symbols of evil
and danger, but originally they had ambivalent meanings. A prime example of this combination of complete opposites is the serpent as a visual
sign of the love of Jesus, while the serpent trampled by a hart was a
reference to Satan being subdued by Christ![265] Possibly the first instance
of the snake as an evil force is in the story of the temptation in the
Garden of Eden. This gave rise to the idea that the snake fears a naked

Figure 187. Domenico Tintoretto,
Saint Jerome in Penitence. Rome:
Barberini Gallery.

265. Evans, *Animal Symbolism*, pp. 115,
223.

266. Ibid., p. 114. Also, Camerarius (*Centuria I*, no. 24, p. 48) pictures several snakes and frogs at the base of a palm, illustrating the motto *Invidia integritatis assecla (assectator?)* ("Envy is virtue's attendant") in Guy de Tervarent, *Attributes et symboles dans l'art profane*, cols. 405–6.

person but attacks a clothed one. When Adam was innocent in his nakedness in the Garden, the serpent could not harm him, but once he and Eve became conscious of, and embarrassed by their nudity, the serpent changed in its attitude toward them—"In like manner, if we do not trouble ourselves about the vanities of this world, we need not fear the assaults of that wily serpent, the devil."[266]

The snake was also an old symbol of prudence and hence of restless inquiry, unable to "leave well enough alone," but this aspect of its inherent meanings does not apply to the Jerome context. In the Jerome story, the snake is a dangerous and evil denizen of the saint's penitential wilderness. The snake was one of the evil creatures that persisted in visual renditions of the saint's story after the other dangerous beasts had been excluded.

The Squirrel

The squirrel, described as one of the "small beasts of gentle nature" by Chaucer in his *Parliament of Fowls*, was a well-known and often-observed creature in Europe, but it seldom occurs in art and is of only minor importance in the symbolic iconography of the Jerome theme. It has been identified in the course of the present study in only seven versions—six paintings and one marble relief. The paintings are: one by Gentile Bellini (Toledo, Ohio, fig. 26); two by Giovanni Bellini (Washington, fig. 22, and Florence); one by Giovanni Mansueti (Bergamo, fig. 36); and two by Lucas Cranach the Elder (Sarasota, fig. 104, and Innsbruck, fig. 94). The sculpture is one attributed to Rossellino (fig. 51). All but one of these show Jerome in penitence in a landscape setting; the Cranach, in Sarasota, shows the saint in his study. This is the only instance of the squirrel in an interior setting. There it is on the edge of the table to the right of the cardinal's hat, in shadow and not too easily discernible. In the other Cranach painting, in Innsbruck, there are two squirrels; in the Gentile Bellini there are also two; in all the others a single one each. In the majority of these works the squirrel is shown sitting up on its haunches with its bushy tail arched over its back. In the Gentile Bellini, however, the two squirrels are merely scampering about on the ground near the lower-left part of the picture; and in Cranach's Innsbruck painting one of the two squirrels is climbing up the trunk of the large tree near the picture's left edge.

267. This emblem is illustrated in Henkel and Schöne, col. 493. The first line echoes Virgil, *Aeneid* 1.207: "*durate, et vosmet rebus servate secundis*," while the second recalls Horace, *Odes* 2.10.17–18: "*. . . non si male nunc, et olim sic erit*" ("If things go badly now, it won't ever be thus").

268. This emblem is from Camerarius, p. 176, no. 88. The sense of the emblem may have caused it to be used in other religious contexts. Thus, in an early sixteenth-century French painting of *The Circumcision* in the De Noyelle Collection (Réau, pl. v), the Christ Child is being offered a squirrel in a cage. Such a caged squirrel may well have been for a child's amusement, much as a small bird on a tether, but as a symbol of wisdom proving mightier than strength it could apply to the Infant Jesus.
In a painting of *Madonna and Child* by Giovanni di Giacomo Gavazzi (Bergamo: S. Alessandro in Colonna), there is a squirrel below and to the left of the Child, Who looks at it and stretches out His arm toward it.

269. The legend of Ratatöskr, the squirrel, is given in Grimm, pp. 796–97.

Although the squirrel never became a commonly used symbol in Christian art, it may be pointed out that a good number of meanings have been associated with it. In one sixteenth-century emblem there is a squirrel sitting up on its haunches, its tail curled over its back, under a downpour of rain, with the explanatory motto:

Durabo, et quondam res expectabo secunda
Quamvis nunc male sit, non male semper erit
("I shall endure and expect once again more favorable things
However bad it is now, it won't be bad forever").[267]

This couplet may reflect the hopeful aspect of the difficult situation attendant upon a supplicating penitent such as Jerome.

Another emblem, showing a squirrel with its tail spread out as a "sail" to traverse a river, informs us that *Vincit solertia vires* ("Inventiveness vanquishes might").[268]

When we recall that the squirrel was often considered, and frequently shown, as a creature habitually gnawing on an acorn or other nut, and that the nut, as first described by Adam of Saint Victor, was an image of Christ, the kernel within it standing for His hidden divinity, the squirrel almost automatically becomes a "seeker after divinity." This interpretation might seem applicable in Cranach's Sarasota and Innsbruck paintings. The probability that the Sarasota picture was commissioned by or for Cardinal Albrecht, whose likeness appears as Saint Jerome, certainly suggests that such an interpretation is not unlikely, because the cardinal, or someone on his staff, must have approved the choice of animals included in the picture.

A squirrel running up or down a vertical tree trunk, as in Cranach's Innsbruck picture of the penitent Jerome, may echo an old Teutonic legend concerning the creature as sowing discord between Heaven and Hell. As Grimm recounted the story, the squirrel kept running up and down the great tree attempting to sow discord between the snake (evil) at its base and the eagle (nobility) in its topmost branches.[269] This attempt to keep alive this conflict was not considered in any way improper; it was a reflection of the antipodal nature of good and evil.

On a less intellectual plane of thought, the squirrel was a part of the popular concept of a forest; it was the most often seen of the creatures of the tall trees.

The Stork

The European white stork, *Ciconia alba*, occurs very rarely in the iconography of Jerome, and in those cases it may be as much a bit of discursive naturalism on the part of the artist as a creature pertinent to the meaning of the composition. Only three instances have been noted and in these the storks are in the far background, not at all close to, or in any significant sense related to, Saint Jerome. A painting of *Saint Jerome in Penitence* by Lucas Cranach the Elder in Innsbruck (fig. 94), and one of *Saint Jerome with Saint Anthony Abbot and a Third Elderly Saint* by Pier Francesco Sacchi, each has a perfectly recognizable white stork in the background. The third case, a bronze relief sculpture of *Saint Jerome in Penitence* by Francesco di Giorgio (fig. 120), has two storks wading in the stream in the background. Because of the lack of color in this case (dark bronze monochrome), these storks cannot be proved to be white storks (there is a second species of stork in Europe, the black stork, *Ciconia nigra*). However, the probability is that Francesco used the white stork, because it is the better known of the two, and the two species seem to have been "merged" in their symbolism.

The stork was a symbol of Filial Devotion. It was also connected with the concept of procreation, as is evidenced by the widespread thought of storks as bringers of babies. In his bestiary Leonardo da Vinci informs us that the stork knows how to cure itself of illness (by drinking salt water), that it has moral judgment (it abandons its companion if the latter is at fault), and shows devotion to its parents when they are too old and weak to care for themselves.[270]

In the Jerome context there is no real evidence as to which, if any, of these ideas is to be sought. Inasmuch as the snake was generally looked upon as a creature of evil, the stork—as a bird believed to attack serpents —may have come to have a corresponding positive virtue. In his *Georgics* (book 2) Virgil wrote:

But when the golden spring reveals the year
And the white bird returns whom serpents fear.

This has been suggested in explanation of a stork shown fighting a snake in Basaiti's *Madonna of the Meadow* (National Gallery, London).[271]

The Swallow

The European barn swallow, *Hirundo rustica*, has been found in only two pictures of Saint Jerome, both of the saint in penitence, one by Bartolomeo di Giovanni (Florence, fig. 44) and one by Domenico Tintoretto (Rome, fig. 187). It is obvious, from the scarcity of its inclusion, that the swallow played no great role in the iconography of Jerome. It was not infrequently introduced into other topics of religious art, primarily as a symbol of Resurrection, because the bird's reappearance in the spring, after its absence throughout the cold winter months, was likened to rebirth. It was also a symbol of maternal care and of domestic contentment, even under conditions of poverty and suffering,[272] which meaning made it particularly pertinent to the frequent votive pictures of the Madonna and Child. Camerarius used a picture of a swallow flying to its nest and four young to illustrate his emblem *Concordia regni* or peaceful rule.[273] Because of this widely accepted meaning people considered it wicked to molest or destroy a swallow's nest, and, conversely, thought it a good omen if swallows built their nests under one's eaves. Neither this meaning nor the resurrection concept was particularly pertinent to the Jerome cycle.

As so often happens with symbols, the swallow came to have quite another meaning in the Low Countries in the fifteenth century. There it came to signify lewdness, because of a tale that the young birds, while still in the nest, were blinded by their own excrement. This led to moralizing along the following line: "As the swallow is blinded by its own excrement, thus do the unchaste" fall into sin and error.[274] On the other hand, following Pliny, Leonardo da Vinci wrote that the swallow opens the eyes of its young when they are blind by bringing celandine to the nest.[275] By and large, the swallow had a favorable connotation. Thus, in northern Italy (Piedmont) one of its common names was "chicken of the Lord"; in Germany, "bird of the Madonna," "Mother of God's bird," and "Mary's bird."[276]

In the picture by Domenico Tintoretto there are two swallows perched on small, thin branches just behind and to the left of the crucifix, to the right of which Jerome is kneeling (fig. 187). In Bartolomeo di

270. MacCurdy, p. 1081.

271. Howe, pp. 87–88.

272. Evans, *Animal Symbolism*, p. 55.

273. *Centuria III*, no. 85, p. 170.

274. Seligmann, p. 102.

275. MacCurdy, p. 1082.

276. Gubernatis, vol. 2, p. 240. Robert Eder, *Mystisch-allegorische Vogelgeschichten und deren Ursprung*, p. 139. D'Arcy W. Thompson has discussed the favorable meanings in "Swallows in the House" (two papers, 1891, 1928).

Giovanni's painting a single swallow is to be seen in flight near the owl perched in the upper-left corner (fig. 44).

The Swan

The swan merits mention in this Bestiary only because there are two of these birds in the remote background of a painting of *Saint Jerome in Penitence* attributed to Bastiani (Brescia), and several of these birds at the right, far from Jerome, in a painting attributed to Patinir, *Saint Jerome in a Landscape* (Chicago: Art Institute). Also, as mentioned in my account of the duck (p. 211), a painting attributed to Jacopo Bellini (Richter Archives 145:III:6 and 7) contains what are either three white ducks or swans. There is no really compelling reason to assume that the presence of these birds is pertinent to the penitent saint in the foreground of any of these pictures, but it is also not impossible to see some argument for their inclusion.

Because of its white plumage the swan was a symbol of Purity, even an emblem of Mary. The old legend of the swan, described by Leonardo da Vinci as pure white, without a blemish, and singing sweetly as it dies[277] caused men to liken it to pious martyrs finding reason for spiritual comfort in their death. There is no reason to credit Saint Jerome with this attitude.

277. MacCurdy, p. 1081; also Evans, *Animal Symbolism*, p. 153. Leonardo was by no means the first to comment on this. Horapollo (Boas, bk. 2, no. 39) noted that the Egyptian priests used the figure of a swan to indicate a musical old man, for the bird "sings most sweetly when old." We still use the expression "swan song" for a last utterance.

The Titmouse

There are several species of titmice in Europe; two of them occur sparingly in the iconography of Saint Jerome, the coal tit, *Parus ater*, and the blue tit, *Parus caeruleus*. The former species occurs in a single instance, in the great *Saint Jerome in Penitence* by Hieronymus Bosch (Ghent, fig. 108); the blue tit in three paintings: Gozzoli, *Madonna and Child with Saints Zenobius, John the Baptist, Jerome, Francis, Peter, and Dominic* (London, fig. 188); Filippino Lippi, *Madonna and Child with Saints Jerome and Dominic* (London, fig. 142); and Patinir, *Saint Jerome in Penitence* (New York). In two of these paintings, by Gozzoli and Filippino Lippi, it is not possible to demonstrate that the tit is meaningfully connected with Jerome any more or less than with the other saints present.

The symbolic use of the various species of tits seems alike, and they may therefore be discussed as "the tit." In Germanic folklore the tit was held in high esteem, as a sacred, inviolable, prophetic, and auspicious creature, as well as a great gossip, whose vocal fluidity enabled it to outwit even Reynard, the sly fox.[278] The esteem with which the tit was held in Spain is reflected in its local names—*cid* ("Lord"), or *cid paxaro* ("sparrow of the Lord"). In the Low Countries the tit was considered a symbol of carelessness, because of its gossipy, talkative nature,[279] and it was also a sign of fertility. These meanings, particularly the last one, are discussed in detail in the chapter on Bosch's painting (p. 137 ff.).

278. Grimm, vol. 2, p. 683.

279. Seligmann, p. 102.

Figure 188. Benozzo Gozzoli, Detail of goldfinch and titmouse from *Madonna and Child and Saints Zenobius, John the Baptist, Jerome, Francis, Peter, and Dominic.* London: The National Gallery.

The Tortoise

280. Friedmann, "Footnotes to the Painted Page: The Iconography of an Altarpiece by Botticini," pp. 10–13.

281. "Haereticorum gravissima peccata significat, qui suis ét coeno ét volutabro luti erroribus immorant [immolant?]."

282. Emblem of *Matrimonium* (no. 100); William S. Heckscher, *Aphrodite as a Nun*, pp. 105–17.

283. William Painter, *The Palace of Pleasure* (originally printed 1566–67), wrote that Venus, "her fote vpon a Tortose, [signifies] the duety of a chaste Woman . . . hir feet not straying or wandering . . . to keep hirselfe within the limits of hir owne house." Similar statements were made by many other writers of the sixteenth and seventeenth centuries. For example, Robert Green stated that chastity is a woman treading on a tortoise, keeping to her own house and not straying abroad, "with every wanton giglet" (in A. B. Grosart's edition).

Tortoises occur in only five versions of "Saint Jerome in Penitence" out of many hundreds examined, but it is also true that they were seldom introduced in any aspect of the whole range of church art. The five instances are: Jacopo Bellini (drawing, Paris, fig. 53); Cranach (Innsbruck, fig. 94); Francesco di Giorgio (bronze relief, Washington, fig. 120); Italian engraving, ca. 1480–1500 (Hind, no. 86); Mansueti (London).

Although the tortoise rarely figured in religious art, it did have a great variety of meanings attached to it. These have been gone into in my discussion of its use by Cranach (p. 120) and by Francesco di Giorgio (p. 168), as well as in another publication, dealing with this creature in two pictures of totally unrelated subjects, *The Holy Women at the Sepulcher* by an imitator of Andrea Mantegna (London: National Gallery) and an altarpiece by Botticini, *The Madonna and Child Enthroned with Saints Benedict, Francis, Sylvester, and Anthony Abbot, and Angels* (New York: Metropolitan Museum of Art).[280] We shall, therefore, consider here chiefly those connotations of the tortoise pertinent to the Jerome story.

To begin with, Saint Jerome himself condemned the creature as a heretical animal of the gravest errors, choosing to dwell in disgrace amid filth and scum.[281] The location given the tortoise in the pictures by Bellini, Cranach, and the anonymous Italian engraver shows nothing of filth or mud, but in Francesco di Giorgio's work, the tortoise is in the mud (?) to the right of Jerome's feet. The Bellini drawing barely shows any details of the terrain, which is essentially barren and desertlike; Cranach places his tortoise in lush grass and leafage near a pheasant. In spite of these differences in suggested habitat, the tortoise in all these cases is still a symbol of evil. In Cranach's painting the creature is especially dark in color, a further suggestion of evil.

The tortoise was also a symbol of reticence and chastity. In his famous and artistically influential compendium of emblems, Alciati used a figure of Venus with one foot on the carapace of a tortoise, an image derived from a Phidian sculpture showing a similarly posed Aphrodite.[282] The Greek writer Pausanius used the image to illustrate the motto *Manere domi et tacitas decet esse puellas* ("Girls should stay at home and be silent"), advising that women should act in this respect like the tortoise, which does not (cannot) leave its shell and is a silent creature (fig. 189). From this concept of Venus as a "stay-at-home" character evolved the resultant one of chastity.[283] This idea of one's own home as the best home, *domus optima*, illustrated by a picture of a tortoise, was incorporated frequently in moralistic emblems (fig. 190).[284]

In connection with its connotations of reticence and chastity, the tortoise also came to be a symbol of Wisdom, a concept actually going back to Pliny, and based originally on the thought that a silent "home body" passed more time in meditation than a person actively wandering about.[285] In view of the fact that Jerome was a great scholar, his association in art with the tortoise might seem suitable in that respect, but this cannot be established. The basic implication of the tortoise remained one of evil; it was listed (Leviticus 11:2–47) among the "abominable" creatures, but, as noted above, it was rarely used in art. One of its few early appearances, in a fourth-century mosaic in the Cathedral of Aquilea, is of a tortoise in combat with a cock, an early Christian symbol of moral combat, the tortoise standing for the forces of darkness and the cock as the herald of dawn, representing the coming of light.[286]

The tortoise did have a connotation of the tomb, and, to a slight degree, of Christ in the tomb. As William Norton Howe mentioned in his brief description of the Mantegna imitator's *Holy Women at the Sepulcher*, the tortoise represented is a pond turtle, which at the beginning of winter constructs an underground chamber and remains there in a comatose state until the onset of warm weather in the spring.[287]

The tortoise was also considered a slow-moving animal, and as such was used to illustrate the old adage *festina lente*, or "make haste slowly,"[288] and related mottoes, among them one of *tardita* ("slowness"). Possibly because of its slow pace and its never seeming to be in a hurry, the tortoise was looked upon as a symbol of longevity. It figured, in the old Egyptian *Book of the Dead* (*Papyrus of Ani*, in the British Museum), among the creatures supposed to have special knowledge of medicinal herbs and other secret remedies for their ills.[289] None of these meanings are discernible in the creature's use in the Jerome context.

Figure 189. *Venus with one foot on a tortoise.* From Alciati, *Emblematum flumen abundans*, 1591.

Figure 190. *Domus optima.* From Camerarius, *Symbolorum et emblematum centuriae quatuor*, 1677.

284. Camerarius, p. 182, no. 91. Something of the extent to which this concept of the "stay at home" virtue was enlarged may be sensed from Cesare Ripa's figure of *Pudicitia*, where Aphrodite, with her foot upon a tortoise, is veiled and draped as a nun. This surprising iconographic use has been thoroughly discussed and explained by Heckscher, pp. 105–17. See

also Henkel and Schöne, cols. 608, 609, 610.

285. Andres Holguin (*La tortuga, simbole del filosofo*) wrote a whole book on the tortoise as a symbol of the philosopher. See also S. Braunfels, in Kirschbaum et al., vol. 4, cols. 69–70.

286. Rudolf Egger, "Ein altchristliches Kampfsymbol," pp. 791–95.

287. *Animal Life in Italian Painting*, p. 105.

288. Ripa, "Festina lente."

289. Cited in Klingender, p. 89.

The Unicorn

290. Salzer, pp. 44–50; Günther, pp. 1–36; Shepard, *The Lore of the Unicorn*; Rowland, pp. 152–57.

This mythical beast is only tangentially involved in the iconography of Saint Jerome, and, to my knowledge, only once at that. It figures as a pseudo-classical decoration on a ruined pagan chapel before which Jerome is kneeling in prayer in Bosch's painting of *Saint Jerome in Penitence*, in the Doge's Palace, Venice (fig. 109). Its meaning in that picture and its very slight connection with the Hieronymite theme is discussed on pages 153 and 267.

The many concepts symbolized by the unicorn have been discussed by many authors, among whom may be mentioned Anselm Salzer, Klaus Günther, Odell Shepard, and Beryl Rowland.[290]

The Wall Creeper

The wall creeper, *Tichodroma muraria*, occurs, so far as I know, in only a single picture of any part of the Jerome cycle—the London *Saint Jerome in Penitence* by Cosimo Tura (frontispiece). Because of this, the bird is discussed in full in the section devoted to this painting (pp. 183–85). As mentioned there, the little wall creeper is extremely rare in religious art, not only in Italian art but in that of all of Europe. Only three instances of its use have been noted: two are by Cosimo Tura, the Jerome picture and a *Madonna with Sleeping Child*, also known as *Madonna dello Zodiaco*, because of the zodiacal signs outlined in gold in the dark blue background. The third instance is Pietro di Domenico's *Adoration of the Shepherds with Galganus and Martin* in the great gallery of Siena (fig. 191).

The wall creeper is that excessively unusual curiosity, a perfectly real and valid species that was "recorded" in art (by Cosimo Tura) long before it ever received identifiable mention by zoologists (or naturalists). Not only this, but its role in folklore and legend appears to have been left unrecorded in documents and has to be reconstructed from the local names applied to it by the common people who knew it before the first compilers of European natural history showed any awareness of its existence. The allegorical significance of this bird, connoting Death, the Madonna ("Muttergottesvogel"), and Resurrection, has been gone into fully elsewhere (pp. 184–85) and need not be repeated here.

In the Madonna picture, now in the Accademia, Venice, it may be pointed out that the Christ Child is sleeping. A sleeping Christ Child is a prefiguration of the dead, martyred Christ, Who gave His Life for the salvation of mankind. The "Death" connotation of the wall creeper, as well as its roles as the "Madonna bird," is thus clearly pertinent in this connection. In this little painting there are two bunches of grapes, one at each of the upper corners, and on each is perched a bird: a wall creeper on the one to the right of the Virgin, and a goldfinch on the other. Bunches of grapes, like the Eucharistic wine, are old symbols of the Blood of Christ, the lifeblood of His religion. It is wholly appropriate in this picture that one of these bunches should involve the bird of Death, the wall creeper, and the other the avian symbol of Resurrection, the goldfinch. Cosimo Tura was an educated, enlightened man with great interest in symbolism and allegory, and it is understandable to find him making such use of these avian symbols.

We know so little about the personality of Pietro di Domenico, on the

Figure 191. Pietro di Domenico, *Adoration of the Shepherds with Galganus and Martin*. Siena: Pinacoteca Nazionale.

other hand, that it is indeed surprising that he included a rather stiffly depicted, but completely identifiable wall creeper, perched away from the main personages of his picture, woodpeckerlike, on one of the upright tree trunks used as a pole to support the roof of the shed, beneath which the adoration is taking place. The reason it is surprising to find this bird in a Sienese picture is that it is a more northern European creature, extending southward in high country to the Alps of Switzerland, Austria, and Italy. Only in winter does it ever come into the north Italian lowlands, and it apparently always has been, as it is today, a rare visitor to Tuscany. Like Cosimo Tura, Pietro also painted the wall creeper correctly in its winter plumage.

In Pietro di Domenico's picture, the bird is a very minor detail, hardly worth considering as significant except as a bit of decoration enlivening a piece of sky between roof poles. Yet the fact that in northern Italy the wall creeper did have local names such as "Madoneta," "Osel della Madona," and "Usel de la Trinita" indicates some apparently unrecorded legends about it that make it appropriate in a picture of the Madonna and Her Child. Not only is the Madonna present, but the Trinity as well, as in the peak of the upper center of the painting is God the Father, and below Him, the white dove of the Holy Spirit.

The Wolf

The wolf enters this Bestiary on the basis of only a single definite use, so far as I know, and of two uncertain ones. The first is a bronze relief of *Saint Jerome in Penitence*, attributed to Filarete by Ulrich Middeldorf (fig. 81).[291] In this plaque the wolf's head, in left profile, intrudes from the composition's right edge behind the kneeling saint. In addition to the wolf, Jerome has associated with him in this small sculpture, two lions and a bear, all, like the wolf, with only their heads showing, and a small snake and a scorpion and a crab in the lower-left corner; a unique faunal assemblage! As mentioned in my discussion of this work in the account of the multiple lions (p. 248), the very uniqueness of the assemblage makes one wonder if the artist had in mind anything beyond a number of feral and dangerous creatures to emphasize the wilderness setting of Jerome's penitential sojourn. Filarete was given to absorbing items from the works of others, sometimes in what seems a rather odd way as far as "ordinary" iconographic usage is concerned.

As for the uncertain cases, a wolf occurs, among a number of other animals, in the left background of Carpaccio's *Meditation on the Passion of Christ* (New York, fig. 32), where its connection with the seated figure of Jerome is only problematical (Job and the dead Christ are also present in the picture, equally removed from the animals in the background and equally susceptible of symbolic connection with them), and in a somewhat faded, but still clear drawing by Jacopo Bellini of *Saint Jerome in the Wilderness* (Paris, fig. 54), where the creature, as far as its zoological accuracy goes, may be a wolf or a jackal (see p. 226). It seems in the latter case that the jackal identification is the more likely, because the *Legenda aurea*, a primary "source" for late medieval and early renais-

291. "Filarete?" pp. 75–86.

292. Mâle, *Religious Art from the Twelfth to the Eighteenth Century*, p. 83.

293. Evans, *Animal Symbolism*, pp. 150–51; Charbonneau-Lassay, pp. 303–13.

294. Hartt, pp. 25–35.

295. Meiss, *Painting in Florence and Siena after the Black Death*, p. 98 fn. Meiss quotes from Alvaro Palayo, a papal aide at Avignon, "Lupi sunt dominantes in ecclesia" ("wolves are dominant in the Church"). In his notes on the three beasts that Dante describes in the opening canto of the *Inferno*, Thomas G. Bergin (*Dante Alighieri: The Divine Comedy*, p. 1, fn.) writes that traditionally the leopard is a sign of Florence, the lion of the House of France, and the she wolf the Papal Court.

Wolves were also used to denote heretics, as in Andrea de Firenze's great Dominican fresco of *The Way to Salvation*

sance concepts of Jerome's penitential wilderness, speaks of the deserts as inhabited by holy men and by jackals.[292]

In the Carpaccio painting the wolf, like the leopard included there, is a dangerous animal, a ravisher of the meek and the helpless.[293] As such, it is part of the emotional background of the meditation by Jerome and Job, but is not certainly connected specifically with either.[294] Aside from this, the wolf was a visual reference, not only to heresy in general, but also to corruption within the Church.[295] Carpaccio's wolf is zoologically not too accurate; it might be a much enlarged fox (!), but it is more likely that the artist intended it for a wolf, an animal he had never seen, whereas its smaller relative he may have known, and used as a basis for his rendition.

Beryl Rowland lists, among other symbolic meanings of the wolf, rapacity, avarice, hypocrisy, false prelates, usurers, magistrates, and accountants (!)[296] The wolf was also a symbol of Siena,[297] a usage obviously of no pertinence in the Jerome context.

in the Spanish Chapel of Santa Maria Novella, Florence, where some of the black and white dogs ("domini canes," or "hounds of the Lord," a visual pun on the Dominicans) are attacking wolves.

296. *Animals with Human Faces*, pp. 161–67.

297. Johannes Wilde, *Michelangelo: The Group of Victory*, p. 4.

The Woodpecker

Woodpeckers, of two species, have been found in only two pictures of Saint Jerome, both by Hieronymus Bosch (Ghent and Venice, figs. 108, 109). Inasmuch as no other instance of their inclusion has been noted, the discussion of woodpecker symbolism in my account of Bosch's paintings (p. 147) need not be repeated here. Suffice it to say that the woodpecker had both good and bad meanings; it was looked upon at times as a symbol of Christ and also of Satan! The latter was the more usual meaning, and the older, as it stems from the *Physiologus*. Thus, in James Carlill's translation (p. 209), we find that when a woodpecker finds a tree to be partly hollow, it builds its nest in it, "So does the Devil with man, for when he finds one faint-hearted in the path of virtue, therein he takes up his abode. . . . But, when he finds one valiant in holiness and faith, therefrom he flies away at once."

Saint Jerome in Illuminated Manuscripts

Figure 192. *Saint Jerome in His Study*, English, 1400–1450. Book of Hours. Oxford: Bodleian Library, MS. Liturg. 401, f. 198ᵛ.

Figure 193. *Saint Jerome in His Study*, Flemish, fifteenth century. Book of Hours. Oxford: Bodleian Library, MS. Liturg. 400, f. 89ᵛ.

194

195

Figure 194. *Saint Jerome in His Study*, English, fifteenth century. Book of Hours known as *Queen Mary's Psalter*. Oxford: Bodleian Library, MS. Auct. D. inf. 2.13, f.209ᵛ.

Figure 195. *Saint Jerome and the Lion*, Flemish, ca. 1450. Book of Hours. Oxford: Bodleian Library, MS. Canon Liturg. 229, f.207ᵛ.

Figure 196. *Saint Jerome and the Lion*, English, late fifteenth-early sixteenth century. *Hours of the Holy Ghost*. Oxford: Bodleian Library, MS. Lat. Liturg. g.5, pl. 163.

Figure 197. *Saint Jerome and the Lion*, English, early fifteenth century. Book of Hours. Oxford: Bodleian Library, MS. Bodley 850, f.70.

Figure 198. Saint Jerome and the Lion, English, ca. 1450–1500. Book of Hours. Oxford: Bodleian Library, MS. Rowl. Liturg. g.3, f.165ᵛ.

Figure 199. *Saint Jerome and the Lion*, French (Norman), ca. 1430–1440. Book of Hours. Oxford: Bodleian Library, MS. Acut. D. inf. 2.11, f.231.

196

198

197

199

200

Figure 200. *Saint Jerome and the Lion*, Flemish, 1514–1520. New Testament. Oxford: Bodleian Library, MS. Corpus Christi Coll. 13, f.68.

Figure 201. *Saint Jerome before a Cave*, Italian (Ferrarese?), ca. 1480. *Officium Beatae Mariae Virginiae.* Oxford: Bodleian Library, MS. Douce 11, f.266.

Figure 202. *Saint Jerome with the Lion*, Italian (Florentine), ca. 1490. *Officium Beatae Mariae Virginiae.* Oxford: Bodleian Library, MS. Canon Liturg. 265, f.14b.

Figure 203. *Saint Jerome in Penitence*, Flemish (?), 1450–1500. Votive Office. Prayers for a Lady. Oxford: Bodleian Library, MS. Douce 12, f.201.

201

202

203

205

204

206

Figure 204. *Saint Jerome in Penitence*, Italian, 1471–1484. Missal. Oxford: Bodleian Library, MS. Canon Liturg. 197, f.223b.

Figure 205. *Saint Jerome and the Lion*, French, late fifteenth century. *The Golden Legend*. Oxford: Bodleian Library, MS. Queen's College 305, f.220.

Figure 206. *Saint Jerome in Penitence*, French, 1500–1525. Oxford: Bodleian Library, MS. Astor A.17, f.153.

Figure 207. *Saint Jerome in Penitence*, Bruges, ca. 1525. Book of Hours. Oxford: Bodleian Library, MS. Astor, A.24, vol. II, f.67.

207

Appendix:
List of Pertinent Renditions of the
Jerome Theme

All the works of art, either mentioned specifically in the text or used as material in arriving at concepts and estimates underlying various historical, statistical, or iconographic discussions, are listed here in abbreviated form, alphabetically by the name of the artist or period. This list, composed of about 1,100 paintings, sculptures, manuscript illuminations, drawings, graphics, and even two pieces of stained glass and one tapestry, could very easily have been extended greatly, if the aim had been purely statistical. However, it seems that the coverage is ample, and that additional examples would not add significantly to the scope of the Bestiary, to the understanding of the symbolism, or to the chronological and geographical span of Hieronymite faunal iconography. The purposes of the list are (1) to show the basis for many statements in the text; (2) to enable readers to identify and to locate any work mentioned; (3) to enable them to see if some example of special interest to them has or has not been included in this survey; (4) to enable readers to "realign" a work according to which list of attributions they prefer to follow. The problem of attributions is always a difficult one when compiling a list partly from up-to-date catalogues and other sources and partly from older attributions made over a span of many decades. I have tried to honor, wherever possible, the attributions currently used by the present owners, whether museums or individuals, but at the same time I have attempted to bring all attributions into line. A publication cutoff date has made it impossible to consider recent changes, such as the Montreal Museum's attribution to Domenico Michelino of the painting here listed as by Andrea di Giusto and the Toledo (Ohio) Museum's "Gentile Bellini," now considered to be "Anonymous Venetian, fifteenth century." For Italian Renaissance paintings Berenson's posthumous lists have been used as a basic reference. The comprehensive "census" of pre-nineteenth-century Italian paintings in American public collections up to the end of 1967 by Burton B. Fredericksen and Federico Zeri enabled me to check their Italian paintings containing Saint Jerome, in North American public collections, against my own list.

It need only be mentioned that I have studied all of these works of art, either in the original or in photographic reproductions, in the course of the present survey.

Giorgio Vasari's description of the lost frescoes of the Jerome story that Gherardo Starnina painted in the Carmine church in Florence suggests that the iconography of the saint was there enlivened to a remarkable degree, at a very early date. However, since Vasari says nothing about the presence of any animals in these scenes, and since nothing else is known about them, Starnina's pictures are not included in this list.

The following abbreviations are used to save needless repetition:

J in W   "Jerome in the Wilderness" (whether the saint is in penitential prayer, or reading, or contemplating, and whether the scene is wilderness or merely "outdoors")

J in S   "Jerome in His Study"

J & L   Jerome removing (or about to remove) the thorn from the lion's foot

J   Jerome pictured as a single figure, standing or enthroned.

In all other instances, as, for example, cases in which Jerome is one among other figures in an altarpiece, the main title of the work is given at sufficient length to render it identifiable. It should be noted that the abbreviated designations are not necessarily mutually exclusive. In some instances, for example, J in W or J in S also portray a thorn-removal scene, as in Colantonio's painting (fig. 1).

The medium of each work is indicated as follows:

(P)   Painting

(S)   Sculpture, whether in the round or in relief

(D)   Drawing

(G)   Graphics, including woodcuts, etchings, and engravings

(M)   Manuscript illuminations

(GL)   Glass

(T)   Tapestry.

If the present location of a piece is unknown, a reference is given to a published illustration of it (cited under the author's last name as listed in the Bibliography) or to an available archival photograph (primarily in the Richter Archives at the National Gallery of Art, Washington). The names of museums and collections are abbreviated in many instances.

Works illustrated in this book are indicated by figure numbers in brackets, following the listing.

Alberti, Cherubino	J in W (G)	(after Michelangelo). Bartsch, vol. 17, p. 69, no. 54.
Altdorfer, Albrecht	J in W (P)	Cologne: Wallraf-Richartz Museum. [Fig. 76]
	J in W (P)	Berlin-Dahlem: Staatliche Museen.
	J in W (G)	Washington: National Gallery of Art; Rosenwald Coll. [Fig. 77]
	J in W (D)	London: British Museum.
	J in W (G)	Waldmann, p. 35.
	J in W (G)	Four versions: Winzinger, nos. 65, 82, 121, 135.

Andrea del Sarto School	J in W (P)	Florence: Uffizi.
Andrea di Giusto	Assumption of Virgin with J and Francis (P)	Tulsa: Philbrook Art Center; Samuel H. Kress Coll.
	J in W (P)	(now attributed to Domenico Michelino) Montreal: Museum of Fine Arts. [Fig. 43]
Andreas, Johannes	J & L (M)	Munich: Stadtbibliothek.
Angelico, Fra, follower (*see also* Domenico di Michelino)	J in W (P)	Boston: Museum of Fine Arts.
Anonymous Twelfth-to-Fourteenth-Century Manuscript Illuminators (all from Princeton Index of Early Christian Art)	J holding book, standing on fantastic beast (M)	Clermont-Ferrand: Bibl. Municipale 1, f. 46^r.
	J seated, writing, ca. 1371–1378 (M)	Cracow: Bibl. Jagiellonska, Lat. 284. Bible I, f. 1^r.
	J seated; lion rearing, 1148 (M)	London: Brit. Mus. Add. 14788–90. I, f. 1^v
	J in S, thirteenth century (M)	Brit. Mus., Burney 3, Bible, Robert of Battle, f. 2^r.
	J in S, second half fourteenth century (M)	Vatican Library, Lat. 50, 51 Bible I.
	J in S, ca. 1400 (M)	Vienna: Nat. Library, 1169 Bible, Martin Korczek, f. 1^r.
Anselmi, Michelangelo	J and Saint Catherine (P)	Milan: Brera.
Antonello da Messina	J in S (P)	London: National Gallery. [Fig. 119]
	J in W (P)	Reggio Calabria: Museo della Magna Grecia.
Antonello de Saliba	Polyptych (P)	Taormina: Duomo.
Antoniazzo Romano	J & L (P)	Venice: Ca'd'Oro.
	J in W (P)	Milan: Poldi-Pezzoli Museum.
Antoniazzo Romano follower	Crucifixion with J and Donors (P)	Berea, Ky.: Samuel H. Kress Coll.
Antonio de Comantes	J in W (P)	Toledo: S. Andres. (Post, vol. 9, p. 279.)
Antonio da Fabriano	J in S (P)	Baltimore: Walters Art Gallery.
Antonio da Ferrara	J. (P)	Urbino: Galleria Nazionale delle Marche.
Antonio da Viterbo	J in W (part of triptych of "Ascension of Virgin") (P)	Vatican.
Antwerp School, ca. 1525	J in W (P)	Cologne: Wallraf-Richartz Museum.
	J in W (P)	Rotterdam: Boymans-van Beuningen Museum.
	J in S (P)	Philadelphia: Johnson Coll.

Aragonese Master   J in S (part of triptych) (P)   *Querschnitt* (April 1926), after p. 280.

Artes Master   J's Lion Driving Camels to Monastery (P)   Valencia: Vidua Montesinas Coll.
                                    (Post, vol. 6, p. 317.)

Austrian, Fifteenth Century   J & L, ca. 1400 (D)   Vienna: National Bibliothek. (Hajós, p. 34.)
                                J & L, "hardly later than 1415" (P)   Austria: Schloss Clam. (Tripp, p. 88.)
                                J & L, ca. 1420 (S)   Vienna: University Art Museum.
                                J & L (M)   *Belles Heures d'Ailly*, f. 186ᵛ. (Hajós, p. 40.)
                                J & L (M)   *Très Belles Heures*, Turin. (Hajós, p. 40.)
                                J & L (G)   Hajós, p. 35.
                                J & L (G)   Hajós, p. 35.

Austrian, Late Fifteenth Century   J & L (S)   Austria: Burg Liechtenstein. (Hajós, p. 34.)

Austrian, Early Sixteenth Century J in W (S)   Vienna: Österreichisches Museum. (Dehio and von Bezold,
                                    vol. 3, pl. 61.)

Austrian, Sixteenth Century Xylo- J in W (G)   Vienna: Albertina.
grapher

Baldung (Hans Baldung Grien)   J in W (G)   Harbison, p. 56, fig. 62.

Baptist Master (French)   J in S (M)   Meiss (1967), p. 250.

Barocci, Federico   J in W (P)   Rome: Borghese Gallery.

Bartolommeo da Forli   J in W (P)   Forlì: Pinacoteca Comunale.

Bartolommeo, Fra   J in W (P)   Berlin-Dahlem: Staatliche Museen.
                                J in W (P)   Norton Hall: Sir W. H. Pollen Coll.

Bartolomeo della Gata   J in W (P)   Arezzo: Sagrestia del Duomo.
                                J in W (P)   Oberlin: Allen Museum.

Bartolomeo di Giovanni   J in W (P)   Florence: Acad. Galleria dell'Accademia. [Fig. 44]
                                J in W (P)   New Haven: Yale University Art Gallery; James Jackson Jarves
                                    Coll. [Fig. 158]
                                J in W (P)   Narni: Pinacoteca.
                                Last Communion of Jerome (P)   Philadelphia: Johnson Coll.
                                J in W (P)   Formerly in Ryan Coll., 1940. (Richter Archives 76:IV:50.)
                                J in W (P)   Palermo: Chiaramonte Bordonaro Coll.
                                Last Communion and Death of Jerome (P)   Baltimore: Walters Art Gallery.

Basaiti, Marco   J in W (P)   Budapest: Musée Hongrois des Beaux-Arts.
                                J in W (P)   Berenson (1969), fig. 591.
                                J in W (P)   Richter Archives 150:IV:5.
                                J in W (P)   Baltimore: Walters Art Gallery.
                                J in W (P)   London: National Gallery.
                                J in W (P)   Venice: Accademia, no. 107.

Basaiti attribution   J in W (P)   Venice: Correr Museum.

Basaiti School   J in W (P)   Budapest: Musée Hongrois des Beaux-Arts. [Fig. 145]

Bassano, Jacopo	J in W (P)	Munich: Alte Pinakothek.
	J in W (P)	Cambridge: Fitzwilliam Museum.
	J in W (P)	Venice: Accademia, no. 652.
	J in W (P)	Venice: Accademia, no. 920.
	J in W (P)	Terre Haute, Ind.: University of Notre Dame.
	J in W (P)	Ponce, Puerto Rico: Museo de Arte de Ponce.
	Madonna and Child with J and Francis (P)	Bassano: Museo Civico.
Bastiani, Lazzaro	Three Episodes from Life of J (P)	Milan: Brera, no. 221. [Fig. 30]
	J in W (P)	Boston: Museum of Fine Arts.
	Death of Jerome (P)	Venice: Accademia.
	J in W (P)	Lugano: Thyssen Coll.
	J in W (P)	Monopoli (Bari): Duomo.
	J in W (P)	Springfield, Mass.: Museum of Fine Arts.
	J in W (P)	Brescia: Bettoni Coll.
Beatrizet, Nic.	J in W (G)	(after Girolamo Muziano). Bartsch, vol. 15, p. 32, no. 255.
Beccafumi, Domenico	J in W (P)	Rome: Doria Pamphili Gallery.
Becerra, Gaspar	J in W (S)	Burgos: Cathedral, Chapel of the Condestable.
Beham, Hans Sebold	J (G)	Seven engravings and four woodcuts, 1519–21. Pauli, nos. 61–67, 893–96.
Belbello da Pavia	J & L (M)	Vatican Library, MS. barb. Lat. 613 f. 1ʳ.
Bellano, Bartolommeo	J (S)	Paris: Louvre.
Bellini, Gentile	J in W (P)	(now attributed to Anonymous Venetian, fifteenth century) Toledo, Ohio: Museum of Art. [Figs. 26–28]
	J in W (P)	Venice: San Marco.
	J in W (P)	Trau (Dalmatia): Duomo.
Bellini, Giovanni	J in W (P)	Washington: National Gallery of Art; Samuel H. Kress Coll. [Figs. 22–25]
	J in W (P)	Florence: Contini-Bonacossi Coll.
	J in W (P)	Birmingham: Barber Institute of Fine Arts.
	J in W (P)	Bergamo: Accademia Carrara.
	J in W (P)	Paris: Musée Jacquemart-André.
	J in W (P)	Marche: S. Francesco.
	J in W (P)	Oxford: Ashmolean Museum.
	J in W (P)	Pesaro: Museo Civico.
Bellini, Giovanni, follower	J in W (P)	London: National Gallery.
Bellini, Jacopo	J in W (P)	Verona: Museo di Castelvecchio. [Fig. 29]
	J in W (D)	Three drawings in London: British Museum. [Fig. 55]
	J in W (D)	Two drawings in Paris: Louvre. [Figs. 53, 54]
	J (P)	Brooklyn, N.Y.: Brooklyn Museum.
Bellini, Jacopo, attribution	J in W (P)	Richter Archives 145:III:6 and 7.
Benaglio, Francesco	J (P)	Washington: National Gallery of Art; Samuel H. Kress Coll. [Fig. 149]

Benson, Abrosius	J in W (P) Philadelphia: Johnson Coll. J in W (P) Antwerp: Musée Mayer van den Burgh. J in W (P) Terre Haute, Ind.: University of Notre Dame. J (P) Brussels: Musées Royaux des Beaux-Arts. J in W (lateral panel of triptych, "Adoration of the Shepherds") (P) Segovia: Ayuntamiento.
Benvenuto di Giovanni	J in W (P) Los Angeles County Museum of Art. J in W (P) London: Wallace Coll.
Bergognone, Ambrogio	J with Saints Ambrose and Catherine (P) Milan: Brera, no. 258. J. in W (P) Milan: Castello Sforzesco. J in W (P) Bergamo: Accademia Carrara.
Bergognone follower	Madonna and Child (P) Bridgeport, Conn.: Museum of Art, Science and Industry; Samuel H. Kress Coll.
Bermejo, Bartolome	Pietà of the Archbishop Despla (P) Barcelona Cathedral.
Bermejo, Bartolome, attribution	J in S (P) Raleigh: North Carolina Museum of Art, no. 169. J (P) New York: Hispanic Society of America.
Bernini, Giovanni Lorenzo	J (S) Siena: Duomo.
Bertucci, Jacopo	J in W (P) Paris: Louvre. J in W (P) Gibbons, pp. 357–62.
Biagio d'Antonio da Firenze	J in W (P) Brunswick, Maine: Bowdoin College; Samuel H. Kress Coll.
Bianchi Ferrari, Francesco	Scenes from Life of J (P) Modena: S. Pietro.
Bicci di Lorenzo	J & L (P) Pescia: S. Antonio Abate. J and Two Other Saints in the Wilderness (P) Perugia: Galleria Nazionale del Umbria.
Blanchard, Jacques	J in S (P) Paris: Louvre (?) (Van de Waal [1964], p. 11.)
Boccaccino, Boccacio	J in W (P) Cremona: Museo Civico.
Boldrini, Leonardo	Madonna with J and Augustine (P) Venice: Museo Correr.
Boldrini, Niccolo	J in W (G) (after Titian). Tietze (1937), fig. 324.
Bolognese, Fourteenth Century	J (P) Bologna: Pinacoteca.
Bolognese School	J with Three Angels (P) Rome: Corsini Gallery.
Bolognese, Seventeenth Century	J in W (P) Lawrence, Kan.: University Art Gallery.
Bonfigli, Benedetto	Pietà with J and Leonard (P) Perugia: S. Pietro. [Fig. 21]
Bonifazio Veronese	Sacra Conversazione (P) Columbia, S. C.: Columbia Museum of Art; Samuel H. Kress Coll.

Bono da Ferrara   J in W (P)   London: National Gallery. [Fig. 62]

Bosch, Hieronymus   J in W (P)   Ghent: Musée des Beaux-Arts. [Figs. 108, 110–115]
                            J in W (P)   Venice: Doge's Palace. [Figs. 109, 116–118]

Bosch School   J in W (P)   Bruges: Musée Communal.

Botticelli, Sandro   J in W (P)   Florence: Uffizi, no. 8389.
                            J in W (P)   Leningrad: Hermitage.
                            Last Communion of Saint Jerome (P)   New York: Metropolitan Museum.
                            J in S (part of triptych) (P)   Rome: Palazzo Rospigliosi.

Botticini, Francesco   J in W (central panel of triptych) (P)   London: National Gallery. [Figs. 38, 39]

Botticini (?)   J in W with Stigmatization of Francis (P)   New Haven: Yale University Art Gallery.

Boucicaut Master   J in S (M)   Paris: Musée Jacquemart-André. [Fig. 12]

Bouts, Aelbert   J in W (P)   Los Angeles: Norton Simon Foundation. [Fig. 69]
                            J in W (P)   Brussels: Musées Royaux des Beaux-Arts. [Fig. 68]

Bouts, Diereck   J (P)   Louvain: St. Peters.

Bouts, Diereck, follower   J in W (P)   Formerly in Brockhaus Coll., Leipzig.

Brandi, Giacinto   J in S (P)   Greenville, S. C.: Bob Jones University.

Brill, Paulus   J in W (P)   Sarasota: Ringling Museum.
                            J in W (P)   Rotterdam: Boymans-van Beuningen Museum, no. 1097.

Brueghel, Pieter   J in W (G)   Boston: Museum of Fine Arts.
                            J in W (D)   Washington: National Gallery of Art.

Bruges, ca. 1525   J in W (M)   Book of Hours. Oxford: Bodleian Library, MS. Astor, A 24, vol. II, f. 67. [Fig. 207]

Bruges School, ca. 1400   J in S (M)   Paris: Bibliothèque Nationale, MS. Fr. 166.f.1.

Brusasorci, Domenico   J in W (P)   Lovere: Accademia Tadini.

Brussels, Early Sixteenth Century   J in W (T)   La Granja de San Ildefonso: Tapestry Museum.

Bugatti, Zanetto   J & L (P)   Bergamo: Accademia Carrara.

Bugiardini, Giulio   J in W (P)   Florence: Museo Bardini.

Buonaccorso, Niccolo di   J in S (P)   Philadelphia: Johnson Coll.

Buonconsiglio, Giovanni   J in W (P)   Venice: Museo Correr.

Butinone, Bernardino   J Reading (P)   Parma: Regia Galleria.

Cabezalero, Juan Martin   J Listening to Voices from Above (P)   Richmond: Cook Coll.

Campagnola, Domenico   J in W (G)   Los Angeles County Museum of Art. [Fig. 56]
                                          J in W (P)   Los Angeles: Norton Simon Foundation. [Fig. 176]
                                          J in W (G)   Hind, vol. 7, pl. 794.

Campagnola, Giulio   J in W (G)   Hamburg: Kunsthalle.

Campi, Antonio   J in S (P)   Madrid: Prado.

Campi, Bernardo   J in W (P)   Cremona: S. Sigismondo.

Campi, Giulio, attribution   Madonna and Child with Jerome and John the Baptist (P)   Agram (Zagreb):
                                          Gemäldegalerie.

Caporali, Bartolommeo   J in S (P)   Naples: Museo Nazionale.

Caravaggio, Michelangelo Merisi da   J Reading (P)   Rome: Borghese Gallery.
                                          J Meditating (P)   Barcelona: Monastery of Montserrat.

Caravaggio School   J in S (P)   Worcester, Mass.: Worcester Art Museum.

Cariani (Giovanni Busi)   J in W (P)   Bergamo: Accademia Carrara. [Fig. 57]
                                          J in W (P)   Bergamo: Conti Suardi Coll.
                                          Resurrection (P)   Milan: Brera, no. 981.
                                          Madonna and Child with Saints (P)   Milan: Brera, no. 116.

Caroselli, Angelo   J in W (P)   Baltimore: Walters Art Gallery.

Caroto, Giovanni Francesco   J in W (in background of Entombment) (P)   Portland, Ore.: Portland Art
                                          Museum; Samuel H. Kress Coll.

Caroto, Giovanni Francesco,
attribution   J in W (in background of Madonna and Child) (P)   Augusta, Ga.: Gertrude
                                          Herbert Memorial Institute of Art; Samuel H. Kress Coll.

Carpaccio, Vittore   J Leading Lion Back to Monastery (P)   Venice: S. Giorgio degli Schiavoni.
                                          [Fig. 31]
                                          Burial of J (P)   Venice: S. Giorgio degli Schiavoni.
                                          Meditation on Passion of Christ (P)   New York: Metropolitan Museum.
                                          [Fig. 32]
                                          J in W (P)   Zogno (Bergamo): Chiesa Parrocchiale.
                                          J in W (P)   Zara (Dalmatia): Duomo.

Carpaccio, Vittore, attribution   J in W (P)   Lugano: Thyssen Coll.

Carracci, Agostino   J in W, 1516 (G)   Boschloo, vol. 2., fig. 102.

Carracci, Annibale   J in W (G)   San Francisco: California Palace of the Legion of Honor;
                                          Achenbach Foundation Coll.

Carracci, Ludovico   J in W (P)   Bologna: S. Martino.

Carrari da Forlì, Baldassare   J in W (P)   Forlì: Pinacoteca Comunale.

Castagno, Andrea del   Trinity with J, Paula, and Eustochium (P)   Florence: SS. Annunziata.
                                       [Fig. 133]

Catena, Vincenzo   J in S (P)   London: National Gallery. [Fig. 2]
                                   J in S (P)   Frankfurt: Städelsches Kunstinstitut.
                                   J in W (P)   Cambridge, Mass.: Fogg Museum.
                                   J in W (P)   Baltimore: Walters Art Gallery. [Fig. 151]
                                   J in W (P)   Paris: Musée Jacquemart-André, no. 2640.

Catena, Vincenzo, attribution   J in W (P)   Paris: Musée Jacquemart-André, no. 736.

Cavarozzi, Bartolomeo   J in S (P)   Florence: Pitti Palace.

Cecco di Pietro   J in S (P)   Raleigh: North Carolina Museum of Art; Samuel H. Kress Coll.
                                       [Fig. 17]

Cenni di Francesco di Ser Cenni   J in S (P)   Pisa: Museo Diocesano.

Cenni di Francesco di Ser Cenni (?)   J in S (P)   San Miniato al Tedesco: S. Domenico.

Cerano, Circle of   J and Angel (P)   Milan: Castello Sforzesco, no. 171.

Cerezo, Matteo de   J in W (P)   Munich: Alte Pinakothek.

Cesare Magni   J (P)   Milan: Castello Sforzesco.

Cesare da Sesto   J in W (P)   Richmond: Cook Coll.
                                   J (P)   Milan: Brera, no. 754.

Ciamberlano, Luca   Death of J (G)   (after Raphael). Bartsch, vol. 20, p. 36, no. 72.

Cima da Conegliano   J in W (P)   London: National Gallery. [Fig. 34]
                                   J in W (P)   Harewood House (York): Earl of Harewood.
                                   J in W (P)   Milan: Brera, 219.
                                   J in W (P)   Florence: Contini-Bonacossi Coll.
                                   J in W (P)   Washington: National Gallery of Art; Samuel H. Kress Coll.
                                       [Fig. 33]
                                   Madonna with Louis and J (P)   Venice: Accademia. [Fig. 182]
                                   Madonna and Child with J and James (P)   Vicenza: Museo Civico.

Civerchio, Vincenzo, attribution   J in W (P)   Formerly in E. L. Tross Coll., Los Angeles (before 1932).
                                       (Richter Archives 134: VIII: 13.) [Fig. 42]

Cock, Jan de   J in W (P)   Cologne: Wallraf-Richartz Museum. [Fig. 70]
                                   J in W (D)   Berlin-Dahlem: Kupferstichkabinett, Staatliche Museen.

Coecke van Aalst, Pieter   J in W (P)   Richter Archives 284: VII: 18.
                                   J in S (P)   Turin: L. R. Piovano Coll.
                                   J in S (P)   Geneva: Musée d'Art et d'Histoire.
                                   J in S (P)   Paris: J. O. Leegenhoek Coll.
                                   J in S (P)   Brussels: Musées Royaux des Beaux-Arts.
                                   J in S (P)   London: Dr. Clark-Kennedy.
                                   J in S (P)   Paris: Frits Lugt Coll.
                                   J in W (P)   Wiesbaden: Gemäldegalerie.

Coello, Sanchez   J and Augustine (P)   Escorial: San Lorenzo el Real.

Coffermans, Marcellus   J in W (P)   Madrid: Prado.

Colantonio, Niccolo Antonio   J in S (P)   Naples: Museo Nazionale. [Fig. 1]

Cologne Master, ca. 1470   J in S (G)   Field, no. 357.

Cornelisz, Jacob   Jerome Altar (P)   Vienna: Kunsthistorisches Museum, no. 101. [Fig. 169]

Correggio (Antonio Allegri) (*see also*   J Contemplating Skull (P)   Madrid: Academia, no. 483.
Costa, Lorenzo)   Madonna di S. Girolamo (P)   Parma: Regia Galleria.

Cort, Cornelis   J (?) in W (G)   (after Muziano). New York: Metropolitan Museum of Art.
                                                     [Fig. 172]
                                                  J in W (G)   (after Muziano). Bierens de Haan, no. 117.
                                                  J in W with angels (G)   (after Jacopo Palma the Younger). Bierens de
                                                     Haan, no. 131.
                                                  J in W (G)   (after Bartolomeo Neroni). Bierens de Haan, no. 140.
                                                  J in W (G)   (after Titian). Bierens de Haan, no. 141.
                                                  J in W (G)   (after Muziano). Bierens de Haan, no. 135.
                                                  J in W (G)   Bierens de Haan, no. 136.
                                                  J (?) Sustained by Angels (G)   (after Bernardino Passeri). New York:
                                                     Metropolitan Museum of Art. [Fig. 170]
                                                  J in W "Altro S. Girolamo" (G)   (after Muziano?). Ugo da Como, p. 109.
                                                  J in W (G)   (after Parmigianino). Ugo da Como, p. 184, no. 35.
                                                  J in W (G)   (after Caraglio). Ugo da Como, p. 184, no. 3.

Costa, Lorenzo   J in W (P)   Ferrara: Pinacoteca Civica.
                                                  J in W (in background of portrait of Cardinal Bibbiena) (P)   Minneapolis
                                                     Institute of Arts. (Attributed to Correggio by Fahy.)
                                                  J in W (P)   Bayonne: Musée Bonnat.
                                                  J in W (P)   Formerly in Palais Athems, Graz.

Costanzo, Marco   J in S (P)   Siracusa: Duomo, Sacristy.

Cotela Master   Jerome and Saint Michael (P)   New York: Hispanic Society of America.

Cozzarelli, Guidoccio   J (at right end of crucifix) (P)   New York: Metropolitan Museum.

Cranach, Lucas, the Elder   J & L with Saint Leopold (P)   Vienna: Kunsthistorisches Museum. [Fig. 92]
                                                  J in W (P)   Vienna: Kunsthistorisches Museum. [Fig. 93]
                                                  J in W (P)   Berlin-Dahlem: Staatliche Museen, no. 565.
                                                  J in W (P)   Formerly owned by Julius Böhler, Ltd. (*Burlington Magazine*
                                                     100: pl. 7.)
                                                  J in W (G)   1509.
                                                  Cardinal Albrecht as J in W (P)   Zollikon, Switzerland: Private Coll.
                                                     (Koepplin and Falk, vol. 1, p. 102.)
                                                  Cardinal Albrecht as J in W (P)   Berlin-Dahlem: Staatliche Museen.
                                                     [Fig. 102]
                                                  J in W (P)   Innsbruck: Tiroler Landesmuseum Ferdinandeum. [Figs. 94–101]
                                                  J in S (P)   Darmstadt: Landesmuseum. [Fig. 103]
                                                  J in S (P)   Sarasota: Ringling Museum. [Figs. 104, 105, 107]

Crespi, Giuseppe Mario J in W (P) London: National Gallery.

Crispin van de Passe Saint Marcus (Jerome?) (G) Boston: Museum of Fine Arts; Harvey D. Parker Coll.

Crivelli, Carlo J in W (predella) (P) London: National Gallery. [Fig. 35]
J in W (P) Formerly in Spiridon Coll., Berlin.

Crivelli, Vittorio J (P) Cambridge, Mass.: Fogg Museum.
J (P) Provincetown, Mass.: Chrysler Coll.

Dalem, Cornelius van J in W (P) Richter Archives 283B: VII: 1.

David, Gerard J in W (P) Frankfurt: Städelsches Kunstinstitut.
J in W (P) London: National Gallery.
J (part of triptych) (P) New York: Metropolitan Museum.

David, Gerard, follower J (grisaille reverse of panel) (P) London: National Gallery.

della Robbia (*see* Robbia, Giovanni della)

Desiderio da Settignano J in W (S) Washington: National Gallery of Art; Widener Coll. [Figs. 45, 46]
J in W (S) New York: Michael Hall Coll.

Diamante, Fra, with Filippo Lippi J & L (P) London: National Gallery. [Fig. 47]

Diamantini, Giuseppe J in W (G) Bartsch, vol. 21, p. 265.

Diana, Benedetto Madonna and Child and Saint Jerome (P) Coral Gables, Fla.: Lowe Art Museum; Samuel H. Kress Coll.
J in W (P) Lugano: Thyssen Coll.
J in W (P) Baltimore: Walters Art Gallery.
J in W (P) Middlebury, Vt.: A. R. Turner Coll.

Domenichino (Domenico Zampieri) Last Communion of J (P) Vatican: Pinacoteca.
J and Angel (P) Madrid: Prado.
J and Angel (P) London: National Gallery, no. 85 [Fig. 4]
J and Angel (P) Venice: Pinacoteca di Concordi.
J in W (P) Glasgow Art Gallery, no. 139; McLellan Bequest, 1854. [Fig. 178]

Domenico di Bartolo J (P) Paris: Louvre.
J (P) Pisa: Duomo.

Domenico di Michelino J in W (P) Dallas Museum of Fine Arts; Samuel H. Kress Coll. [Fig. 159]
J in W (P) Prato: Galleria Comunale.
Dream of Jerome (P) Chartres (Dep. Louvre): Musée des Beaux-Arts.

Donatello attribution J (S) Faenza: Pinacoteca.

Dossi, Battista J in W (P) Paris: Louvre.

Dossi, Dosso

J in W (P) Moscow: Pushkin Museum.
J in S (P) Milan: Crespi Gallery.
J in W (P) Vienna: Kunsthistorisches Museum, no. 510. [Fig. 160]
J in W (P) Rome: Conte Leonardo Vitetti.

Dossi, Dosso, attribution

J in S (P) Amsterdam: Rijksmuseum.

Dürer, Albrecht

J & L, 1492 (G) (Title page of *Epistolare beati Hieronymi*) Basle: N. Kessler.
J in S, 1492 (G) Washington: National Gallery of Art; Rosenwald Coll.
J in W, 1497 (G) Washington: National Gallery of Art; Rosenwald Coll.
J in W, 1498 (P) Raveningham Hall (Norwich): Lt. Col. Sir Edmund Bacon Coll.
J in S. 1511 (G) Washington: National Gallery of Art; Rosenwald Coll. [Fig. 88]
J by a Pollard Willow, 1512 (G) Washington: National Gallery of Art; Rosenwald Coll. [Fig. 89]
J in W, 1512 (G) Washington: National Gallery of Art; Rosenwald Coll.
J in S, 1514 (G) Washington: National Gallery of Art; Rosenwald Coll. [Fig. 83]
J in S, ca. 1520 (D) Berlin-Dahlem: Kupferstichkabinett, Staatliche Museen. [Fig. 91]
J in S, 1521 (P) Lisbon: Museo Nacional.

Dutch, Seventeenth Century

J in S (P) Claremont, Calif.: Pomona College.

Ecija Master

J in W (P) Puerto de Santa Maria: Parish Church. (Post, vol. 10, p. 100.)
J in S (P) Schilling, p. 179, fig. 3.

El Greco (Domenico Theotokopoulos)

J in W (P) Washington: National Gallery of Art. [Fig. 79]
J in W (P) Florence: Contini-Bonacossi Coll.
J in W (P) New York: Hispanic Society of America.
J in W (P) Edinburgh: National Gallery of Scotland.
J as Cardinal (P) Three versions: London: National Gallery; New York: Frick Collection; New York: Metropolitan Museum (Lehmann Coll.)

Elsheimer, Adam

J in W (P) Bergamo: Accademia Carrara. [Fig. 78]

English, ca. 1400

J Adoring Vision of Christ (M) Oxford: Bodleian Library, MS. Aubrey 31, f. 201v.

English, ca. 1400–1450

J & L (M) Oxford, Bodleian Library, MS Bodley 850, f. 70. [Fig. 197]
J in S (M) Oxford, Bodleian Library, MS Auct. D., inf.2.13, f. 209ᵛ; in Book of Hours known as *Queen Mary's Psalter*. [Fig. 194]
J in S (M) San Marino, Calif.: Henry E. Huntington Library, HM 1144, f. 179.
J & L (M) Oxford: Bodleian Library, Book of Hours, MS. Liturg. 401, f. 198ᵛ. [Fig. 192]

English, ca. 1450–1500

J in S (M) Oxford: Bodleian Library, Book of Hours, MS. Rowl. Liturg. g.3, f. 165ᵛ. [Fig. 198]

English, Late Fifteenth–Early Sixteenth Century

J & L (M) Oxford: Bodleian Library, Hours of the Holy Ghost, MS. Lat. Liturg. g.5, f. 163. [Fig. 196]

Enzola, Gianfrancesco

J in W (S)   Washington: National Gallery of Art; Samuel H. Kress Coll.
J & L (S)   Washington: National Gallery of Art; Samuel H. Kress Coll.

Fenzoni, Ferraù

J in W (P)   New London, Conn.: Lyman Allyn Museum.

Ferrarese, Fifteenth Century

J in W (P)   (formerly attributed to Mantegna). Washington: National
   Gallery of Art; A. W. Mellon Coll. [Fig. 148]
J in W (G)   Hind, vol. 4, pl. 422.
J in W (P)   Longhi (1934), pl. 36.
J & L (P)   Bisogni, fig. 45.
J in W (P)   Bologna: Pinacoteca.
J in W (P)   Bergamo: Accademia Carrara, no. 280.
J in W (P)   Richter Archives 252:I:30.
J Pardoning the Robbers (P)   Milan: Brera, no. 226.
J's Death (P)   Milan: Brera, no. 226 bis.
Obsequies of J (P)   Venice: Museo Correr.
J Reading (P)   Ferrara: Pinacoteca Civica.
J in S (P)   Ravenna: Accademia.

Ferrari, Defendente

J in W (P)   Turin: Museo Civico, no. 210.
J in W (P)   Turin: Museo Civico, no. 398.
J in W (P)   Turin: Museo Civico, no. 290.
J in W (P)   Avigliana (Turin): S. Giovanni.
J in W (P)   Buttigliera Alta (Turin): S. Antonio di Ranverso.

Ferrari, Gaudenzio

J in W (in background of Visitation) (P)   Milan: Brera, no. 37.
J and Donor (P)   Milan: S. Giorgio al Palazzo.

Filarete (Antonio di Pietro
Averlino) attribution

J in W (S)   Cambridge: Fitzwilliam Museum, on indefinite loan from J. G.
   Pollard Coll. [Fig. 81]

Filippo da Verona

J in W (P)   Berenson (1969), fig. 483.

Fiorenzo di Lorenzo

J in W (P)   New Haven: Yale University Art Gallery.
J in W (P)   Bergamo: Accademia Carrara, no. 539.
J in W (P)   Baltimore: Walters Art Gallery.

Flemish, Fifteenth Century

J in W (M)   New York: Pierpont Morgan Library, M.46, *Hours of the
   Virgin.*
Jerome Legend (M)   New York: Pierpont Morgan Library, no. M.675
   (Voragine, *La Légende dorée.*) [Fig. 155]
J in W (D)   Chicago: Art Institute.
J & L (S)   Bode, fig. 105.
J & L (M)   Oxford: Bodleian Library, MS. Liturg. 98, f. 138ᵛ.
J in W (M)   Oxford: Bodleian Library, MS. Douce 12, f. 201. [Fig. 203]
J in S (M)   Oxford: Bodleian Library, MS. Liturg. 400, f. 89ᵛ. [Fig. 193]
J in W (M)   Oxford: Bodleian Library, MS. Douce 20, f. 176ᵛ.
J (M)   Oxford: Bodleian Library, MS. Canon Liturg. 229, f. 207ᵛ. [Fig. 195]
J in W (P)   Richter Archives 276:I:16.
J in W (P)   Palermo: Lanzadi Mazzarino Coll.

Flemish, Sixteenth Century

J in W (M)   Oxford: Bodleian Library, MS. Astor A.29, vol. II, f. 67.
J in S (P)   Antwerp: Musée Royal des Beaux-Arts, no. 5087.
J in S (M)   Oxford: Corpus Christi College, MS. 13 f. 68. [Fig. 200]
J in W (P)   Rome: Pallavicini Gallery.

	J in W (P)	Granada: Capella Real.
	J in W (P)	Granada: Capella Real.
	J in W (P)	Madrid: Museo Arqueologico Nacional.
	J in W (P)	Hagerstown, Md.: Washington County Museum.
	J in W (P)	Detroit Institute of Arts.
	J in W (P)	New York: Manhattanville College.
	J in W (P)	Ashland, Ohio: Ashland College.
	J in S (P)	Granada: Comte de las Infantas Coll.
	J in S (P)	Burgos: Cathedral Cloister.
	J in S (P)	Briviesca (Burgos): S. Maria la Mayor.
	J in S (P)	Madrid: Alexandro de Araoz Coll.
	J in S (P)	Madrid: Rodriguez Bauza Coll.
	J in S (P)	New York: Metropolitan Museum.
Flemish (or Lombard?), Seventeenth Century	J in W (P)	Turin: Museo Civico d'Arte Antico.
Flemish (or Michel Wolgemut?)	Cycle of Jerome Legend (triptych) (P)	Ain: Musée.
Florentine Anonymous Fine Manner, ca. 1480–1500	J in W (G)	(after Pollaiuolo). Washington: National Gallery of Art; Rosenwald Coll. [Fig. 131]
Florentine, 1420–1465	J in W, J in S (P)	Pisa: Museo Nazionale di S. Matteo.
Florentine, 1460–1470	J in W (G)	Hind, vol. 2, pl. 38.
	J in W (G)	Hind, vol. 2, pl. 39.
Florentine, Fifteenth Century	J in W (P)	Brunswick (Maine): Bowdoin College.
	J in W (P)	Princeton University Art Gallery.
Florentine, Sixteenth Century	Allegory of Jerome (P)	Chicago: Art Institute.
Fogolino, Marcello	J in W (P)	Liverpool: Walker Art Gallery.
Foppa, Vincenzo	J in W (P)	Bergamo: Accademia Carrara, no. 279.
	J in W (P)	Budapest: Museum no. 1372.
Francés, Nicolás	J in S (P)	Dublin: National Gallery of Ireland. [Fig. 154]
Francesco di Antonio	J's Dream (P)	Paris: Musées Nationaux. (Berenson [1963], fig. 719.)
Francesco di Giorgio	J in W (S)	Washington: National Gallery of Art; Samuel H. Kress Coll. [Figs. 120, 122–125, 128]
Francesco dai Libri (Il Vecchio)	J in W (P)	Formerly owned by Cesare Laurenti, Venice.
	Legend of Jerome (P)	Milan: Brera.
	Death of Jerome (P)	Venice: Museo Correr.
Francia, Francesco	Crucifixion with J (P)	Bologna: Museo Civico.
Franco, Battista	J in W (G)	Bartsch, vol. 16, p. 131, no. 138.
Frankentaler School	J & L (P)	Innsbruck: Tiroler Landesmuseum Ferdinandeum.

French "Medieval"	J & L (S) Brou: Cathedral.
French, Twelfth Century	J & L (capital of portal) (S) Autun: Abbey Church.
French (Paris), ca. 1300	*Legenda aurea* (M) San Marino, Calif.: Henry E. Huntington Library, HM 3027, f. 136. [Fig. 156]
French, ca. 1418	J & L (M) New York: Pierpont Morgan Library, MS 866, f. 144^v.
French (Norman), 1420–1440	J in S (M) Oxford: Bodleian Library, MS. Auct. D. inf. 2.11.f.231^v. [Fig. 199]
French, ca. 1430–1435	J & L (M) New York: Pierpont Morgan Library, MS. 46.
French, ca. 1440	J in S (P) Rotterdam: Boymans-van Beuningen Museum.
French, Early Fifteenth Century	J & L (M) Paris: Bibliothèque Nationale, MS. Lat. 1161, f. 268. J in S (M) Baltimore: Walters Art Gallery, Ms. 721, f. 277^v. J in S (M) *Book of Hours of Jean, Duc de Berry*. New York: Metropolitan Museum, Cloisters. J in S (M) *Bible Moralisée*. Paris: Bibliothèque Nationale, MS. F.166, f. A. [Fig. 14] J in S (M) New York: Metropolitan Museum, Cloisters. Jerome Translating Scripture (P) Richter Archives 304A:V:95.
French (Amiens), ca. 1450	J in S (M) San Marino, Calif.: Henry E. Huntington Library, HM 1807, f. 134.
French Gold Scroll Master, ca. 1450	J in S (M) San Marino, Calif.: Henry E. Huntington Library, HM 1125,f.147. [Fig. 163]
French, ca. 1480	Dream of J in *Heures de Louis de Laval* (M) Paris: Bibliothèque Nationale, MS. Lat. 920. f.308^v. [Fig. 10]
French (Burgundian), ca. 1490	J in W (M) San Marino, Calif.: Henry E. Huntington Library, HM 1148 f. 27.
French, Late Fifteenth Century	J & L (M) Oxford: Bodleian Library, MS. Queen's College 305 f. 220. [Fig. 205]
French (Burgundian), ca. 1500	J in W (P) Beaune: Hospital St. Esprit.
French, 1500–1525	J in W (M) Oxford: Bodleian Library, MS. Astor A.17.f.153. [Fig. 206]
French, Sixteenth Century	J in W (M) San Marino, Calif.: Henry E. Huntington Library, HM 1124, f. 180.
Frueauf, Rueland, the Younger	J & L (P) Heidrich, pl. 71.
Fungai, Bernardino	J & L (P) Chiusi: S Secondiano (Duomo). J in W (P) Chiusi: S. Secondiano (Duomo).
Gandolfi, Gaetano	J with Angel (P) Bazzano, near Bologna: Paris Church.

Garofalo (Benvenuto Tisi)	Madonna and Child with Jerome (P) Dallas Museum of Fine Arts; Samuel H. Kress Coll. J in W (P) New Orleans: Issac Delgado Museum. J in W (P) Bolzano: Museo Dell'Alto Adige. J in W (P) Berlin-Dahlem: Staatliche Museen, no. 243. J in W (P) Rome: Museo da Palazzo Venezia.
Gassel, Lucas	J in W (P) Antwerp: Musée Royal des Beaux-Arts, no. 931.
Gavazzi, Giovanni di Giacomo	Madonna and Child (P) Tulsa: Philbrook Art Center; Samuel H. Kress Coll.
Genga, Girolamo	J in W (D) Richter Archives 259:XIV:8.
Gentile da Fabriano	Coronation of Virgin with Saints (P) Milan: Brera, no. 497.
Gentileschi, Orazio	J in W (P) Turin: Museo Civico.
German, Fifteenth Century	J & L (G) Schreiber, nos. 1535 and 1537. J & L (G) Ring, fig. 7. J & L (P) Munich: Alte Pinakothek. J (GL) Detroit Institute of Arts. J in W (G) Combe, p. 35. J in S (G) Washington: National Gallery of Art; Rosenwald Coll. [Fig. 166] J in S (P) Frankfurt: Städelsches Kunstinstitut. Penitent J with Saints Margaret and John the Apostle (P) Richter Archives 292 I:IX:60. J in W (G) Los Angeles County Museum of Art.
Ghiberti, Lorenzo	J (S) Florence: first door of Baptistry.
Ghirlandajo, Domenico	J in S (P) Florence: Ognissanti. [Fig. 84]
Ghirlandajo, Ridolfo	J in W (P) Florence: S. Trinita. J in W (P) Florence: Uffizi, no. 4660.
Giambono, Michele, attribution	J in S (P) Richter Archives 144:VII:28.
Giordano, Luca	J (P) Paris: L. A. Gaboviand Coll. (Richter Archives 125: I: 100.) Jerome Contemplating the Last Judgment (P) Madrid: Prado.
Giovanni del Biondo	J (P) Florence: S. Croce.
Giovanni di Paolo, attribution	J in S (P) Siena: Pinacoteca Nazionale, no. 180. J & L (P) Siena: S. Girolamo. J & L (book cover) (P) Siena: Archivio di Stato. J (P) Siena: Museo dell'Opera del Duomo.
Giovanni Francesco da Rimini	J (left panel of triptych) (P) Perugia: Galleria Nazionale del'Umbria.
Giovanni Francesco Toscani	J in W (P) Princeton, N.J.: Princeton University Art Gallery.
Giovenone, Girolamo	J in W (P) Vercelli: Museo Borgogna. J in W (P) Turin: Museo Civico.
Giraldi, Alessandra	J in W (P) Vienna: Eissler Coll. (Venturi, fig. 69.)

Girolamo da Carpi	J in W (P) Ferrara: S. Paolo.
Girolamo dai Libri	Nativity with Saints (P) Verona: Museo Civico, no. 290.
Girolamo di Giovanni da Camerino (?)	J in W (P) Formerly in Cavaliere Vinci Coll., Fermo. (Described in Crowe and Cavalcaselle, vol. 3, p. 158 fn.)
Girolamo (Pennacchi) da Treviso	J in W (P) Bergamo: Piccinelli Coll. J (P) Treviso: Museo Civico.
Girolamo di Benvenuto	J (P) Lewisburg, Pa.: Bucknell University; Samuel H. Kress Coll.
Girolamo da Santa Croce	Madonna and Child Enthroned with J and John the Baptist (P) Venice: Museo Correr.
Goltzius, H.	J in W (G) (after Palma il Giovanne). Bartsch, vol. 3, p. 81, no. 266.
Gomez, Juan	Jerome Cycle (P) Escorial: San Lorenzo el Real.
Gossaert (*see* Mabuse, Jan)	
Goya, Francisco	J in W (P) Los Angeles: Norton Simon Foundation.
Gozzoli, Benozzo	J in W (P) Montefalco: S. Francesco. [Fig. 183] J and a "Beato" (P) Lugano: Thyssen Coll. Madonna and Child and Saints (P) London: National Gallery, no. 283. [Fig. 188] J & L (P) Montefalco: S. Francesco. J and Other Saints (P) Formerly owned by Paul Bottenwieser, Berlin. (Richter Archives 64:VI:7.) Entombment of Christ (P) Rotterdam: Boymans-van Beuningen Museum, no. 2550.
Grünewald, Hans	J in W (G) Bartsch, vol. 7, p. 312, no. 34. J in W (G) Bartsch, vol. 7, p. 312, no. 35.
Guercino (Giovanni Francesco Barbieri)	J in W (P) Leningrad: Hermitage. J Hears Trumpet of Last Judgment (P) Rimini: S. Girolamo. J with Angel (P) Three paintings: Vaduz: Liechtenstein Coll. J with Angel (P) Paris: Louvre, no. 1141. J with Vision of Madonna and Child (P) Paris: S. Thomas Equinas. J in W (P) Los Angeles County Museum of Art. [Fig. 162]
Günther, Matthäus	J with Angel (P) Bressanone (formerly Brixen): Monastery Church.
Hagnower, Niklas, attribution	J (S) Colmar: Unterlinden Museum.
Hemessen, Jan van	J in W (P) Windsor: Royal Coll. J (P) Six paintings: Modena, Genoa, Vienna (two), Parma, Prague. J in S (P) Salzburg: Museum. J in W (P) Leningrad: Hermitage. J in S (P) Brussels: Musées Royaux des Beaux-Arts.

Hemessen, Jan van, attribution	Jerome, Roch and Sebastian (P)	Paris: Petit Palais.
Hemmel d'Andlau, Peter	J & L (GL)	Ulm: Cathedral.
Herrera the Elder, Francisco de	J in W (P)	Rouen: Musée des Beaux-Arts.
Herri met de Bles	J in W (P)	Richter Archives 279A:VIII:47.
	J in W (P)	Brooklyn, N.Y.: Brooklyn Museum.
Hugo van der Goes follower (Master of Saint Gudule)	J in S (P)	Richter Archives 277:IX:1.
Inglés, Jorge (?)	J in S (P)	Valladolid: Museum. (Post, vol. 4, p. 71.)
Isenbrandt, Adrian (seven or more pictures, of which these may suffice)	J in W (P)	Philadelphia: Johnson Coll.
	J in W (P)	Leningrad: Hermitage. [Fig. 72]
	J in W (central panel of triptych) (P)	Hamburg: Kunsthalle, no. 753.
Italian, Thirteenth Century	J in S (M)	Oxford: Bodleian Library, MS. Lat. bib. f. 3, f. 1.
	J in S (M)	Oxford: Bodleian Library, MS. Douce 113, f. 2.
Italian, Fourteenth Century	J and Dragon (M)	Oxford: Bodleian Library, MS. Canon Bibl. Lat. 49, f. 1. [Fig. 147]
Italian, Fifteenth Century	J in W (M)	Oxford: Bodleian Library, MS. Canon Liturg. 168, f. 451^v.
	J & L (M)	Oxford: Bodleian Library, MS. Canon Liturg. 168, f. 451^v.
	J writing (M)	Oxford: Bodleian Library, MS. Canon Liturg. 168, f. 451^v.
	J in W (M)	Oxford: Bodleian Library, MS. Canon Liturg. 197, f. 223b. [Fig. 204]
	J in W (M)	Oxford: Bodleian Library, *Officium Beatae Mariae Virginiae*, MS. Douce 11, f. 266. [Fig. 201]
	J & L (M)	Oxford: Bodleian Library, *Officium Beatae Mariae Virginiae*, MS. Canon Liturg. 265, f. 14b. [Fig. 202]
	J in W (G)	Hind, vol. 2, no. 84.
	J in W (G)	Hind, vol. 2, no. 85.
	J in W (G)	Hind, vol. 2, no. 86.
	J in W (G)	Hind, vol. 2, no. 313.
	J in W (G)	Hind, vol. 2, no. 316.
	J in S (P)	Amherst, Mass.: Amherst College.
Italian, Sixteenth Century	J (M)	Oxford: Bodleian Library, MS. Douce 29, f. 23^v.
	J in W (P)	Rouen: Musée des Beaux-Arts.
	J in W (P)	Baltimore: Walters Art Gallery, no. 1119.
	J in W (P)	Baltimore: Walters Art Gallery, no. 1680.
	J in W (P)	Los Angeles County Museum of Art, no. 49.11.7.
	J in W (P)	St. Meinrad, Ind.: Archabbey.
Italian, Seventeenth Century	J in S (P)	Washington: Georgetown University.
	J in W (G)	Palo Alto, Calif.: Stanford University, no. 60.207.
	Four Doctors of the Church (S)	Denver: Museum of Art.
Jacopino da Bologna	J in S (panel of triptych) (P)	Bologna: Pinacoteca.
Jacopo da Valencia	J in W (P)	Boston: Museum of Fine Arts.

Jacopo de Barbari   J in S (G) Hind, vol. 7, pl. 706.

Jacopo della Quercia   J in S with Lion (S) Lucca: S. Frediano. [Fig. 18]

Janssens, Jan   J with Angel (P) Ghent: St. Michael's Church.

Juan de Juanes   J in W (P) London: Pritchard Coll.

Klocker, Hans   Madonna and Child with Saint Leonard and J. (S) Innsbruck: Tiroler
              Landesmuseum Ferdinandeum.

Kulmbach, Hans Süss von   J and John the Baptist (P) Nürnberg: St. Sebald.

Langetti, Giovanni Battista   Vision of J (P) Cleveland Museum of Art.

LaTour, Georges de   J in W (P) Grenoble: Musée de Peinture et de Sculpture.
              J's Dream (P) Nantes: Musée des Beaux-Arts.
              J in W (P) Stockholm: National Museum.
              J in S (P) Paris: Louvre.

Lattanzio da Rimini   J in W (P) New York: Edgar Speyer Coll.

Leiden School, Sixteenth Century J in S (P) Amsterdam: Rijksmuseum.

Leonardo da Vinci   J in W (P) Vatican: Pinacoteca. [Fig. 48]

Lianori, Pietro   J & L (panel of triptych) (P) Bologna: Pinacoteca.

Liberale da Verona   J, Francis, and Paul (P) Verona: Museo Civico, no. 625.

Ligozzi, Jacopo   J in W (P) Arezzo: Casa Vasari.

Liguria School   J (panel in polyptych) (P) Baltimore: Walters Art Gallery, no. 636.

Limbourg Atelier attribution   Madonna with J, Sixtus, and a Cardinal (P) Glasgow Art Gallery.

Limbourg, Jean de (probably)   Twelve Scenes of J's Life (M) In *Les Belles Heures de Jean, Duc de Berry*.
              New York: Metropolitan Museum, Cloisters. [Figs. 5–9]

Lippi, Filippino   J in W (P) Florence: Uffizi. [Fig. 185]
              J in W (P) Marseilles: Musée des Beaux-Arts.
              J in S (P) El Paso Museum of Art; Samuel H. Kress Coll.
              Madonna and Child with J and Dominic (P) London: National Gallery, no.
               293. [Figs. 142, 143]

Lippi, Filippo   J and Francis in Wilderness (P) Altenburg: Lindenau Museum.
              J, John the Baptist, and Ansanus (P) Cambridge, Mass.: Fogg Museum.

Lippi, Filippo, attribution, and Fra J in W (P) Cambridge, Mass.: Fogg Museum.
Diamante attribution

Liss (or Lys), Johann   Vision of J (P) Venice: S. Niccolo dei Tolentini.
              Vision of J (P) Cambridge, Mass.: Fogg Museum.

Lochner, Stefan   J in S (P)   Cologne: Private Coll. (Richter Archives 336:XIII:19.)
                                         J (P)   London: National Gallery, no. 705.

Lochner, Stefan, attribution   J in S (P)   Raleigh: North Carolina Museum of Art. [Fig. 15]

Lombard, Lambert   J in W (P)   Borgharen: J. Timmers Coll. (Timmers, fig. 130.)

Lombard School, Fifteenth Century   J & L (P)   Bergamo: Accademia Carrara, no. 277. [Fig. 167]

Lombard School, Sixteenth Century   Hermit Saints (P)   Milan: Brera, no. 954.
                                         J in S (P)   Rome: Doria Pamphili Gallery.
                                         J in W (G)   Kristeller, p. 40.

Lombardo, Pietro   J (S)   Venice: San Stefano.

Lombardo, Tullio, workshop   J & L (S)   Brescia: Museo Civico.

Lorenzo Monaco   J in S (P)   Amsterdam: Rijksmuseum, no. 1641–B1.

Lorenzo Monaco (?)   J in W (P)   Meiss (1974), p. 135, fig. 2.

Lorenzo Veneziano   J (P)   Berlin-Dahlem: Staatliche Museen.

Loth, Carl   J in W (P)   Formerly in Scholz-Forni Coll., Hamburg. (Richter Archives
                                           199:III:18.)

Lotto, Lorenzo   Madonna and Saints (P)   London: National Gallery.
                                         J in W (P)   Allentown, Pa.: Allentown Art Museum, Samuel H. Kress Coll.
                                         J in S (P)   Hamburg: Kunsthalle. (Richter Archives 168:III:18.)
                                         J in W (P)   Madrid: Prado.
                                         J in W (P)   Paris: Louvre.
                                         J in W (P)   Rome: Castel San Angelo.
                                         J in W (P)   Rome: Doria Pamphili Gallery.
                                         J in S (P)   Rome: Zocca Coll.
                                         J in W (P)   Sibiu, Romania: Castle of Peles.
                                         J in W (P)   Berenson (1969), fig. 789.

Lucas van Leyden (or Leiden)   J in W (P)   Berlin-Dahlem: Staatliche Museen. [Fig. 73]
                                         J in W (P)   Rotterdam: Boymans-van Beuningen Museum.
                                         J in W (G)   Delen, vol. 2, pl. xix.
                                         J in S (G)   Bartsch, vol. 7, p. 398, no. 114.
                                         J in W (G)   Bartsch, vol. 7, p. 397, no. 112.
                                         J in W (G)   Bartsch, vol. 7, p. 398, no. 113.

Luini, Bernardino   J in W (P)   Formerly in Crespi Gallery, Milan.
                                         J in W (P)   Milan: Poldi-Pezzoli Museum, no. 652.
                                         J in W (predella) (P)   Como: Duomo.
                                         J in S (P)   Vienna: Harrach Coll.
                                         J in W (P)   Vienna: Kunsthistorisches Museum.
                                         J in W (P)   Vienna: Kunsthistorisches Museum, no. 583.

Mabuse (Gossaert), Jan   J in W (P)   Washington: National Gallery of Art; Samuel H. Kress Coll.
                                           [Fig. 71]

Maccagnino, Angelo, attribution J in W (P) Private coll. (Longhi, rev. ed., pl. 2.)

Macchiavelli, Zanobi J & L (P) Berenson (1969), fig. 805.
J Forgives Thieves (P) Berenson (1969), fig. 807; also illus. in *Pantheon* 26 (1968): 240.

Magnasco, Alessandro J in W (P) Dresden: Gemäldegalerie.
J with Angel of Last Judgment (P) Florence: Uffizi.

"Mainardi" (Ghirlandajo follower) attribution J in W (P) Florence: Gallerie Fiorentine.

Maino, Fray Juan Bautista J in W (P) Stockholm: National Museum.

Mansueti, Giovanni J in W (P) Bergamo: Accademia Carrara, no. 152. [Fig. 36]
J in W (P) Formerly owned by Arthur Hughes, London. (Burlington Fine Arts Club, pl. xix.)
J in W (P) Bristol: City Art Gallery.
J Appearing to Augustine (P) Berenson (1969), fig. 375.

Mansueti, Giovanni, Studio J in W (P) Richter Archives 153:II:7.

Mantegna, Andrea J in W (P) São Paulo, Brazil: Museu de Arte. [Fig. 181]
J in W (predella of polyptych 105). (P) Milan: Brera.

Marinus van Roemerswael J in S (P) Madrid: Prado.
J in S (P) Philadelphia: Johnson Coll.
J in S (P) Montreal Museum of Fine Arts, no. 188.
J in S (P) Ponce, Puerto Rico: Museo de Arte de Ponce, no. 58-0046.
J in S (P) Antwerp: Musée Royal des Beaux-Arts, no. 990.
J in S (P) Stockholm: National Museum.

Marmion, Simon J and Donor (P) Philadelphia: Johnson Coll.

Masaccio J (one of four panels) (P) Berlin-Dahlem: Stattliche Museen, no. 58D.

"Masaccio" (with Andrea di Giusto) J in W (P) Altenburg: Lindenau Museum.

Masaccio, Circle of, (Giovanni di Francesco Toscani attribution) J in W (P) Princeton University Art Gallery.

Masolino da Panicale J and John the Baptist (P) London: National Gallery.

Massone, Giovanni J Enthroned (P) Philadelphia: Johnson Coll.

Massys, Cornelis J in W (P) Antwerp: Musée Royal des Beaux-Arts, no. 830.

Massys, Jan J in S (P) Madrid: Prado.
J in S (P) Vienna: Kunsthistorisches Museum.

Massys, Quentin J in S (P) Philadelphia: Johnson Coll.

Massys, Quentin, follower J in S (P) New York: Metropolitan Museum.

Master B. R.   J in W (G)   Mayor, fig. 434.

Master of the Banderoles   J in W (G)   Hollstein, vol. 12, p. 51.

Master of Brussels Adoration   J in W (P)   Greenville, S. C.: Bob Jones University.

Master of Death of the Virgin   J in S (G)   Mayor, fig. 88.

Master E. S.   J in S (in Saint John in Wilderness) (G)   Shestack, no. 62.

Master Esiguo   J (P)   New Brunswick, N. J.: Rutgers University.

Master of the Gerona Martyrology   J in S (M)   Vienna: Österreichisches National bibliothek, Korczek Bible, col. 1169, f. 1ʳ. (M. Frinta, fig. 3.)

Master (Meister) von Grossgmain   J & L (P)   Lugano: Thyssen Coll.

Master of Half Lengths   J & L (P)   Zurich: Kunsthaus.
                                         J in W (P)   Rotterdam: Boymans-van Beuningen Museum.
                                         J in W (P)   Kansas City, Mo.: Nelson Gallery.

Master (Meister) des Heiligen   J (S)   Modena: Galleria Estense.
Altaren   J (S)   London: Victoria and Albert Museum.

Master (Meister) des Heiligen   J with Two Holy Women and Donor (P)   Munich: Alte Pinakothek.
Hieronymus   J in S (P)   Firmenich-Richartz, p. 97.

Master of the Heiligentafel   J in W (G)   Hollstein, vol. 12, p. 182.

Master of Liesborn   Saints Ambrose, Exuperius, and J (P)   London: National Gallery, no. 254.

Master (Meister) des Marienlebens   J and Saints Bernard (?), Giles, and Benedict (?) (P)   London: National Gallery, no. 250.

Master of the Osservanza Triptych   J in W (P)   Siena: Pinacoteca Nazionale, no. 216.

Master of Pozuelo   J in W (P)   Los Angeles: Loyola University.

Master P. W. of Cologne   J in W (G)   Washington: National Gallery of Art; Rosenwald Coll.

Master of Saint Gudule (*see* Hugo
van der Goes)

Master of the Saint Lucy Legend   J & L (right panel of triptych) (P)   Los Angeles County Museum of Art.
attribution   [Fig. 164]

Master of Saint Ursula Legend   J in W (P)   Richter Archives 278:V:22.

Master of the Sherman Predella   J in W (P)   Boston: Museum of Fine Arts.

Master of the Spes Nostra   Allegory of Transience (P)   Amsterdam: Rijksmuseum.

Master of Staffalo   J (P)   Greenville, S.C.,: Bob Jones University.

Master of Upper Rhine	J & L (P)	Frankfurt: Städelsches Kunstinstitut.
Matteo di Giovanni	J in S (P)	Cambridge, Mass.: Fogg Museum.
	J & L (P)	Siena: Duomo; Museo dell'Opera.
	Two Episodes from Life of J (P)	Chicago: Art Institute.
Matteo de Gualdo	J in W (P)	Turin: Sabauda Gallery.
Mattioli, Ludovico	J in W (G)	Calabi, pl. 83.
Maveolo da Cazano	J (P)	Brooklyn, N. Y.: Brooklyn Museum.
Mayno, Juan Bautista	J in W (P)	Grenoble: Musée de Peinture et de Sculpture.
Mazzola-Bedoli, Girolamo	Annunciation (J in W in background) (P)	Milan: Ambrosiana, no. 127.
Mazzolino, Ludovico	J in W (P)	New York: New-York Historical Society, B.373.
Meloni, Marco	J in W (P)	Formerly in Silbermann Coll., Vienna, 1934.
	J in W (P)	Modena: Galleria Estense.
	J (P)	Florence: Spinelli Sale, 1934.
Memling, Hans	J & L (P)	Ring, fig. 3.
	J (wing of altarpiece) (P)	Lübeck: Cathedral.
	Mass of Saint Gregory (P)	New York: Metropolitan Museum.
Memling, Hans, attribution	J & L (P)	Brussels: Musées Royaux des Beaux-Arts.
Mestrovic, Ivan	Jerome the Priest (S)	Washington: House of the Croatian Franciscan Fathers. [Fig. 82]
Mezzastris (Pier Antonio da Foligno)	J in W (P)	Foligno: Palazzo Trinci.
Michelangelo Buonarroti	J in W (D)	Paris: Louvre.
Michelangelo (unknown artist, after lost drawing by)	J in W (G)	Paris: Bibliothèque Nationale. (Tolnay [1960], fig. 253.)
Mino da Fiesole	Jerome Legend (S)	Four reliefs: Rome: S. Maria Maggiore; Museo di Palazzo Venezia. [Fig. 49]
Moderno	J in W (S)	Washington: National Gallery of Art; Samuel H. Kress Coll.
Moderno, style of	J in W (S)	Washington: National Gallery of Art; Samuel H. Kress Coll.
Mola, Pier Francesco	J Writing (P)	Vatican: Pinacoteca.
Monogrammist, 1520	J in S (G)	Bartsch, vol. 7, p. 472, no. 1.
Montagna, Bartolomeo	J in W (P)	Bergamo: Accademia Carrara, no. 545. [Fig. 37]
	J in W (P)	Milan: Brera, no. 807.
	J in W (P)	Milan: Poldi-Pezzoli Museum.
	J in W (P)	Ottawa: National Gallery of Canada.
	J in W (P)	Lugano: Thyssen Coll.

Montagna, Benedetto   J in W (G)   Washington: National Gallery of Art; Rosenwald Coll.
                             J in W (G)   Hind, vol. 7, pl. 743.
                             J in W (G)   Hind, vol. 7, pl. 756.

Montañes, J. Martinez   J in W (S)   near Seville: Monastery of San Isidoro del Campo.
                             J in W (S)   Llerena: Convent of Santa Clara (Proske, pl. 10).
                             J (in retable of Immaculate Conception) (S)   Seville: Cathedral.

Morales, Luis de   J in W (P)   Dublin: National Gallery of Ireland.

Moretto da Brescia (Alessandro   J in W (P)   Vaduz: Liechtenstein Coll.
Bonvicino)   Madonna and Child with J and Saint Bartholomew (P)   Vatican: Pinacoteca,
                                 no. 150.
                             J in W (P)   Isolabella (Lago Maggiore): Palazzo Borromeo.
                             J in W (P)   Los Angeles County Museum of Art.
                             J, Francis, and Margaret of Cortona (P)   Brescia: San Francesco.
                             J in W (P)   Stockholm: National Museum.
                             J, Bernardino, and other Saints (P)   London: National Gallery.

Moretto attribution   J in W (P)   Washington: Howard University; Samuel H. Kress Coll.

Moroni, Giovanni Battista   J in W (P)   Bergamo: Accademia Carrara no. 75.
                             J Reading (P)   Harewood House (York): Lord Harewood.

Moroni, Giovanni Battista (?)   J in W (P)   Allentown, Pa.: Allentown Art Museum; Samuel H. Kress Coll.

Murillo, Bartolome Esteban   J in W (P)   Madrid: Prado.

Muziano, Girolamo (see also   J in W (P)   Vatican: Pinacoteca, no. 369.
Cort, Cornelius, and Sadeler, Johann)   J in W (P)   Rome: Borghese Gallery.
                             J in W (P)   Richter Archives 225:V:1.
                             J in W (P)   Bologna: Pinacoteca.

Muziano, Girolamo (?)   J in W (P)   Bergamo: Accademia Carrara (two other versions there also).

Nasini, Giuseppe   J with Angel (P)   Florence: San Lorenzo.

Navarrete, Fernandez de   J in W (P)   Escorial: San Lorenzo el Real. (Zarco Cuevas, p. 12.)

Neapolitan, Fifteenth Century   J in S (P)   Naples: Museo Nazionale.

Nelli, Ottaviano   J & L (P)   Orleans: Musée des Beaux-Arts.

Neri di Bicci   Saint Ursula and Saint Jerome (P)   Worcester, Mass.: Worcester Art
                                 Museum.

Neroccio dei Landi   J (one of four panels of saints) (P)   Philadelphia: Johnson Coll.

Neroni, Bartolomeo (Il Riccio)   Coronation of Madonna (P)   Siena: Pinacoteca Nazionale, no. 444, 447.
(see also Cort, Cornelis)

Netherlands, Sixteenth Century   J in W (P)   Brussels: Musées Royaux des Beaux-Arts, no. 979a.
                             J in S (P)   Antwerp: Musée Royal des Beaux Arts, no. 5087.
                             J in W (P)   Hamburg: Kunsthalle.

	J in W (P) Richter Archives 284:XII:14.
	J & L (S) Utrecht: Aartsbischoppelijk Museum.
	J and Donor (P) Antwerp: Musée Royal des Beaux-Arts, no. 32.
Niccolo da Foligno	Madonna and Child with Saints (P) Rome: Barberini Gallery.
Niccolo di Buonaccorso	J in S (P) Philadelphia: Johnson Coll.
Niccolo di Liberatore da Foligno	J (P) Boston: Museum of Fine Arts.
Niccolo di Maestro Antonio d'Ancona	J in W (P) Turin: Galleria Sabauda.
Niccolo di Naldo	J in S (P) Siena: Duomo, Sacristy, Capella del Lire.
Nicoletto da Modena	J in W (G) Hind, vol. 6, pl. 679.
North Italian, Late Fifteenth or Early Sixteenth Century	J in W (S) Washington: National Gallery of Art; Samuel H. Kress Coll. (Pope-Hennessy [1965], no. 317.) J in W (S) Washington: National Gallery of Art; Samuel H. Kress Coll. (Pope-Hennessy [1965], no 346.) J (S) Washington: National Gallery of Art; Samuel H. Kress Coll. (Pope-Hennessy [1965], no. 369.)
North Italian, Seventeenth Century	J with Angel of Last Judgment (P) Vercelli: SS. Annunziata.
Nuzi, Allegretto	J (P) Houston: Museum of Fine Arts.
Oggiono, Marco d'	J (P) Palermo: Chiaramonte Bordonaro Coll.
Oliverio, Alessandro	J in W (P) Richter Archives 227:IX:12. Roch between J and Sebastian (P) Venice: S. Maria della Salute.
Orazio, Marinali	J in W (S) Vicenza: Museo Civico.
Ortolano (Giovanni Battista Benvenuti)	J in W (P) Cambridge: Fitzwilliam Museum, no. 160.
Pacchia, Girolamo del	J in S (P) Siena: San Girolamo.
Pacher, Michael	Saint Wolfgang Altarpiece (P) Munich: Alte Pinakothek. J in S (P) Augsburg. (Richter Archives 343: IV: 29.)
Paduan, Fifteenth Century	J in W (S) Washington: National Gallery of Art; Samuel H. Kress Coll. (Pope-Hennessy [1965], no. 319.)
Paduan (?) or Venetian (?), Early Sixteenth Century	J in W (S) Washington: National Gallery of Art; Samuel H. Kress Coll. (Pope-Hennessy [1965], no. 320.) [Fig. 121]
Palma, Jacopo il Giovane (see also Cort, Cornelis)	J in W (P) Moscow: Museum of Fine Arts. J & L (P) Parrocchiale: S. Giorgio delle Pertiche. J in S (P) Venice: Accademia.
Palma, Jacopo il Giovane, attribution	J in W (P) Richter Archives 190: XIII:16.

Palmezzano, Marco

J in W (P)   Faenza: Pinacoteca.
J in W (P)   Rome: Barberini Gallery, no. 715.
J in W (P)   Formerly in Roerich Museum, New York.
J in W (P)   Venice: Conte Vittorino Cini.

Panetti, Domenico

J (P)   Indianapolis: John Herron Art Institute.

Paolo da San Leocadio

J in W (P)   Barcelona: Despujol Coll. (Bosque, p. 184.)

Parenzano, Bernardino

Christ Bearing Cross between J and Augustine (P)   Modena: Pinacoteca
   Estense.

Paris Bordone

J in W (P)   Philadelphia: Johnson Coll. [Fig. 58]
Rest on Flight into Egypt with J (P)   Berenson (1969), no. 1135.
Sacra Conversazione (P)   Los Angeles County Museum of Art; Paul Rodman
   Mabury Coll. [Fig. 186]

Parmigianino (Francesco Mazzola)

Vision of J (P)   London: National Gallery.

Passeri, Bernardino (see also Cort,
Cornelius)

Madonna and Child with Saints (P)   Bologna: Pinocateca.
Death of J (P)   Cambridge, Mass.: Fogg Art Museum. [Fig. 171]
Body of J (?) Supported by Angels (P)   Bremen: J. H. Beckmann Coll.
   (Bierens de Haan, fig. 38, opp. p. 143.)

Patinir, Joachim

J in W (P)   Karlsruhe: Kunsthalle.
J in W (P)   Paris: Louvre.
J in W (P)   Madrid: Prado.
J in W (P)   London: National Gallery.
J in W (in triptych) (P)   New York: Metropolitan Museum.

Patinir workshop

J in W (P)   Venice: Ca'd'Oro.
J in W (P)   Wuppertal-Elberfeld: Von der Heydt Museum.
J in W (in triptych) (P)   Palermo: di Trabia Coll.
J in W (P)   Formerly owned by Frederick Mont, New York.
J in W (P)   Formerly in Hellberg Coll., Stockholm.
J in W (P)   New York: Wildenstein Coll.
J in W (P)   Chicago: Art Institute.

Paudiss, Christoph

J in W (P)   Munich: Alte Pinakothek.

Pedralbes Master

Triptych of Crucifixion with Saint Macarius and J (P)   Barcelona: Muntades
   Coll. (Post, vol. 7, fig. 7.)

Pellegrino, Aretusi (il Munari)

Jerome Legend (P)   Modena: S. Pietro. [Fig. 168]

Pencz, Joerg

J in S (P)   Richter Archives 340:IV:3.

Pereda y Salgado, Antonio di

J in W (P)   Madrid: Prado.

Perugino, Pietro (Vannucci)

J in W (P)   Assisi: Sacro Convento; F. M. Perkins Coll.
J in W (P)   Baltimore: Walters Art Gallery.
J in W (P)   Caen: Musée des Beaux-Arts.
J in W (P)   Hampton Court, (Middlesex), no. 1196.
J in W (P)   Perugia: Pinacoteca, no. 242.

J in W (P)   Formerly owned by Dr. J. Hasson, Shenfield (Berkshire, England).

J in W (panel of triptych) (P)   Washington: National Gallery of Art; A. W. Mellon Coll. [Figs. 66, 180]

J in W (with Holy Children in background) (P)   Washington: National Gallery of Art; Samuel H. Kress Coll. [Fig. 65]

J in W (with Holy Children in background) (P)   Rome: Palazzo Barberini.

J in W (P)   Vienna: Kunsthistorisches Museum.

Baptist with J, Francis, Sebastian, and Anthony of Padua (P)   Perugia: Galleria Nazionale dell 'Umbria, no. 280.

Crucifixion with J and Saint Christopher (P)   Rome: Borghese Gallery.

Crucifixion with Magdalene, Jerome, and Baptist (P)   Florence: Uffizi.

Perugino follower

J in W (P)   San Diego: Fine Arts Gallery.

Pesellino, Francesco

Crucifixion with J and Francis (P)   Washington: National Gallery of Art; Samuel H. Kress Coll.

Madonna with J (P)   New York: Metropolitan Museum.

Madonna with J (P)   Philadelphia: Johnson Coll.

J & L (predella) (P)   London: National Gallery.

Pfisterer, Jacob

J in W (P)   Innsbruck: Tiroler Landesmuseum Ferdinandeum.

Piazza, Martino

J in W (P)   Milan: Castello Sforzesco.

Last Communion and Miracle of J (P)   Bloomington: Indiana University.

Piero della Francesca

J in W (P)   Berlin-Dahlem: Staatliche Museen.

Jerome with kneeling Monk (P)   Venice: Accademia.

Piero di Cosimo

J in W (P)   Florence: Museo Horne, no. 31.

J in W (D)   New York: Metropolitan Museum; R. Lehmann Coll.

Pietro da Cortona

J in W (P)   Detroit Institute of Arts.

Pietro de Po

J in W (G)   (after Domenichino). Bartsch, vol. 20, p. 17, no. 251.

Pino, Marco

J (P)   New London, Conn.: Lyman Allyn Museum.

Pinturicchio, Bernardino

J & L (P)   Rome: S. Maria del Popolo.

J in W (P)   Rome: S. Maria del Popolo.

J in W (P)   Rome: Galleria Corsini.

J in W (P)   Perugia: Pinacoteca, no. 1495.

Crucifixion with J and Christopher (P)   Rome: Borghese Gallery

Pisan, Late Thirteenth–Early Fourteenth Century

J in W (P)   Cracow: M. Tomaszewski Coll. (Muzeum Krakow, fig. 14.)

Pisan, Fourteenth Century

J in W (P)   Pisa: Galleria San Matteo, no. 159. [Fig. 52, left]

J in S (P)   Pisa: Galleria San Matteo, no. 159. [Fig. 52, right]

Pisanello follower (Francesco dei Franceschi?)

J in W (P)   London: Present whereabouts unknown. [Fig. 63]

Poccette, Il

J in W (P)   Forlì: S. Mercuriale.

Poelemburg, Cornelis   J in W (P)   Bergamo: Accademia Carrara, no. 451.

Polidoro, Lanziani   Madonna with J (P)   Cambridge, Mass.: Fogg Museum.

Pollaiuolo, Antonio   J in W (D)   Florence: Uffizi.
J (P)   Pistoia: San Domenico.

Pollaiuolo, Antonio (after), probably by Finiguerra   J in W (G)   Hind, vol. 2, no. 58.

Pontormo (Jacopo Carruci da)   J in W (P)   Hanover: Kestner-Museum, no. 279.

Portillo Master   J in S (P):   New York: Proskauer Coll. (Post, vol. 9, p. 411.)

Poussin, Nicolas   J in W (P)   Madrid: Prado.

Previtale, Andrea   J in W (with Martyrdom of Stephen) (P)   Bergamo: Accademia Carrara.
J in W (P)   Oxford: Ashmolean Museum.

Procaccini, Giulio Cesare   J and Angel (P)   Milan: Brera, no. 346.

Provence School, ca. 1440–1450   J in S (P)   Rotterdam: Boymans-van Beuningen Museum, no. 2467.

Pseudo Pier Francesco Fiorentino   J and Saint Francis (after Filippo Lippi) (P)   Bergamo: Accademia Carrara, no. 514. [Fig. 173]

Pynas, Jan Symons   J in W (D)   Palo Alto: Stanford University.

Raffaelino del Garbo   Madonna and Child with Saints and Angels (P)   San Francisco: M. H. DeYoung Memorial Museum; Samuel H. Kress Coll. [Fig. 161]

Raimondi, Marcantonio   J in W (G)   Bartsch, vol. 14, p. 132, no. 152.
J in W (G)   (after Raphael). Bartsch, vol. 14, p. 88, no. 101.
J in W (G)   (after Raphael). Bartsch, vol. 14, p. 88, no. 102.

Raphael (Raffaello Santi) (?)   J in W (P)   London: Lady Wantage Coll. (Richter Archives 117A:IV:54.)
J in W (P)   Amsterdam: Goudstikker Coll.

Rembrandt van Ryn.   J in W (G)   Washington: National Gallery of Art; Rosenwald Coll. [Fig. 74]
J in W (G)   Washington: National Gallery of Art; Rosenwald Coll. [Fig. 75]
J in W, ca. 1653 (G)   Mayor (1971), no. 505.
J in W (G) J (?), 1642, in S (G)   Van de Waal (1964).
J in W, ca. 1652 (D)   Copenhagen: Kobberstiksamlingen.

Reni, Guido   J and Angel (P)   Vienna: Kunsthistorisches Museum, no. 633.
J and Angel (P)   Detroit: Institute of Arts.
J in W (P)   London: National Gallery.

Rexach, Juan   J (P)   Palma: Gallerias Costa. (Post, vol. 6, fig. 22.)

Ribera, Giuseppe de   J in W (P)   Leningrad: Hermitage.
J in W (P)   Madrid: Prado.
J in W (G)   Bartsch, vol. 20, p. 80, no. 3.

	J in W (P) Detroit: Institute of Arts.	
	J Listening to Angel's Trumpet (two versions) (G) Bartsch, vol. 20, p. 80, nos. 3, 4, also p. 80, no. 4.	
	J in W (P) Ponce: Museo de Arte de Ponce.	
	J in W (P) Cambridge, Mass.: Fogg Museum	
	J in W (P) Milan: Brera, no. 613.	
	J in W (P) Baltimore: Walters Art Gallery.	
	J in W (P) Omaha: Joslyn Museum.	
	J in S (P) Terre Haute, Ind.: University of Notre Dame.	
	J with Angel (P) Rome: Doria Gallery.	
	J with Angel (P) Naples: Museo Nazionale.	
Ribera School	J in W (P) Rome: Corsini Gallery.	
	J in W (P) Milan: Castello Sforzesco, no. 196.	
	J in W (P) Staten Island, N.Y.: Staten Island Institute.	
Ricci, Marco	J in W (P) Rome: Corsini Gallery.	
Ricci, Sebastiano	J in W (P) Rimini: Pinacoteca.	
Riemenschneider, Tilman	J & L (S) Erfurt: Herr Domprobst Würschmitt Coll.	
	J & L (S) Cleveland Museum of Art.	
Riemenschneider follower	J & L (S) Karlstadt: Parish Church. [Fig. 157]	
	J (S) Würzburg: Mainfrankisches Museum.	
Robbia, Andrea della	J in W (S) Assisi: S. Maria Degli Angeli. [Fig. 50]	
	J in W (S) Pieve: S. Fiora.	
Robbia, Giovanni della	J & L (in Hexagonal Ciborio) (S) Galatrona: S. Giovanni Battista.	
	Several panels of Legend of J (S) Arcevia: S. Medardo.	
Robbia, Giovanni della, attribution	J in W (S) Formerly in Bardini Coll., New York.	
Robbia, Luca della	J and Angels (bronze relief) (S) Florence: Duomo.	
Roberti, Ercole di	J before Dead Christ at Tomb (P) London: National Gallery.	
	J in W (P) Sir Thomas Barlow Coll. (*Burlington Magazine* 91 [1949], pp. 242–45.)	
	J in W (P) Ferrara: Pinacoteca Civica.	
	J in W (P) Milan: Bargellesi Coll.	
Robetta, Cristoforo (?)	J in W (G) London: British Museum.	
Romanino, Girolamo	J in W (P) Brescia: Pinacoteca Martinengo, no. 1214.	
	J in W (P) Milan: Crespio Morbio Coll.	
	J in W (one panel in triptych) (P) London: National Gallery, no. 297.	
	Madonna and Child with James and J (P) Atlanta: High Museum of Art; Samuel H. Kress Coll. [Fig. 152]	
Rondinelli, Niccolo	J (P) Venice: S. Crisogono.	
Rosa, Salvator	J in W (P) Sarasota: Ringling Museum.	
	J with Angel of Last Judgment (P) Fabriano: Duomo.	

Rossellino, Antonio, attribution   J in W (S)   Formerly in Bardini Coll., New York (to 1940). [Fig. 51]

Rossello di Jacopo (Franchi)   J Writing (one panel of triptych) (P)   Florence: Spedale degli Innocenti.

Rubens, Peter Paul   J in W (P)   Dresden: Gemäldegalerie.
                                        J in W (P)   Richter Archives 286C: III: 13.
                                        J in S (P)   Potsdam-Sanssouci: Bildergalerie.

Saavedra, Antonio del Castillo   J in W (P)   Madrid: Prado.

Sabatelli, Luigi   J & L (P)   Fiesole: San Girolamo.

Sacchi, Pier Francesco   J, Anthony Abbot, and a Third Elderly Saint (P)   Richter Archives
                                           126: XII: 5.
                                        Jerome, Martin and Beggar, and Anthony Abbot (P)   Berlin-Dahlem:
                                           Staatliche Museen.
                                        J in W (P)   Wichita, Kan.: Wichita Art Association.

Sadeler, Johann   J in W   (Knipping, p. 64).
                                        J in W (G)   (after Girolamo Muziano). Milan: Dubini Coll.

Salimbeni, Lorenzo, and Jacopo da   Legend of J (P)   *Burlington Magazine* 68 (1936): 95–97.
Sanseverino

Salimbeni, Ventura   J (P)   Rome: Doria Pamphili Gallery.

Salzburg Xylographer, ca. 1500   J in S (G)   Vienna: Albertina.

Sammachini, Orazio   Madonna and Child with J and Magdalene (P)   Los Angeles: University of
                                           California.

Sano di Pietro   J in W (P)   Paris: Louvre. [Fig. 41]
                                        J in W (P)   Siena: Pinacoteca Nazionale. [Fig. 80]
                                        J & L (P)   Paris: Louvre [Fig. 146]
                                        J in W (P)   Grosseto: Duomo.
                                        J in W (P)   New York: Metropolitan Museum.
                                        J (in triptych) (P)   Boston: Museum of Fine Arts.
                                        J in W (D)   Florence: Uffizi.

Santa Croce, Francesco da   Vision of J (P)   Venice: Museo Correr, no. 75.
                                        Madonna with J and Catherine (P)   Baltimore: Walters Art Gallery.

Santa Croce, Girolamo de   J in W (P)   Turin: Galleria Sabauda.

Santi, Giovanni   J Enthroned in Wilderness (P)   Vatican: Pinacoteca, no. 326. [Fig. 20]

Santi di Tito   J in W (P)   Rome: San Giovanni dei Fiorentini.

Sardinian, Fifteenth Century   J and Augustine (P)   San Simeon, Calif.: Hearst Castle.

Sassetta (Stefano di Giovanni)   J in W (panel of triptych) (P)   Boston: Museum of Fine Arts.

Savery, Roelandt   J in W (P)   Bonn: Landesmuseum. [Fig. 177]

Savoldo, Giovanni Girolamo	J in W (P) London: National Gallery, no. 3092. J in W (P) Oxford: Ashmolean Museum.
Scacco, Cristoforo	J in W (P) Fondi: Duomo.
Schäufelein, Hans Leonhard	J in W (P) Nürnberg: Germanisches Museum.
Scheere, Herman, Studio	J in S (M) ca. 1405. *Millar Hours*, English. San Marino, Calif.: Henry E. Huntington Library, HM 19913, f. 122. [Fig. 13]
Scheere, Herman, remote follower of	J in S (M) San Marino, Calif.: Henry E. Huntington Library, HM 28175, f. 73.
Scolari, Giuseppe	J in W (G) Boston: Museum of Fine Arts (second state). New York: Metropolitan Museum
Scorel, Jan van	J in W (P) Breda: Funeral Chapel of Engelbrecht II von Nassau. (Hoogewerff, fig. 57.)
Sebastiano da Reggio	J in W (G) (after painting by Marcello Venusti, after a lost drawing by Michelangelo). Tolnay (1960), fig. 252.
Segovia School	J in S (P) Madrid: Lazare Coll. (Post, vol. 4, p. 457.)
Sellaio, Jacopo del	J in W (P) Altenburg: Lindenau Museum. J in W (P) New Haven: Yale University Art Gallery. J in W (P) Budapest: Museum of Fine Arts. J in W (P) Breslau: Schlesisches Museum. J in W (P) Frankfurt: Paul Bottenwieser Coll. J in W(P) Stockholm: National Museum. J in W with Temptation of Saint Anthony (P) Göttingen: Gemäldegalerie. J in W (P) Cracow: National Museum. J in W with Mary of Egypt and Baptist (P) Milan: Contessa Rasini. J in W (P) Florence: Horne Foundation. J in W (P) Paris: Louvre. J in W (P) Sarasota: Ringling Museum. J in W (P) Seattle Art Museum. J in W (P) I Tatti, Florence. [Fig. 174] J in W (P) London: Courtauld Institute. J in W (P) Princeton, N.J.: Princeton University Art Gallery. J and Saint Francis (P) El Paso Museum of Art; Samuel H. Kress Coll. [Fig. 40]
Sellaio (?)	Nativity with J and other Saints (P) New Haven: Yale University Art Gallery.
Serodine, Giovanni	J in S (P) Greenville, S.C.: Bob Jones University.
Sienese, Late Fourteenth Century	J in S (P) Philadelphia: Johnson Coll. J in W (S) Siena: Duomo. J with Three Cardinals (P) Pittsburgh: Carnegie Institute.
Signorelli, Luca	J (P) Paris: Louvre. J (P) Assisi: Sacro Convento. Augustine's Vision (P) London: National Gallery. Madonna and Child with Saints (P) London: National Gallery, no. 1847.

Silesian, ca. 1500   J in W (P)   Breslau: Schlesisches Museum für Kunstgewerbe. (Troche, p. 129.)

Simone dei Crocifissi   J & L (in polyptych) (P)   Athens, Ga.: University of Georgia; Georgia Museum of Art; Kress Study Coll. [Fig. 153]

Sodoma (Giovanni Antonio Bazzi)   J in W (P)   Harewood House (York): Lord Harewood.
                                  J in W (P)   London: National Gallery, no. 3947.
                                  J (P)   Baltimore: Walters Art Gallery, no. 1680.
                                  J in W (P)   Milan: Morelli Coll. (Richter Archives 100:I:32.)

Sogliani, Giovanni Antonio (?)   J in W (P)   Compton Wyngates (Warwick): Marquess of Northampton.
                                  J Writing (P)   Dublin: National Gallery of Ireland.

Solario, Andrea   J in W (P)   Barnard Castle (Yorkshire): Bowes Museum.
                                  J in W (P)   Florence: Gualino Coll.
                                  J (P)   Milan: Ambrosiana.
                                  J in W with Francis Receiving Stigmata (P)   Milan: Brera.

Lo Spagna (Giovanni di Pietro)   J in W (P)   Paris: Louvre, no. 1511.
                                  J in W (P)   San Diego: Fine Arts Gallery.
                                  J in W (P)   Indianapolis: John Herron Art Institute.

Spanish, Sixteenth Century   J in W (P)   Cincinnati Art Museum.
                                  Death of J (P)   Cambridge, Mass.: Fogg Museum.

Spanish Tradition in south of France   J in S (P)   Paris: Louvre.

Springinklee, Hans   J in S (G)   Bartsch, vol. 7, p. 57, no. 329.

Squarcione, Francesco   J (one panel of polyptych) (P)   Padua: Museo Civico.

Stefano di Antonio   J with Magdalen and Saint Francis (P)   Boston: Gardner Museum.

Strada, Vespasiano   J in W (G)   Bartsch, vol. 18, p. 310, no. 18.

Stuber, Wolfgang   Martin Luther in His Study (G)   Vienna: Albertina. [Fig. 90]

Sustris, Lambert   J in W (P)   Formerly in Holford Coll., London.
                                  J in W (P)   Oxford: Ashmolean Museum, no. 400.
                                  J in W (P)   Stockholm: National Museum.

Taddeo di Bartolo   J (P)   New Haven: Yale University Art Gallery.

Teniers, David the Younger   J in W (P)   Frankfurt: Städelsches Kunstinstitut.

Terbrugghen, Hendrick   J in W (P)   Rotterdam: Boymans-van Beuningen Museum, no 2435.

Tiberio d'Assisi   Madonna and Child with Saints (P)   Vatican: Pinacoteca.
                                  Madonna and Child with Saints (P)   Assisi: S. Damiano, Capella di San Gerolamo.

Tiepolo, Giovanni Battista   Death of J (P)   Milan: Poldi Pezzoli Museum.
                                  J in W (P)   Chicago: Art Institute.

	J and Angels (D) Los Angeles: Armand Hammer Coll.
	Temptation of J (D) Copenhagen: Statens Museum for Kunst.
Tintoretto, Domenico	J in W (P) Rome: Barberini Gallery. [Fig. 187]
Tintoretto, Jacopo	Madonna Appearing to J (P) Venice: Accademia, no. 785.
	J in W (P) Vienna: Kunsthistorisches Museum, no. 696.
Tintoretto School	J in W (P) Vienna: Kunsthistorisches Museum.
Titian (Tiziano Vecellio)	J in W (P) Paris: Louvre.
	J in W (P) Florence: Uffizi.
	J in W (P) Milan: Brera. [Fig. 59]
	J in W (P) Rome: Accademia di San Luca.
	J in W (P) Lugano: Thyssen Coll.
	J in W (P) Escorial: Nuevos Museos.
Titian attribution (or School)	J in W (P) Formerly in W. J. Davies Coll. (Richter Archives 178:V:5); woodcut by Boldrini after this painting. [Fig. 175]
	J in W (P) Bergamo: Accademia Carrara, no. 209.
	J in W (P) Sacramento, Calif.: Crocker Art Gallery.
	J in W (P) Formerly in Belloni Coll., Florence.
	J in W (G) Paris: Bibliothèque Nationale. (Rosand and Muraro, p. 32, fig. 1.)
	J in W, ca. 1516 (G) (designed by Titian, woodcut by Ugo da Carpi). Rosand and Muraro, p. 93, fig. 6.
Tomaso da Modena	J in S (P) Treviso: S. Niccolo. [Fig. 11]
	J & L (P) Modena: Galleria Estense.
Torrigiano, Pietro	J in W (S) Seville: Museum of Fine Arts.
Troger, Paul	J with Angel of Last Judgment (D) Salzburg: Städtliches Museum.
Tura, Cosimo	J in W (P) London: National Gallery. [Frontispiece and figs. 132, 134, 139, 141]
Tura, Cosimo, attribution	J in W (M) Cleveland Museum of Art.
Tuscan, Fourteenth Century	J in W (P) Princeton, N.J.: Princeton University Art Museum.
Ulocrino	J in W (S) Washington: National Gallery of Art; Samuel H. Kress Coll. (Pope-Hennessy [1965], fig. 340.) [Fig. 165]
	J in W (S) Washington: National Gallery of Art; Samuel H. Kress Coll. (Pope-Hennessy [1965], fig. 341.)
	J in W (S) Washington: National Gallery of Art; Samuel H. Kress Coll. (Pope-Hennessy [1965], fig. 342.)
Ulocrino attribution	J in W (S) Washington: National Gallery of Art; Samuel H. Kress Coll. (Pope-Hennessy [1965], fig. 350.)
Umbrian School	J (P) Amsterdam: Goudstikker Coll. (Richter Archives 102:I:5.)
	J in W (in background of Madonna and Child) (P) Tulsa: Philbrook Art Center; Samuel H. Kress Coll.
Urgel Master	J in W (P) Barcelona: Museum of Catalan Art. (Post, vol. 7, 36.)

van Cleve, Joos (including workshop)

J in S (P)   London: Duke of Fife.
J in S (P)   Milan: Private collection.
J in W (P)   Vienna: Holzapfel Coll.
J in S (P)   Dayton, Ohio: Art Institute, no. 59-159.
J in S (P)   Cambridge, Mass.: Busch Reisinger Museum.
J in S (P)   Princeton, N.J.: Princeton University Art Gallery.
J in S (P)   Madrid: Prado.
J in W (P)   Worcester, Mass.: Worcester Art Museum.
J in W (P)   Muskegon, Mich.: Hackley Art Gallery.
J in S (P)   West Palm Beach, Fla.: W. Norton Gallery.

van der Weyden, Rogier

J & L (P)   Detroit Institute of Fine Arts.
J & L (P)   Brussels: Musées Royaux des Beaux-Arts. [Fig. 67]
J and Donor (P)   New York: Metropolitan Museum.
Pietà (P)   London: National Gallery, no. 6265.

van Dyck, Anthony

J in W (P)   Dresden: Gemäldegalerie.
J and Angel (P)   Rotterdam: Willem van der Vorm Coll.
J and Angel (P)   Stockholm: National Museum.
J in W (P)   Richter Archives 288D:I:79.
J in W (P)   Richter Archives 288C:V:51.
J in W (P)   Oldenburg: Landesmuseum.

van Eyck, Jan

J in S (P)   Detroit Institute of Arts. [Fig. 16]

van Oost, Jakob, the Elder

J listening to Trumpet (P)   Bruges: St. John's Hospital.

van Somer, Hendrick

J Reading (P)   Rome: Corsini Gallery, no. 2330.

van Staveren, Jan

J in W (P)   Copenhagen: Statens Museen for Kunst.

van Vliet, Joris

J in W (G)   Cambridge, Mass.: Fogg Museum.

Vasari, Giorgio

J Tempted (P)   Florence: Pitti Palace, no. 393.

Vasari attribution

J in W (P)   Chicago: Art Institute, no. 64.64.

Vasquez, Antonio

J in W (P)   Valladolid: Museo Nacional de Escultura. (Post, vol. 14, p. 81.)

Venetian, Fifteenth Century

J (one of a series of panels) (P)   Columbia, S.C.: Museum of Art; Samuel H. Kress Coll.
J and Angels (P)   Venice: Museo Correr.
J in W (P)   Bergamo: Accademia Carrara, no. 280.
J (P)   New York: Metropolitan Museum.

Venetian, Sixteenth Century

J (P)   Los Angeles County Museum of Art.

Venetian, Seventeenth Century

J Reading (P)   Brescia: Pinacoteca Martinengo, no. 909.

Veneto-Byzantine

J & L (P)   Chicago: David and Alfred Smart Gallery, University of Chicago; Samuel H. Kress Coll. [Fig. 19]
J & L (P)   London: National Gallery.

Venusti, Marcello

J in W (P)   Rome: S. Maria della Pace.

	J in W (D) (after a lost drawing by Michelangelo). Rotterdam: Boymans-van Beuningen Museen, no. 238. (Tolnay [1960], fig. 251.)
Verla, Francesco	J in W (P) Formerly (?) in S. Fidenzio, Verona.
Veronese (Paolo Caliari)	J and Donor (P) Dulwich: College Art Gallery. J in W (P) Murano: S. Pietro Martire. J in W (P) Washington: National Gallery of Art; Samuel H. Kress Coll. [Fig. 60] J in W (D) Vienna: Albertina. J in W (P) Chicago: Art Institute. J in W (P) Venice: S. Andrea della Zerada.
Veronese, Fifteenth Century	J in S (P) Amherst, Mass.: Amherst College; Samuel H. Kress Coll.
Verrocchio, Andrea and Assistants	Crucifixion with J and Anthony Abbot (P) Argiano: S. Maria e Angiolo.
Vico, Enea	J in W (G) Bartsch, vol. 15, p. 285, no. 10.
Vignon, Claude	J in S (P) Greenville, S.C.: Bob Jones University.
Vincent, François-André	J and Trumpeting Angel (P) Montpellier: Musée Fabre.
Vittoria, Alessandro	J (S) Venice: S. Maria dei Frari. J (S) Venice: SS. Giovanni e Paolo.
Vivarini, Alvise	J in W (P) Washington: National Gallery of Art; Samuel H. Kress Coll. [Fig. 61] J in W (P) Boston: Museum of Fine Arts. J (P) Denver Art Museum.
Vivarini, Antonio	J, Francis, and Anthony Abbot (P) Poughkeepsie, N.Y.: Vassar College. Bernardino between J and Louis of Toulouse (P) Venice: S. Francesco d. Vigna. J in W (P) Formerly owned by H. M. Clark, London.
Vivarini, Antonio, and Giovanni d'Alemagna	J (P) Baltimore: Walters Art Gallery. J (in polyptych) (P) Venice: S. Zaccaria. J (P) Columbia, S.C.: Museum of Art. J (P) New York: Metropolitan Museum.
Vivarini, Antonio, and Bartolomeo Vivarini	J (in polyptych) (P) Bologna: Pinacoteca.
Vivarini, Bartolomeo	J (P) Boston: Museum of Fine Arts.
von Saaz, Jan	J & L (P) Prague: National Museum. (Hajós, p. 35.)
Vouet, Simon	J and Angel (P) Washington: National Gallery of Art; Samuel H. Kress Coll. [Fig. 3]
Wechtlin, Hans	J in W (G) Basel: Kunstmuseum, Kupferstichkabinett.
Zanetti, Bartolomeo	J in W (G) Breslauer, no. 119.

Zenale, Bernardo   Madonna and Child and Saints (P)   Denver Art Museum; Samuel H. Kress
                               Coll.

Zoan, Andrea   J in W (G)   Hind, vol. 6, pl. 590.

Zoppo, Marco   J in W (P)   Baltimore: Walters Art Gallery.
                           J in W (P)   Baltimore: Walters Art Gallery, no. 543. [Fig. 64]
                           J in W (P)   Bergamo: Accademia Carrara.
                           J in W (P)   Lugano: Thyssen Coll.
                           J in W (P)   Bologna: Pinacoteca, no. 778.
                           J in W (P)   Bologna: Collegio di Spagna, Cappella.
                           J in W (P)   London: Seilern Coll.

Zurbaran, Francesco   J (P)   San Diego: Museum of Fine Arts.
                           J, Paula, and Eustochium (P)   Washington: National Gallery of Art; Samuel
                               H. Kress Coll.
                           Temptation of J (P)   Guadalupe: Hieronymite Monastery.

Bibliography

Adam of Saint-Victor. *Sequentiae*. In Migne, *Patrologia Latina*, vol. 196, col. 1433. (*See also* Gautier, Leon)

Aelian (Claudius Aelianus). *De natura animalium*. Translated by Lynn Thorndike. In *History of Magic*, vol. 1. New York: Macmillan Co., 1923.

Albertus, Magnus. Two editions consulted: *Opera omnium*, vol. 20. Lugdini: Petri Iammy, 1651; and *Animalium*, vol. 12. Paris, Vives: Augusti Borgnet, 1891.

Alciati, Andrea. *Emblematum flumen abundans*. Translated by Henry Green. London, Manchester: Holbein Society, 1871.

Aldrovandus, Ulysses. *Ornithologiae hoc est, de avibus historiae*. Bk. 12. Bologna: Nicolai Tebaldini, 1640–1646.

Andrea, Giovanni. *Hieronymianus*. Cologne: Conrad Winters, 1482. Partly reprinted in J. Klapper, *Aus der Frühzeit des Humanismus*, pp. 255–71. Breslau: M. and H. Markus, 1926.

Aristotle. *The Works of Aristotle*. Edited and translated by J. A. Smith and W. D. Ross. Vol. 4. Oxford: Clarendon Press, 1910.

———. *Historia animalium*. Translated by D'Arcy Wentworth Thompson. Oxford: Clarendon Press, 1910.

Arrigoni degli Oddi, Ettore. *Ornitologia italiana*. Milan: U. Hoepli, 1929.

Augustine, Saint. Sermo cclxii: "De ascensione Domini." In Migne, *Patrologia Latina*, vol. 38, col. 1210.

———. "Enarratio in Psalmum lxvi." In Migne, *Patrologia Latina*, vol. 36, col. 804. 1865.

Bachofen, Johann Jacob. *Der Baer in der Religion des Altertums*. Basle: C. Meyri, 1863.

Bächtold-Stäubli, Hans. *Handwörterbuch des deutschen Aberglaubens*. Berlin and Leipzig: W. de Gruyter and Co., 1927–1938.

Baer, Eva. *Sphinxes and Harpies in Medieval Islam Art: An Iconographical Study*. Oriental Notes and Studies, no. 9. Jerusalem: The Israel Oriental Society, 1965.

Bainton, Roland H. *Studies on the Reformation*. Boston: Beacon Press, 1963.

Baldass, Ludwig. "Cranach's büssender Hieronymus von 1502." *Jahrbuch der Preussischen Kunstsammlungen* 49 (1928): 76–81.

———. *Albrecht Altdorfer*. Vienna: Gallus Verlag K. G., 1941.

———. *Hieronymus Bosch*. New York: Harry N. Abrams, in association with Verlag Anton Schroll & Co., Vienna, 1960.

Baltrusaitis, Jurgis. *Le Moyen Âge fantastique*. Paris: A. Colon, 1955.

———. *Réveils et prodiges: Le Gothique fantastique*. Paris: A. Colon, 1960.

Barb, Alfons A. "Der Heilige und die Schlangen." *Mitteilungen der Anthropologischen Gesellschaft* 82 (Vienna, 1952): 1–21.

Bartholomew Anglicus. *Batman upon Bartholome, His Booke De Proprietatibus Rerum*. Translated by John de Trevisa. London, 1582.

———. *Medieval Lore . . . Gleanings from the Encyclopedia of Bartholomew Anglicus on the Properties of Things*. Edited by R. Steele. London: A. Moring, 1905.

Bartsch, Adam von. *Le Peinte graveur*, 21 vols. Vienna: J. W. Degen, 1803–1811

———. *Le Peinte graveur illustré: Illustrations to Adam Bartsch's "Le Peinte graveur."* Vols. 12–21. University Park, Pa.: Pennsylvania State University Press, 1971.

Basil, Saint. *Exegetic Homilies*. Translated by Sister Agnes Clare Way, C.D.P. In *The Fathers of the Church*, vol. 46. Washington: Catholic University of America Press, 1965.

Bax, Dirk. *Ontcijfering van Jeroen Bosch*. The Hague: Martinus Nijhoff, 1948–1949.

Bean, Jacob, and Stampfle, Felice. *Drawings from New York Collections: I. The Italian Renaissance: Metropolitan Museum of Art, Pierpont Morgan Library*. Greenwich, Conn.: New York Graphic Society, 1965.

Beckwith, John. *The Adoration of the Magi in Whalebone*. Victoria and Albert Museum Monograph 28. London: Victoria and Albert Museum, 1966.

Behling, Lottlisa. *Die Pflanze in der mittelalterliche Tafelmalerei*. Weimar: H. Böhlaus Nachfolger, 1957.

Beissel, Stefan. "Zur Geschichte der Tiersymbolik in der Kunst des Abendlandes." *Zeitschrift für christliche Kunst* 14 (1901):275–86.

Benesch, Otto. *The Art of the Renaissance in Northern Europe*. Rev. ed. London: Phaidon Press, 1965.

———. *German Painting from Dürer to Holbein*. Skira Editions, Geneva. New York: World Publishing Co., 1966.

———. "Hieronymus Bosch and the Thinking of the Middle Ages, II." In *Collected Writings*, vol. 2. New York: Phaidon Publishers, 1971 (originally published in *Konsthistorisk Tidskrift* 26 [Stockholm, 1957]: 103–27).

Berchorius, Petrus. *Reductorium morale super totam Bibliam*. Nuremberg, 1583.

Berenson, Bernard. *Venetian Painting in America: The Fifteenth Century*. New York: Frederick Fairchild Sherman, 1916.

———. *The Study and Criticism of Italian Art*. Third Series. London: G. Bell and Sons, 1927.

———. *Italian Pictures of the Renaissance*. Oxford: Clarendon Press, 1932.

———. *The Drawings of the Florentine Painters*. Vol. 2. Chicago: University of Chicago Press, 1938.

———. *Italian Pictures of the Renaissance: Venetian School*. 2 vols. New York: Phaidon Publishers, 1957.

———. *Italian Pictures of the Renaissance: Florentine School*. 2 vols. London: Phaidon Press, 1963.

———. *Italian Pictures of the Renaissance: Central Italian and Northern Italian Schools*. 3 vols. New York: Phaidon Publishers, 1968.

———. *Homeless Paintings of the Renaissance*. Edited by Hanna Kiel. Bloomington: Indiana University Press, and London: Thames & Hudson, 1969.

Bergström, Ingvar. "Disguised Symbolism in 'Madonna' Pictures and Still Life." *Burlington Magazine* 97 (London, 1955): 303–8, 340–49.

———. *Dutch Still-Life Painting in the Seventeenth Century*. Translated by Christina Hedström and Gerald Taylor. New York: Thomas Yoseloff, 1956.

———. "Medicina, Fons et Scrinium: A Study in van Eyckian Symbolism and and its Influence in Italian Art. *Konsthistorisk Tidskrift* (1957): 1–20.

———. "Den fångne fågeln. Särtryck ur Symbolister." *Tidskrift for Konstvetenskap* 30 (1957): 11–38.

Berry, Ana Margarita. *Animals in Art*. London: Chatto and Windus, 1929.

Berti, Luciano. *Masaccio*. University Park, Pa., and London: Pennsylvania University Press, 1967.

Bier, Justus. "Riemenschneider's St. Jerome and Other Works in Alabaster." *Art Bulletin* 33 (1951): 226–34.

Bierens de Haan, J.C.J. *L'Oeuvre gravé de Cornelis Cort: Graveur Hollandais 1537–1578*. The Hague: Martinus Nijhoff, 1948.

Biese, Alfred. *Development of Feeling for Nature in the Middle Ages*. New York: Burt Franklin, 1905.

Bisogni, Fabio. "Contributo per un problema Ferrarese." *Paragone* 23 (1972): 69–79, figs. 41–47.

Blanke, Fritz. "Ikonographie der Reformationszeit: Fragen um ein Cranach Bild (Toledo, Ohio. Mus. Art)." *Theologische Zeitschrift* 7 (1951): 467–71.

Blankenberg, Wera von. *Heilige und dämonische Tiere: die Symbolsprache der deutschen Ornamentik im frühen Mittelalter.* Leipzig: Koehler und Amelang, 1943.

Boas, George. *The Hieroglyphics of Horapollo.* Bollingen Series, no. 23. New York: Pantheon Books, 1950.

Bochart, Samuel. *Hierozoicon sive bipartitum opus de animalibus Sacrae Scripturae autore Samuele Bocharto.* Lugduni Batavorum et Traiecti ad Rhenum, 1712 (original ed. 1663, London).

Bode, Wilhelm. "Tonabdrücke von Reliefarbeiten niederländischer Goldschmiede aus dem Kreise der Künstler des Herzogs von Berry." *Amtliche Berichte aus den Königlichen Kunstsammlungen* 38 (1916–1917): col. 3/5 ff.

Bodmer, Heinrich. *Leonardo. Des Meisters Gemälde und Zeichnungen.* Stuttgart: Deutsche Verlags Anstalt, 1931.

Boehmer, Heinrich. *Luther and the Reformation in the Light of Modern Research.* Translated by E. S. G. Potter. London: G. Bell and Sons, 1930.

Bollandist Fathers. *Acta sanctorum, Septembris, viii.* Antwerp: Apud Bernardum Alb. vander Plassche, 1762. (Life of Saint Jerome is by Father Joannes Stiltinck [Joanne Stiltingo], pp. 657–63.)

Boschius, Jacobus. *Symbolographia; Sive de arte Symbolico.* Augsburg and Dillingen: J. C. Bencard, 1701.

Boschloo, A. W. A. *Annibale Carraci in Bologna.* 2 vols. The Hague: Government Publishing Office, 1974.

Bosque, Andrée de. *Artisti italiani in Spagnia, dal XIVᵉ siecolo ai re cattolici.* Milan: Alfieri and Lacroix, 1968.

Brandi, Cesare. *Quattrocentisti Senesi.* Milan: Ulrico Hoepli, 1949.

Bree, Charles Robert. *A History of the Birds of Europe, Not Observed in the British Isles.* 2d ed. 5 vols. London: Goombridge, 1875–1876.

Breslauer, Martin. *A Miscellany of Books, Autographs, and Manuscripts on Many Subjects.* List 39. London, 1971.

Brinton, Selwyn. *Francesco di Giorgio Martini of Siena.* 2 vols. London: Besant and Co., 1934–1935.

Brown, Robert, Jr. *The Unicorn.* London: Longmans Green, 1881.

Browne, Sir Thomas. *Pseudodoxia Epidemica.* London: T. H. for E. Dod, 1646.

Buchner, E. "Altdorfer's Büssender Hieronymus." *Wallraf-Richartz Jahrbuch* 1, n.s. (1930): 161–69.

Buffon, G. L. L., Comte de. *Histoire naturelle des oiseaux.* Vol. 2. Paris: Impre-Royale, 1790.

Bulard, Marcel. *Le Scorpion, symbole du peuple juif dans l'art religieux des XIVᵉ, XVᵉ, XVIᵉ siècles, à propos de quatre peintures murales de la chapelle Saint-Sébastien, à Lanslevillard (Savoie).* Paris: E. de Boccard, 1935.

Burlington Fine Arts Club. *Early Venetian Pictures and Other Works of Art.* London: Burlington Fine Arts Club, 1912.

Cabrol, Ferdinand, and Leclercq, Henri. *Dictionnaire d'archéologie chrétienne et de liturgie.* Vol. 5. Paris: Letouzey et Ané. 1922.

Cahier, Charles. *Nouveaux mélanges d'archéologie.* Paris: Firmin Didot, 1874.

Calabi, Augusto. *L'Incisione italiana.* Milan: Fratelli Treves Editori, 1931.

Camerarius, Joachim. *Symbolorum et emblematus ex animalibus quadrupedibus desumtorum centurea altera collecta.* Nürnberg: Kauffmann, 1595.

———. *Symbolorum emblematum centuriae quattuor.* Mayenne: Ludovici Bourgeat, Academiae Bibliopolae, 1677.

Carlill, James, trans. *The Physiologus.* In *The Epic of the Beast, Consisting of English Translations of the History of Reynard the Fox and Physiologus.* Introduction by William Rose. London: George Routledge and Sons, n.d. (1924?).

Carritt, David. "Dürer's St. Jerome in the Wilderness," *Burlington Magazine* 99 (1957): 363–67.

Carroll, William Meredith. *Animal Conventions in English Renaissance Non-Religious Prose (1550–1600).* New York: Bookman Associates, 1954.

Cartari, Vincenzo. *Le imagini colla sposizione degli dei degli antiche.* Venice, 1556.

Castelfranco, J. *The Paintings of Leonardo da Vinci.* New York: Random House, n.d.

Cavalca, Fra Domenico. *Volgarizzamento delle vite de S. S. Padri.* 2 vols. Milan: Istituto Editoriale Italiano, 1926.

Charbonneau-Lassay, Louis. *Le Bestiaire du Christ.* Bruges: Desclée de Brouwer, 1940.

Chastel, André. *Arte et humanisme à Florence au temps de Laurent le Magnifique.* Paris: Presses Universitaires de France, 1961.

—————. *The Age of Humanism: Europe 1480–1530.* London: Thames and Hudson, 1963.

Choulant, Johann Ludwig. *Graphische Incunabeln für Naturgeschichte und Medizin. Geschichte und Bibliographie der ersten naturhistorischen und medizinischen Drucke des XIV und XV Jahrhunderts, welche mit illustrierenden Abbildungen versehen sind.* Leipzig: R. Weigel, 1858.

Clark, Kenneth. *One Hundred Details from Pictures in the National Gallery.* London: National Gallery, 1938.

Class, E. *Auffassung und Darstellung der Tierwelt in französischen Roman de Renart.* Tübingen: G. Schnürlen, 1910.

Coletti, Luigi. *Catalogo delle cose d'arte e di antichita d'Italia.* Treviso, Roma, 1935.

Collins, A. H. *Symbolism of Animals and Birds Represented in English Church Architecture.* London: Sir I. Pitman & Sons, 1913.

Combe, Jacques. *Iheronimus Bosch.* Translated by Ethel Duncan. Paris: Pierre Tisné, 1946.

Como, Ugo da. *Girolamo Muziano.* Bergamo: Istituto italiana d'arte grafiche, 1930.

Contreras y Lopez del Ayala, Juan de, Marques de Lozoya. *The Escorial: The Royal Palace at La Granja de San Ildefonso.* New York: Meredith Press, 1967.

Corominas, Juan. *Diccionario critico etimologico de la lingua castellana.* 4 vols. Madrid: Gredos, 1954–1957.

Crombie, A. C. *Medieval and Early Modern Science.* 2d rev. ed. Vol. 1. New York: Doubleday and Co., 1959.

Crowe, J. A., and Cavalcaselle, G. B. *A History of Painting in North Italy.* Vol. 1. London: John Murray, 1871.

—————. *A New History of Painting in Italy from the II to the XVI Century.* Edited by Edward Hutton. 3 vols. New York: E. P. Dutton; London: J. M. Dent, 1909.

Curtius, Ernst Robert. *European Literature and the Latin Middle Ages.* Translated by W. R. Trask. New York: Pantheon Books, 1953.

Danckert, Werner. "Mutter Ente: Eine arkäische Göttin des Mittelmeerkreises und ihr Nachleben in europäischer Volksdichtung." *Antaios* 5 (1964): 535–50.

D'Ancona, A., and Comparetti, D. *Le antiche rime volgari secondo la lezione del Codice Vaticano 3793.* 5 vols. Bologna: G. Romagnoli, 1875–1888.

Dante Alighieri. *The Divine Comedy.* Translated and edited by Thomas G. Bergin. New York: Appleton-Century Crofts, 1955.

Davies, Martin. *The Earlier Italian Schools.* London: National Gallery, 1951.

Dawson, Warren R. "The Lore of the Hoopoe." In *The Bridle of Pegasus: Studies in Magic, Mythology, and Folklore,* pp. 126–42. London: Methuen & Co., 1930.

Dehio, Georg, and Bezold, Gust. von. *Denkmäler der deutschen Bildhauerkunst.* Vol. 3, pl. 61. Berlin: Ernst Wasmuth, a–g, 1905.

Delen, Adrien J. J. *Histoire de la gravure dans les anciens Pays-Bas et dans les provinces Belges des origines jusqu'a la fin du XVIIIᵉ siècle.* 3 vols. Paris: Librairie Nationale d'Art et d'Histoire, 1924–1935.

Demonts, Louis. "Le Maître de l'Annonciation d'Aix des Van Eyck à Antonello de Messine." *Revue de l'art ancien et moderne* 53 (1928): 257–80.

Deonna, Woldemar. "Mercure et le scorpion." *Latomus* 17 (1958): 614–58.

Didron, Adolphe Napoleon. *Christian Iconography.* Translated by E. J. Millington. 2 vols. New York: Frederick Ungar Publishing Co., 1965.

Dierbach, Johann Heinrich. *Flora Mythologica oder Pflanzenkunde in Bezug auf Mythologie und Symbolik.* Wiesbaden: Dr. Martin Sandig, 1970.

Dowling, Alfred E. P. Raymond. *The Flora of the Sacred Nativity.* London: Kegal Paul, Trench, Trübner and Co., 1890.

Druce, George C. "The Medieval Bestiaries: Their Influence on Ecclesiastical Decorative Art." *Journal of the British Archeological Association* 25, n.s. (1919–20): 41–82; 26: 35–79.

Druce, George C., trans. *The Bestiary of Guillaume LeClerc* (originally written in 1210–1211). Printed for private circulation. Ashford, Kent: Headley Brothers, Invicta Press, 1936.

Duchaussoy, Jacques. *Le Bestiaire divin ou le symbolique des animaux.* Paris: Le Colombe; Editions du Vieux Colombier, 1958.

Duval, Y. M. "Saint Augustin et le commentaire sur Jonas de Saint Jérôme." *Revue des Études Augustiniennes* 12 (1968): 9–40.

Dvořák, Max. *Idealism and Naturalism in Gothic Art.* Translated by R. J. Klawster. Terre Haute, Ind.: University of Notre Dame, 1967.

Eder, Robert. "Mystisch-allegorische Vogelgeschichten und deren Ursprung." In *Mitteilungen des Ornithologischen Vereins in Wien* 14 (1890): 126–28; 141–43; 191–92; 205–6; 223–25; 244–46; 297–98; 312–14; 324–26; vol. 15 (1891): 9–10; 32–33; 54–56; 116–18; 138–41; 169–71; 183–85; 193–95; 224.

Egger, Rudolf. "Ein altchristliches Kampfsymbol." *Byzantion* 5 (1929): 791–95.

Eisenberg, Marvin. "The Penitent St. Jerome by Giovanni Toscani." *Burlington Magazine* 118 (1976): 274–83.

Eiswirth, Rudolf. *Hieronymus' Stellung zur Literatur und Kunst.* Wiesbaden: Otto Harrassowitz, 1955.

Erffa, Hans Martin von. "Grus Vigilans." *Philobiblion, eine Vierteljahrsschrift für Buch und Graphik-Sammler* 1 (1957): 286–308.

Evans, Arthur Humble. *Turner on Birds: A Short and Succinct History of the Principal Birds Noticed by Pliny and Aristotle.* First published by Doctor William Turner, 1544. Cambridge: Cambridge University Press, 1903

Evans, Edward Payson. *Animal Symbolism in Ecclesiastical Architecture.* New York: Henry Holt, 1896.

Evans, Joan. *Art in Mediaeval France.* London, New York, and Toronto: Oxford University Press, 1948.

Fahy, Everett. "A Portrait of a Renaissance Cardinal as St. Jerome." *Minneapolis Institute of Arts Bulletin* 59 (1970): 5–19.

Fazio, Bartolommeo. *Bartholomaei facii de viris illustribus.* Edited by L. Mehus. Florence, 1745.

Fehrle, Eugen. "Der Hahn in Aberglauben." *Schweizerisches Archiv für Volkskunde* 16 (1912): 65 ff.

Fenyö, Ivan. *Albrecht Dürer.* Budapest: Corvina, 1956.

Ficarro, Angelo. *La posizione di S. Girolamo nella storia della cultura.* Milan. Vol. 1, 1916; vol. 2, 1920.

Field, Richard S. *Fifteenth Century Woodcuts and Metalcuts.* Washington: National Gallery of Art, 1965.

Firmenich-Richartz, Eduard. "Der Meister des heiligen Hieronymus." *Wallraf-Richartz Jahrbuch* 1 (1934): 99–100.

Fonck, Father Leopold, S. J. "Hieronymi scientia naturalis exemplis illustratus." In *Biblica: commentarii editi a pontificio istituto biblico,* vol. 1, pp. 481–99. Rome: Piazza Della Pilotta 35, 1920.

Forstner, Dorothea. *Die Welt der Symbole.* Innsbruck, Vienna, Munich: Tyrolia Verlag, 1961.

Fox-Daxies, Arthur Charles. *A Complete Guide to Heraldry.* London: T. C. and E. C. Jack, 1925.

Fränger, Wilhelm. *The Millennium of Hieronymus Bosch.* Translated by Eithne Wilkins and Ernst Kaiser. Chicago: University of Chicago Press, 1951.

Frazer, J. G. *The Golden Bough.* Vol. 4. London: Macmillan, 1935.

Fredericksen, Burton B. *The Cassone Paintings of Francesco di Giorgio.* Los Angeles: J. Paul Getty Museum, 1969.

Fredericksen, Burton B., and Zeri, Federico. *Census of Pre-Nineteenth-Century Italian Paintings in North American Public Collections.* Cambridge, Mass.: Harvard University Press, 1973.

Friedländer, Max J. "Der Hl. Hieronymus von Marinus van Reymerswale." *Pantheon* 13 (1934): 33–36.

—————. *Early Netherlandish Painting from van Eyck to Brueghel.* New York: Phaidon Publishers, 1956.

Friedländer, Max J., and Rosenberg, Jacob. *Die Gemälde von Lucas Cranach.* Berlin: Deutscher verein für Kunstwissenschaft, 1932.

Friedmann, Herbert. *The Symbolic Goldfinch: Its History and Significance in European Devotional Art.* Bollingen Series VII. New York: Pantheon Books, 1946.

—————. "The Iconography of a Madonna and Child by Giovanni Baronzio in the Kress Collection, National Gallery of Art, Washington." *Gazette des Beaux Arts* 35, (May–December 1949): 345–52.

—————. "A Painting by Pantoja and the Legend of the Partridge of St. Nicholas of Tolentino." *Art Quarterly* 22 (1959): 45–55.

—————. "Two Paintings by Botticelli in the Kress Collection." In *Studies in the History of Art Dedicated to William E. Suida on his Eightieth Birthday,* pp. 116–23. London: Phaidon Press, 1959.

—————. *Bartolome Bermejo's "Episcopal Saint": A Study in Medieval Spanish Symbolism.* In *Smithsonian Miscellaneous Collections,* vol. 149, no. 8, pp. 1–21. Washington: Smithsonian Institution, 1966.

—————. "Footnotes to the Painted Page: The Iconography of an Altarpiece by Botticini." *Bulletin of the Metropolitan Museum of Art* (Summer 1969): 1–17.

Friedreich, J. B. *Die Symbolik und Mythologie der Natur.* Würzburg, 1859.

Frinta, Mojmir, S. "The Master of the Gerona Martyrology and Bohemian Illustration." *Art Bulletin* 46, (1964): 283–306.

Fuhrmann, Ernst. *Das Tier in der Religion.* Munich: Muller, 1922.

Galichon, Emil. "Domenico Campagnola: Peintre graveur du XVIe siecle." *Gazette des Beaux-Arts* 17 (1864): 456–61, 536–53.

Garver, Milton Stahl. "Sources of the Beast Similes in the Italian Lyric of the Thirteenth Century." *Romanische Forschungen* 21 (1908): 276–300.

Gauckler, Paul. *Catalogue du Musée Alaoui.* Suppl. Paris, 1910.

Gautier, Leon. *Oeuvres poetiques d'Adam de Saint-Victor.* 3d. ed. Paris, 1894.

Gaya Nuño, Juan Antonio. *La pintura española fuera de España.* Madrid: Espasa-Calpe, S.A., 1958.

Gesner, Konrad. *Historia animalium.* Bk. 3. Zurich, 1555.

Gibbons, Felton. "Jacopo Bertucci of Faenza." *Art Bulletin* 50 (1968): 357–62.

Giehlow, Karl. "Die Hieroglyphenkunde des Humanismus in der Allegorie der Renaissance, besonders der Ehrenpforte Kaiser Maximilian I." *Jahrbuch der Kunsthistorischen Sammlungen des allerhöchsten Kaiserhauses* 32 (1915): 1–232.

Gilles, René. *Le Symbolism dans l'art religieux.* Paris: Mercure de France, 1943.

Giovannino de Grassi. *Taccuino di disegni di Giovannino de Grassi.* Codice della Biblioteca Civica di Bergamo. Bergamo: Edizione Monumenta Bergonensis, 1961.

Goloubew, Victor. *Les Dessins de Jacopo Bellini au Louvre et au British Museum.* 2 vols. Brussels: G. van Oest & Co., 1908–1912.

Gombrich, E. H. "Icones Symbolicae: The Visual Image in Neo-Platonic Thought." *Journal of the Warburg and Courtauld Institute* 11 (1948): 163–92.

———. *Symbolic Images: Studies in the Art of the Renaissance.* London: Phaidon Press, 1972.

Goode, James M. *The Outdoor Sculpture of Washington, D.C.* Washington: Smithsonian Institution Press, 1974.

Gower, John. "Confessio Amantis." In *The Collected Works of John Gower,* edited by G. C. Macaulay. 4 vols. Bk. 3, 11. 2599–2616. Oxford: University Press, 1899–1902.

Grimm, Jacob. *Teutonic Mythology.* 4th ed. Translated by J. S. Stallybrass. 4 vols. New York: Dover Publications, 1966.

Grosart, A. B. *The Life and Complete Works in Prose and Verse of Robert Green.* 15 vols. London: E. Stock, 1881–1896.

Grossman, M. L., and Hamlet, J. *Birds of Prey of the World.* New York: Clarkson N. Potter, 1964.

Gubernatis, Angelo de. *Zoological Mythology.* Vol. 2. London: Trübner & Co., 1872.

Guillaume Le Clerc. *See* Druce, George C., trans.

Guldan, Ernst. *Eva und Maria: Eine Antithese als Bildmotiv.* Graz Köln: Böhlau, 1966.

Gundersheimer, Werner L. *Ferrara: The Style of a Renaissance Despotism.* Princeton, N.J.: Princeton University Press, 1973.

Günther, Klaus. "Das Einhorn: Die eklektische natur-und-symbolgeschtliche Betrachtung eines Fabeltieres." *Sitzungsberichte der Gesellschaft Naturforschender Freunde zu Berlin* 7 (1967): 1–36.

Gurney, John Henry. *Early Annals of Ornithology.* London: H. F. & G. Witherby, 1921.

Haig, Elizabeth. *The Floral Symbolism of the Great Masters.* London: Kegal Paul, Trench, Trübner and Co., 1913.

Hajós, Giza. "Ein unbekanntes Hieronymusrelief aus der Burg Liechtenstein in Niederösterreich." *Oesterreichische Zeitschrift für Kunst und Denkmalspflege* 26 (1972): 32–44.

Hall, Edwin. "Cardinal Albergati, St. Jerome, and the Detroit Van Eyck." *Art Quarterly* 31 (1968): 2–34.

———. "More about the Detroit Van Eyck: The Astrolabe, the Congress of Arras and Cardinal Albergati." *Art Quarterly* 34 (1971): 181–201.

Hall, Joseph. *The Works of Joseph Hall.* Vol. 12, p. 10. Oxford: D. A. Talboys. 1839.

Hand, John. *Joos van Cleve and the Saint Jerome in the Norton Gallery and School of Art*. West Palm Beach, Fla.: Norton Gallery, 1972.

Harbison, Craig. Introduction to the exhibition, "Symbols in Transformation: Iconographic Themes at the Time of the Reformation. An Exhibition of Prints in Memory of Erwin Panofsky." Princeton, N.J.: Princeton University Press, 1969.

Harthan, John P. "Medieval Bestiaries." *Geographic Magazine* 22 (1949): 182–90.

Hartmann, Grisar, S. J. *Luther*. 6 vols. Translated by E. M. Lamond. London: K. Paul Trench, Trübner & Co., 1918.

Hartt, Frederick. "Carpaccio's Meditation on the Passion." *Art Bulletin* 22 (1940): 25–35.

———. *Michelangelo Drawings*. New York: Harry N. Abrams, 1971.

Headley, John M. *Luther's View of Church History*. New Haven: Yale University Press, 1963.

Heckscher, William S. "Bernini's Elephant and Obelisk." *Art Bulletin* 29 (1947): 155–82.

———. "Aphrodite as a Nun." *The Phoenix* 7 (1953): 105–17.

———. "Dornauszieher." In *Reallexikon zur deutschen Kunstgeschichte*, edited by Otto Schmitt. Vol. 4, cols. 289–99. Stuttgart: Alfred Druckenmüller Verlag, 1958.

———. "Reflections on Seeing Holbein's Portrait of Erasmus at Longford Castle." In *Essays in the History of Art* (Festschrift Rudolf Wittkower), pp. 128–48. New York: Phaidon Press, 1967.

Heider, Gustav Adolph. *Schöngraben über Thiersymbolik und das Symbol des Löwen in der christlichen Kunst*. Vienna, 1849.

Heidrich, Ernst. *Die Altdeutsche Malerei*. Jena: Eugen Diederichs Verlag, 1909. Rev. ed by Hans Möhle, 1941.

Heinemann, Fritz. *Giovanni Bellini e i Belliniani*. 2 vols. Venice: N. Pozza. 1962.

Henkel, A., and Schöne, A. *Emblemata. Handbuch zur Sinnbildkunst des XVI und XVII Jahrhunderts*. Stuttgart: J. B. Metzlersche, 1967.

Herodotus. *The History of Herodotus*. Translated by George Rawlinson; edited by Manuel Komroff. New York: Tudor Publishing Co., 1956.

Hervieux, L., ed. *Les Fabulistes Latins: Odonis fabulis addita, collectio secunda. XXI:* "De quadam bestia que vocatur harpia." Vol. 4, p. 401. Paris: Firmin-Didot, 1896.

Herzog, Sadja. *Gossaert, Italy, and the National Gallery's Saint Jerome Penitent*. Reports and Studies in the History of Art. pp. 59–73. Washington: National Gallery of Art, 1970.

Hess, Hanns. *Die Naturanschauung der Renaissance in Italien*. Marburg: Verlag des Kunstgeschichtlichen Seminars, 1924.

Hill, Sir George Francis. *Drawings by Pisanello, a Selection with Introduction and Notes*. Paris and Brussels: G. Van Oest, 1929.

Hill, G. F., and Pollard, G. *Renaissance Medals from the Samuel H. Kress Collection of the National Gallery of Art*. London: Phaidon Press, 1967.

Hiller, Irmgard, and Vey, Horst. Katalog den deutschen und niederländischen Malerei bis 1550. Cologne: Wallraf-Richartz Museum, 1969.

Hind, Arthur M. *Early Italian Engraving: A Critical Catalogue with Complete Reproductions of All Prints Described*. 7 vols. London: B. Quaritch, 1938–1948.

———. *A History of Engraving and Etching from the 15th Century to the Year 1914: being the 3d and fully rev. ed. of "A Short History of Engraving and Etching."* New York: Dover Publications, 1963.

Hinton, N. D. "The Owl and the Nightingale." In *New Catholic Encyclopedia*, vol. 10, p. 841. New York: McGraw Hill & Co., 1967.

Hirn, Yjro. *The Sacred Shrine: A Study of the Poetry and Art of the Catholic Church.* London: Faber and Faber, 1958.

Holbrook, R. *Dante and the Animal Kingdom.* New York: Columbia University Press, 1902.

Holguin, Andres. *La tortuga, simbolo del filosofo.* Bogotá: Ediciones Mito., 1961.

Hollstein, F. W. H. *Dutch and Flemish Etchings, Engravings, Woodcuts, 1400–1750.* Vols. 1–19. Amsterdam: M. Hertzberger, 1949–1976.

Honorius of Autun. "Dominica in septuagesima" in *Speculum Ecclesiae.*" In Migne, *Patrologia Latina,* vol. 172, cols. 855–57. Paris, 1895.

Hoogewerff, Godefridus Joannes. *Jan van Scorel peintre de la Renaissance Hollandaise.* The Hague: Martinus Nijhoff, 1923.

Hopf, Ludwig. *Thierorakel und Orakelthiere in alter und neuer Zeit.* Stuttgart: Kohlhammer, 1888.

Horapollo. *See* Boas, George.

Houghton, W. *Gleanings from the Natural History of the Ancients.* London: Cassel, Petter, & Galpin, 1879.

Howe, William Norton. *Animal Life in Italian Painting.* London: George Allen & Co., 1912.

Howey, M. Oldfield. *The Cat in the Mysteries of Religion and Magic.* New York: A. Richmond, 1931.

Hubert, J., Porcher, J., and Volbach, W. F. *The Carolingian Renaissance.* New York: George Braziller, 1970.

Hugo of Folieto. "De bestiis et aliis rebus." Appendix to the writings of Hugo of St. Victor, in Migne, *Patrologia Latina,* vol. 177. Paris, 1879.

Hugo of Saint Victor. "De arca Noë morali." In Migne, *Patrologia Latina,* vol. 176, cols. 617–80; "De arca Noë mystica," in Migne, *Patrologia Latina,* vol. 176, cols. 681–703. Paris, 1880.

Huhn, Vital. "Löwe und Hund als Symbole des Rechts." *Mainfränkisches Jahrbuch für Geschichte und Kunst* 7 (Würzburg, 1955): 1–63.

Huizinga, Johan. *The Waning of the Middle Ages.* New York: Doubleday Anchor Books, 1954 (originally published in London, 1924).

Hulme, F. Edmund. *The History, Principles and Practice of Symbolism in Christian Art.* London: Swan Sonnenschein & Co., 1892.

Isidore, Saint, of Seville. *Etimologias. Version castellana.* Edited by Luis Cortes y Gongora. Bk. 12, *Los Animales,* Chap. 7, "de Aves." Madrid: Biblioteca de Autores Cristianos, 1951.

———. *Originum sive etymologiarum.* Bk. 20. Edited by W. M. Lindsey. Oxford: Oxford University Press, 1911.

Iversen, Erick. *The Myth of Egypt and its Hieroglyphs.* Copenhagen: Gad, 1961.

Jacobus da Voragine. *See* Voragine, Jacobus de.

James, M. R., ed. *The Bestiary: being a reproduction in full of the manuscript Ii.4.26 in the University Library, Cambridge, with supplementary plates from other manuscripts of English origin, and a preliminary study of the Latin bestiary as current in England.* London: Roxburgh Club, 1928.

Jameson, Anna. *Sacred and Legendary Art.* 9th ed. Vol. 1. London: Longmans, Green, & Co., 1883.

Janson, Horst W. *Apes and Ape Lore in the Middle Ages and the Renaissance.* Studies of the Warburg Institute. London: University of London. 1952.

Jean, L. F. *Dictionnaire de zoologie ou histoire naturelle (encyclopedia theologique) de l'abbe Migne.* Paris, 1853.

Jerome, Saint. "Commentaria in Jonam Prophetam." In Migne, *Patrologia Latina,* vol. 25, cols. 1147–49. Paris, 1880.

————. *Dogmatic and Polemical Works*. Translated by John N. Hritzu. "On the Perpetual Virginity of the Blessed Mary, against Helvidius." In *The Fathers of the Church*, vol. 53, pp. 11–43. Washington: Catholic University of America Press, 1965.

————. *Select Letters. See* Wright, F. A.

Jesse, Wilhelm. "Beiträge und Volkskunde zur Ikonographie des Hasen." *Volkskunde-Arbeit* (1934): 158–75.

Jungblut, Renate. *Hieronymus Darstellung und Verehrung eines Kirchenvaters*. Bamberg; Kleinoffsetdrückerei Kurt Urlaub, 1967.

Kaftal, G. *Iconography of the Saints in Tuscan Painting*. Florence: Sansoni. 1952.

————. *Iconography of the Saints in the Central and Southern Italian Schools of Painting*. Florence: Sansoni, 1965.

Katzenellenbogen, A. *Allegories of the Virtues and Vices in Mediaeval Art from Early Christian Times to the XIIIth Century*. Studies of the Warburg Institute, vol. 10. London: Warburg Institute, 1939.

Keller, O. *Die Antike Tierwelt*. 2 vols. Leipzig: W. Engelmann, 1909–13. (Offset reproduction, Hildesheim, G. Olms, 1963.)

Kellermann, Volkmar. "Der Hirsch." *Germanien* 12 (1940): 128–36; 168–75.

Killermann, Seb. "A. Dürer's Pflanzen und Tierzeichnungen." *Studien der deutschen Kunstgeschichte* 119. Strasbourg, 1910.

————. *Die Vogelkunde des Albertus Magnus (1207–1280)*. Regensburg: Verlagsanstalt vorm. G. J. Manz, 1910.

Kirschbaum, Engelbert; Bandmann, Günter; Braunfels, Wolfgang; Kollwitz, Johannes; and others. *Lexikon der Christlichen Ikonographie*. 4 vols. Rome, Freiburg, Basel, Vienna: Herder, 1968–1972.

Klapper, Joseph. *Aus der Frühzeit des Humanismus, Dichtungen zu Ehren des Heiligen Hieronymus*. Bausteine, Festschrift Max Koch zum 70 Geburtstag. Breslau, M. and H. Marcus, 1926.

————. "Schriften Johanns von Neumarkt." In *Vom Mittelalter zur Reformation*. Vol. 6, pt. 2, esp. pp. 17–19; 499–500. Berlin: Weidmann, 1932.

Klibansky, Raymond; Panofsky, Erwin; and Saxl, Fritz. *Saturn and Melancholy: Studies in the History of Natural Philosophy, Religion, and Art*. New York: Basic Books, 1964.

Klingender, Francis. *Animals in Art and Thought to the End of the Middle Ages*. Cambridge, Mass.: Massachusetts Institute of Technology Press, 1971.

Knipping, John Baptist. *Die iconografi van de contra-reformatie in de Nederlanden*. 2 vols. Hilversum: P. Brand, 1939–1940.

Knortz, Karl. *Die Insekten in Sage, Sitte und Literatur*. Annaberg: Grasers Verlag, 1910.

Knowles, David. *The Evolution of Medieval Thought*. Baltimore: Helicon Press, 1962.

Koch, Robert A. *Joachim Patinir*. Princeton, N. J.: Princeton University Press, 1968.

Koepplin, Dieter, and Falk, Tilman. *Lukas Cranach Gemälde Zeichnungen Druckgraphic*. Basel and Stuttgart: Birkhauser Verlag. 1974 (vol. 1); 1977 (vol. 2).

Kolloff, Edward. *Die sagenhafte und symbolische Thiergeschichte des Mittelalters*. In Friedrich von Raumer, *Historisches Taschenbuch*, ser. 4, vol. 8, pp. 177–269. Leipzig: F. A. Brockhaus, 1867.

Kramer, G. H. *Elenchus vegetabilium et animalium per austriam inferiorem observatum*. Vienna, 1756.

Kris, Ernst. *Georg Haefnagel und der wissenschaftliche Naturalismus*. Festschrift für Julius von Schlosser zum 60 Geburtstage. Zürich, Leipzig, Wien: Amalthea Verlag. 1927.

Kristeller, Paul. *Die lombardische Graphik der Renaissance*. Berlin: Bruno Cassirer, 1913.

Kuhn, Charles L. "Herman Scheere and English Illuminations of the Early Fifteenth Century." *Art Bulletin* 22 (1940): 138–56.

———. *German and Netherlandish Sculpture 1280–1800. The Harvard Collection*. Cambridge, Mass.: Harvard University Press, 1965.

Kuhns, L. Oscar. *The Treatment of Nature in Dante's "Divina Commedia."* New York: Edward Arnold. 1897.

Künstle, Karl. *Ikonographie der Christlichen Kunst*. Vol. 2, pp. 299–307. Freiburg im Breisgau: Herder und Co., C. M. B. H. Verlagsbuchhandlung, 1926.

Kuretsky, Susan Donahue. "Rembrandt's Tree Stump: An Iconographic Attribute of St. Jerome." *Art Bulletin* 56 (1974): 571–80.

Lauchert, Friedrich. *Geschichte des Physiologus*. Strasbourg: K. J. Trübner, 1889.

LeClerc, Guillaume. *See* Druce, George C.

Leeuw, Gerardus Nander. "Gallicinium De Haan in der oudste Hymmen der Westersche Kerk." *Mededeelingen der Nederländsche Akademie van Wetenschappen* (1941), n.s., vol. 4, no. 19, pp. 833–51.

Lehmann-Brockhaus, Otto. "Tierdarstellungen der Fiori di Virtu." *Mittheilungen des Kunsthistorischen Instituts in Florenz* 6 (1940–1941): 1–32.

Lehrs, Max. *Geschichte und kritischer Katalog des deutschen, niederländischen und französischen Kupferstichs im XV. Jahrhunderts*. 9 vols. Vienna: Gesellschaft für vervielfältigende Kunst, 1908–34.

Leisegang, Hans. "Das Mysterium der Schlange: Ein Beitrag zur Erforschung des griechischen Mysterienkultes und seines Fortlebens in der christlichen Welt. *Eranos-Jahrbuch* (1939): 151–250.

Leonardo da Vinci. *See* MacCurdy, Edward.

Lewinsohn, Morus Richard. *Animals, Men, and Myths*. London: Gollancz, 1954.

Liebmann, Michael J. "On the Iconography of the 'Nymph of the Fountain' by Lucas Cranach the Elder." *Journal of Warburg and Courtauld Institute* 31 (1968): 434–37.

Lilienfein, Heinrich. *Lukas Cranach und seine Zeit*. Bielefeld und Leipzig: Velhagen und Klasing, 1942.

Lindsay, Thomas M. *A History of the Reformation*. New York: Charles Scribner & Sons, 1936.

Linfert, Carl. *Hieronymus Bosch: The Paintings*. Garden City, N.Y.: Phaidon Publishers; Doubleday & Co., 1959.

Linnaeus, Carolus. *Systema naturae*, 10th ed., Vol. 1. Uppsala, 1758.

Lipffert, Klementine. *Symbol-Fibel*. Kassel: Johannes Stauda-Verlag, 1961.

Lisini, A. *Le tavolette dipinti di biccherna e di gabella del R. Archivio di Stato in Siena*. Florence: L. S. Olschki, 1904.

Lloyd, Joan Barclay. *African Animals in Renaissance Literature and Art*. Oxford: Clarendon Press, 1971.

Longhi, Roberto. *Officina Ferrarese*. Rome: Le Edizioni d'Italia. 1934. Rev. ed. Florence: Sansoni, 1956.

Lortz, Joseph. *The Reformation in Germany*. Translated by Ronald Walls. Vol. 2. New York: Herder and Herder, 1968.

Lother, Helmut. *Der Pfau in der altchristlichen Kunst*. Leipzig: Dieterich, 1929.

Lüdecke, Heinz. *Lucas Cranach d.Ä. im Spiegel seiner Zeit. Aus Urkunden, Chroniken, Briefen, Reden und Gedichten*. Auftrage der Deutschen Akademie der Künste herausgegeben. Berlin, Rutten, und Loening, 1953.

Lurker, M. "Das Tier in der Bildwelt des Hieronymus Bosch." *Studium generale* 20 (1967): 212–20.

Lutze, Eberhard, and Wiegand, Eberhard. *Die Gemälde des 13. bis 16. Jahrhunderts. Kataloge des Germanischen Nationalmuseums zu Nürnberg.* 2 vols. Leipzig: K. F. Koehler, 1937.

Luz, W. A. "Der Kopf des Kardinals Albrecht bei Dürer, Cranach, und Grünewald." *Repertorium für Kunstwissenschaft* 45 (1925): 41–77.

McCulloch, Florence Turner. *Medieval and French Bestiaries.* University of North Carolina, Studies in the Romance Languages and Literatures, no. 33. Chapel Hill: University of North Carolina Press, 1962.

MacCurdy, Edward. *The Notebooks of Leonardo da Vinci.* New York: George Braziller, 1954.

McKenzie, Kenneth. "Per la storia die bestiarii italiani." *Giornalo storico della letteratura italiana* 64, (1914): 35–371.

Macku, Anton. "Zur Symbolik an Pilgrams Kanzel des Wiener Stephansdomes." In *Der Dom* (Mitteilungsblatt des Wiener Domerhaltungsvereins). Vol. 2. Vienna, 1969.

Mâle, Emil. *The Gothic Image. Religious Art in France of the Thirteenth Century.* Translated by Dora Nussey. New York: Harper Torchbooks, 1958 (originally published in 1913 by E. P. Dutton & Co.).

———. *Religious Art from the Twelfth to the Eighteenth Century.* (Original French title, *L'Art religieux du XIIe au XVIIIe siècle.*) New York: Noonday Press, 1958.

Mariacher, Giovanni. *Il Museo Correr di Venezia. Dipinti dal XIV al XVI Secolo.* Venice: Neri Pozza Editore, 1957.

Marle, Raimond van. *The Development of the Italian Schools of Painting.* 18 vols. The Hague: Martinus Nijhof, 1923–38.

Marlier, Georges. *Erasme et la peinture flamande de son temps.* (Esp. Chap. 6, "Saint Jérôme, patron des humanistes chrétiens," pp. 169–216.) Damme: Musée van Maerlant, 1954.

Marquand, Allan. *Luca della Robbia.* Princeton, N.J.: Princeton University Press, 1914.

———. *Giovanni della Robbia.* Princeton, N.J.: Princeton University Press, 1920.

———. *Andrea della Robbia.* Princeton, N.J.: Princeton University Press, 1922.

———. *The Brothers of Giovanni della Robbia.* Princeton, N.J.: Princeton University Press, 1928.

Martin, E. W. *The Birds of the Latin Poets.* Palo Alto, Calif.: Leland Stanford University Publications; University Series, 1914.

Martinez, C. Lopez. "San Jeronimo penitente; magnifica escultura de Juan Martinez Montañes." (Esp. Arte no. 87, pp. 267–81.) *Rev. Archivio,* 1949.

Mather, Frank Jewett, Jr. *A History of Italian Painting.* New York: Henry Holt & Co., 1923.

Maurer, Friedrich. *Der altdeutsche Physiologus.* Altdeutsche Textbibiolthek, no. 67. Tübingen: Niemeyer, 1967.

Mayor, A. H. *Late Gothic Engravings of Germany and the Netherlands.* New York: Dover Publications, 1968.

———. *Prints and People.* New York: Metropolitan Museum of Art, 1971.

Megenberg, Konrad von. *Das Buch der Natur* (1481). Translated by Franz Pfeiffer. Hildesheim: Georg Olms Verlagsbuchhandlung, 1962.

Meinhof, Werner. "Leonardos Hieronymus." *Repertorium für Kunstwissenschaft* 52 (1931): 101–24.

Meiss, Millard. "Jan van Eyck and the Italian Renaissance." In *Venezia e l'Europa.* Proceedings of the Eighteenth International Congress of Art Historians, pp. 58–69. Venice, 1956.

———. "French and Italian Variations on an Early Fifteenth Century Theme: St. Jerome in His Study." *Gazette des Beaux-Arts* 62 (1963): 147–70.

———. *Painting in Florence and Siena after the Black Death*. New York: Harper Torch Books, Harper & Row, 1964, (first published by Princeton University Press, 1951).

———. *Giovanni Bellini's St. Francis in the Frick Collection*. Princeton, N.J.: Princeton University Press, 1964.

———. *French Painting in the Time of Jean de Berry*. London: Phaidon Press, 1967.

———. *French Painting in the Time of Jean de Berry, the Boucicaut Master*. London: Phaidon Press, 1968.

———. *The Great Age of Fresco: Giotto to Pontormo*. New York: Metropolitan Museum of Art, 1968.

———. *The Great Age of Fresco: Discoveries, Recoveries, and Survivals*. New York: George Braziller, in association with the Metropolitan Museum of Art, 1970.

———. "Scholarship and Penitence in the Early Renaissance: The Image of St. Jerome." *Pantheon* 32 (1974): 134–40.

Meiss, Millard, and Beatson, Elizabeth H. *The Belles Heures of Jean, Duke of Berry*. New York: George Braziller, 1974.

Melito (S. Melitonis Clavis). "De Avibus." Chap. 8 of Pitra, J. B., *Analecta novissima spicilegii solesmensis*. 3 vols. Graz: Akademische Druck-u Verlagsanstalt, 1963.

Ménard, René. *La Mythologie dans l'art ancien et moderne*. Paris: Librairie Ch. Delagrave, 1880.

Middeldorf, Ulrich. *Medals and Plaquettes from the Sigmund Morgenroth Collection*. Chicago: Art Institute, 1944.

———. "Filarete?" *Mitteilungen des Kunsthistorischen Institutes in Florenz* 17 (1973): 75–86.

Migne, Jacques Paul. *Patrologia Latina*. 221 vols. and supplements. Paris, 1844–1903.

Millar, Eric G. *English Manuscript Illuminations from the 10th to the 13th Centuries*. Paris: G. Van Oest, 1926.

Mode, Heinz. *Fabulous Beasts and Demons*. London: Phaidon Press, 1975.

Möller, Lise Lotte. *Bestiarium: Tiere in der Kunst der letzteren fünf Jahrtausende*. Hamburg: Museum für Kunst und Gewerbe, 1962.

Molsdorf, Wilhelm. *Christliche Symbolik der Mittelalterischen Kunst*. Graz: Akademische Druck-u Verlagsanstalt, 1968.

Mone, Franz Joseph. *Lateinische Hymnen des Mittelalters*. Vol. 2. *Marienlieder*. Freiburg im Breisgau: Herder, 1854.

Monroy, Ernst Friedrich von. *Embleme und Emblembucher in den Niederlanden 1560–1630*. Utrecht: Haentjens Dikker and Gumbert, 1964.

Monteiro, Mariana. *The Life of Saint Jerome, The Great Doctor of the Church, in Six Books, from the Original Spanish of the Reverend Father Fray José de Siguenza*. London: Sands and Co., 1907.

Morris, F. O. *A History of British Birds*. 2d ed. Vol. 1. London: Bell and Daldy, 1870.

Morrona, Alessandro da. *Pisa illustrata nelle arti del disegno*. 2d ed. 3 vols. Livorno: G. Marenigh, 1812.

Moschos, Joannes, and Sophronius, Patriarch of Jerusalem. "Pratum Spirituale." In Migne, *Patrologia Latina*, vol. 74, cols. 172–74. Paris, 1878.

Moya, Salvador de. "Biblioteca Geneologica Latina." *Revista Geneologica Latin*. Suppl. São Paulo,, 1961.

Muller, Herbert J. *The Uses of the Past: Profiles of Former Societies*. New York: Oxford University Press, 1957.

Münch, Hans. *Der Wiedehopf*. Die Neue Brehm-Bücherei. Leipzig: Akademische Verlagsgesellschaft Geest und Portig, 1952.

Murphy, Francis Xavier, ed. *A Monument to Saint Jerome*. (Esp. pp. 155–63, by E. P. Burke.) New York: Sheed and Ward, 1952.

Muzeum Narodowe Zbiory Czartoryskich Krakow. *La Peinture italienne des XIVᵉ et XVᵉ siècles*. Cracow Museum, 1961.

National Gallery of Art. *Summary Catalogue of European Paintings and Sculptures*. Washington: National Gallery of Art, 1965.

Neckam, Alexander. *De naturis rerum*. Edited by Thomas Wright. London: Longman, Roberts, and Green, 1863.

Neumarkt, Johanns von. *Schriften*. In J. Klapper, *Vom Mittelalter zur Reformation*, vol. 7, pt. 2. Berlin: Weidmann, 1932.

Newton, Alfred. *A Dictionary of Birds*. London: Adam and Charles Black, 1893–1896.

Norris, C. "The St. Jerome from Sanssouci." *Burlington Magazine* 95 (1953): 391.

Odo of Cheriton. *Les Fabulistes Latin: Odonis fabulis addita, collectio secunda*. XXI: "De quadam bestia que vocatur harpia." Edited by L. Hervieux. Vol. 4, p. 401. Paris: Firmin-Didot, 1896.

Oertel, Robert. *Frühe Italienische Malerei in Altenburg*. Berlin: Henschelverlag Kunst und Gesellschaft, 1961.

Offner, Richard. "A Saint Jerome by Masolino." *Art in America* 8 (1920): 68–76.

Oswald, F. "Die Darstellungen des Hl. Hieronymus beim Meister des Bartholomäusaltares." *Wallraf-Richartz Jahrbuch*, 23 (1961): 342–46.

Owst, Gerald Robert. *Preaching in Medieval England: An Introduction to Sermon Manuscripts of the Period c. 1350–1450*. Cambridge: Cambridge University Press, 1926.

Pächt, Otto. "Early Italian Nature Studies and the Early Calendar Landscape." *Journal of the Warburg and Courtauld Institutes* 13 (1950): 13–47.

———. "Zur Entstehung des 'Hieronymus im Gehäuse.'" *Pantheon* 21 (1963): 131–42.

Painter, William. *The Palace of Pleasure* (originally printed 1566–1567). Edited by J. Jacobs. 3 vols. London: David Nutt, 1890.

Palliser, Mrs. Bury (Fanny M.). *Historic Devices, Badges, and War-Cries*. London: Sampson Lowe, Son, and Marston, 1870.

Palluchini, Rodolfo. *La pittura veneziana del trecento*. Venice and Rome: Istituto per la Collaborazione Culturale, 1964.

Pangritz, Walter. *Das Tier in der Bibel*. Munich: Reinhardt, 1963.

Panofsky, Dora. "The Textual Basis of the Utrecht Psalter Illustrations." *Art Bulletin* 25 (1943): 50–58.

Panofsky, Erwin. "A Letter to St. Jerome: A Note on the Relationship between Petrus Christus and Jan van Eyck." In *Studies in Art and Literature for Belle da Costa Greene*, pp. 102–8. Princeton, N.J.: Princeton University Press, 1954.

———. *Albrecht Dürer*. 2 vols. Princeton, N.J.: Princeton University Press, 1955.

———. *The Life and Art of Albrecht Dürer*. Princeton, N.J.: Princeton University Press, 1955.

———. *Early Netherlandish Painting*. 2 vols. 2d printing. Cambridge, Mass.: Harvard University Press, 1958. (Paperback ed., 1971.)

———. *Renaissance and Renascences in Western Art*. Copenhagen: Russack & Co., 1960.

———. *Studies in Iconology: Humanistic Themes in the Art of the Renaissance* New York: Harper Torch Books, Harper & Row, 1962 (originally published, 1939, by Oxford University Press, New York).

———. "The Mouse that Michelangelo Failed to Carve." In *Essays in Memory of Karl Lehmann*, edited by Lucy Freeman Sandler, pp. 242–51. New York: Institute of Fine Arts, New York University, 1964.

———. *Studies in Titian, Mostly Iconographic*. New York: New York University Press, 1969.

Panzer, Friedrich. *Beitrag zur deutschen Mythologie*. Munich: 1848–1855.

Parmelee, Alice. *All the Birds of the Bible: Their Stories, Identification and Meaning*. New York: Harper Brothers, 1959.

Parshall, Peter W. "Albrecht Dürer's 'St. Jerome in his Study': A Philological Reference." *Art Bulletin* 53 (1971): 303–5.

Pauli, Gustav. *Hans Sebald Beham: Ein Kritisches Verzeichnis seiner Kupferstiche, Radirungen und Holzschnitte*. Strassburg: J. H. Ed. Heitz (Heitz und Mündel), 1901.

Perocco, Guido. *Carpaccio: Nella scuola di S. Giorgio degli Schiavoni*. Venice: Ferdinando Ongania, 1964.

Pfeiffer, Franz. *See* Megenberg, Konrad.

Philip, Lotte Brand. "The Peddler by Hieronymus Bosch: A Study in Detection." *Nederlands Kunsthistorisch Jaarboek* 9 (1958): 1–81.

Phipson, Emma. *Animal Lore of Shakespeare's Time*. London: K. Paul, Trench and Co., 1883.

Pierre de Beauvais. *French Prose Bestiary*. In *Mélanges d'archéologie, d'histoire, et de littérature*. Edited by C. Cahier and A. Martin. Vol. 2, no. 16, p. 157: "De la arpie, sa natur." Paris: Fermin-Didot, 1851.

Pigler, A. "Astrology and Jerome Bosch." *Burlington Magazine* 92 (1950): 132–36.

———. *Barockthemen. Eine Auswahl von Verzeichnissen zur Ikonographie des 17. und 18. Jahrhunderts*. Vol. 1. Budapest: Verlag der Ungarischen Akademie der Wissenschaften, 1956.

———. "La Mouche peinte: Un talisman." *Bulletin du Musée Hongrois des Beaux-Arts* 24 (1964): 47–64.

Pillion, Louise. "La Légende de Saint Jérôme d'après quelques peintures italiennes du XVe siècle au Musée du Louvre." *Gazette des Beaux-Arts*, ser. 3, vol. 39 (1908): 303–18.

———. "Trois faits de la légende de Saint Jérôme illustrés dans une prédelle de Signorelli." *Revue de l'Art Chrétien* 53 (1910): 31.

Pinedo, Ramiro de. *El simbolismo en la escultura medieval española*. Madrid: Espasa-Calpe, 1930.

Piper, Ferdinand. *Mythologie und Symbolik der Christlichen Kunst von der ältesten Zeit bis ins sechzehnte Jahrhundert*. Vol. 1 (esp. pp. 377–93). Weimar: Druck und Verlag des Landes-Industrie-Comptoirs, 1847.

Pitra, Jean Baptiste. *Analecta novissima spicilegii solesmensis*. 3 vols. Graz: Akademische Druck-und Verlagsanstalt, 1963. (*See* Melito.)

Planiscig, Leo. *Desiderio da Settignano*. Vienna: Verlag Anton Schroll & Co., 1942.

Pliny (Plinius, Caius Secundus). *Libri naturalis historiae*. Venice: J. Spira, 1469.

———. *Natural History*. Translated by John Bostock and H. T. Riley. 6 vols. London: Bell, 1855–1890. (*See also* Rackham, H.)

Pöllmann, O. B., Father Ansgar. "Von der Entwicklung des Hieronymus-Typus in der älteren Kunst." *Benediktinische Monatsschrift* 2 (1920): 438–522.

Pope, Hugh. "St. Jerome: Bird-watcher and Naturalist." *Clergy Review* 26 (1946): 237–52.

Pope-Hennessy, John. *Italian Renaissance Sculpture*. London: Phaidon Press, 1958.

———. *Italian Bronze Statuettes*. London: Phaidon Press, 1961.

———. *Renaissance Bronzes from the Samuel H. Kress Collection.* London: Phaidon Press for the Samuel H. Kress Foundation, New York, 1965.

———. *Essays on Italian Sculpture.* New York and London: Phaidon Press, 1968.

Popham, A. E., and Pouncey, Philip. *Italian Drawings in the British Museum: Fourteenth and Fifteenth Centuries.* 2 vols. London: British Museum, 1950.

Popitz, Klaus. *Tiere und Pflanzen in der Graphik.* Berlin-Dahlem: Staatliche Museen Berlin Kunstbibliothek, 1967.

Pordenone. Exhibition catalogue: *San Girolamo nella pittura e nell' incisione dell '500, '600, '700.* Pordenone: Centro Studi, 1968.

Post, Chandler Rathfon. *A History of Spanish Painting.* 14 vols. in 20. Cambridge, Mass.: Harvard University Press, 1930–66.

Praz, Mario. *Studies in Seventeenth Century Imagery.* 2d ed. Rome: Edizioni di Storia e letteratura, 1964.

Procacci, Ugo. "Opere sconosciute d'arte toscana." *Rivista d'Arte* 14 (1932): p. 474, figs. 6, 7.

———. "Una 'vita' inedita del Muziano." *Arte Veneta* (1954): 242–64.

Proske, Beatrice Gilman. *Juan Martinez Montañes, Sevillian Sculptor.* New York: Hispanic Society, 1967.

Rackham, H. trans. *Pliny, Natural History.* 10 vols. Loeb Classical Library edition. Cambridge, Mass.: Harvard University Press, 1938–1940.

Radowitz, Joseph Maria von. "Devisen und Mottos des spätern Mittelalters." In *Gesammelte Schriften*, vol. 1. Berlin: G. Reimer, 1852.

Randall, Lilian M. C. "The Snail in Gothic Marginal Warfare." *Speculum* 37 (1962): 358–67.

———. *Images in the Margins of Gothic Manuscripts.* Los Angeles and Berkeley: University of California Press, 1966.

Réau, Louis. "Le Saint Jérôme d'Albert Dürer au Musee de Lisbonne." *Gazette des Beaux-Arts,* ser. 5, vol. 18 (1928): 297–304.

———. *French Painting in the XIVth, XVth, and XVIth Centuries.* Translated by Mary Chamot. London, Paris, New York: Hyperion Press, 1939.

———. *Histoire de la peinture au Moyen-Age: La Miniature.* Melun: Librairie d'Argence, 1946.

———. *Iconographie de l'art chrétien.* Vols. 1–3. Paris: Presses universitaires de France, 1955–58.

Redslob, Edwin. *Gemäldegalerie Berlin-Dahlem, Ehemals Kaiser-Friedrich-Museum.* Baden-Baden: Holle Verlag, 1964.

Reusner, Nicolaus. *Emblemata Nicolai Reusneri.* Frankfurt: Ioannem Feyerabendt, 1581.

Reuterswärd, Patrick. *Sinn und Nebensinn bei Dürer: Randbemerkungen zur 'Melancolia I.' Gestalt und Wirklichkeit.* Edited by R. Muhler. Festgabe für Ferdinand Weinhandl. Berlin, 1967.

———. *Hieronymus Bosch.* Uppsala: Acta Universitatis Uppsaliensis, 1970.

Richardson, E. P. "The Detroit St. Jerome by Jan van Eyck." *Art Bulletin* 19 (1956): 232–33.

Richter, G. M. "Pisanello Studies I." *Burlington Magazine* 55 (1929): 59–66.

Ring, Grete. "St. Jerome Extracting the Thorn from the Lion's Foot." *Art Bulletin* 27 (1945): 188–94.

Ripa, Cesare. *Iconologia de Cesare Ripa accresciuta dell'Abate Cesare Orlandi;* 5 vols. Perugia: P. Constantini, 1764–1767.

Roberts, Helen I. " 'St. Augustine in St. Jerome's Study:' Carpaccio's Painting and its Legendary Source." *Art Bulletin* 41 (1959): 283–301.

Robin, Percy Ansell. *Animal Lore in English Literature.* London: John Murray, 1932.

Roggen, D. "J. Bosch: Literatuur en Folklore." *Gentsche Bijdragen tot de Kunstgeschiedenis* 6 (Ghent, 1939–1940): 107–26.

Rolland, Eugène. *Faune populaire de la France*. Vol. 2: *Les Oiseaux sauvages, noms vulgaires, dictons, proverbes, légendes, contes et superstitions*. Paris: Maisonneuve & Cie., 1879; vol. 10: *Les Oiseux sauvages, seconde partie*, 1915.

Rosand, David, and Muraro, Michelangelo. *Titian and the Venetian Woodcut*. Washington: International Exhibitions Foundation, 1976.

Rosen, Felix. *Die Natur in der Kunst: Studien eines Naturforschers zur Geschichte der Kunst*. Leipzig: B. G. Teubner, 1903.

Rosenberg, Jakob. "On the Meaning of a Bosch Drawing." In *De Artibus Opuscula, Essays in Honor of Erwin Panofsky*, pp. 422–26. New York: New York University Press, 1961.

———. "Lucas Cranach the Elder: A Critical Appreciation." In *Record of the Art Museum, Princeton University*, vol. 28, no. 1, pp. 27–53. Princeton, N.J., 1969.

Rowland, Beryl. *Animals with Human Faces*. Knoxville: University of Tennessee Press, 1973.

Rudolphi, Friedrich. *Gotha Diplomatica; oder Ausführliche Historische Beschreibung des Fürstenthums Sacshen-Gothe*. Frankfurt am Main und Leipzig, 1717.

Ruhmer, Eberhard. *Grünewald: The Paintings* (with two essays by J. K. Huysmans). New York: Phaidon Publishers, 1958.

———. *Tura, Paintings and Drawings*. New York: Phaidon Publishers, 1958.

———. *Cranach*. New York: Phaidon Publishers, 1963.

Runge, Paul. *Die Lieder und Melodien der Geiszler des Jahres 1349 nach den Aufzeichnung Hugo's von Reutlingen*. Leipzig: Breitkopf und Härtel, 1900. (An offset reproduction of this work was issued in Wiesbaden in 1969 by Breitkopf and Härtel.)

Rupprich, Hans. *Dürer's Stellung zu den agnostischen und kunstfeindlichen Strömungen seiner Zeit*. Munich: Verlag Bayerischen, Akademie der Wissenschaft, 1959.

Salmi, M. *Mostra storica nazionale della miniatura*. Florence, 1953.

———. *Cosme Tura*. Milano Istituto Editoriale Electa, 1957.

Salter, Emma Gurney. *Nature in Italian Art*. London: Adam & Charles Black, 1912.

Salzer, Anselm. *Die Sinnbilder und Beiworte Mariens in der deutschen Literatur und lateinischer Hymnenpoesie des Mittelalters. Mit Berücksichtigung der patristischen Literatur*. Linz: K.u.k. Hofbuchdruckerei Jos. Feichtingers Erben, 1893.

Sälzle, Karl. *Tier und Mensch, Gottheit und Dämon: Das Tier in der Geistesgeschichte der Menschheit*. Munich: Bayerische Landwirtschaftsverlag, 1965.

Santillana, Giorgio di. *The Age of Adventure: The Renaissance Philosophers*. New York: Mentor Books, New American Library, 1956.

Schapiro, Meyer. "Muscipula diaboli: The Symbolism of the Merode Altarpiece by the Master of Flemalle." *Art Bulletin* 27 (1945): 182–87.

Scheller, R. W. *A Survey of Medieval Model Books*. Haarlem: Teylers Tweede Genootschap, 1963.

Schilder, F. A. "Die ethnologische Bedeutung der Porzellanschnecke." *Ethnologie* 58 (1926): 313–20.

Schilling, Edmund. "Täfelchen mit dem heiligen Hieronymus." *Zeitschrift für Kunstwissenschaft* 11 (1957): 175–84.

Schmitt, O. "Baum." In *Reallexikon zur deutschen Kunstgeschichte*, vol. 2, pp. 63–73. Stuttgart-Waldsee, 1948.

Schreiber, Wilhelm L. *Handbuch der Holz und Metallschnitte des XV. Jahrhunderts*. Vol. 3. Leipzig: K. W. Hiersemann, 1927.

Schubring, Paul. *Die Plastik Sienas im Quattrocento*. Berlin: G. Grotesche Verlagsbuchhandlung, 1907.

Schwarz, Heinrich, and Plagemann, Volker. "Eule." In *Reallexikon zur deutschen Kunstgeschichte*, vol. 6, cols. 267–322. Stuttgart: Alfred Druckemüller Verlag, 1970.

Seligmann, K. "Hieronymus Bosch: 'The Peddler'" *Gazette des Beaux-Arts* 42 (1953): 97–104.

Seymour, Charles. *Masterpieces of Sculpture from the National Gallery of Art*. Washington: National Gallery of Art, 1949.

Seznec, Jean. *The Survival of the Pagan Gods: The Mythological Tradition and Its Place in Renaissance Humanism and Art*. Translated by Barbara Sessions. New York: Bollingen Series, Pantheon Books, 1953. (Originally published in French as "*La Survivance des dieux antiques.*" Studies of the Warburg Institute, XI, 1940.)

Shapley, Fern R. "Giovanni Bellini and Cornaro's Gazelle." *Gazette des Beaux-Arts*, ser. 6 (1945): 27–30.

———. *Paintings from the Samuel H. Kress Collection. Italian Schools, XIII–XV Century*. London: Phaidon Press, 1966.

———. *Paintings from the Samuel H. Kress Collection. Italian Schools, XV–XVI Century*. London: Phaidon Press, 1968.

Shepard, Odell. *The Lore of the Unicorn*. London: G. Allen and Unwin, 1930.

Shestack, Alan. *Master E. S. Five Hundredth Anniversary Exhibition*. Philadelphia: Museum of Art, 1967.

Simrock, Karl Joseph. *Handbuch der deutschen Mythologie*. 2d ed. Bonn: A. Marcus, 1864.

Sindona, Enio. *Pisanello*. Translated by John Ross. New York: Harry N. Abrams, 1961.

Skinner, C. M. *Myths and Legends of Flowers, Trees, Fruits, and Plants*. 5th imp. Philadelphia: J. R. Lippincott Co., 1925.

Slive, Seymour. *Frans Hals*. National Gallery of Art: Kress Foundation. Studies in the History of European Art. Vols. 1, 2, 3. London: Phaidon Press, 1970–1974.

Smith, Earl Baldwin. *The Dome*. Princeton, N.J.: Princeton University Press, 1950.

Snyder, James. *Bosch in Perspective*. Englewood Cliffs, N.J.: Prentice-Hall, 1973.

Spitz, Lewis W. *The Religious Renaissance of the German Humanists*. Cambridge, Mass.: Harvard University Press, 1963.

Stange, Alfred. *Deutsche Malerei der Gotik*. Berlin: Deutschen Kunstverlag München, 1960.

Stauch, Lieselotte. "Drache." In *Reallexikon zur deutschen Kunstgeschichte*, vol. 4, cols. 342–66. Stuttgart: Alfred Druckemüller Verlag, 1958.

Stechow, Wolfgang. *Northern Renaissance Art 1400–1600: Sources and Documents*. Englewood Cliffs, N.J.: Prentice-Hall, 1966.

———. "*Peter Paul Rubens's Deborah Kip, Wife of Sir Balthasar Gerbier, and Her Children.*" Studies in the History of Art. Washington: National Gallery of Art, 1973.

Strieder, Pieter. *Deutsche Malerei der Renaissance*. Königstein im Taunus: Langewiesche Nachfolger Köster, 1966.

Strompen, C. "Maddonnenbilder Lucas Cranach's in Innsbruck." *Zeitschrift des Ferdinandeums für Tirol und Vorarlberg*, ser. 3, vol. 39 (1895): 305–34.

Strümpell, Anna. "Hieronymus im Gehäuse." *Marburger Jahrbuch für Kunstwissenschaft* 2 (1925–26): 173–252.

Stuart, Dorothy M. *A Book of Birds and Beasts, Legendary, Literary, and Historical*. London: Methuen, 1957.

Sühling, F. *Die Taube in christlichen Altertum*. Freiburg, 1930.

Suida, Wilhelm E. "Über eine Darstellung des heiligen Hieronymus von Albrecht Dürer." *Reportorium für Kunstwissenschaft* 23 (1900): 315.

———. "Tizians Darstellungen des heiligen Hieronymus." *Kirchenkunst* 5 (1933): 158.

———. *A Catalogue of Paintings in the John and Mable Ringling Museum of Art.* Sarasota, Fla.: Ringling Museum of Art, 1949.

———. *Italian Paintings and Northern Sculpture from the Samuel H. Kress Collection: Atlanta Art Association Galleries.* Atlanta: Atlanta Art Gallery, 1958.

Supino, Igino Benvenuto. *Jacopo della Quercia.* Bologna: Casa Editrice Apollo, 1926.

Swainson, Charles. *Provincial Names and Folk Lore of British Birds.* London: E. Stack, 1885.

Taylor, Henry Osborn. *The Medieval Mind.* 4th ed. 2 vols. London: Macmillan and Co., 1938.

Tertullian (Quintus Septimus Florens Tertullianus). *Apologeticus, De spectaculis.* With an English translation by T. R. Glover. Cambridge, Mass.: Harvard University Press, 1960.

Tervarent, Guy de. *Attributes et symboles dans l'art profane, 1450–1600.* Vol. 2. Geneva: Librairie E. Droz, 1959.

Thompson, D'Arcy Wentworth. "Swallows in the House." *Classical Review* 5 (1891): 231.

———. *A Glossary of Greek Birds.* Oxford: Clarendon Press, 1895.

———. "On Bird and Beast in Ancient Symbolism." *Transactions, Royal Society of Edinburgh* 38 (1897): 179–92.

———. "Swallows in the House." *Classical Review* 42 (1928): 245.

Thulin, Oskar. "Um Cranachs Künstlertum und Persönlichkeit." In *Luther, Mitteilungen d. Luthergesellschaft,* pp. 87–96. Munich, 1955.

Tietze, Hans. "Der heilige Hieronymus von Lukas Cranach." *Kunst und Künstler* 27 (1929): 314–16.

———. *Titian: Paintings and Drawings.* Vienna: Phaidon Press, 1937.

Tietze, Hans, and Tietze-Conrat, E. "Tizian Studien." *Jahrbuch der Kunsthistorischen Sammlungen in Wien,* n.s., 10 (1936): 137–92.

———. "Domenico Campagnola's Graphic Art." *Print Collectors' Quarterly* 26 (1939): 311–33; 445–69.

———. *The Drawings of the Venetian Painters of the 15th and 16th Centuries.* New York: J. J. Augustin. 1944.

Timmers, J. J. M. *Symboliek en Iconographie der christelijke Kunst.* Roermond-Maaseik: J. J. Romen en Zonen, 1947.

Toesca, Pietro. *La pittura e la miniatura nella Lombardia. Dai più antichi monumenti alla metà del quattrocento.* Turin: Giulio Einaudi editore, 1966.

Tolnay, Charles de. *Hieronymus Bosch.* Basel: Les Editions Holbein, 1937.

———. *Michelangelo.* Vol. 5. *The Final Period.* Princeton, N.J.: Princeton University Press, 1960.

———. *Hieronymus Bosch.* London: Reynal & Co., in association with William Morrow & Co., 1966.

Topsell, Edward. *The historie of foure-footed beastes, describing the true and lively figure of every beast, with a discourse of their severall names, conditions, kindes, vertues . . . collected out of all the volumes of Conradus Gesner and all other writers to this present day.* London: W. Iaggard, 1607.

Townsend, Horace. *Catalogue of Collection of Signor Stefano Bardini to be Sold April 23–27, 1918.* New York: American Art Association, 1918.

Tripp, G. "Restaurierung gotischer Fresken in Schloss Clam." *Oesterreichische Zeitschrift für Kunst und Denkmalspflege* 6 (1952): 88–90.

Troche, Ernst Günter. "Schlesische Quellen zur altniederländischen Malerei." *Pantheon* 21 (1938): 128–31.

Turner, A. Richard. *The Vision of Landscape in Renaissance Italy*. First paperback ed. Princeton, N.J., and London: Princeton University Press, 1974.

Vaccari, Alberto, S. J. "Un prossimo centenario o la morte di San Girolamo." *La Civilita Cattolica* 68, (1918): 202–16; 503–13.

———. "Le antiche vite di San Girolamo." In *Miscellanea Geronimiana*, pp. 1–18. Rome: Tip. Poliglotta Vaticano, 1920.

van de Waal, H. "Rembrandt's Faust Etching: A Socinian Document and the Iconography of the Inspired Scholar." *Oud-Holland* 79, no. 1 (1964): 11–12; 37–44.

———. "Hommage au Professor Panofsky." *Gazette des Beaux-Arts*, period 6, vol. 71 (1968), p. 261.

Vasari, Giorgio. *The Lives of the Painters, Sculptors, and Architects*. Translated by A. B. Hinds. Vol. 1, p. 185. London and Toronto: J. M. Dent and Sons (Everyman's Library), 1927.

Vavala, E. Sandberg. "Story of Jerome: Predella Attributed to the Brothers Salimbeni of San Severino." *Burlington Magazine* 68 (1936): 95–97.

Venturi, Adolfo. "Francesco di Giorgio Martini scultore." *l'Arte* 26 (1908): 197–228.

———. *L'arte e San Girolamo*. Milan: Fratelli Treves, 1924.

Vincent of Beauvais. *Speculum naturale*. 2 vols. Bk. 16, chap. 94, cols. 1211–12, "de Harpya." Strasbourg: Adolf Rusch, 1478 (or later).

Vinycomb, John. *Fictitious and Symbolic Creatures in Art*. London: Chapman and Hall, 1906.

Virgil. *The Aeniad of Virgil*. Translated by C. Day Lewis. London: The Hogarth Press, 1961.

Volkmann, Ludwig. *Bilderschriften der Renaissance. Hieroglyphik und Emblematic in ihren Beziehungen und Fortwirkungen*. Leipzig: K. W. Hiersemann, 1923.

Vollmer, Hans. *Allgemeines Lexikon der Bildenden Künstler von der Antike bis zum Gegenwart*. Vols. 22, 34. Leipzig: Verlag von E. A. Seemann, 1940.

Voragine, Jacobus de. *Legenda aurea* (3 editions consulted):

    1. Jacobi a Voragine. *Legenda aurea: Vulgo historia Lombardica dicta ad optimorum librorum fidem*. Edited by Th. Graesse. Reproductio phototypica editionis tertiae 1890. Osnabrück: Otto Zeller, 1965.

    2. *The Golden Legend or Lives of the Saints, as Englished by Wm. Caxton*. Edited by F. S. Ellis. Vol. 5. London: Temple Classic Series, 1900.

    3. *The Golden Legend of "Jacobus de Voragine."* Translated and adapted from the Latin by Granger Ryan and Helmut Ripperger. Part 2. London, New York, Toronto: Longmans, Green and Co., 1941.

Waddell, Helen J. *Beasts and Saints*. London: Constable & Co., 1934.

Waetzoldt, Wilhelm. *Dürer and his Times*. Translated by R. H. Boothroyd. London: Phaidon Press, 1950.

Waldmann, Emil. *Albrecht Altdorfer*. London: Medici Society, 1923.

Wardle, William L. "Beelzebub." In *Encyclopaedia Brittanica*, ed. 14, vol. 3, pp. 313. London, Chicago, New York, 1936.

Weicker, Georg. *Der Seelenvogel in der alten Literatur und Kunst*. Leipzig, 1902.

Weise, Georg. *Dürer und die Ideale der Humanisten*. Tübingen: Kunsthistorisches Institut der Universität, 1953.

Weiss, Roberto. "Some Van Eyckian Illuminations from Italy: Representations of St. Jerome." *Journal of the Warburg and Courtauld Institutes* 18 (1955): 319–21.

Wellmann, Max. "Der Physiologus: Eine religionsgeschichtlichnaturwissenschaftliche Untersuchung." *Philologus*, suppl., vol. 22, pt. 1 (1930): 1–116.

Wertheim Aymes, Clement Antoine. *Hieronymus Bosch: Eine Einführung in seine geheime Symbolik*. Amsterdam: V. H. Van Ditmar, N. V., 1957.

Wescher, Paul. "Zanetto Bugatto and Rogier van der Weyden." *Art Quarterly* 25 (1962): 209–13.

White, T. H. *The Bestiary. A Book of Beasts, Being a Translation from a Latin Bestiary of the Twelfth Century*. New York: Capricorn Books. G. P. Putnam's Sons, 1966.

Wilczynski, Beatrice. "Matteo di Giovanni: Two Episodes of St. Jerome." *Chicago Art Institute Quarterly* 50 (1956): 74–76.

Williamson, George C., ed. *Anonimo (Marcantonio Michiel)*. Translated by Paolo Mussi. (Reissue.) New York, London: Benjamin Blom, 1969.

Wind, Edgar. "Studies in Allegorical Portraiture. I. Albrecht von Brandenburg as St. Erasmus." *Journal of the Warburg and Courtauld Institutes* 1 (1937). 142–82.

Windelband, W. *Lehrbuch der Geschichte der Philosophie*. (Esp. Chap. 4, "Philosophie der Renaissance.") Tübingen: J. C. B. Mohr, 1916.

Winzinger, Franz. *Albrecht Altdorfer Graphik*. Munich: R. Piper & Co., 1963.

Wittkower, Rudolf. "Miraculous Birds." *Journal of the Warbourg and Courtauld Institutes* 1 (1938): 253–57.

———. "Eagle and Serpent: A Study in the Migration of Symbols." *Journal of the Warbourg and Courtauld Institutes* 1 (1938): 293–325.

———. "Desiderio da Settignano's 'St. Jerome in the Desert.'" Studies in the History of Art. Washington: National Gallery of Art, 1972.

Wright, F. A. *Select Letters of St. Jerome*. Loeb Classical Library. London: William Heinemann; New York: G. P. Putnam's Sons, 1933.

Wright, Thomas. *Popular Treatises on Science Written during the Middle Ages in Anglo-Saxon, Anglo-Norman, and English*. London: Historical Society of London, 1841.

Wustmann, R. "Von einigen Tieren und Pflanzen bei Dürer." *Zeitschrift für bildende Kunst* 22 (1911): 109–16.

Zarco Cuevas, R. P. Fr. Julian, O.S.A. *Pintores españoles en San Lorenzo el Real de el Escorial*. Madrid: Instituto de Valencia de Don Juan, 1931.

Zeri, Federico. See Frederickson, Burton B.

Zimmerman, E. H. "Beiträge zur Ikonographie Cranachscher Bildnisse." *Zeitschrift des deutschen vereins für Kunstwissenschaft* 9 (1942): 3–52.

Zircle, Conway. "Animals Impregnated by the Wind." *Isis* 25 (1936): 95–130.

Index

This book was produced by the Smithsonian Institution Press, Washington, D.C. Printed by Eastern Press, New Haven, Conn. Set in Linotype Janson by The Maryland Linotype Composition Company, Inc., Baltimore, Md. The text paper is seventy-pound Glatfelter Springforge Offset with Holliston Roxite vellum cover and Multicolor Antique endsheets. Designed by Elizabeth Sur.